EDUCATION
and SOCIETY

EDUCATION
and SOCIETY

Edited by

W. Warren Kallenbach
San Jose State College

Harold M. Hodges, Jr.
San Jose State College

With an Introduction by

Robert J. Havighurst
University of Chicago

Charles E. Merrill Books, Inc., Columbus, Ohio

Library of Congress Catalog Card Number: 63-18591

First Printing . . . . . September, 1963
Second Printing . . . . July, 1964
Third Printing . . . . May, 1966

To

A. G. Jelinek

and

Emory S. Bogardus

PREFACE

This book fulfills the ever-increasing demand among educators for a truly professional source book in the realm of sociology, anthropology, and psychology: a book with information that is simultaneously lucid and *first-hand*. What was formerly an intellectual luxury has now become virtually mandatory. To teach or to administer today's schools with no more than a rudimentary knowledge of the American social fabric is, in fact, all but unthinkable. The editors, in their quest to satisfy this need, have turned to those at the apex of the behavioral sciences—to such acknowledged authorities as David Riesman, Ralph Linton, Talcott Parsons, Kingsley Davis, Gordon Allport, Clyde Kluckhohn, Henry A. Murray, Albert K. Cohen, Robert J. Havighurst, Ernest W. Burgess, Howard Becker, and others. There are provocative essays on our national purpose by Adlai Stevenson and Max Lerner, but as is the case for many of the readings in this collection, the reader will have to derive the implications of their statements for himself. "Peninsula People," by Harold M. Hodges, Jr., a study of social stratification in a California "megalopolis," is presented here for the first time. The study is current and still continuing.

In their selection of articles, the editors have treated the central questions—the areas where education and the social sciences most fruitfully converge—with a judicious blend of intellectual vigor, sprightliness, and depth of insight. Each chapter of the book is preceded by an introduction that clarifies and integrates basic themes and expands on the issues raised in the articles, but the introductions are not meant to take the place of the readings that follow.

The nine chapters into which the book has been divided deal, in turn, with:

> The social nature of contemporary education
>
> The nature and dynamics of culture and social change
>
> The acquisition of personality
>
> The changing role of the family
>
> The culture of the school
>
> Deviant behavior (with emphasis on casual sequences and the areas of delinquency and prejudice)
>
> The dynamics of mass culture and mass leisure
>
> The role of social class in American culture
>
> The relationship between education and national goals

ACKNOWLEDGMENTS

We are most appreciative of the personal suggestions for the direction and content of the text from Professors **Robert J. Havighurst** and **David Riesman.**

We are equally grateful to the authors whose writings are, in most cases, required reading in our respective undergraduate classes. The book now serves to put them all, plus some promising new ones, under one roof.

Thanks are extended to the publishers and individual authors who granted permission to reprint the various readings. Readings are, with few exceptions, complete articles or chapters. (Some footnotes or paragraphs are omitted for reasons of space only.)

Without question, no book can be planned, written, edited, and printed without careful editorial guidance. The Charles E. Merrill staff maintained the best relationship with us, and to them we make this last acknowledgment.

San Jose State College

W. Warren Kallenbach
Harold M. Hodges, Jr.

TABLE OF CONTENTS

XI

CHAPTER SIX—Deviant Behavior, 265

CHAPTER SEVEN—Mass Culture, 327

CHAPTER EIGHT—Social Class, 375

CHAPTER NINE—Our National Purpose and Education, 421

INTRODUCTION

By Robert J. Havighurst

Why should a teacher know more than his subject? If he teaches history, why should he know more than history? Or if he teaches science, why should he know more than science?

No teacher can *teach* successfully if he knows nothing of the students whom he teaches or of the society in which he teaches. He might be able to work as a scholar in his special field without knowing much about anything else. He might write novels without knowing about students; he might do research work in chemistry without having much knowledge of society; he might study society as a sociologist without knowing about students as persons. In other words, he might be a specialist and a scholar and operate within the four walls of his subject; but if he is a teacher, he must know something about society and something about students.

For this reason a prospective teacher studies sociology and psychology—and especially those parts of sociology and psychology which bear most directly on education.

He studies the social foundations of education, so that as a teacher he will be ready to teach boys and girls from families of various social classes, or various race and nationality groups. He finds out by studying the social foundations of education what it means to say that education should aim to increase the life chances of underprivileged youth, and how this can be done. He learns by studying the social foundations of education how to serve as a teacher in a foreign culture, if he should want to go abroad to work. Or, if his ambition is to become a principal or superintendent of schools, he learns enough about people and about communities to understand this kind of job.

This book of readings is a collection of examples of research in the sociology of education, not re-written and simplified for easier reading, but chosen so as to give the student quick access to some of the best and most significant work, which will supplement his textbook.

The readings let the researchers speak directly to the student about educational matters. They give a body of information on sociological factors that influence education or are influenced by education.

Since the readings deal with social foundations of education, they do not cover the entire field of sociology, but they concentrate on such relevant topics as: social development of the personality, social class and social mobility, the family, the school culture, school and community, urban and metropolitan development, population trends, the dynamics of prejudice, juvenile delinquency, and mass communication.

From a more general, philosophical point of view, some of the readings deal with education as an instrument created and maintained by society to maintain and to improve itself.

EDUCATION
and SOCIETY

Chapter One

THE SOCIAL NATURE OF MAN AND EDUCATION

More and more, teacher education programs are including the social foundations of education in the pattern of required courses. Why is this so? In the Introduction to *Education and Society,* Professor Havighurst asks — and ably answers — a related question: Why should the teacher know more than his subject?

Achievement of our educational goals is facilitated by knowledge of the learner and the society in which he lives. These are not independent, isolated bodies of knowledge; you must know and understand the relationships between each. You cannot describe or attempt to predict about the one without describing or attempting to predict about the other. This book of readings is designed to enable the reader to gain further knowledge and understanding of the individual acting and reacting within his particular society.

Our first selection in this book of readings is titled, "The Typical American," but could just as well have been called the typical (middle-class or upper-class) European or Latin American. The brief, and choice, essay illustrates the principle of cultural diffusion. That American society, one of the world's most advanced industrial complexes, owes so much to earlier, simpler peoples is plainly evident. It is a striking illustration of Linton's estimate that no society in the world has created more than ten per cent of the elements of its total culture.

In the other selection of this brief introductory chapter, Ralph W. Tyler and Richard I. Miller provide a survey of current social trends—

1

each with its related blessings and challenges. The greatest challenge—after survival—is whether most of mankind can vigorously adapt and utilize these rapidly changing physical, social, intellectual, and emotional environments. The final chapter of the book, Chapter Nine, helps us with some directions for our adaptations and utilizations.

THE TYPICAL AMERICAN*

by Ralph Linton

Our solid American citizen awakens in a bed built on a pattern which originated in the Near East but which was modified in Northern Europe before it was transmitted to America. He throws back the covers made from cotton, domesticated in India, or linen, domesticated in the Near East, or wool from sheep, also domesticated in the Near East, or silk, the use of which was discovered in China. All of these materials have been spun and woven by processes invented in the Near East. He slips into his moccasins, invented by the Indians of the Eastern woodlands, and goes to the bathroom, whose fixtures are a mixture of European and American inventions, both of recent date. He takes off his pajamas, a garment invented in India, and washes with soap invented by the ancient Gauls. He then shaves, a masochistic rite which seems to have been derived from either Sumer or ancient Egypt.

Returning to the bedroom, he removes his clothes from a chair of southern European type and proceeds to dress. He puts on garments whose form originally derived from the skin clothing of the nomads of the Asiatic steppes, puts on shoes made from skins tanned by a process invented in ancient Egypt, and cut to a pattern derived from the classical civilizations of the Mediterranean, and ties around his neck a strip of bright-colored cloth which is a vestigial survival of the shoulder shawls worn by the seventeenth-century Croatians. Before going out for breakfast he glances through the window, made of glass invented in Egypt, and if it is raining, puts on overshoes made of rubber discovered by the Central American Indians and takes an umbrella, invented in southeastern Asia. Upon his head he puts a hat made of felt, a material invented in the Asiatic steppes.

On his way to breakfast he stops to buy a paper, paying for it with coins, an ancient Lydian invention. At the restaurant a whole new series of borrowed elements confronts him. His plate is made of a form of pottery invented in China. His knife is of steel, an alloy first made

*From Ralph Linton, *The Study of Man,* pp. 326-327. Copyright, 1936, D. Appleton-Century Co. Inc. Reprinted by permission of the publishers, Appleton-Century-Crofts, Inc.

in southern India, his fork a medieval Italian invention, and his spoon a derivative of a Roman original. He begins breakfast with an orange, from the eastern Mediterranean, a cantaloupe from Persia, or perhaps a piece of African watermelon. With this he has coffee, an Abyssinian plant, with cream and sugar. Both the domestication of cows and the idea of milking them originated in the Near East, while sugar was first made in India. After his fruit and first coffee he goes on to waffles, cakes made by a Scandinavian technique from wheat domesticated in Asia Minor. Over these he pours maple syrup, invented by the Indians of the Eastern woodlands. As a side dish he may have the eggs of a species of bird domesticated in Indo-China, or thin strips of the flesh of an animal domesticated in Eastern Asia, which have been salted and smoked by a process developed in northern Europe.

When our friend has finished eating, he settles back to smoke, an American Indian habit, consuming a plant domesticated in Brazil in either a pipe, derived from the Indians of Virginia, or a cigarette, derived from Mexico. If he is hardy enough he may even attempt a cigar, transmitted to us from the Antilles by way of Spain. While smoking he reads the news of the day, imprinted in characters invented in Germany. As he absorbs the accounts of foreign troubles he will, if he is a good conservative citizen, thank a Hebrew deity in an Indo-European language that he is 100 per cent American.

SOCIAL FORCES AND TRENDS*

by Ralph W. Tyler and Richard I. Miller

We are living in one of the most decisive eras of history. Certainly there have been critical times in the past, but never before have so many forces combined in a single period to provide great opportunities as well as great perils.

Rapid advances in science and technology, rising aspirations of people throughout the world, economic growth, bureaucratic development, and population growth have been important factors in the radical change our society has undergone since the turn of the century. Some

*From Ralph W. Tyler and Richard I. Miller, "Social Forces and Trends," *National Education Association Journal,* Volume 51, No. 6 (September 1962), pp. 26-28. Copyright © 1962 by the National Education Association of the United States. Reprinted by permission.

other forces that have made our lives so different from our forebears' include increased leisure time for workers, urbanization, and international interdependence.

These changes have solved certain problems, but they have created others, many of which our schools are called upon to meet. The new problems, in many instances, require new methods of solution.

THE SCIENTIFIC REVOLUTION

Breath-taking developments in science and technology, with deep ramifications for our social structure, have overshadowed all other changes. A man born sixty years ago in the horse-and-buggy age may live to see the dawn of interplanetary travel and machines capable of thinking.

As machines rapidly relieve men of much manual and mental effort, they also will cause increasing social upheaval and uncertainty as well as great shifts in the pattern of employment. There will be fewer and fewer opportunities in unskilled and skilled labor and greater demands for scientists, engineers, teachers, persons in the health professions, and in other fields requiring post high school education.

It is interesting to see how rapidly the occupational picture has been changing. At the turn of the century, for example, about one worker in 250 was an engineer; the ratio today is one in 50. The number of electricians has increased by ninety percent since 1920. The number of scientists in all fields in 1958 was estimated at 300,000; in 1959, at 313,000. By 1970 the figure is expected to increase about seventy-five percent over 1959. In the past twenty years, the number employed in the health services has increased fivefold.

Mathematics and physics will be among the fastest growing fields in the next ten years. The largest scientific professions—chemistry and biological sciences—will also grow rapidly, although not so fast as the fields of mathematics and physics. Our schools will not only be called upon to educate students for these occupations, but they will, of necessity, also be asked to help in the readjustment to new living conditions and patterns of thought.

In addition to fundamental changes in the structure of our society, the scientific revolution has brought about a profoundly different way of looking at the world. Science—as method—is a way of thinking about problems. While the steps used in this process may vary considerably, the procedure of thought, the so-called scientific method, follows a more or less similar pattern—one that represents a radical departure from the scholasticism and ecclesiastical thinking of earlier periods. The scientific method starts from no answered suppositions about the universe and the nature of man; it is a way of looking at the world which stresses objectivity and rational selection of alternatives.

It has been said that the method of invention was, more than anything else, responsible for the scientific and technological revolution. In any case, science and technology have been instrumental, by their very nature, in developing faith in the rational powers of man as perhaps his surest salvation.

Yet a serious gap has developed between the cleverness of our inventions and our ability to make wise social decisions about them. Education is challenged to help close the gap; to help educate a generation of citizens who will be able to make wise social decisions about the fruits of science and technology.

Rather than being awed or overwhelmed by the dizzy pace of the scientific revolution, we should systematically analyze appropriate aspects of it to determine the educational implications. Then we need to make decisions about the tasks of the school, taking into account our basic values and the reality of our situation.

LEISURE TIME

Americans now spend an estimated forty billion dollars per year, or eight percent of the gross national product, on leisure-time activities. This expenditure is only 12 billion dollars less than the 1962 national defense budget and greater than all federal income-tax receipts; it is more than the combined spending for new housing and new automobiles.

The use of leisure time has both personal and social significance. For the individual, it can be an opportunity to select from a wide variety of leisure-time possibilities those compatible with his way of life and enjoyable to him. To society, it can be a means of developing wholesome values and training for effective group life. The extent to which leisure time serves these important purposes is greatly dependent upon the schools. The development of interests in intellectual, social, and aesthetic experiences is a fundamental task of the school.

URBANIZATION

The cluster of problems related to urbanization represents the most serious domestic challenge facing the American people and their schools today. Two dimensions of urbanization—the movement to suburbia and the slum problem—deserve special attention.

In 1950, seventy percent of the urban population was in the central cities and thirty percent in the suburban fringe areas. By 1960, the ratio was 60-40. This pattern of transfer has been particularly characteristic in many older Eastern cities like New York and Boston.

Generally speaking, the residents of suburbia are predominantly middle-class; they value material success and social mobility. They are leaving the central city areas largely to individuals in the lower socio-economic brackets.

This exodus of middle-class people to the suburbs draws leadership and money from the central city area, which results in a depreciation of the neighborhood and the growth of slums as less money becomes available to fight congestion and obsolescence. As the exodus to the suburbs continues, even less money and leadership is left behind to stop the downward cycle.

The type of people living in the slums today has also changed. James B. Conant in *Slums and Suburbs* has noted that the current slum dweller is no longer the white foreign immigrant from a stable society bound by traditional pride of family and strong church connections— the immigrant that knew his predecessors had worked their way out of slum poverty and that he or his children could do the same thing.

The culturally deprived or disadvantaged youth growing up in the slum areas today has less chance to escape his environment than the immigrant child of fifty years ago despite a much higher level of prosperity in the country. Figures show that in 1961 the unemployment rate among nonschool youths under twenty years of age was approximately seventeen percent, or *three times* the national average. In some slum areas, over fifty percent of the male youth were out of school and out of work.

The Conant report re-emphasizes a plea made twenty-five years ago in a report *(How Fare American Youth?)* by the American Youth Commission of the American Council on Education. In the 1937 report, issued during America's worst depression, the Commission called upon the American people to unite in an effort to help slum youth to become what they had a right and an obligation to be — full-time workers, responsible members of their families, and constructive members of their communities.

Additional factors make the need for action today more urgent than ever before. For example, some sociologists and educators consider that this tendency toward class stratification poses a serious problem to the American concept of the school as an important laboratory of democracy, enrolling all the children of all the people.

Does the increasing social class segregation of children in the public schools tend to produce more rigidity in the vertical social class structure and make the Horatio Alger tradition less realistic to future generations of Americans? Will the schools in the slums be able to develop the kinds of young people needed as the United States moves further into an urban-industrial society?

POPULATION GROWTH

The electric clock and chart in the lobby of the Department of Commerce Building in Washington tell us that in the United States there is one birth every 7.5 seconds, one death every 19 seconds, one immigrant every 1.5 minutes, and one emigrant every 23 minutes. What this means in terms of population growth is that the United States makes a net gain of one person every 10.5 seconds, or over 8,000 persons each day and about 3 million each year.

How will the schools meet the needs of a nation likely to grow to 196 million by 1965, 260 million by 1980, and 350 million by the turn of the twenty-first century?

The continuing need for additional classrooms cannot be overlooked by our educators and government leaders. Population growth during the sixties will require new classrooms for 8.1 million additional youths.

The classroom shortage in 1959 was reported to be 135,000 rooms; in 1960 the shortage was placed at 142,100 rooms. Almost two million children are attending schools in overcrowded buildings and 685,000 are on curtailed or half-day sessions. The shortage is most acute in burgeoning surburban areas around our larger cities.

The ill effects of overcrowding are all too obvious — less time for instructional purposes, more discipline problems, and inadequate physical conditions for learning.

Even if the construction of new classrooms catches up with the population growth, the chronic shortage of adequately prepared teachers remains. New instructional technological devices can aid the teacher in stimulating and guiding learning, but they do not take the place of the teacher. The effective use of these new devices requires planning and direction by a well-trained professional person.

The number of new teachers is increasing, partly because of the increase in college graduates and partly because of higher teacher pay scales. However, funds must be increased to expand our college programs for teacher education; and teacher salaries, especially in urban areas, must continue to rise to meet the competition for talent from private industry and from other governmental agencies.

International Interdependence and Conflict

While United States involvement in world affairs is not new, the heightened nature of our involvement has created new responsibilities for our schools.

The study of world affairs in the public schools must be selective. Teaching the particular aspects of this complex subject must be determined in part by the maturity of the students, the purposes of education, and the time available in the school day. But international relations in our present age is as vital an area for citizen understanding and action as local political issues were a generation ago.

All teaching of international relations should stress objective analysis and searching evaluation of the issues. Too often teaching in this area includes an uncritical acceptance of clichés and generalities. Encouraging the student to reason for himself is especially crucial. The successful brainwashing of some American soldiers during the Korean War indicated that these soldiers were unable to analyze critically what they found to be convincing arguments when these arguments were presented with unfamiliar premises and with the rationale of conclusions flowing from them.

Conclusion

The lives of all of us are undergoing rapid transformations at a pace never before recorded in history. The birth of new nations, the impact of new technology, the stirring of new ideas, and even the ascent into a new dimension of the universe—everywhere is change. Whether its final effects are desirable or undesirable will depend to a large extent upon men's attitudes toward change and their ability to deal with new problems with intelligence and courage. The development of men capable and eager to meet the problems and the opportunities of the future is a major task for the schools to work out now.

Chapter Two

THE NATURE OF CULTURE

You cannot touch or feel or see *culture*. Yet every man, woman, and child who has progressed beyond infancy "has" it. He must have it. Lacking culture, he could not survive. Were it not for culture, in fact, we and our ancestors would never have peopled the earth. If you, the reader, lacked a cultural heritage, you would not be reading these— or any—words. You would be little more than a gibbering, incomprehensible idiot, less capable of mere survival than a member of the very earliest tribe of prehistoric men.

Culture may be likened to the air around us: it is so much with us, so intangible a part of our everyday environment, that we take it for granted. While most of us are at least vaguely aware of the air we breathe, only the sophisticated in our midst realize that something more than raw, inherent "human nature" is responsible for mankind's superiority over his fur-clad, tree-climbing primate cousins. That "something" is what the social scientist chooses to call culture.[1]

---

[1] One of the better definitions of culture—because it explains so much so succinctly—is John Cuber's; culture, in his words, consists of ". . . continually *changing . . . patterns . . .* of *learned* behavior . . . and the products of learned behavior (including attitudes, values, knowledge, and material objects) . . . which are *shared* by . . . and *transmitted* among . . . members of society" [italics ours]. All cultures, everywhere, are (1) forever *changing*—perhaps at a barely perceptible snail's pace (in a nonliterate tribe, for instance), perhaps at a dazzlingly rapid pace (as in midcentury America), but never quite the same from one year to the next; (2) *patterned,* rather than a grab-bag of unrelated items (cultural items, material and nonmaterial, must be interrelated in order to function and make society cohesive, operational, and predictable); (3) *learned* (since it cannot be

11

It should hardly seem surprising, then, that the culture concept is thought by many to be the most important single contribution the social sciences have yet evolved in their continuing effort to comprehend and explain man and his social milieu. And when we have read — and intellectually digested—Professor Clyde Kluckhohn's "Queer Customs," we will readily concur with the sociologist who observed that it is ". . . almost impossible to exaggerate the importance of culture in human life. Neither a single individual, a particular social group, nor an entire society can be understood without reference to culture."[2]

To affirm the overwhelming consequence of culture is not to deny the critical role enacted by heredity; this will be abundantly apparent when we examine the dynamics of personality in the next chapter of the book. It is true that our genetic inheritance explains our unique ability, as a species, to create and transmit culture; inherent differences in individual strength, vigor, and intellectual capacity will help account for important individual variations on the basic cultural themes. But heredity altogether fails to explain why *Homo sapiens* has undergone no fundamental biological changes in many thousands of years yet has moved from a mastery of crude stone implements to a mastery of nuclear energy. Nor will biology explain racial, national, and ethnic differences any more than it will explain the differences which so visibly demarcate Mississippi sharecroppers from residents of the Klamath Indian reservation — or the Arunta aborigines of northern Australia from the Bedouin nomads who roam the Rub' al Khali wastes.

Professor Kluckhohn's provocative essay is of special relevance for the educator, the person who will administer America's schools or teach its children. For ours is an era when the school, more than ever before, will open its doors to children of divergent ethnic and social-class backgrounds. These children will enter the schoolroom with cultural equipment (and consequent personality and value configurations) which can only be comprehended by those who have mastered the revealing truths inherent in the culture concept. And to know the meaning of culture is to discern the major points in the Kluckhohn selection; the relativity of values—of "right" and "wrong," "good" and "bad"; the fallacy of the *"nature* versus *nurture"* controversy; the

---

biologically transmitted, culture can only be acquired by learning); (4) *shared* (standing alone, the property of one or a few individuals, it would simply be unique behavior), and (5) *transmitted* (if not passed on from parents to offspring, from generation to generation—culture would wither on the vine), John Cuber, *Sociology: A Synopsis of Principles,* 4th edition (New York: Appleton-Century-Crofts, Inc., 1959), p. 60.

    [2]*Ibid.*

danger of cultural or biological determinism; and the meaning and significance of cultural variability, social institutions, culture lag, manifest and latent cultural functions, subculture, and ethnocentrism. To fail to grasp the essence and ramifications of culture, finally, is to fail to understand much else in this book—and in life—the dynamics of juvenile delinquency, for example, and personality growth, marital adjustment and maladjustment, and bigotry.

The Lonely Crowd first appeared in 1950. A short while later the book had become a best seller, and its chief author, David Riesman, had become a celebrity. His novel thesis, that Western civilization (and America in particular) was producing a profound shift in the character and orientation of its people, had excited the imagination of academician and layman alike. Typing friend and foe as "other-directed" or "inner-directed" became the most sophisticated of parlor games.

Riesman, it is true, was hardly the first to call attention to the intimate ties between personality and culture; similar distinctions had been advanced in the past by such theorists as Durkheim, Cooley, and Tonnies—not to mention a whole new school of anthropology. Yet Riesman and his collaborators, Reuel Denney and Nathan Glazer, were interested in something more: (1) the direction in which Western (and American) cultural development was moving, (2) the dynamics which explained and accompanied this drift, and (3) the consequences for society and the individual. Above all, the authors of *The Lonely Crowd* were concerned with the plight of contemporary man—with the impact of industrialization upon humanity.

Tradition-direction, inner-direction, other-direction: these were Riesman's character constructs which justly captivated the public fancy. From the very beginning, there has been disagreement about the meaning of what Riesman chose to call "social character." Some contend that the author was describing *categories* or *classes* of people; others would hold that the other-directed (or inner- or tradition-directed) person is precisely a person — an *individual* with a particular style of personality configuration. But if the issue was not altogether clear when *The Lonely Crowd* first appeared, Riesman himself recently clarified the point beyond cavil. *The Lonely Crowd,* he observed in 1960, ". . . did not move outward from individuals toward society, but rather the other way around; we started with society and with particular historical developments within society."[3] The authors, he points out, did not

---

[3] David Riesman, *"The Lonely Crowd*: A Reconsideration in 1960," S. M. Lipset and Leo Lowenthal (eds.), *Culture and Social Character, The Works of David Riesman Reviewed* (New York: The Free Press of Glencoe, 1961), p. 427.

assume that an individual would be a replica of his social role; it is thus "impossible to classify a particular individual as other-directed or inner-directed."[4] Even if such a classification were attempted, he concluded, it might help us understand a person's relations to others, and his way of meeting problems, but it would tell us little ". . . of what would strike us if we were his friend."[5]

What, then, is tradition-direction? And inner- and other-direction? The selection from *The Lonely Crowd* will afford us an answer. But certain points warrant elaboration. In theory, the tradition-directed character type was—and is—most prevalent in that type of society which is variously known as folk, rural, agrarian, or *Gemeinschaft*. "Primitive" tribes, isolated villages in remote corners of Europe, ancient China, India, Japan, and most of feudal-era Europe are examples. Unique as each such society was, they had at least one quality in common: they were dominated by centuries-old tradition. Virtually every task, occupational calling, and custom was substantially identical to what it had been for countless generations past; and each was so clearly explicit, so obvious, that it was understood by the bright and the dull, the young and the old. Each and every person performed according to type. Whether serf, warrior, shaman, candlestick maker, or midwife, he knew his station and its accompanying role, and he played it according to "the rules."

The tradition-directed character type began to disappear when it was no longer "functional": when the tradition-oriented societies were shaken by the torrent of change, innovation, and discovery that accompanied in turn the Renaissance, the Reformation, and the commercial and industrial revolutions. A man with a new sort of value configuration was called for in an era that denounced much of the past and worshiped experimentation, individuation, and "progress"; he was the "inner-directed" man, unfettered by rigidly grooved, predetermined patterns of conduct and values. Although an individualist, relatively insensitive to the approval or disapproval of his peers, the inner-directed man was not quite the self-determined, autonomous man that many mistakenly assume. Instead, "his" values and principles, deeply embedded in his conscience in his earliest years, were largely those of his parents.

Other-directedness, finally, is an emergent character type: the product of a socio-economic climate that has increasingly come to ap-

---

⁴ *Ibid*, p. 428.
⁵ *Ibid*.

prove teamwork, group integration, and gregariousness — and to disparage rugged, "others-be-damned" individualism. The latter, innerdirected mode of conformity, ("conformism," we must remind ourselves, is not synonymous with other-directedness alone; the traditiondirected and inner-directed personalities merely conformed in different ways to different people), flourished in an era when originality, toughmindedness, independence, and daring were economic virtues. Henry Ford and Andrew Carnegie — both "self-made" millionaires — would seem to popularly exemplify the values of this era — an era that now appears to have been a *transitional* age. The psychic mainspring of the other-directed mode of conformity is a need to "fit" and belong — to be accepted by one's peers as a "good guy." If the inner-directed man wondered, above all else, "how to succeed" in the world of money and power, the other-directed mentality is primarily sensitive to the need to win acceptance. The former was geared to a world of burgeoning industrialization, social change and the breakdown of traditional values; the other-directed man appears to be a product of the post-industrial era — an era characterized more by what William L. Whyte, Jr. calls the "organization man" and C. Wright Mills terms the "New middle class." In contrast to the reckless, devil-take-the-hindmost inner-directed sort, the other-directed person is essentially a "team-man" who can quickly adjust to any new interpersonal situation, however novel.

In "The Folk-Urban-Suburban Continuum: A Conceptual Overview of America Yesterday, Today, and Tomorrow," Hodges places much of the tradition-inner-other-directed thesis into sharper historical focus. As the author warns, his continuum is a logical construct an ideal-type scheme that will help clarify the sweeping changes which have restructured so much of America's cultural and economic configuration during the past century. The Perdidans—the fictional southern European villagers whom the author chose as his hypothetical example — might as easily have been Polish, Italian, Irish, or Bohemian, any of the "new immigrants" from southern or central Europe who flooded the nation between 1880 and 1920. The reader might profitably refer to the folk-urban-suburban concept (and the accompanying chart) as he reads the sections of the book pertaining to personality growth, the family, mass culture, social class, delinquency, and prejudice. For each topic will become more meaningful if viewed against the context of the rapid social change which has marked the past American century.

Leo Gurko's article contrasts sharply with the other selections in this chapter of the book. Polemical, often angry, and laden with personal value judgments, it is, nonetheless, worthy of inclusion because it is representative of a growing body of literature: appraisals of mid-century American culture that focus upon what the authors take to be dominant — and consequential — elements in the American "character." Gurko is only one of many[6] whose observations have struck respondent chords in many American readers. Most such endeavors are sprightly, imaginative, and incisive, but it is possible that their popularity is at least in part due to the fact that we are among the world's most self-conscious, self-analytical people. "Who . . . is the American?" asked Crèvecoeur, an early European observer. Ever since, to the delight of American readers, a host of authorities, recognized and self-styled, have been volunteering answers.[7] The appetite for such national pulse-taking analyses appears to be continuing unabated.

Works such as Gurko's should not be confused with the generally more cautious and scholarly studies of "national character" that have enjoyed increasing popularity since the end of World War II. Authored in the main by anthropologists — Margaret Mead, Ruth Benedict, Geoffrey Gorer, Clyde Kluckhohn, Otto Klineberg, and Gregory Bateson were among pioneers in the field — studies such as these have been concerned, in Mead's words, with ". . . establishing regularities to be found in the character of all those who have been reared within . . . a given nation state."[8] Still a fledgling scientific endeavor, the study of national character is increasingly calling for interdisciplinary co-operation among such students of personality as the cultural anthropologist, social psychiatrist, sociologist, cultural historian, and social psychologist. And whether we are impressed with the level of precision and authenticity that interpretations of national character have attained, we must agree with Clyde Kluckhohn and Henry A. Murray's observation that "most white citizens of the United States, in spite of regional, ethnic, and class differences, have features of personality which distinguish them from Englishmen, Australians, or New Zealanders."

---

[6] See, for example, Lynes' *A Surfeit of Honey,* Potter's *People of Plenty,* Larrabee's *The Self-Conscious Society,* Griffith's *Waist-High Culture,* Kronenberger's *Company Manners,* Macdonald's *Masscult & Midcult,* Commager's *The American Mind,* and Barzun's *The House of Intellect;* written in varying styles and at variant levels of discourse, each is a highly readable interpretation of key elements in American life.

[7] Among the earliest and most famous were Count Alexis de Tocqueville, Lord James Bryce, and Harriet Martineau.

[8] Margaret Mead, "National Character and the Science of Anthropology," S. M. Lipset and Leo Lowenthal (eds.), *Culture and Social Character, The Work of David Riesman Reviewed,* (New York: The Free Press of Glencoe, 1961), p. 19.

QUEER CUSTOMS: THE CONCEPT OF CULTURE*

by Clyde Kluckhohn

Why do the Chinese dislike milk and milk products? Why would the Japanese die willingly in a Banzai charge that seemed senseless to Americans? Why do some nations trace descent through the father, others through the mother, still others through both parents? Not because different peoples have different instincts, not because they were destined by God or Fate to different habits, not because the weather is different in China and Japan and the United States. Sometimes shrewd common sense has an answer that is close to that of the anthropologist: "because they were brought up that way." By "culture," anthropology means the total life way of a people, the social legacy the individual acquires from his group. Or culture can be regarded as that part of the environment that is the creation of man.

This technical term has a wider meaning than the "culture" of history and literature. A humble cooking pot is as much a cultural product as is a Beethoven sonata. In ordinary speech a man of culture is a man who can speak languages other than his own, who is familiar with history, literature, philosophy, or the fine arts. In some cliques that definition is still narrower. The cultured person is one who can talk about James Joyce, Scarlatti, and Picasso. To the anthropologist, however, to be human is to be cultured. There is culture in general, and then there are the specific cultures such as Russian, American, British, Hottentot, Inca. The general abstract notion serves to remind us that we cannot explain acts solely in terms of the biological properties of the people concerned, their individual past experience, and the immediate situation. The past experience of other men in the form of culture enters into almost every event. Each specific culture constitutes a kind of blueprint for all of life's activities.

One of the interesting things about human beings is that they try to understand themselves and their own behavior. While this has been particularly true of Europeans in recent times, there is no group which has not developed a scheme or schemes to explain man's actions. To the insistent human query "why?" the most exciting illumination anthropology has to offer is that of the concept of culture. Its explanatory importance is comparable to categories such as evolution in biology, gravity in physics, disease in medicine. A good deal of human behavior can be understood, and indeed predicted, if we know a people's design for living. Many acts are neither accidental nor due to personal peculiarities nor caused by supernatural forces nor simply mysterious. Even those of us who pride ourselves on our individualism follow most of the time a pattern not of our own making. We brush our teeth on arising. We put on pants — not a loincloth or a grass skirt. We eat three meals a day—not four or five or two. We sleep in a bed — not in a hammock or on a sheep pelt. I do not have to know the individual and his life history to be able to predict these and countless other regularities, including many in the thinking process, of all Americans who are not incarcerated in jails or hospitals for the insane.

To the American woman a system of plural wives seems "instinctively" abhorrent. She cannot understand how any woman can fail to be jealous and uncomfortable if she must share her husband with other women. She feels it "unnatural" to accept such a situation. On the other hand, a Koryak woman of Siberia, for example, would find it hard to understand how a woman could be so selfish and so undesirous of feminine companionship in the home as to wish to restrict her husband to one mate.

Some years ago I met in New York City a young man who did not speak a word of English and was obviously bewildered by American ways. By "blood" he was as American as you or I, for his parents had gone from Indiana to China as missionaries. Orphaned in infancy, he was reared by a Chinese family in a remote village. All who met him found him more Chinese than American. The facts of his blue eyes and light hair were less impressive than a Chinese style of gait, Chinese arm and hand movements, Chinese facial expression, and Chinese modes of thought. The biological heritage was American, but the cultural training had been Chinese. He returned to China.

Another example of another kind: I once knew a trader's wife in Arizona who took a somewhat devilish interest in producing a cultural reaction. Guests who came her way were often served delicious sandwiches filled with a meat that seemed to be neither chicken nor tuna fish yet was reminiscent of both. To queries she gave no reply until each had eaten his fill. She then explained that what they had eaten was not chicken, not tuna fish, but the rich, white flesh of freshly killed rattlesnakes. The response was instantaneous — vomiting, often violent vomiting. A biological process caught in a cultural web.

A highly intelligent teacher with long and successful experience in the public schools of Chicago was finishing her first year in an Indian school. When asked how her Navaho pupils compared in intelligence with Chicago youngsters, she replied, "Well, I just don't know. Sometimes the Indians seem just as bright. At other times they just act like dumb animals. The other night we had a dance in the high school. I saw a boy who is one of the best students in my English class standing off by himself. So I took him over to a pretty girl and told them to dance. But they just stood there with their heads down. They wouldn't even say anything." I inquired if she knew whether or not they were members of the same clan. "What difference would that make?"

"How would you feel about getting into bed with your brother?" The teacher walked off in a huff, but, actually, the two cases were quite comparable in principle. To the Indian the type of bodily contact involved in our social dancing has a directly sexual connotation. The incest taboos between members of the same clan are as severe as between true brothers and sisters. The shame of the Indians at the suggestion that a clan brother and sister should dance and the indignation of the white teacher at the idea that she should share a bed with an adult brother represent equally nonrational responses, culturally standardized unreason.

All this does not mean that there is no such thing as raw human nature. The very fact that certain of the same institutions are found in all known societies indicates that at bottom all human beings are very much alike. The files of the Cross-Cultural Survey at Yale University are organized according to categories such as "marriage ceremonies," "life crisis rites," "incest taboos." At least seventy-five of these categories are represented in every single one of the hundreds of cultures analyzed. This is hardly surprising. The members of all human groups have about the same biological equipment. All men undergo the same poignant life experiences such as birth, helplessness, illness, old age, and death. The biological potentialities of the species are the blocks with which cultures are built. Some patterns of every culture crystallize around focuses provided by the inevitables of biology: the difference between the sexes, the presence of persons of different ages, the varying physical strength and skill of individuals. The facts of nature also limit culture forms. No culture provides patterns for jumping over trees or for eating iron ore.

There is thus no "either-or" between nature and that special form of nurture called culture. Cultural determinism is as one-sided as biological determinism. The two factors are interdependent. Culture arises out of human nature, and its forms are restricted both by man's biology and by natural laws. It is equally true that culture channels biological processes — vomiting, weeping, fainting, sneezing, the daily habits of food intake and waste elimination. When a man eats, he is reacting to an internal "drive," namely, hunger contractions consequent upon the lowering of blood sugar, but his precise reaction to these internal stimuli cannot be predicted by physiological knowledge alone. Whether a healthy adult feels hungry twice, three times, or four times a day and the hours at which this feeling recurs is a question of culture. *What* he eats is of course limited by availability, but is also partly regulated by culture. It is a biological fact that some types of berries are poisonous; it is a cultural fact that, a few generations ago, most Americans considered tomatoes to be poisonous and refused to eat them. Such selective, discriminative use of the environment is characteristically cultural. Whether a man eats to live, lives to eat, or merely eats and lives is only in part an individual matter, for there are also cultural trends. Emotions are physiological events. Certain situations will evoke fear in people from any culture. But sensations of pleasure, anger, and lust may be stimulated by cultural cues that would leave unmoved someone who has been reared in a different social tradition.

Except in the case of newborn babies and of individuals born with clear-cut structural or functional abnormalities we can observe innate endowments only as modified by cultural training. In a hospital in New Mexico where Zuni Indian, Navaho Indian, and white American babies are born, it is possible to classify the newly arrived infants as unusually active, average, and quiet. Some babies from each "racial" group will fall into each category, though a higher proportion of the white babies will fall into the unusually active class. But if a Navaho baby, a Zuni baby, and a white baby — all classified as unusually active at birth — are again observed at the age of two years, the Zuni baby will no longer seem given to quick and restless activity — *as compared with the white child* — though he may seem so as compared with the other Zunis of the same age. The Navaho child is likely to fall in between as contrasted with the Zuni and the white, though he will probably still seem more active than the average Navaho youngster.

It was remarked by many observers in the Japanese relocation centers that Japanese who were born and brought up in this country, especially those who were reared apart from any large colony of

Japanese, resemble in behavior their white neighbors much more closely than they do their own parents who were educated in Japan.

I have said "culture channels biological processes." It is more accurate to say "the biological functioning of individuals is modified if they have been trained in certain ways and not in others." Culture is not a disembodied force. It is created and transmitted by people. However, culture, like well-known concepts of the physical sciences, is a convenient abstraction. One never sees gravity. One sees bodies falling in regular ways. One never sees an electromagnetic field. Yet certain happenings that can be seen may be given a neat abstract formulation by assuming that the electromagnetic field exists. Similarly, one never sees culture as such. What is seen are regularities in the behavior or artifacts of a group that has adhered to a common tradition. The regularities in style and technique of ancient Inca tapestries or stone axes from Melanesian islands are due to the existence of mental blueprints for the group.

Culture is a way of thinking, feeling, believing. It is the group's knowledge stored up (in memories of men; in books and objects) for future use. We study the products of this "mental" activity; the overt behavior, the speech and gestures and activities of people, and the tangible results of these things such as tools, houses, cornfields, and what not. It has been customary in lists of "culture traits" to include such things as watches or lawbooks. This is a convenient way of thinking about them, but in the solution of any important problem we must remember that they, in themselves, are nothing but metals, paper, and ink. What is important is that some men know how to make them, others set a value on them, are unhappy without them, direct their activities in relation to them, or disregard them.

It is only a helpful shorthand when we say "The cultural patterns of the Zulu were resistant to Christianization." In the directly observable world of course, it was individual Zulus who resisted. Nevertheless, if we do not forget that we are speaking at a high level of abstraction, it is justifiable to speak of culture as a cause. One may compare the practice of saying "syphilis caused the extinction of the native population of the island." Was it "syphilis" or "syphilis germs" or "human beings who were carriers of syphilis"?

"Culture," then, is "a theory." But if a theory is not contradicted by any relevant fact and if it helps us to understand a mass of otherwise chaotic facts, it is useful. Darwin's contribution was much less the accumulation of new knowledge than the creation of a theory which put in order data already known. An accumulation of facts, however large, is no more a science than a pile of bricks is a house. Anthropology's demonstration that the most weird set of customs has a consistency and an order is comparable to modern psychiatry's showing that there is meaning and purpose in the apparently incoherent talk of the insane. In fact, the inability of the older psychologies and philosophies to account for the strange behavior of madmen and heathens was the principal factor that forced psychiatry and anthropology to develop theories of the unconscious and of culture.

Since culture is an abstraction, it is important not to confuse culture with society. A "society" refers to a group of people who interact more with each other than they do with other individuals — who cooperate with each other for the attainment of certain ends. You can see and indeed count the individuals who make up a society. A "culture" refers to the distinctive ways of life of such a group of people. Not all social events are culturally patterned. New types of circumstances arise for which no cultural solutions have as yet been devised.

A culture constitutes a storehouse of the pooled learning of the group. A rabbit starts life with some innate responses. He can learn from his own experience and perhaps from observing other rabbits. A human infant is born with fewer instincts and greater plasticity. His main task is to learn the answers that persons he will never see, persons long dead, have worked out. Once he has learned the formulas supplied by the culture of his group, most of his behavior becomes almost as automatic and unthinking as if it were instinctive. There is a tremendous amount of intelligence behind the making of a radio, but not much is required to learn to turn it on.

The members of all human societies face some of the same unavoidable dilemmas, posed by biology and other facts of the human situation. This is why the basic categories of all cultures are so similar. Human culture without language is unthinkable. No culture fails to provide for aesthetic expression and aesthetic delight. Every culture supplies standardized orientations toward the deeper problems, such as death. Every culture is designed to perpetuate the group and its solidarity, to meet the demands of individuals for an orderly way of life and for satisfaction of biological needs.

However, the variations on these basic themes are numberless. Some languages are built up out of twenty basic sounds, others out of forty. Nose plugs were considered beautiful by the predynastic Egyptians but are not by the modern French. Puberty is a biological fact. But one culture ignores it, another prescribes informal instructions about sex but no ceremony, a third has impressive rites for girls only, a fourth for boys and girls. In this culture, the first menstruation is welcomed as a happy, natural event; in that culture the atmosphere is full of dread and supernatural threat. Each culture dissects nature according to its own system of categories. The Navaho Indians apply the same word to the color of a robin's egg and to that of grass. A psychologist once assumed that this meant a difference in the sense organs, that Navahos didn't have the physiological equipment to distinguish "green" from "blue." However, when he showed them objects of the two colors and asked them if they were exactly the same colors, they looked at him with astonishment. His dream of discovering a new type of color blindness was shattered.

Every culture must deal with the sexual instinct. Some, however, seek to deny all sexual expression before marriage, whereas a Polynesian adolescent who was not promiscuous would be distinctly abnormal. Some cultures enforce lifelong monogamy, others, like our own, tolerate serial monogamy; in still other cultures, two or more women may be joined to one man or several men to a single woman. Homosexuality has been a permitted pattern in the Greco-Roman world, in parts of Islam, and in various primitive tribes. Large portions of the population of Tibet, and of Christendom at some places and periods, have practiced complete celibacy. To us marriage is first and foremost an arrangement between two individuals. In many more societies marriage is merely one facet of a complicated set of reciprocities, economic and otherwise, between two families or two clans.

The essence of the cultural process is selectivity. The selection is only exceptionally conscious and rational. Cultures are like Topsy. They just grew. Once, however, a way of handling a situation becomes institutionalized, there is ordinarily great resistance to change or deviation. When we speak of "our sacred beliefs," we mean of course that they are beyond criticism and that the person who suggests modification or abandonment must be punished. No person is emotionally indifferent to his culture. Certain cultural premises may become totally out of accord with a new factual situation. Leaders may recognize this and reject the old ways in theory. Yet their emotional loyalty continues in the face of reason because of the intimate conditionings of early childhood.

A culture is learned by individuals as the result of belonging to some particular group, and it constitutes that part of learned behavior which is shared with others. It is our social legacy, as contrasted with our organic heredity. It is one of the important factors which permits us to live together in an organized society, giving us ready-made solutions to our problems, helping us to predict the behavior of others, and permitting others to know what to expect of us.

Culture regulates our lives at every turn. From the moment we are born until we die there is, whether we are conscious of it or not, constant pressure upon us to follow certain types of behavior that other men have created for us. Some paths we follow willingly, others we follow because we know no other way, still others we deviate from or go back to most unwillingly. Mothers of small children know how unnaturally most of this comes to us — how little regard we have, until we are "culturalized," for the "proper" place, time and manner for certain acts such as eating, excreting, sleeping, getting dirty, and making loud noises. But by more or less adhering to a system of related designs for carrying out all the acts of living, a group of men and women feel themselves linked together by a powerful chain of sentiments. Ruth Benedict gave an almost complete definition of the concept when she said, "Culture is that which binds men together."

It is true any culture is a set of techniques for adjusting both to the external environment and to other men. However, cultures create problems as well as solve them. If the lore of a people states that frogs are dangerous creatures, or that it is not safe to go about at night because of witches or ghosts, threats are posed which do not arise out of the inexorable facts of the external world. Cultures produce needs as well as provide a means of fulfilling them. There exist for every group culturally defined, acquired drives that may be more powerful in ordinary daily life than the biologically inborn drives. Many Americans, for example, will work harder for "success" than they will for sexual satisfaction.

Most groups elaborate certain aspects of their culture far beyond maximum utility or survival value. In other words, not all culture promotes physical survival. At times, indeed, it does exactly the opposite. Aspects of culture which once were adaptive may persist long after they have ceased to be useful. An analysis of any culture will disclose many features which cannot possibly be construed as adaptations to the total environment in which the group now finds itself. However, it is altogether likely that these apparently useless features represent survivals, with modifications through time, of cultural forms which were adaptive in one or another previous situation.

Any cultural practice must be functional or it will disappear before long. That is, it must somehow contribute to the survival of the society or to the adjustment of the individual. However, many cultural functions are not manifest but latent. A cowboy will walk three miles to catch a horse which he then rides one mile to the store. From the point of view of manifest function this is positively irrational. But the act has the latent function of maintaining the cowboy's prestige in the terms of his own subculture. One can instance the buttons on the sleeve of a man's coat, our absurd English spelling, the use of capital letters, and a host of other apparently nonfunctional customs. They serve mainly the latent function of assisting individuals to maintain their security by preserving continuity with the past and by making certain sectors of life familiar and predictable.

Every culture is a precipitate of history. In more than one sense history is a sieve. Each culture embraces those aspects of the past which, usually in altered form and with altered meanings, live on in the present. Discoveries and inventions, both material and ideological, are constantly being made available to a group through its historical contacts with other peoples or being created by its own members. However, only those that fit the total immediate situation in meeting the group's needs for survival or in promoting the psychological adjustment of individuals will become part of the culture. The process of culture building may be regarded as an addition to man's innate biological capacities, an addition providing instruments which enlarge, or may even substitute for, biological functions, and to a degree compensating for biological limitations — as in ensuring that death does not always result in the loss to humanity of what the deceased has learned.

Culture is like a map. Just as a map isn't the territory but an abstract representation of a particular area, so also a culture is an abstract description of trends toward uniformity in the words, deeds, and artifacts of a human group. If a map is accurate and you can read it, you won't get lost; if you know a culture, you will know your way around in the life of a society.

Many educated people have the notion that culture applies only to exotic ways of life or to societies where relative simplicity and relative homogeneity prevail. Some sophisticated missionaries, for example, will use the anthropological conception in discussing the special modes of living of South Sea Islanders, but seem amazed at the idea that it could be applied equally to inhabitants of New York City. And social workers in Boston will talk about the culture of a colorful and well-knit immigrant group but boggle at applying it to the behavior of staff members in the social-service agency itself.

In the primitive society the correspondence between the habits of individuals and the customs of the community is ordinarily greater. There is probably some truth in what an old Indian once said, "In the old days there was no law; everybody did what was right." The primitive tends to find happiness in the fulfillment of intricately involuted cultural patterns; the modern more often tends to feel the pattern as repressive to his individuality. It is also true that in a complex stratified society there are numerous exceptions to generalizations made about the culture as a whole. It is necessary to study regional, class, and occupational subcultures. Primitive cultures have greater stability than modern cultures; they change—but less rapidly.

However, modern men also are creators and carriers of culture. Only in some respects are they influenced differently from primitives by culture. Moreover, there are such wide variations in primitive cultures that any black-and-white contrast between the primitive and the civilized is altogether fictitious. The distinction which is most generally true lies in the field of conscious philosophy.

The publication of Paul Radin's *Primitive Man as a Philosopher* did much toward destroying the myth that an abstract analysis of experience was a peculiarity of literate societies. Speculation and reflection upon the nature of the universe and of man's place in the total scheme of things have been carried out in every known culture. Every people has its characteristic set of "primitive postulates." It remains true that critical examination of basic premises and fully explicit systematization of philosophical concepts are seldom found at the non-literate level. The written word is an almost essential condition for free and extended discussion of fundamental philosophic issues. Where dependence on memory exists, there seems to be an inevitable tendency to emphasize the correct perpetuation of the precious oral tradition. Similarly, while it is all too easy to underestimate the extent to which ideas spread without books, it is in general true that tribal or folk societies do not possess competing philosophical systems. The major exception to this statement is, of course, the case where part of the tribe becomes converted to one of the great proselytizing religions such as Christianity or Mohammedanism. Before contact with rich and powerful civilizations, primitive peoples seem to have absorbed new ideas piecemeal, slowly integrating them with the previously existing ideology. The abstract thought of non-literate societies is ordinarily less self-critical, less systematic, nor so intricately elaborated in purely logical dimensions. Primitive thinking is more concrete, more implicit — perhaps more completely coherent than the philosophy of most individuals in larger societies which have been influenced over long periods by disparate intellectual currents.

No participant in any culture knows all the details of the cultural map. The statement frequently heard that St. Thomas Aquinas was the last man to master all the knowledge of his society is intrinsically absurd. St. Thomas would have been hard put to make a pane of cathedral glass or to act as a midwife. In every culture there are what Ralph Linton has called "universals, alternatives, and specialties." Every Christian in the thirteenth century knew that it was necessary to attend mass, to go to confession, to ask the Mother of God to intercede with her Son. There were many other universals in the Christian culture of Western Europe. However, there were also alternative cultural patterns even in the realm of religion. Each individual had his own patron saint, and different towns developed the cults of different saints. The thirteenth-century anthropologist could have discovered the rudiments of Christian practice by questioning and observing whomever he happened to meet in Germany, France, Italy, or England. But to find out the details of the ceremonials honoring St. Hubert or St. Bridget he would have had to seek out certain individuals or special localities where these alternative patterns were practiced. Similarly, he could not learn about weaving from a professional soldier or about canon law from a farmer. Such cultural knowledge belongs in the realm of the specialties, voluntarily chosen by the individual or ascribed to him by birth. Thus, part of a culture must be learned by everyone, part may be selected from alternative patterns, part applies only to those who perform the roles in the society for which these patterns are designed.

Many aspects of a culture are explicit. The explicit culture consists in those regularities in word and deed that may be generalized straight from the evidence of the ear and the eye. The recognition of these is like the recognition of style in the art of a particular place and epoch. If we have examined twenty specimens of the wooden saints' images made in the Taos valley of New Mexico in the late eighteenth century, we can predict that any new images from the same locality and period will in most respects exhibit the same techniques of carving, about the same use of colors and choice of woods, a similar quality of artistic conception. Similarly if, in a society of 2,000 members, we record 100 marriages at random and find that in 30 cases a man has married the sister of his brother's wife, we can anticipate that an additional sample of 100 marriages will show roughly the same number of cases of this pattern.

The above is an instance of what anthropologists call a behavioral pattern, the practices as opposed to the rules of the culture. There are also, however, regularities in what people say they do or should do. They do tend in fact to prefer to marry into a family already connected with their own by marriage, but this is not necessarily part of the official code of conduct. No disapproval whatsoever is attached to those who make another sort of marriage. On the other hand, it is explicitly forbidden to marry a member of one's own clan even though no biological relationship is traceable. This is a regulatory pattern—a Thou Shalt or a Thou Shalt Not. Such patterns may be violated often, but their existence is nevertheless important. A people's standards for conduct and belief define the socially approved aims and the acceptable means of attaining them. When the discrepancy between the theory and the practice of a culture is exceptionally great, this indicates that the culture is undergoing rapid change. It does not prove that ideals are unimportant, for ideals are but one of a number of factors determining action.

Cultures do not manifest themselves solely in observable customs and artifacts. No amount of questioning of any save the most articulate in the most self-conscious cultures will bring out some of the basic attitudes common to the members of the group. This is because these basic assumptions are taken so for granted that they normally do not enter into consciousness. This part of the cultural map must be inferred by the observer on the basis of consistencies in thought and action. Missionaries in various societies are often disturbed or puzzled because the natives do not regard "morals" and "sex code" as almost synonymous. The natives seem to feel that morals are concerned with sex just about as much as with eating — no less and no more. No society fails to have some restrictions on sexual behavior, but sex activity outside of marriage need not necessarily be furtive or attended with guilt. The Christian tradition has tended to assume that sex is inherently nasty as well as dangerous. Other cultures assume that sex in itself is not only natural but one of the good things of life, even though sex acts with certain persons under certain circumstances are forbidden. This is implicit culture, for the natives do not announce their premises. The missionaries would get further if they said, in effect, "Look, our morality starts from different assumptions. Let's talk about those assumptions," rather than ranting about "immorality."

A factor implicit in a variety of diverse phenomena may be generalized as an underlying cultural principle. For example, the Navaho Indians always leave part of the design in a pot, a basket, or a blanket unfinished. When a medicine man instructs an apprentice he always leaves a little bit of the story untold. This "fear of closure" is a recurrent theme in Navaho culture. Its influence may be detected in many contexts that have no explicit connection.

If the observed cultural behavior is to be correctly understood, the categories and presuppositions constituting the implicit culture must be worked out. The "strain toward consistency" which Sumner noted in the folkways and mores of all groups cannot be accounted for unless one grants a set of systematically interrelated implicit themes. For example, in American culture the themes of "effort and optimism," "the common man," "technology," and "virtuous materialism" have a functional interdependence, the origin of which is historically known. The relationship between themes may be that of conflict. One may instance the competition between Jefferson's theory of democracy and Hamilton's "government by the rich, the wellborn, and the able." In other cases most themes may be integrated under a single dominant theme. In Negro cultures of West Africa the mainspring of social life is religion; in East Africa almost all cultural behavior seems to be oriented toward certain premises and categories centered on the cattle economy. If there be one master principle in the implicit culture, this is often called the "ethos" or *Zeitgeist*.

Every culture has organization as well as content. There is nothing mystical about this statement. One may compare ordinary experience. If I know that Smith, working alone, can shovel 10 cubic yards of dirt a day, Jones 12, and Brown 14, I would be foolish to predict that the three working together would move 36. The total might well be considerably more; it might be less. A whole is different from the sum of its parts. The same principle is familiar in athletic teams. A brilliant pitcher added to a nine may mean a pennant or may mean the cellar; it depends on how he fits in.

And so it is with cultures. A mere list of the behavioral and regulatory patterns and of the implicit themes and categories would be like a map on which all mountains, lakes, and rivers were included —but not in their actual relationship to one another. Two cultures could have almost identical inventories and still be extremely different. The full significance of any single element in a culture design will be seen only when that element is viewed in the total matrix of its relationship to other elements. Naturally, this includes accent or emphasis, as well as position. Accent is manifested sometimes through frequency, sometimes through intensity. The indispensable importance of these questions of arrangement and emphasis may be driven home by an analogy. Consider a musical sequence made up of three notes. If we are told that the three notes in question are A, B, and G, we receive information which is fundamental. But it will not enable us to predict the type of sensation which the playing of this sequence is likely to evoke. We need many different sorts of relationship data. Are the notes to be played in that or some other order? What duration will each receive? How will the emphasis, if any, be distributed? We also need, of course, to know whether the instrument used is to be a piano or an accordion.

Cultures vary greatly in their degree of integration. Synthesis is achieved partly through the overt statement of the dominant conceptions, assumptions, and aspirations of the group in its religious lore, secular thought, and ethical code; partly through habitual but unconscious ways of looking at the stream of events, ways of begging certain questions. To the naive participant in the culture these modes of categorizing, of dissecting experience along these planes and not others, are as much "given" as the regular sequence of daylight and darkness or the necessity of air, water, and food for life. Had Americans not thought in terms of money and the market system during the depression they would have distributed unsalable goods rather than destroyed them.

Every group's way of life, then, is a structure—not a haphazard collection of all the different physically possible and functionally effective patterns of belief and action. A culture is an interdependent system based upon linked premises and categories whose influence is greater, rather than less, because they are seldom put in words. Some degree of internal coherence which is felt rather than rationally constructed seems to be demanded by most of the participants in any culture. As Whitehead has remarked, "Human life is driven forward by its dim apprehension of notions too general for its existing language."

In sum, the distinctive way of life that is handed down as the social heritage of a people does more than supply a set of skills for making a living and a set of blueprints for human relations. Each different way of life makes its own assumptions about the ends and purposes of human existence, about what human beings have a right to expect from each other and the gods, about what constitutes fulfillment or frustration. Some of these assumptions are made explicit in the lore of the folk; others are tacit premises which the observer must infer by finding consistent trends in word and deed.

In our highly self-conscious Western civilization that has recently made a business of studying itself, the number of assumptions that are literally implicit, in the sense of never having been stated or discussed by anyone, may be negligible. Yet only a trifling number of Americans could state even those implicit premises of our culture that have been brought to light by anthropologists. If one could bring to the American scene a Bushman who had been socialized in his own culture and then trained in anthropology, he would perceive all sorts of patterned regularities of which our anthropologists are completely unaware. In the case of the less sophisticated and less self-conscious societies, the unconscious assumptions characteristically made by individuals brought up under approximately the same social controls bulk even larger. But in any society, as Edward Sapir said, "Forms and significances which seem obvious to an outsider will be denied outright by those who carry out the patterns; outlines and implications that are perfectly clear to these may be absent to the eye of the onlooker."

All individuals in a culture tend to share common interpretations of the external world and man's place in it. To some degree every individual is affected by this conventional view of life. One group unconsciously assumes that every chain of action has a goal and that when this goal is reached tension will be reduced or will disappear. To another group, thinking based upon this assumption is meaningless— they see life not as a series of purposive sequences, but as a complex of experiences which are satisfying in and of themselves, rather than as means to ends.

The concept of implicit culture is made necessary by certain eminently practical considerations. Programs of the British Colonial services or of our own Indian service, which have been carefully thought through for their continuity with the overt cultural patterns, nevertheless fail to work out. Nor does intensive investigation reveal any flaws in the setup at the technological level. The program is sabotaged by resistance which must be imputed to the manner in which the members of the group have been conditioned by their implicit designs for living to think and feel in ways which were unexpected to the administrator.

What good is the concept of culture so far as the contemporary world is concerned? What can you do with it? Much of the rest of this book will answer these questions, but some preliminary indications are in order.

Its use lies first in the aid the concept gives to man's endless quest to understand himself and his own behavior. For example, this new idea turns into pseudo problems some of the questions asked by one of the most learned and acute thinkers of our age, Reinhold Niebuhr. In his recent book *The Nature and Destiny of Man* Niebuhr argues that the universally human sense of guilt or shame and man's capacity for self-judgment necessitate the assumption of supernatural forces. These facts are susceptible of self-consistent and relatively simple explanation in purely naturalistic terms through the concept of culture. Social life among human beings never occurs without a system of conventional understandings which are transmitted more or less intact from generation to generation. Every individual is familiar with some of these and they constitute a set of standards against which he judges himself. To the extent that he fails to conform he experiences discomfort because his childhood training put great pressure on him to follow the accepted pattern, and his now unconscious tendency is to associate deviation with punishment or withdrawal of love and protection. This and other issues which have puzzled philosophers and scientists for countless generations become understandable through this fresh concept.

The principal claim which can be made for the culture concept as an aid to useful action is that it helps us enormously toward predicting human behavior. One of the factors limiting the success of such prediction thus far has been the naive assumption of a minutely homogenous "human nature." In the framework of this assumption all human beings are motivated by the same needs and goals. In the cultural framework we see that, while the ultimate logic of all peoples may be the same (and thus communication and understanding are possible), the thought processes depart from radically different premises—especially unconscious or unstated premises. Those who have the cultural outlook are more likely to look beneath the surface and bring the culturally determined premises to the light of day. This may not bring about immediate agreement and harmony, but it will at least facilitate a *more* rational approach to the problem of international understanding and to diminishing friction between groups within a nation.

Knowledge of a culture makes it possible to predict a good many of the actions of any person who shares that culture. If the American Army was dropping paratroopers into Thailand in 1944, under what circumstances would they be knifed, under what circumstances would they be aided? If one knows how a given culture defines a certain situation, one can say that the betting odds are excellent that in a future comparable situation people will behave along certain lines and not along others. If we know a culture, we know what various classes of individuals within it expect from each other—and from outsiders of various categories. We know what types of activity are held to be inherently gratifying.

Many people in our society feel that the best way to get people to work harder is to increase their profits or their wages. They feel that it is just "human nature" to want to increase one's material possessions. This sort of dogma might well go unchallenged if we had no knowledge of other cultures. In certain societies, however, it has been found that the profit motive is not an effective incentive. After contact with whites, the Trobriand Islanders in Melanesia could have become fabulously rich from pearl diving. They would, however, work only long enough to satisfy their immediate wants.

Administrators need to become conscious of the symbolic nature of many activities. American women will choose a job as hostess in a restaurant rather than one as a waitress at a higher salary. In some societies the blacksmith is the most honored of individuals while in others only the lowest class of people are blacksmiths. White children in schools are motivated by grades; but children from some Indian tribe will work less hard under a system that singles the individual out from among his fellows.

Understanding of culture provides some detachment from the conscious and unconscious emotional values of one's own culture. The phrase, "some detachment," must be emphasized. An individual who viewed the designs for living of his group with complete detachment would be disoriented and unhappy. But I can prefer (i.e., feel affectively attached to) American manners while at the same time perceiving certain graces in English manners which are lacking or more grossly expressed in ours. Thus, while unwilling to forget that I am an American with no desire to ape English drawing-room behavior, I can still derive a lively pleasure from association with English people on social occasions. Whereas if I have no detachment, if I am utterly provincial, I am likely to regard English manners as utterly ridiculous, uncouth, perhaps even immoral. With that attitude I shall certainly not get on well with the English, and I am likely to resent bitterly any modification of our manners in the English or any other direction. Such attitudes clearly do not make for international understanding, friendship, and cooperation. They do, to the same extent, make for a too rigid social structure. Anthropological documents and anthropological teachings are valuable, therefore, in that they tend to emancipate individuals from a too strong allegiance to every item in the cultural inventory. The person who has been exposed to the anthropological perspective is more likely to live and let live both within his own society and in his dealings with members of other societies; and he will probably be more flexible in regard to needful changes in social organization to meet changed technology and changed economy.

Perhaps the most important implication of culture for action is the profound truth that you can never start with a clean slate so far as human beings are concerned. Every person is born into a world

defined by already existing culture patterns. Just as an individual who
has lost his memory is no longer normal, so the idea of a society's
becoming completely emancipated from its past culture is inconceivable.
This is one source of the tragic failure of the Weimar constitution in
Germany. In the abstract it was an admirable document. But it failed
miserably in actual life partly because it provided for no continuity
with existent designs for acting, feeling, and thinking.

Since every culture has organization as well as content, administrators and lawmakers should know that one cannot isolate a custom
to abolish or modify it. The most obvious example of failure caused
by neglect of this principle was the Eighteenth Amendment. The legal
sale of liquor was forbidden, but the repercussions in law enforcement,
in family life, in politics, in the economy were staggering.

The concept of culture, like any other piece of knowledge, can
be abused and misinterpreted. Some fear that the principle of cultural
relativity will weaken morality. "If the Bugabuga do it why can't we?
It's all relative anyway." But this is exactly what cultural relativity
does *not* mean.

The principle of cultural relativity does not mean that because
the members of some savage tribe are allowed to behave in a certain
way that this fact gives intellectual warrant for such behavior in all
groups. Cultural relativity means, on the contrary, that the appropriate-
ness of any positive or negative custom must be evaluated with regard
to how this habit fits with other group habits. Having several wives
makes economic sense among herders, not among hunters. While
breeding a healthy skepticism as to the eternity of any value prized by
a particular people, anthropology does not as a matter of theory deny
the existence of moral absolutes. Rather, the use of the comparative
method provides a scientific means of discovering such absolutes. If all
surviving societies have found it necessary to impose some of the same
restrictions upon the behavior of their members, this makes a strong
argument that these aspects of the moral code are indispensable.

Similarly, the fact that a Kwakiutl chief talks as if he had delusions
of grandeur and of persecution does not mean that paranoia is not a real
ailment in our cultural context. Anthropology has given a new perspective to the relativity of the normal that should bring greater
tolerance and understanding of socially harmless deviations. But it has
by no means destroyed standards or the useful tyranny of the normal.
All cultures recognize some of the same forms of behavior as pathological. Where they differ in their distinctions, there is a relationship
to the total framework of cultural life.

There is a legitimate objection to making culture explain too much. Lurking, however, in such criticisms of the cultural point of view is often the ridiculous assumption that one must be loyal to a single master explanatory principle. On the contrary, there is no incompatibility between biological, environmental, cultural, historical, and economic approaches. All are necessary. The anthropologist feels that so much of history as is still a living force is embodied in the culture. He regards the economy as a specialized part of the culture. But he sees the value in having economists and historians, as specialists, abstract out their special aspects—so long as the complete context is not entirely lost to view. Take the problems of the American South, for example. The anthropologist would entirely agree that biological (social visibility of black skin, etc.), environmental (water power and other natural resources), historical (South settled by certain types of people, somewhat different governmental practices from the start, etc.), and narrowly cultural (original discrimination against Negroes as "heathen savages," etc.) issues are all inextricably involved. However, the cultural factor is involved in the actual working out of each influence— though culture is definitely not the whole of it. And to say that certain acts are culturally defined does not always and necessarily mean that they could be eliminated by changing the culture.

The needs and drives of biological man, and the physical environment to which he must adjust, provide the stuff of human life, but a given culture determines the way this stuff is handled—the tailoring. In the eighteenth century a Neapolitan philosopher, Vico, uttered a profundity which was new, violent—and unnoticed. This was simply the discovery that "the social world is surely the work of man." Two generations of anthropologists have compelled thinkers to face this fact. Nor are anthropologists willing to allow the Marxists or other cultural determinists to make of culture another absolute as autocratic as the God or Fate portrayed by some philosophies. Anthropological knowledge does not permit so easy an evasion of man's responsibility for his own destiny. To be sure, culture is a compulsive force to most of us most of the time. To some extent, as Leslie White says, "Culture has a life and laws of its own." Some cultural changes are also compelled by economic or physical circumstances. But most of an economy is itself a cultural artifact. And it is men who change their cultures, even if — during most of past history — they have been acting as instruments of cultural processes of which they were largely unaware. The record shows that, while situation limits the range of possibility, there is always more than one workable alternative. The essence of the cultural process is selectivity; men may often make a choice. Lawrence Frank probably overstates the case:

In the years to come it is probable that this discovery of human origin and development of culture will be recognized as the greatest of all discoveries, since heretofore man has been helpless before these cultural and social formulations which generation after generation have perpetuated the same frustration and defeat of human values and aspirations. So long as he believes this was necessary and inevitable, he could not but accept this lot with resignation. Now man is beginning to realize that his culture and social organization are not unchanging cosmic processes, but are human creations which may be altered. For those who cherish the democratic faith this discovery means that they can, and must, undertake a continuing assay of our culture and our society in terms of its consequences for human life and human values. This is the historic origin and purpose of human culture, to create a human way of life. To our age falls the responsibility of utilizing the amazing new resources of science to meet these cultural tasks, to continue the great human tradition of man taking charge of his own destiny.

Nevertheless, to the extent that human beings discover the nature of the cultural process, they can anticipate, prepare, and—to at least a limited degree—control.

Americans are now at a period in history when they are faced with the facts of cultural differences more clearly than they can take with comfort. Recognition and tolerance of the deeper cultural assumptions of China, Russia, and Britain will require a difficult type of education. But the great lesson of culture is that the goals toward which men strive and fight and grope are not "given" in final form by biology nor yet entirely by the situation. If we understand our own culture and that of others, the political climate can be changed in a surprisingly short time in this narrow contemporary world providing men are wise enough and articulate enough and energetic enough. The concept of culture carries a legitimate note of hope to troubled men. If the German and Japanese peoples behaved as they did because of their biological heredity, the outlook for restoring them as peaceful and cooperative nations would be hopeless. But if their propensities for cruelty and aggrandizement were primarily the result of situational factors and their cultures, then something can be done about it, though false hopes must not be encouraged as to the speed with which a culture can be planfully changed.

THE LONELY CROWD*

by David Riesman
with Nathan Glazer and Reuel Denney

HIGH GROWTH POTENTIAL: TRADITION-DIRECTED TYPES

The phase of high growth potential characterizes more than half the world's population: India, Egypt, and China (which have already grown immensely in recent generations), most preliterate peoples in Central Africa, parts of Central and South America, in fact most areas of the world relatively untouched by industrialization. Here death rates are so high that if birth rates were not also high the populations would die out.

Regions where the population is in this stage may be either sparsely populated, as are the areas occupied by many primitive tribes and parts of Central and South America; or they may be densely populated, as are India, China, and Egypt. In either case, the society achieves a Malthusian bargain with the limited food supply by killing off, in one way or another, some of the potential surplus of births over deaths— the enormous trap which, in Malthus' view, nature sets for man and which can be peaceably escaped only by prudent cultivation of the soil and prudent uncultivation of the species through the delay of marriage. Without the prevention of childbirth by means of postponement of marriage or other contraceptive measures, the population must be limited by taking the life of living beings. And so societies have "invented" cannibalism, induced abortion, organized wars, made human sacrifice, and practiced infanticide (especially female) as means of avoiding periodic famine and epidemics.

Though this settling of accounts with the contradictory impulses of hunger and sex is accompanied often enough by upheaval and distress, these societies in the stage of high growth potential tend to be stable at least in the sense that their social practices, including the "crimes" that keep population down, are institutionalized and patterned.

*From David Riesman with Nathan Glazer and Reuel Denney, *The Lonely Crowd, Abridged,* New Haven: Yale University Press, pp. 9-25. Copyright 1950, 1953, © 1961 by Yale University Press. Reprinted by permission.

Generation after generation, people are born, are weeded out, and die to make room for others. The net rate of nature increase fluctuates within a broad range, though without showing any long-range tendency, as is true also of societies in the stage of incipient decline. But unlike the latter, the average life expectancy in the former is characteristically low: the population is heavily weighted on the side of the young, and generation replaces generation far more rapidly and less "efficiently" than in the societies of incipient population decline.

In viewing such a society we inevitably associate the relative stability of the man-land ratio, whether high or low, with the tenacity of custom and social structure. However, we must not equate stability of social structure over historical time with psychic stability in the life span of an individual: the latter may subjectively experience much violence and disorganization. In the last analysis, however, he learns to deal with life by adaptation, not by innovation. With certain exceptions, conformity is largely given in the "self-evident" social situation. Of course nothing in human life is ever really self-evident; where it so appears it is because perceptions have been narrowed by cultural conditioning. As the precarious relation to the food supply is built into the going culture, it helps create a pattern of conventional conformity which is reflected in many, if not in all, societies in the stage of high growth potential. This is what I call tradition-direction.

A DEFINITION OF TRADITION-DIRECTION

Since the type of social order we have been discussing is relatively unchanging, the conformity of the individual tends to reflect his membership in a particular age-grade, clan, or caste; he learns to understand and appreciate patterns which have endured for centuries, and are modified but slightly as the generations succeed each other. The important relationships of life may be controlled by careful and rigid etiquette, learned by the young during the years of intensive socialization that end with initiation into full adult membership. Moreover, the culture, in addition to its economic tasks, or as part of them, provides ritual, routine, and religion to occupy and to orient everyone. Little energy is directed toward finding new solutions of the age-old problems, let us say, of agricultural technique or medicine, the problems to which people are acculturated.

It is not to be thought, however, that in these societies, where the activity of the individual member is determined by characterologically grounded obedience to traditions, the individual may not be highly prized and, in many instances, encouraged to develop his capabilities, his initiative, and even, within very narrow time limits, his aspirations. Indeed, the individual in some primitive societies is far more appreciated and respected than in some sectors of modern society. For the individual in a society dependent on tradition-direction has a well-defined functional relationship to other members of the group. If he is not killed off, he "belongs"— he is not "surplus," as the modern unemployed are surplus, nor is he expendable as the unskilled are expendable in modern society. But by very virtue of his "belonging," life goals that are *his* in terms of conscious choice appear to shape his destiny only to a very limited extent, just as only to a limited extent is there any concept of progress for the group.

In societies in which tradition-direction is the dominant mode of insuring conformity, relative stability is preserved in part by the infrequent but highly important process of fitting into institutionalized roles such deviants as there are. In such societies a person who might have become at a later historical stage an innovator or rebel, whose belonging, as such, is marginal and problematic, is drawn instead into roles like those of the shaman or sorcerer. That is, he is drawn into roles that make a socially acceptable contribution, while at the same time they provide the individual with a more or less approved niche. The medieval monastic orders may have served in a similar way to absorb many characterological "mutations."

In some of these societies certain individuals are encouraged toward a degree of individuality from childhood, especially if they belong to families of high status. But, since the range of choice, even for high-status people, is minimal, the apparent social need for an individuated type of character is also minimal. It is probably accurate to say that character structure in these societies is very largely "adjusted," in the sense that for most people it appears to be in tune with social institutions. Even the few misfits "fit" to a degree; and only very rarely is one driven out of his social world.

This does not mean, of course, that the people are happy; the society to whose traditions they are adjusted may be a miserable one, ridden with anxiety, sadism, and disease. The point is rather that change, while never completely absent in human affairs, is slowed down as the movement of molecules is slowed down at low temperature; and the social character comes as close as it ever does to looking like the matrix of the social forms themselves.

In Western history the Middle Ages can be considered a period in which the majority were tradition-directed. But the term tradition-directed refers to a common element, not only among the people of precapitalist Europe but also among such enormously different types of people as Hindus and Hopi Indians, Zulus and Chinese, North African Arabs, and Balinese. There is comfort in relying on the many writers who have found a similar unity amid diversity, a unity they express in such terms as "folk society" (as against "civilization"), "status society" (as against "contract society"), *"Gemeinschaft"* (as against *"Gesellschaft"*), and so on. Different as the societies envisaged by these terms are, the folk, status, and *Gemeinschaft* societies resemble each other in their relative slowness of change, their dependence on family and kin organization, and—in comparison with later epochs— their tight web of values. And, as is now well recognized by students, the high birth rate of these societies in the stage of high growth potential is not merely the result of a lack of contraceptive knowledge or techniques. A whole way of life—an outlook on change, on children, on the place of women, on sexuality, on the very meaning of existence —is the basis of distinction between the societies in which human fertility is allowed to take its course and toll and those which prefer to pay other kinds of toll to cut down on fertility by calculation, and, conceivably, as Freud and other observers have suggested, by a decline in sexual energy itself.

TRANSITIONAL GROWTH: INNER-DIRECTED TYPES

Except for the West, we know very little about the cumulation of small changes that can eventuate in a breakup of the tradition-directed type of society, leading it to realize its potential for high population growth. As for the West, however, much has been learned about the slow decay of feudalism and the subsequent rise of a type of society in which inner-direction is the dominant mode of insuring conformity.

Critical historians, pushing the Renaissance ever back into the Middle Ages, seem sometimes to deny that any decisive change occured at all. On the whole, however, it seems that the greatest social and characterological shift of recent centuries did indeed come when men were driven out of the primary ties that bound them to the Western medieval version of tradition-directed society. All later shifts, including the shift from inner-direction to other-direction, seem unimportant by comparison, although of course this latter shift is still under way and we cannot tell what it will look like when—if ever—it is complete.

A change in the relatively stable ratio of births to deaths, which characterizes the period of high growth potential, is both the cause and consequence of other profound social changes. In most of the cases known to us a decline takes place in mortality prior to a decline in fertility; hence there is some period in which the population expands rapidly. The drop in death rate occurs as the result of many interacting factors, among them sanitation, improved communications (which permit government to operate over a wider area and also permit easier transport of food to areas of shortage from areas of surplus), the decline, forced or otherwise, of infanticide, cannibalism, and other inbred kinds of violence. Because of improved methods of agriculture the land is able to support more people, and these in turn produce still more people.

Notestein's phrase, "transitional growth," is a mild way of putting it. The "transition" is likely to be violent, disrupting the stabilized paths of existence in societies in which tradition-direction has been the principal mode of insuring conformity. The imbalance of births and deaths puts pressure on the society's customary ways. A new slate of character structures is called for or finds its opportunity in coping with the rapid changes—and the need for still more changes—in the social organization.

A Definition of Inner-Direction

In Western history the society that emerged with the Renaissance and Reformation and that is only now vanishing serves to illustrate the type of society in which inner-direction is the principal mode of securing conformity. Such a society is characterized by increased personal mobility, by a rapid accumulation of capital (teamed with devastating technological shifts), and by an almost constant *expansion:* intensive expansion in the production of goods and people, and extensive expansion in exploration, colonization, and imperialism. The greater choices this society gives—and the greater initiatives it demands in order to cope with its novel problems—are handled by character types who can manage to live socially without strict and self-evident tradition-direction. These are the inner-directed types.

The concept of inner-direction is intended to cover a very wide range of types. Thus, while it is essential for the study of certain problems to differentiate between Protestant and Catholic countries and their character types, between the effects of the Reformation and the effects of the Renaissance, between the puritan ethic of the European north and west and the somewhat more hedonistic ethic of the European east and south, while all these are valid and, for certain purposes, important distinctions, the concentration of this study on the development of modes of conformity permits their neglect. It allows the grouping together of these otherwise distinct developments because they have one thing in common: *the source of direction for the individual is "inner" in the sense that it is implanted early in life by the elders and directed toward generalized but nonetheless inescapably destined goals.*

We can see what this means when we realize that, in societies in which tradition-direction is the dominant mode of insuring conformity, attention is focused on securing strict conformity in generally observable words and actions, that is to say, behavior. While behavior is minutely prescribed, individuality of character need not be highly developed to meet prescriptions that are objectified in ritual and etiquette—though to be sure, a social character *capable* of such behavioral attention and obedience is requisite. By contrast, societies in which inner-direction becomes important, though they also are concerned with behavioral conformity, cannot be satisfied with behavioral conformity alone. Too many novel situations are presented, situations which a code cannot encompass in advance. Consequently the problem of personal choice, solved in the earlier period of high growth potential by channeling choice through rigid social organization, in the period of transitional growth is solved by channeling choice through a rigid though highly individualized character.

This rigidity is a complex matter. While any society dependent on inner-direction seems to present people with a wide choice of aims— such as money, possessions, power, knowledge, fame, goodness—these aims are ideologically interrelated, and the selection made by any one individual remains relatively unalterable throughout his life. Moreover, the means to those ends, though not fitted into as tight a frame of social reference as in the society dependent on tradition-direction, are nevertheless limited by the new voluntary associations—for instance, the Quakers, the Masons, the Mechanics' Associations—to which people tie themselves. Indeed, the term "tradition-directed" could be misleading if the reader were to conclude that the force of tradition has no weight for the inner-directed character. On the contrary, he is very considerably bound by traditions: they limit his ends and inhibit his choice of means. The point is rather that a splintering of tradition takes place, connected in part with the increasing division of labor and stratification of society. Even if the individual's choice of tradition is largely determined for him by his family, as it is in most cases, he cannot help becoming aware of the existence of competing traditions— hence of tradition as such. As a result he possesses a somewhat greater degree of flexibility in adapting himself to every changing requirement and in return requires more from his environment.

As the control of the primary group is loosened—the group that both socializes the young and controls the adult in the earlier era—a new psychological mechanism appropriate to the more open society is "invented": it is what I like to describe as a psychological gyroscope.[1] This instrument, once it is set by the parents and other authorities, keeps the inner-directed person, as we shall see, "on course" even when tradition, as responded to by his character, no longer dictates his moves. The inner-directed person becomes capable of maintaining a delicate balance between the demands upon him of his life goal and the buffetings of his external environment.

This metaphor of the gyroscope, like any other, must not be taken literally. It would be a mistake to see the inner-directed man as incapable of learning from experience or as insensitive to public opinion in matters of external conformity. He can receive and utilize certain signals from outside, provided that they can be reconciled with the limited maneuverability that his gyroscope permits him. His pilot is not quite automatic.

Huizinga's *The Waning of the Middle Ages* gives a picture of the anguish and turmoil, the conflict of values, out of which the new forms slowly emerged. Already by the late Middle Ages people were forced to live under new conditions of awareness. As their self-consciousness and their individuality developed, they had to make themselves at home in the world in novel ways. They still have to.

INCIPIENT DECLINE OF POPULATION: OTHER-DIRECTED TYPES

The problem facing the societies in the stage of transitional growth is that of reaching a point at which resources become plentiful enough or are utilized effectively enough to permit a rapid accumulation of capital. This rapid accumulation has to be achieved even while the social product is being drawn on at an accelerated rate to maintain the rising population and satisfy the consumer demands that go with the

---

[1] Since writing the above I have discovered Gardner Murphy's use of the same metaphor in his volume *Personality* (New York, Harper, 1947).

way of life that has already been adopted. For most countries, unless capital and techniques can be imported from other countries in still later phases of the population curve, every effort to increase national resources at a rapid rate must actually be at the expense of current standards of living. We have seen this occur in the U.S.S.R., now in the stage of transitional growth. For western Europe this transition was long-drawn-out and painful. For America, Canada, and Australia—at once beneficiaries of European techniques and native resources—the transition was rapid and relatively easy.

The tradition-directed person, as has been said, hardly thinks of himself as an individual. Still less does it occur to him that he might shape his own destiny in terms of personal, lifelong goals or that the destiny of his children might be separate from that of the family group. He is not sufficiently separated psychologically from himself (or, therefore, sufficiently close to himself), his family, or group to think in these terms. In the phase of transitional growth, however, people of inner-directed character do gain a feeling of control over their own lives and see their children also as individuals with careers to make. At the same time, with the shift out of agriculture and, later, with the end of child labor, children no longer become an unequivocal economic asset. And with the growth of habits of scientific thought, religious and magical views of human fertility—views that in an earlier phase of the population curve made sense for the culture if it was to reproduce itself—give way to "rational," individualistic attitudes. Indeed, just as the rapid accumulation of productive capital requires that people be imbued with the "Protestant ethic" (as Max Weber characterized one manifestation of what is here termed inner-direction), so also the decreased number of progeny requires a profound change in values—a change so deep that, in all probability, it has to be rooted in character structure.

As the birth rate begins to follow the death rate downward, societies move toward the epoch of incipient decline of population. Fewer and fewer people work on the land or in the extractive industries or even in manufacturing. Hours are short. People may have material abundance and leisure besides. They pay for these changes however—here, as always, the solution of old problems gives rise to new ones—by finding themselves in a centralized and bureaucratized society and a world shrunken and agitated by the contact—accelerated by industrialization—of races, nations, and cultures.

The hard enduringness and enterprise of the inner-directed types are somewhat less necessary under these new conditions. Increasingly, *other people* are the problem, not the material environment. And as people mix more widely and become more sensitive to each other, the surviving traditions from the stage of high growth potential—much disrupted, in any case, during the violent spurt of industrialization—become still further attenuated. Gyroscopic control is no longer sufficiently flexible, and a new psychological mechanism is called for.

Furthermore, the "scarcity psychology" of many inner-directed people, which was socially adaptive during the period of heavy capital accumulation that accompanied transitional growth of population, needs to give way to an "abundance psychology" capable of "wasteful" luxury consumption of leisure and of the surplus product. Unless people want to destroy the surplus product in war, which still does require heavy capital equipment, they must learn to enjoy and engage in those services that are expensive in terms of man power but not of capital—poetry and philosophy, for instance. Indeed, in the period of incipient decline, nonproductive consumers, both the increasing number of old people and the diminishing number of as yet untrained young, form a high proportion of the population, and these need both the economic opportunity to be prodigal and the character structure that allows it.

Has this need for still another slate of character types actually been acknowledged to any degree? My observations lead me to believe that in America it has.

A DEFINITION OF OTHER-DIRECTION

The type of character I shall describe as other-directed seems to be emerging in very recent years in the upper middle class of our larger cities: more prominently in New York than in Boston, in Los Angeles than in Spokane, in Cincinnati than in Chillicothe. Yet in some respects this type is strikingly similar to the American, whom Tocqueville and other curious and astonished visitors from Europe, even before the Revolution, thought to be a new kind of man. Indeed, travelers' reports on America impress us with their unanimity. The American is said to be shallower, freer with his money, friendlier, more uncertain of himself and his values, more demanding of approval than the European. It all adds up to a pattern which, without stretching matters too far, resembles the kind of character that a number of social scientists have seen as developing in contemporary, highly industrialized and bureaucratic America: Fromm's "marketer," Mills' "fixer," Arnold Green's "middle class male child."

It is my impression that the middle-class American of today is decisively different from those Americans of Tocqueville's writings who nevertheless strike us as so contemporary, and much of this book will be devoted to discussing these differences. It is also my impression that the conditions I believe to be responsible for other-direction are affecting increasing numbers of people in the metropolitan centers of the advanced industrial countries. My analysis of the other-directed character is thus at once an analysis of the American and of contemporary man. Much of the time I find it hard or impossible to say where one ends and the other begins. Tentatively, I am inclined to think that the other-directed type does find itself most at home in America, due to certain unique elements in American society, such as its recruitment from Europe and its lack of any feudal past. As against this, I am also inclined to put more weight on capitalism, industrialism, and urbanization — these being international tendencies — than on any character-forming peculiarities of the American scene.

Bearing these qualifications in mind, it seems appropriate to treat contemporary metropolitan America as our illustration of a society—so far, perhaps, the only illustration—in which other-direction is the dominant mode of insuring conformity. It would be premature, however, to say that it is already the dominant mode in America as a whole. But since the other-directed types are to be found among the young, in the larger cities, and among the upper income groups, we may assume that, unless present trends are reversed, the hegemony of other-direction lies not far off.

If we wanted to cast our social character types into social class molds, we could say that inner-direction is the typical character of the "old" middle class—the banker, the tradesman, the small entrepreneur, the technically oriented engineer, etc.—while other-direction is becoming the typical character of the "new" middle class—the bureaucrat, the salaried employee in business, etc. Many of the economic factors associated with the recent growth of the "new" middle class are well known. They have been discussed by James Burnham, Colin Clark, Peter Drucker, and others. There is a decline in the numbers and in the proportion of the working population engaged in production and extraction—agriculture, heavy industry, heavy transport—and an increase in the numbers and the proportion engaged in white-collar work and the service trades. People who are literate, educated, and provided with the necessities of life by an ever more efficient machine industry and agriculture, turn increasingly to the "tertiary" economic realm. The service industries prosper among the people as a whole and no longer only in court circles.

Education, leisure, services, these go together with an increased consumption of words and images from the new mass media of communications. While societies in the phase of transitional growth step up the process of distributing words from urban centers, the flow becomes a torrent in the societies of incipient population decline. This process, while modulated by profound national and class differences, connected with differences in literacy and loquacity, takes place everywhere in the industrialized lands. Increasingly, relations with the outer world and with oneself are mediated by the flow of mass communication. For the other-directed types political events are likewise experienced through a screen of words by which the events are habitually atomized and personalized—or pseudo-personalized. For the inner-directed person who remains still extant in this period the tendency is rather to systematize and moralize this flow of words.

These developments lead, for large numbers of people, to changes in paths to success and to the requirements of more "socialized" behavior both for success and for marital and personal adaptation. Connected with such changes are changes in the family and in child-rearing practices. In the smaller families of urban life, and with the spread of "permissive" child care to ever wider strata of the population, there is a relaxation of older patterns of discipline. Under these newer patterns the peer-group (the group of one's associates of the same age and class) becomes much more important to the child, while the parents make him feel guilty not so much about violation of inner standards as about failure to be popular or otherwise to manage his relations with these other children. Moreover, the pressures of the school and the peer-group are reinforced and continued—in a manner whose inner paradoxes I shall discuss later—by the mass media: movies, radio, comics, and popular culture media generally. Under these conditions types of character emerge that we shall here term other-directed. To them much of the discussion in the ensuing chapter is devoted. *What is common to all the other-directed people is that their contemporaries are the source of direction for the individual—either those known to him or those with whom he is indirectly acquainted, through friends and through the mass media. This source is of course "internalized" in the sense that dependence on it for guidance in life is implanted early. The goals toward which the other-directed person strives shift with that guidance: it is only the process of striving itself and the process of paying close attention to the signals from others that remain unaltered throughout life.* This mode of keeping in touch with others permits a close behavioral conformity, not through drill in behavior itself, as in the tradition-directed character, but rather through an exceptional sensitivity to the actions and wishes of others.

Of course, it matters very much who these "others" are: whether they are the individual's immediate circle or a "higher" circle or the anonymous voices of the mass media; whether the individual fears the hostility of chance acquaintances or only of those who "count." But his need for approval and direction from others—and contemporary others rather than ancestors—goes beyond the reasons that lead most people in any era to care very much what others think of them. While all people want and need to be liked by some of the people some of the time, it is only the modern other-directed types who make this their chief source of direction and chief area of sensitivity.

The inner-directed person, though he often sought and sometimes achieved a relative independence of public opinion and of what the neighbors thought of him, was in most cases very much concerned with his good repute and, at least in America, with "keeping up with the Joneses." These conformities, however, were primarily external, typified in such details as clothes, curtains, and bank credit. Or, indeed, the conformities were to a standard, evidence of which was provided by the "best people" in one's milieu. In contrast with this pattern, the other-directed person, though he has his eye very much on the Joneses, aims to keep up with them not so much in external details as in the quality of his inner experience. That is, his great sensitivity keeps him in touch with others on many more levels than the externals of appearance and propriety. Nor does any ideal of independence or of reliance on God alone modify his desire to look to the others—and the "good guys" as well as the best people—for guidance in what experiences to seek and in how to interpret them.

THE THREE TYPES COMPARED

One way to see the structural differences that mark the three types is to see the differences in the emotional sanction or control in each type.

The tradition-directed person feels the impact of his culture as a unit, but it is nevertheless mediated through the specific, small number of individuals with whom he is in daily contact. These expect of him not so much that he be a certain type of person but that he behave in the approved way. Consequently the sanction for behavior tends to be the fear of being *shamed*.

The inner-directed person has early incorporated a psychic gyroscope which is set going by his parents and can receive signals later on from other authorities who resemble his parents. He goes through life less independent than he seems, obeying this internal piloting. Getting off course, whether in response to inner impulses or to the fluctuating voices of contemporaries may lead to the feeling of *guilt*.

Since the direction to be taken in life has been learned in the privacy of the home from a small number of guides, and since principles, rather than details of behavior, are internalized, the inner-directed person is capable of great stability. Especially so when it turns out that his fellows have gyroscopes too, spinning at the same speed and set in the same direction. But many inner-directed individuals can remain stable even when the reinforcement of social approval is not available—as in the upright life of the stock Englishman isolated in the tropics.

Contrasted with such a type as this, the other-directed person learns to respond to signals from a far wider circle than is constituted by his parents. The family is no longer a closely knit unit to which he belongs but merely part of a wider social environment to which he early becomes attentive. In these respects the other-directed person resembles the tradition-directed person: both live in a group milieu and lack the inner-directed person's capacity to go it alone. The nature of this group milieu, however, differs radically in the two cases. The other-directed person is cosmopolitan. For him the border between the familiar and the strange—a border clearly marked in the societies depending on tradition-direction—has broken down. As the family continuously absorbs the strange and reshapes itself, so the strange becomes familiar. While the inner-directed person could be "at home abroad" by virtue of his relative insensitivity to others, the other-directed person is, in a sense, at home everywhere and nowhere, capable of a rapid if sometimes superficial intimacy with and response to everyone.

The tradition-directed person takes his signals from others, but they come in a cultural monotone; he needs no complex receiving equipment to pick them up. The other-directed person must be able to receive signals from far and near; the sources are many, and the changes rapid. What can be internalized, then, is not a code of behavior but the elaborate equipment needed to attend to such messages and occasionally to participate in their circulation. As against guilt-and-shame controls, though of course these survive, one prime psychological level of the other-directed person is a diffuse *anxiety*. This control equipment, instead of being like a gyroscope, is like a radar.

THE FOLK-URBAN-SUBURBAN CONTINUUM: A CONCEPTUAL OVERVIEW OF AMERICA YESTERDAY, TODAY, AND TOMORROW*

by Harold M. Hodges, Jr.

"Culture," "personality," and "social class": the student who cannot comprehend these concepts cannot comprehend even the most rudimentary facts about man and society. Yet there is another conceptual scheme which must be mastered by any one who would discern the uniformities which lend consistency and continuity to the seeming chaos of today's world. This is the "folk-urban" typology.[1]

In its briefest terms, the folk-urban device is a frame of reference which will help us conceptualize social reality; it is an "ideal type" construct—a continuum with polar extremes, "folk" at the one end and "urban" at the other, which do not exist in reality. Actual societies tend to be *more* or *less* folk or urban in coloration. Nor can any single society be located at any exact point along the continuum; for all societies, even the most isolated and "primitive," are in a constant state of flux and change.

For our purposes the concept will help us to (1) fathom the dynamics and consequences of industrialization and urbanization, and (2) understand how raw-boned immigrants have bridged the vast cultural gap between old world and new in scarcely three generations. It is certainly a concept which will enable us to better understand the ethnic and racial minorities which are still in our midst . . . .

Even today the majority of the world's peoples live in what amount to folk-structured societies. And less than one hundred years ago a significant proportion of our own ancestors were members of folk

---

---

[1] The folk-urban concept is not altogether new; similar schemes have been proposed in the past by Ferdinand Tonnies *(Gemeinschaft-Gesellschaft)*, Emile Durkheim (organic-mechanical), Howard Becker (sacred-secular), Robert Redfield (folk-urban), Kingsley Davis (rural-urban), and, more recently, many sociologists (communal-associational).

societies. The concept, in a word, can be viewed along two dimensions: geographical and historical. In the first instance we might compare such contemporary societies as the French with the Yegali aborigines of the Seychelles Islands; in the second, we might contrast the early nineteenth-century American with the American of our own time.[2] We have elected the historical comparison, for it is the purpose of this essay to illustrate and help explain the Americanization process which converted millions of European-born peasants (and American-born farmers and villagers as well) into the urbanized people we know today.

To illustrate our example the more vividly, we shall take a hypothetical people, the Perdidans, as representative of the "new immigrants" —Poles, Croats, Italians, Slovenes, Rumanians—who packed the holds of New York-bound ships in the several decades just before World War I. Unlike the Scandinavians, Germans, and English who had preceded them, those who emigrated from Perdida, Italy, Austria-Hungary, and other southern and eastern European countries were primarily of agrarian, peasant stock, were Roman Catholic, and found their new homes in America's burgeoning new industrial complexes. In consequence, the acculturation process which they and their children faced was of a totally different character from the process encountered by the Germans, Scandinavians, and Czechs who settled in the northern tier of Great Lakes states or by those Irish who moved west with the Army and the railroads.[3] To learn what happened to the Perdidan peasant and what his grandchildren are doing today is to gain a penetrating insight into the marrow of a changing America. We shall look, too, into the immediate future—into the "mass society" which appears to be our cultural destiny. Thus we shall *extend* the folk-urban polarity by adding a new, and baldly hypothetical, dimension: the "suburban."

The Perdidans of 1900, like the Perdidans of centuries past, lived in a diminutive valley high on the arid slopes of a pine-mantled escarpment of the Pyrenees mountains. Sustained by a precarious one-crop economy, the natives of Perdida — like the residents of the Spanish province of Huesca on the one side and the French department of Hautes Pyrenees on the other—were mired in a semi-serf status barely

---

[2] There are, of course, Americans who even today adhere to a way of life that is heavily permeated with folk-like characteristics (hillbillies, for example, or inhabitants of remote hamlets); rural peoples who move to the cities afford more tangible, visible examples.

[3] Many Irish, of course, remained in eastern seaboard cities; but though akin to the "new immigrants" in their loyalty to Catholicism and their village backgrounds, the fact that they were an English-speaking people immeasurably eased their assimilation into American culture.

removed from feudalism. Dominated by ancient customs, folkways, and mores, the social fabric of the entire community was tied up in two core institutions: the Roman Catholic Church and the family. All attended masses and confessions, and the priest was confidant and close friend to every man, woman, and child in the village.

And next to the village priest the most important man was the head of the family — often a grandfather or great-grandfather. The family was patriarchal — father-dominated; women and (above all) children played a secondary, very subservient role. Aside from the village priest, candlestick maker, and perhaps a smithy, butcher and baker, there were no "specialists." Almost totally self-sufficient, each family built its own home, raised its own foodstuffs, delivered its own babies, made its own clothing (from shearing the family sheep through weaving, cutting, and sewing). But more important and meaningful than this family self-sufficiency was the intense family loyalty which colored every thread of every villager's life. In a larger sense this same intense in-group loyalty pervaded the entire village. Outsiders and strangers, even if they came from neighboring villages, were greeted with either suspicion or hostility.

Coupled with a stagnant, unchanging agrarian-handicraft economy and a blended sense of loyalty and obligation to the family, this local-ized ethnocentrism saw only rare villagers leaving for a new and more challenging life in the distant outside world. Not only were people essentially happy and well-adjusted in such a setting, but they *knew* no other, more exciting way of life. In short, an intensive *conservatism* marked every sphere of life. This was the well-ordered existence their ancestors had known, and this was the sort of life they wanted to live.

For the Perdidan villager (and his counterpart throughout Europe and the rural USA) other areas of life were just as rigidly static and unvaried. The pattern of life was so simple and clearcut that even the unintelligent could play their prescribed roles without confusion or conflict. People knew what was expected of them and they knew what to expect of others. Only a handful of the villagers were literate. Nor did masses of peasants need to be literate. Formal schooling was for the priest, the doctor, the aristocrat, and the city folk. If one were born into a family which had farmed for generations, *he* would be a farmer — and so would his children and his children's children.

But this way of life was not to last. A series of devastating droughts depleted the always-meager potato crop; and the potato was the staple in the villagers' diet. Then came a stream of letters from the few who had migrated to America. Surfeited with more money and an easier life than they had ever known in Perdida, they painted a gleaming picture of the "land of plenty." The villagers responded. *En masse,* within a two-year span, the *entire* village packed its scant possessions and jammed the holds of New York-bound immigrant ships.

Like the Germans and Irish before them — and the Italians and Puerto Ricans yet to come—the Perdidan villagers flocked to the big city. For this was where the jobs were. The industrial revolution, spawned 30 years before in the wake of the Civil War, had re-structured the face of America. And the coal-blackened factories were necessarily located in the cities; this was where transportation lines converged and where the massive reservoir of labor was concentrated.

The newest immigrants, handicapped by language and skill barriers, were at the bottom of the totem pole. They obtained the least skilled jobs and, even though women and children worked, they could only find homes in the blighted segments of the city which fringed the manufacturing district. These dilapidated slum and tenement areas were known as "zones of transition." The term was an apt one. For these overcrowded "hell's kitchens" were transitional in a twofold respect: they had once been respectable middle-class homes, but their owners had fled, property values tumbled, and buildings fell into disrepair as the manufacturing districts drew closer; more significantly, these slums (in New York, Boston, Pittsburgh, Philadelphia, Chicago — in virtually every American metropolis geared to a growing industry) were the *temporary* stopping places for wave after wave of immigrants. As the invading immigrant group prospered and acquired the economic wherewithal and social graces, it moved into "better" areas of the city. But a new influx of immigrants — often from a different country — took its place. The sequence was repeated again and again. When they arrived at the early 1900's, the Perdidans were simply the newest wave in this decades-old pattern.

As the Perdidan villagers gradually settled down in their new milieu, another process familiar to successive influxes of immigrants took place. Instead of moving in helter-skelter fashion to scattered parts of the zone of transition, the villagers all settled within an area bounded by one or two blocks. This world was too new and frightening to go it alone, so they sought out familiar faces. Soon, as old friends and cliques reconsolidated, old customs and ways of life re-emerged. Thus the Perdidans became a "cultural island" — a tight little in-group similar to the scores of surrounding "little Bohemias" and "little Germanys."

But — and *here begins the first significant shift* — this snug little island with its old-fashioned way of life was only for the elderly. The *children,* those too young to remember Perdida and those born in the new world, began to revolt. It was gradual at first, just a restless chafing as the second-generation Perdidan-Americans returned home from school or factory to discover their parents just a little obsolete and embarrassingly "foreign." It was the beginning of the end. And the beginning of the beginning. For these children were on their way to becoming Americans. As time elapsed, embarrassment would turn to chagrin as their parents desperately clung to the only way of life they could understand.

The Americanization process was not an easy one. The awkward young Perdidans were as culturally maladroit as the by-now Americanized Irish had been before them. They had roundly rejected their parents' way of life, but they had not yet mastered the subtler intricacies of the urban, middle-class American way. They were *marginal men* — people "without a culture" or, better, people on the edges of two cultures. The consequence, as it had often been for their antecedents from other countries, was an almost inevitable blend of confusion, resentment, and chaos which many sociologists have aptly labeled "social disorganization."[4] The majority of Perdidan-Americans, it is true, ultimately solved the dilemma of marginality and achieved some measure of social, economic, and psychological stability in adulthood. Obtaining semi-skilled, skilled, and often clerical jobs, they abandoned the ethnic enclaves where their parents still lived and found new homes in the more "respectable" workingmen's neighborhoods just inside the suburban peripheries of the city.[5] But a minority, especially those who had engaged in norm-violating escapades as full-fledged members of delinquent gangs, never became law-abiding adults.[6] Some turned to underworld careers and others became opiate addicts or panhandlers. Others, too — more so (significantly) in the second generation than in the immigrant or the third generations — were victimized by mental illness (especially the schizophrenic and paranoiac psychoses), alcoholism, marital discord, and even suicide.[7]

---

[4] Not all immigrants went through so jarring an indoctrination; the Scandinavians in particular, and many Germans and Bohemians, migrated directly to an agrarian middle west where the way of life was similar to what they had known in the old country.

[5] In this process, many gave up familistic loyalties for more individualistic motives; they now paid allegiance only to the immediate "nuclear" family of wife and children.

[6] See Chapter Six for an elaboration on the matter of delinquency.

[7] Marginality—the sense of norm and role confusion which the sociologist identifies as *"anomie"*—was compounded for the *adolescent* second-generation Perdidan. For adolescence, even for children of old American stock, is frequently a period of agony, uncertainty, and revolt against parental standards, in short another type of marginality.

Born sometime between 1935 and 1945, the modal *third*-generation Perdidan (no longer, in fact, a "hyphenated" American) is characteristically a suburban-dwelling, middle-class American. Like his blue-collar father, he is still upward-mobile, and if he did not manage to attend college, his recently born children are almost certain to obtain the bachelor's degrees which open the door to professional — and upper-middle-class—status. He has completed the folk-urban-suburban cycle.[8] "Suburban," like "urban" and "folk," is less a geographical entity than it is a cultural (and social psychological) concept; more abstract and metaphysical than concrete, it represents a synthetic compound of characteristics lifted out of real social situations. People, in a word, need not dwell in "suburbia" to share the congeries of values and life styles which we label "suburban." Nor do all who are suburban in this context share all the characteristics we have listed. Suburbanism, finally, is less a *fait accompli* than it is an emergent process. In consequence, the qualities which we attach to it are necessarily tentative and hypothetical.

The more memorable ravages of urbanization — the norm-shattering dislocations which paralleled the industrialization of America during the last third of the nineteenth century and the first third of the twentieth—appear to have spent their energies.[9] Suburbanism, to some observers, represents the American reaction to the debilitating experience of urbanization — a re-stabilizing sociological "return to the womb" (or better, in Erich Fromm's words, an "escape from freedom").[10] If this be true—and only educated guesswork can be adduced as evidence — urbanization represented a painful *transitional* phase of our history; we have now, in almost full-circle fashion, re-entered an

---

[8] The portrait of the "typical" immigrant group painted in these pages is, for purposes of dramatic simplification, consciously broad-stroked. Although the overall pattern was strikingly similar for many, each wave of immigrants actually encountered experiences unique to its own national group. Despite a common "folk" heritage, there were also significant differences—in terms of language, customs, mores, folkways, and religion—among Germans, Poles, Irish, Scandinavians, Italians, Perdidans, and central Europeans. And the west coast ethnics, especially (the Japanese, Chinese, Filipino, and, to a lesser extent, the Mexican), came from uniquely variant cultural backgrounds and encountered a different type of reception from native Americans.

[9] The pace may continue for awhile in those major metropolitan complexes— New York, Detroit, Los Angeles, Seattle, Chicago and San Francisco—which are still witnessing massive influxes of migrant ethnics.

[10] Most students of personality agree that human behavior is actuated in times of stress by a "strain for consistency"—a deepfelt need for harmony, balance, and freedom from anxiety—which wards off threats of discord. Societies (and small groups as well) may be impelled by similar tension-alleviating mechanisms. For if they are to endure, societies, like humans, must be integrated units.

era of relative predictability and stability. Whatever its origins, a firmer, more homogeneous "mass society" (see Chapter Seven) has made its appearance and promises to engulf even the remotest hinterlands of the United States. The following chart highlights the more significant contours of the folk, urban, and suburban eras. Clarity and economy dictate that the descriptions be terse and simplified. The reader must be warned, too, that any given industrial society will contain all three elements; in consequence, the boundaries which separate "folk," "urban," and "suburban" are in reality blurred and overlapping.

(The footnotes below refer to references cited in the chart on pages 57-59.)

[1] Redfield, Robert, "The Folk Society," *American Journal of Sociology,* 52 (January, 1947), p. 294.

[2] "The component relations are structured into a rigidly unified whole by the inflexible, unchanging, all-powerful culture pattern," Wilson, Logan, and Kolb, William L., *Sociological Analysis* (New York: Harcourt, Brace and Company), 1949, p. 345.

[3] In this complex, diversified society, with its myriad groups and competing interests, the pervasive hold of tradition has been largely broken, and the comparative uniformity of thought has been replaced by an almost endless variety," Ely Chinoy, *Sociology* (N. Y.: Random House, 1961), p. 90.

[4] See Fava, Sylvia F., "Suburbanism as a Way of Life," *American Sociological Review,* 21 (February, 1956), pp. 35-36; Gist, Noel, "Ecological Decentralization and Rural-Urban Relationships," *Rural Sociology,* 17 (December, 1952), pp. 33 1ff, and Martin, W., *The Rural-Urban Fringe* (Eugene, Oregon: The University of Oregon Press, 1953), pp. 60-68.

[5] Although the city is secondary in character, one author warns, it is at the same time "a congeries of interlocking and overlapping primary groups," Davis, Kingsley, *Human Society* (N. Y.: The Macmillan Company, 1961), p. 332.

[6] Chinoy, Ely, *Sociological Perspective* (N. Y.: Random House, 1954), p. 33.

[7] Chinoy, *Sociology, op. cit.,* p. 89.

[8] Davis, *op. cit.,* p. 331.

[9] For amplification of this point, see Potter, David M., *People of Plenty, op. cit.,* Chapter III.

[10] See Lynes, Russell, *Surfeit of Honey, op. cit.*

[11] See Riesman, David, "Some Observations on Changes in Leisure Attitudes," *Antioch Review,* 12 (December, 1952), pp. 417-436.

Folk Culture:

I: Tradition-oriented; strong resistance to change and novel ideas; pattern of life static, unvarying, community centered ... "behavior is traditionally spontaneous, uncritical, and personal" ... rigidly unified culture.[2]

II: Social controls vested in mores, folkways rather than codified laws ... controls enforced by informal community pressures, threat of gossip or ostracism ... behavior regulated by firm, inflexible custom ... little allowance for individual choice, no tolerance for deviates, dissenters ...

III: Social relationships long-lasting, intimate, personal; dependence upon others for approval, affection ... slight privacy and anonymity ... dominance of primary and quasi-primary groups (family, neighborhood) ...

IV: Little division of labor except between men and women ... "range of alternative patterns of behavior open to individuals is held to a minimum"[6] ... emphasis on ascribed (hereditary) rather than achieved (competitive) statuses ... people know what to expect of others ... sex and age roles rigidly prescribed, starkly different ...

Urban Culture:

I: Future-oriented; undergoing rapid change and consequent breakdown of traditional values, practices ... social structure loosely articulated ... composed of welter of conflicting, competing groups and ideologies.[3]

II: Mores have been weakened and folkways redefined; legal norms and laws have supplanted unwritten codes; few universally accepted beliefs, values, standards of behavior ... mass movement of heterogeneous peoples to the city broke control exerted by family, neighbors ... complex formal agencies of control, such as police ...

III: Relations with others more transitory, impersonal, superficial, anonymous (people expose only segments of their total selves in everyday interaction) ... indifference toward strangers replaces rural hospitality (or hostility) ...[5]

IV: Proliferation of social roles and intricate division of labor ... few fixed, ascribed positions (individuals must seek out and compete for positions) ... "individuals must fit into a complex social structure in which they occupy social statuses and play many different and unrelated roles." Tendency for sex and age roles to converge, become more alike (and more confusing) ...

Suburban Culture (?):

I: Comfort-oriented; security and freedom from want becoming ideals ... social structure increasingly cohesive, well integrated ... quest for certainty ... cult of adjustment supplants cult of individualism ... re-emergence of community, nation-wide norms ... consensus ...

II: Social controls re-invested in neighborhood, family ... increase of informal primary-type contacts strengthens role of peer group ... rural and quasi-rural values take root[4] ...

III: Relations with others less superficial, transitory ... growing dependence upon others for approval, affection ... friendships, cliques increasingly based on mutual interests and values ... social distance between strangers less marked ...

IV: Sex, age roles, continue to converge (children act "older," adults "younger") ... roles becoming better-defined yet more flexible ... others becoming more predictable ...

FOLK CULTURE:

V: Component parts of society are closely articulated, fitting together with a minimum of friction or conflict . . . little or no social disorganization (divorce, delinquency, suicide, etc.) . . . although life strict and narrow, level of adjustment was relatively high.

VI: Pattern of life dictated by custom; "tradition-direction" prevails . . little urge to challenge status quo, innovate, or flaunt tradition . . . .

VII: Particularistic social system (with emphasis upon inherited, feudal-like status) . . . rigid social-class structure . . . intense conservatism pervades all segments of life . . . people tend to accept their own assigned statuses as inevitable . . . governments (like family, community) often autocratic, aristocratic . . .

VIII: Ethnocentrism and correlative suspicion of "outsiders" . . . intolerance toward deviates from prescribed norms . . little or no acquaintance with other communities, other values and ways of life . . .

URBAN CULTURE:

V: Communal dissensus replaces consensus . . . social organization increasingly atomistic and ill-defined . . . value orientations of various subcultures automatically clash . . . soaring rates of social disorganization . . . uncertainties beget *anomie*, marginality, mental illness . .

VI: Philosophy of "rugged" individualism, experimentation . . . "progress" becomes goal . . . emergence of "inner-directed" character . . deviates, mavericks, "characters" become more common . . .

VII: Universalistic social system (emphasis upon individual achievement, same norms for all) . . more open, permeable social-class system (and consequent emergence of class consciousness, status striving, conspicuous consumption) . . . emergence of rags-to-riches theme . . . emergence of labor as political force, resurgence of political liberalism, democratic government.

VIII: Growing contacts and familiarity with people from diverse cultural backgrounds encourages tolerance . . . "people rub elbows with and become indifferent to extremes of all kinds"[8] . . . but early phases of growth promote ethnic and racial conflict.

SUBURBAN CULTURE (?):

V: Increasing communal consensus . . . gradual dissipation of religious, ethnic, racial subcultures (with consequent attenuation of value clashes) . . indications various indices of social disorganization (divorce, delinquency, etc.) leveling off, occasionally decreasing . . .

VI: Lesser encouragement, toleration of deviates, mavericks . . . emergence of "other-directed" character type . . emphasis upon "teamwork," group harmony, "togetherness" . . .

VII: Trend toward "mass society" with correlative mass middle-class-dominated culture . . . lesser proportion in upper and lower classes . . . class lines increasingly vague, boundaries more and more fluid, class-linked value and life-style differences less marked . . masses more liberal politically but left-wing radicalism blunted; labor, business, and other power units countervail, balance . .

VIII: Diminution of ethnic and racial conflict and increase of libertarianism (popular belief in civil liberties) . . increasing cosmopolitanism, breakdown of regional and national barriers (in face of rear-guard, die-hard ultra-nationalists, hyper-conservatives) . . .

FOLK CULTURE:

IX: Community is economically self-sufficient...a simple technology in which virtually every one is a primary producer ...minimal division of labor...agrarian and handicraft economy with minimal competition (mutual aid is frequent)...

X: Simple, "folk" type entertainment (folk songs, carnivals, fairs)...emphasis more on participants than spectators...simple leisure tastes involving community-wide or family-wide participation...

XI: Patriarchal, male-dominant family systems...marriages based on tradition, utility...marital unions stable, life-long ...life familistic (family centered) in orientation...extended families frequent ...family occupies central place in social structure, performs major obligations (educational, religious, economic) ...

XII: Scanty, informal education except for clergy, aristocrats...slight value attached to formal schooling (emphasis more upon practical knowledge)...illiteracy widespread....

URBAN CULTURE:

IX: Increasingly complex economic system with elaborate division of labor...quick transfer of goods and services...gradual demise of individual enterpriser and increasing potency of big business ...but specialization, competition continue to prevail...

X: More "sophisticated" (and synthetic, manufactured) entertainment fare...growth of "spectatoritus," mushrooming of competitive spectator sports...increasing potency and pervasiveness of mass media...variegated tastes and publics...work and leisure sharply distinguished...

XI: Children, wives break free of father domination...children leave families as they gain economic independence...marriages increasingly based on "love-at-first-sight" romances (with spouse often from totally different backgrounds)...life decreasingly familistic, increasingly individualistic...family loses central role...divorce rates soar...families become smaller...

XII: Emergence of mass education, progressive ideology...education increasingly democratic, available to all...burgeoning of school population...professionalization of teaching...illiteracy disappearing..."diploma" goal for all...

SUBURBAN CULTURE (?):

IX: Post-industrial economy of "plenty,"[9] service economy dominant...increasing dominance of corporation (and demise of "Main Street" businessman)...automation of industry increases...series of "common markets" supplant national competition, trade barriers...

X: Mass media of communication increasingly geared to demands and taste of "lowest common denominator"...new spectator sports supplant old (but increase in participant sports)..."upper bohemian" market for sophisticated entertainment challenges mass market[10]...proliferation of specialized hobby groups"[11]...

XI: Families increasingly democratic, companionship in nature...marriages increasingly stable...marriages more homogamous ("likes marry likes")...families become larger...resurgence of single-family dwellings, family-centered activities...long-time trend toward earlier marriages reversed...

XII: Increasing proportion of population attends school, mean years of schooling continue to rise...popular reaction against excesses of "progressive education" movement...greater demand for college preparation...college degree becomes prerequisite for "upper-middle-class" status...

THE AMERICAN FEAR OF SOLITUDE*

by Leo Gurko

The American can endure almost all states except solitude. At home in the world of material objects and gadgets, gregarious in the company of others, he is restless and uneasy in the company of himself. His society is crammed to the bursting point with organizations of every description which he joins in multiple numbers less to be with his fellows than to get away from himself. He is an Elk, American Legionnaire, Rotarian, Kiwanian, Moose, Mason or a Knight of Columbus. He attends church for reasons more social than religious. He joins societies that seek to prevent World War III, or protect ownerless animals and attaches himself to the countless booster clubs that dot the civic landscape with posters advertising Belleville or Dead Lick as the biggest little city in the country. He attends innumerable conventions with unflagging enthusiasm. Bars, taverns, bowling alleys, poolrooms, gymnasiums, country clubs, are social centers that attract him in large clusters. When he is not in formal contact with others, he is at home listening to the radio, or sitting in stupefied silence in front of a television set, or watching a movie, one in a dark crowd. He is never alone if he can help it.

From her listening post on the campus of Smith College, Mary Ellen Chase reports *(Woman's Day,* October, 1949) the same flight from solitude: "I am particularly impressed by the repeated aversion, which countless girls express, to being by themselves. I hear every morning frenzied appeals for company. 'Wait for me! I'm coming! Don't go without me.' As we stream onward by scores across the campus, I overhear the same desolations repeated again and again: 'I had the most boring evening. Not a soul came to my room.' 'I can't possibly go alone. It would be just awful.' 'I don't think there's another girl in the college from Idaho (or Dakota, or Montana). Whatever shall I do after Chicago, all that train ride alone?' 'If I only had a roommate, it might help some. At least I'd have someone to talk to at night.'

*From "The American Fear of Solitude," by Leo Gurko, *Tomorrow Magazine,* Volume 9 (April 1950), pp. 5-10. Copyright by Garrett Publications, Inc., 1950. Reprinted by permission.

'She's nice, you know, but she must be a bit queer. She's forever going off all by herself! ' "

Moreover, solitude is associated with failure. One of the key words in American life is popularity, the tense pursuit of which has crushed many a youthful spirit. Since popularity implies not being by oneself, it makes the exclusive company of that self difficult to maintain with comfort and painful to contemplate.

The most diligent promoters of the cause of popularity have been the advertisements. The whole cleanliness industry, a major one in the United States, gears its publicity releases to the keynote of what will people think of you. The whole fashion industry, equally high-powered, directs its appeals to an identical standard of social success.

The body must be not only well-barbered, clean, and fashionably clothed, it must also be young. Youth is the time when the flesh counts most and the mind least; it is hence the period of maximum popularity. It is not so much the spirit of youth that is glorified as its physical energy and surface attractiveness. Middle age has become a bogey which scares millions into concealing its telltale signals. Industries have been built on the fear of baldness in men and wrinkles on the faces of women. Massages, girdles for men, an enormous beauty-parlor trade equipped with superb machines, diets, weight-removing salons, rejuvenation fads, and a host of other devices to dam the inroads of age, flourish throughout the country.

The body is the key to popularity; and popularity the key to success. This is a major tenet of the advertising industry, with its daily barrage of coaxing, wheedling, threatening, fear-producing, envy-arousing messages. The whole pull of that industry is from the inside out, a terrific centrifugal force drawing the individual away from the center of himself to the periphery and beyond. As such, it is clearly a latter-day product of all the forces in American history which have shied away from meditation and self-searching, and concentrated on go-getting in the world of flesh and space unstained by thought. Seen from this side, the life of the American is one long unbroken flight from his inward self.

The impulse to become lost in something at once larger and outside oneself runs very strongly in other directions. In the most sequestered areas, revivalism of every description stretches back into the past and has taken deep root. With its mixture of religion and eroticism, revivalism has flourished not simply among the superstitious but among those to whom life for one reason or another has not been satisfactory, the emotionally undernourished, the sexually frustrated, those who can no longer endure reality.

Of the many ways in which God is pursued in America, revivalism is perhaps the most glandular and frenzied, and comes close to defining contact with the Almighty as a kind of ecstatic oblivion. In this orgiastic state, anything can happen. The voluntary abandonment of personality, which is the end-product of revivalism, is a sacrificial self-yielding into the hands of someone else, a kind of triumphant suicide very strange indeed within the bosom of democratic society, where the individual personality is, in theory, a most precious and triumphant possession. So desperate a craving for otherness is a potent sign of how tedious, unpleasant, or unendurable one's own self has become.

Americans are not only a God-pursuing but also a devil-worshiping people. Not the devil in the shape of Lucifer with a handsome swarthy face and horns. Nothing so romantic, literary, or primitive. The devil rather as scapegoat, upon whose single shoulders manifold troubles can be heaped, the "fall guy," whom we can blame for errors we sub-consciously suspect to be our own. Thurman Arnold, in his drily searching book *The Folk-Lore of Capitalism,* has studied the devil-hunting proclivities of the American people in politics. For a long time, the government was the devil responsible for all ills, and its agents, the politicians, crooked, conniving, and corrupt characters who leeched upon the population. With the collapse of 1929 and the new role of the government as a great rescue agency under the New Deal, the devil became the big businessman, the "economic royalist," as Franklin D. Roosevelt called him in a memorable epithet, who had brought about the depression as a consequence of his greedy policies and was doing all in his power to block any attempts at recovery not under his spon-sorship. In foreign affairs before 1939, fascism and communism were the twin devils powerful enough to shield our own errors and in-adequacies. Since the end of the Second World War, it has been com-munism alone, concentrated in what has come to be a dread name, Soviet Russia, that has been the villainous agent responsible for the ills of the world.

Whatever percentage of contemporary troubles can be attributed to the communists, by no effort of the imagination, however staggering, can all of them be so ascribed. A goodly share of them are of our own making, and will not disappear merely because we refuse to accept responsibility. Our refusal is as much a flight from ourselves and the reality encasing us as is revivalism, the more dangerous because it is a collective and not simply an individual matter.

Another symptom of the same evasion is the national faith in experts, and the eagerness to believe them without qualification or reserve. The enormous specialization that accompanied the spread of industrialism broke up life into smaller and smaller segments, and made the custodian of each segment growingly important. In due course, this custodian developed into the expert who, by virtue of his total knowledge of a single area and total ignorance of everything else, set up shop as middleman between his area and the public at large. His total ignorance of all else was an integral element in his functioning as expert, the theory being that his very concentration upon a single sphere at the expense of every other kind of knowledge was a strong, indeed an indispensable, qualification for his career.

And a striking fact about the American scene is that a man who succeeds in one field of enterprise is listened to with awed respect when he comments on any other, no matter how far removed. Rarely has ignorance commanded so high a price and brought so rich a reward.

Belief in the expert, however, is more than a tailored product of economics. It has been immensely stimulated by our reluctance to think for ourselves and accept responsibility for the things that happen. The expert is a convenient mechanism for doing our thinking and a superb scapegoat when things go astray.

We listen eagerly to their voices and when the wrong tune is called, they, not we, absorb the blame. Among the more firmly orbited authorities are the newspaper columnists. They combine the roles of gossip and pundit, ministering to the reader's passion for "inside" information and his need for a settled frame of reference.

Suspicious of every form of physical and political authority, America is laden with a vast bureaucracy of authority in the areas of morals, intellect, and personal conduct.

This contradiction extends elsewhere. In *The American Character,* D. W. Brogan comments on it with regard to war: "The American people . . . have always been antimilitarist but never antimilitary. They have combined a rational and civilized horror of war's waste and in-humanity with a simple end . . . natural pleasure in the trappings of war."

Even in politics, where by theory and tradition the fuehrer princi-ple has been rejected from the start, eagerness to submit to strong leadership survives, and in difficult times swells into urgency. The dangerous instance of Huey Long, who headed the fastest-growing American fascist movement in the 1930's, revealed how viable was that eagerness. Long rose above the swarm of promise-makers through his resourceful and intelligent personality, oozing with eloquence, humor, and in instinctive rapport with the dissatisfied lower middle class of the towns and the dissatisfied small tenant farmers of the country, the group that provided Hitler with his mass base in Germany. It was the impact of his magnetic self, with its enormous assurance, perhaps even more than his invitation to quick wealth, that held those who flocked to his banner. The quest for certainty is never more easily achieved than in the arms of some bold fellow who persuades you that he knows all the answers. Americans, while freer from this form of persuasiveness than certain European peoples, are nevertheless more prone to it than naive libertarians conceive.

And it is not just political demagogues and regressive orators who exercise the spell. Franklin D. Roosevelt acquired after a time a hold upon the affection of millions of his constituents that far transcended the specific ideology of the New Deal. He assumed the role of the Great White Father soon after his advent to the presidency when conditions began to improve. An idolatrous cult arose round Roosevelt, as violent and passionate in its way as the cult of Roosevelt-haters (less numerous but no less emotional). It prospered on the mystical assumption that so long as Roosevelt remained president, all was well, and the storm of grief that greeted his death had overtones of hysteria that suggested the passing of a demigod.

There is little evidence to suggest that Roosevelt had dynastic ambitions, despite the calumnious accusations of his enemies, or even wished to serve as an all-protecting father to millions of insecure Americans. But he served as such, whether he wanted to or not, to the millions who were no longer willing to rely upon themselves psychologically in the ceaseless struggle with the problems of life.

The vacuum created by his death left his idolatrous devotees in a state of acute emotional distress. There ensued a period of spy hunts, witch hunts, thorough control, loyalty oaths, and relentless searching out not simply of subversive doctrine but of liberal doctrine as well, made acute by fear of Russia and the atom bomb, and given a final impetus by loss of the great man. A formidable consciousness sprang up of an anchorage lost, of lines gone slack and sudden pressures reversing upon one's own self. Candidates seeking to fill the vacuum sprang up on every side, none of them up to the stature of the man they were seeking to replace, but all of them under various banners promising the moon.

The common historical complaint against the great man, even the well-intentioned liberal one, is that he lives for them, leaving them incapacitated to lead their own after he departs. For all of Roosevelt's part in educating the electorate in progressive ideas (always carefully within the fundamental framework of capitalism), he kept many of his more enthusiastic followers in an infantile emotional state. For them, recovery has been a slow and painful process, as it appears to be in almost every instance of self-avoidance.

The same principle operates with other emergent leaders of whatever social persuasion, whether ruthless and aggressive like Father Coughlin, or mild and passive like Dr. Townsend.

These yearnings for self-relinquishment do not, of course, dominate the American political scene, as they do so strongly in Germany, but they characterize it. If not visible at any given moment, they are assuredly lying under the surface just out of sight. They bestrew the road to maturity, cutting off access to those farther reaches of the mind where the making of decisions and the bearing of personal responsibility reside. The hero-worshiping instinct in America has flowered in other fields less dangerous than politics.

Roosevelt aside, no president in this country has won the popularity or received so huge a press as Clark Gable. Or exercised the spell cast by Greta Garbo. Or aroused as much discussion as did the feats of Babe Ruth, Jack Dempsey, Bill Tilden, Red Grange, or Bobby Jones. The luminaries of the sports world have been the petted darlings of the public since the end of the First World War, but they are mere satellites in the terrific luminosity of the movie stars. The lives of the stars have had almost as great an impact, and to many fans are as fascinating and important as the movies themselves. This is more than normal curiosity about spectacular figures; it amounts to frenzy.

Such fervor denotes the impulse to subserve one's real self as completely as possible, and creates a gap into which the spectacular self being worshiped can flow. This impulse has of course a universal range, and it would be absurd to regard its habitat as exclusively the United States. But the shapes it assumes in America are unique; not the least of them is the extraordinary, movie-worshiping cult, fittingly revolving around an art form created in America and enjoying here its largest efflorescence.

Among the prevailing causes of the flight from self is a slackening belief in the powers of the individual. Nearly everything that has happened since 1914 has conspired to batter away at the individual, and infect him with a sense of helplessness. America has of course been the last great country to feel the inroads of this reduction in the stock of free will, but even here signs of it are widespread. As with so many feelings, it is more evident in its symptoms than in its roots. One very large symptom is the extraordinary vogue of historical romances and cowboy sagas. Both have one element in common: the portraiture of characters in an earlier age who were free agents. The less this seems possible today the more demonstrations of it from the past are welcomed.

The flight from self for whatever reason—internal or external, symptomized by an inability to be alone, the distrust of mind, an excessive belief in the virtues of popularity, the cult of youth and the body beautiful—sooner or later reverts to the starting point, for the self, no matter how many doors are slammed upon it, remains unavoidable. All the hasheesh in India cannot keep the addict from awakening to a world which seems crueler and less bearable than ever. No matter how much liquor is consumed, how many fraternal associations, poolroom camaraderies, pyramid clubs, and bowling-alley groups are organized, no matter the number of movie tidbits, batting averages, and scoring records immersing the fan in a warm sea of gratifying statistics, the self remains the zone to which all roads of flight must in the end return. As with the smoker of hasheesh, the journey leaves the voyager in a weakened state, less able to cope with reality than when he started, just as long submission to a dictator leaves a people less able to govern themselves when he is removed. The total effect is a reduced capacity to cope with experience when the person in flight comes full circle back to it.

Reality, when it must finally be dealt with, throws us in some ways into disequilibrium. The whole history of the postwar period, dominated as it has been by the fear and hatred of Russia, is a succinct illustration. To subordinate all other problems to the point where they command little attention in order to concentrate on the menace of communism, is to oversimplify life with precisely that emotional immaturity characteristic of people in flight. Particularly is this true of ideological warfare, for which the American has been least prepared. He is more inclined to take refuge in the hydrogen bomb as a weapon against Russian expansion than to define and advance democracy. He is better at producing armaments than at spreading dissension in the ranks of the enemy. He would rather fight a hot war than a cold one. Though belonging to the greatest nation of advertisers the world has ever seen, he is ill at ease in the field of propaganda, and the appeal to men's minds is an art that he approaches slowly and hesitantly. A long succession of almost physical victories at home and abroad stretches behind him, but his moral and intellectual triumphs have been few.

Confronted with a physical challenge he has been a heroic and undiscourageable figure. His record on less tangible issues is not so admirable. The Negro slaves were legally freed by the Civil War but their subsequent progress toward equality has been painfully slow, and discrimination against them remains one of the painful blots on American democracy. The First World War was fought to save the world for democracy and end wars forever. We won that conflict on the battle-field but lost it everywhere else. The tensions that have followed World War II, being as much ideological in character as physical, have found us handling the physical end (UNRRA, the Marshall Plan, the Berlin Airlift) with great competence, while the ideological end (the Voice of America, the elimination of Nazis and their industrial supporters in Germany, the promotion of democracy in Greece, the propaganda war with the Russians, the witch hunts at home, themselves a sign of acute disequilibrium, directed not only at communists but at persons with liberal and radical ideas) has limped a long way behind.

To these defeats in the realm of principle, the flights from self have made notable contributions. They have insulated sections of the public from contact with the world before them, making it appear difficult and hostile out of all real proportion. They have bred the illusion that the self can be avoided when it cannot; and fostered the conviction that reality can be permanently shut off. They have encouraged a contempt for tackling experience on any but the material level and thus created their own particular brand of anti-intellectualism. Finally, by developing and hardening into institutional forms, they have made immensely more complicated the return to reality and the dealing with it by the reintegrated whole self of the whole man.

In these several ways, they exist as major obstacles on the already arduous journey toward national maturity.

Where once an alternative existed between thinking or not, the issue now is between thinking one way or another. The age of anxiety, as Auden called it, jogs the intellect as well as the nerves, and there is no dodging it. Even living from day to day requires argument, debate, meditation, analysis—all the stages and processes of thought—in order to cope, however sketchily, with the phenomenally rapid kaleidoscope of communism and capitalism, the Atlantic Pact, democracy and tyranny, the exhaustion of the earth's food resources, and scores of other over-bearing issues leaping out of newspapers, radios, newsreels, leaflets, confidential letters, out of the very overheated, supercharged air of the time.

Since crises can no longer be side-stepped, they must be faced, and by degrees, sometimes halting, sometimes rapid, America has been facing them since the black October of 1929. It has been proven over and over that force alone will not solve them. The immense prosperity of the twenties did not avert the crash. The immense potential strength of the United States did not keep Nazi Germany from defying us or fascist Japan, with one seventh of our steel production, from assaulting us. Our emergence as the greatest armed and industrialized power on earth has not kept the Soviet Union from challenging us everywhere.

Power has become powerless unless allied to principle. Since principle cannot be formulated without rational thought or sustained without its constant encouragement, an atmosphere of intellectual suppression is a drag on the national interest. Assuming, of course, that the principle to which our force is tied is essentially democratic. If so, the relationship between the free exercise of the mind and the carrying forward of democratic policies on the largest scale is intimate and deep-flowing. The recognition of this is one of the pressing imperatives of our time.

Signs of independent thinking on the part of the citizenry abound. Our organs of communication and propaganda have developed enormously in this century, yet it is plain that their ability to control the reactions of the public has not increased proportionately. Proof of this lies everywhere. While the great majority of newspapers and magazines have supported the Republicans in presidential campaigns since 1932, the electorate has voted Democratic. The frightful beating given the "scientific" polls in the campaign of 1948 remains one of the memorable events in the psychological history of the times. Big-scale advertising, whatever its initial effects, has bred in the public mind a thickening core of resistance. A steady market has been created for consumers' reports analyzing the wide and frequently incompatible differences that exist between advertising claims and actualities. The dockets of the Federal Trade Commission are crowded with cases of prosecution for advertising fraud, news of which, in however small a way, has seeped into the general consciousness.

In many ways then, the American is less credulous, less likely to take things at their face value, than he once was. The very weight of the machinery of persuasion that has sprung up under the spur of technology has created in the public a counter machinery of disbelief, and made it much less the gullible, superstitious, moronic mass that Mencken accused it of being a generation ago. There is evidence indeed that the American people are brighter than their leaders.

The public may not be the fount of all wisdom which the mystique of democracy sometimes claims, but neither is it the stupid philistine mass that culture snobs and reactionary critics often claim. Large sections of it are surely alert to art and expression that are not bogged down in obscurantism. The unrelenting pressures of the age of technology have shaken everyone to the point where the most violent and ingenious forms of escape have been created side by side with unprecedented curiosity about the meaning of life. It is this curiosity, rising from the ruins of the old credulous faith in the power of muscle and money to solve all difficulties and dissolve all crises, which provides the solid basis for a great expansion of creative work in America.

American society has not been in so great a state of fluidity as regards influence with the public since the end of the Civil War, when preachers, poets, professors, eighteenth-century aristocrats, nineteenth-century agrarian radicals were ousted from positions of leadership and replaced by the entrepreneurs. Whether into this promising situation, men of ideas, regardless of profession, can again make their way remains to be seen. Their opportunity has not been so bright for a century.

The flexibility of American institutions is the most specific insurance that this and other opportunities will remain open. So long as this malleability survives, all changes are possible, even radical alterations in the present, still parlous state of the thinking man.

The challenge of the American future lies not in the elimination or discrediting of materialism (which would be impossible) but in its intelligent and self-enlightened pursuit. On the cultural level, one sign of this enlightenment would be the viewing of art and creative thought as vital and rewarding activities. On the material level, a supreme example of it is the Tennessee Valley Authority; in a word, an application of organized reason and technological efficiency in the interests of maximum human well-being. The healing of the split between highbrow and lowbrow, that Van Wyck Brooks defined many years ago, remains a major item on the national agenda. When they exist once again in a state of fusion and mutual respect, a long step will have been taken toward the restoration of the wholeness of American life.

The inescapable pressures of our time are already beginning to force the contending sides together. In the completion of that process lies the major hope that the nation will face the crises ahead with a renewed integration of self.

This is the objective beckoning us as the twentieth century enters its second half.

Chapter Three

CULTURE AND PERSONALITY

"Culture" and "personality"—the concepts are inseparably linked; neither can be understood without reference to the other. Let us take, for example, the process of personality acquisition. Man, we know, is not born with "human nature." The newborn infant comes into the world equipped only with the *potential* for becoming human; but his potential, to be realized, must be nurtured. Thus the concept "socialization": the process of inducting the individual into the social world, of re-shaping original (biological) nature into human (learned) nature. Socialization, in short, is the procedure "by which someone learns the ways of a given society or social group so that he can function within it"[1]—so that he can become an effective, participating, norm-abiding member of society. If the individual is to acquire a personality, he must simultaneously "acquire culture."

To stress the common, recurrent features of the socialization process is not to deny those unique, singular features which differentiate individual from individual any more than it is to deny the hereditary base upon which personality is built. It is simply to stress the more characteristic, culturally stamped components of personality.

Ralph Linton observes in "The Individual, Culture and Society" that the individual "takes the bait of immediate personal satisfaction and is caught upon the hook of socialization; he would learn to eat in response to his own hunger drive, but his elders teach him to 'eat like a

[1] Frederick Elkin, *The Child and Society, The Process of Socialization* (New York: Random House, Inc., 1960), p 4.

71

gentleman.' " Thus Linton, like the other contributors to this chapter, stresses the complex interdependence between the individual, his society, and his culture. In fact, Linton claims that to understand the individual —and personality in general—we must understand the individual's social environment.

In this article, Linton makes other important points: different as man is from his subhuman relatives, the differences which demarcate man from beast are after all only differences of degree—of intensity— not of kind.[2] What is more, unlike man, animals can survive and function with the aid of instincts; mankind could not survive infancy without the constant aid and presence of others. Linton also focuses on man's most compelling psychic needs: the needs for emotional response, long-term security, and novelty of experience.

The piece by Clyde Kluckhohn and Henry A. Murray (the former an anthropologist, the latter a psychologist) is adapted from *Personality in Nature, Society and Culture,* a trail-blazing interdisciplinary book of readings that they edited. Like the other authors in this chapter, Kluck-hohn and Murray stress the singularity of every individual; but they also warn that the behavioral scientist, be he clinical or social psychol-ogist, psychiatrist, cultural anthropologist, or sociologist, must neces-sarily concern himself most with the patterns and uniformities that humans share in common, for without knowledge of uniformities, there can be no science of man. Yet in seeking constancies and regularities, the authors admit, we are in danger of becoming "determinists"— converts to the assumption that one, basic factor (heredity, culture, or the economic system, for example) determines all else. Kluckhohn and Murray contend that "most human beings (including scientists) crave simple solutions and tend to feel that because simple questions can be asked there must be simple answers." For this reason, there are fre-quent instances of both overestimation and underestimation of the role of heredity in the formation of personality. Today's student of person-

---

[2] One of the very first (and most important) lessons the student of sociology must learn is that whatever distinctions he would deal with or conceptualize— delinquent and non-delinquent, neurotic and non-neurotic, prejudiced and un-prejudiced, normal and abnormal—are not all-or-none black-and-white differences, but matters of *degree.* Most such differences can be most graphically plotted along a *continuum,* with either end (or pole) representing the extremes. Between the polar extremities are man-made, purely imaginary units of measurement (inches, pounds, "I.Q." points) which help us describe and comprehend whatever varia-tions we are examining. In consequence, whatever dividing lines we draw (be-tween, say, culture and heredity) are arbitrary; in reality, "boundary lines" are blurred and overlapping.

ality, the authors caution, must be particularly wary of succumbing to *environmental* determinism.

In examining the intricate relationships between culture and personality, the authors advise, we must not forget that *subcultural* memberships—social class, regional, or ethnic, for instance—are often of over-riding significance. The fact that J. Godrick Pontefract is an upper-class Bostonian and that Morcomb Yegal is a slum-dwelling migrant, may be much more meaningful than the fact that both are citizens of the United States. We must remember, too, Kluckhohn and Murray advise, how unwittingly culture-bound the vast majority of us are. "Culture acts," they write, "as a set of blinders . . . through which men view their environments." Our cultural and subcultural affiliations function, in short, to distort or pervert our perceptions of the world around us. No matter what our degree of sophistication, we are all unfailingly ethnocentric. Recognition of this fact would seem of particular relevance for the educator. For he, perhaps more than anyone else, must increasingly work with, judge, and understand youngsters of every conceivable subcultural background. Individual differences and cultural differences, he must realize, are often one and the same.

In the process of becoming socialized, each of us, gradually but progressively, adopts what we take to be appropriate ways of acting and behaving: as a child, a son, a boy, a brother, a student, we realize—however subconsciously—that we are expected to do certain things in certain ways. Simultaneously, we are learning what we may expect from others in related positions. We are engaged in role-playing. In "Status and Role," Ralph Linton explains what this process involves and why, without it, mankind would have failed to survive as a species. The reader will quickly realize that "status" and "role" are not concrete, tangible entities; they are concepts—means of visualizing and explaining reality. With these concepts firmly in hand, we realize that the occupant of a status (for example, a mother) is expected to perform certain roles (caring for and training her children, cooking, housekeeping). We shall learn, too, that these two concepts are inseparable: that there can be no roles to play without accompanying statuses. What is more, every role is a "self-other" role; the status "husband" is meaningless without the status "wife", and so with teacher and pupil, employer and employee, etc. Without these roles, which may be likened to ready-made suits of clothes, there would be only chaos and anarchy, and life and human relations would be totally unstructured and unpredictable. Social roles, in a word, are central, cementing ingredients in the cultural matrix; without them, there could be no human societies.

That each of us enacts roles, Linton makes clear, does not make soulless automatons of us. Especially in the more flexible, innovative, and less tradition-bound industrial societies, occupants of various statuses are allowed considerable leeway in role-playing. "Husband," "actor," "attorney," "adolescent": each such role can be played in innumerable ways in our society; yet whatever variations each allows, most of us know roughly what to expect of husbands, actors, attorneys, and adolescents. The matter, however, is more complicated than this. Every person, for one thing, plays a vast multiplicity of roles during his lifetime. Sometimes several such roles (good mother, loving wife, efficient housekeeper, charming hostess) almost automatically clash with or hinder one another. Other roles may be vaguely defined because they are relatively new ("divorcee," for example, or "married student") or because they are undergoing re-definition (today's "grandmother," for instance, in comparison to the frail, rocking-chair variety of yesteryear). Some, finally, are unhappy with the statuses they fill or are dissatisfied with the performance of their role. In each such instance, it should be noted—whether a matter of role conflict, role definition, role require-ments, or role performance—the occupant of the status is rarely aware of the nature and causes of his dilemma. He is probably "unhappy," but it is quite unlikely that he knows "what is wrong."[3]

The most salient feature of Linton's selection is his consideration of "ascribed" and "achieved" statuses. The former, in simple terms, comprises those positions (such as age or sex statuses) that we are automatically assigned; the latter relates to positions (such as occupa-tional or marital statuses) that we choose of our own volition.[4] Yet ascribed statuses, even though assigned at birth, are not the same the world over. How a "boy" behaves and how a "girl" behaves is, in fact, far more a matter of cultural definition than of biological definition.[5] Thus, what we take to be inherently "masculine" behavior might easily (and legitimately) be considered feminine-type behavior in another society. And so too, as Linton points out, with age: the roles assigned

---

[3] Karen Horney, Henry Stack Sullivan, Erich Fromm, and many other psy-chiatrists who are sympathetic with the *interpersonal interaction* school of thought hold that such subconscious role difficulties as these constitute key ingredients in many neurotic personality makeups.

[4] The ascribed-achieved distinction is in a sense more theoretical than actual; the role of "husband," for example, is technically an achieved one. But, once chosen, the husband role prescribes a rather rigid set of duties, obligations, and functions which are undeniably "ascribed" in coloration.

[5] For a more detailed and sprightly account of such culturally patterned male-female differences, see Margaret Mead's *Male and Female* (N. Y.: Mentor Books, 1955).

adolescents—and hence the way adolescents act—vary considerably from one society to the next. The "teen-age" subculture, which we are coming to take so for granted in America, is unknown in the majority of the world's societies.

Kingsley Davis, in "The Sociology of Parent-Youth Conflict," reiterates and amplifies a point made by Linton in the preceding article: puberty (the biological transition from childhood to adulthood) and adolescence (the sociological shift from immaturity to maturity) do not necessarily coincide, for the latter is not biologically ordained; it is a matter of cultural definition. Age—"adolescence," "middle age," and "old age"—is, except at the very polar extremes of the life cycle, as much or more a question of cultural interpretation as it is a strictly physiological phenomenon.

Culture, in a word, is not as subservient to the dictates of heredity as is commonly imagined, and much that is thought to be innate to the human species is in reality a product of cultural influence. Thus adolescence, as Davis makes clear, can be handled in a number of ways. The author examines four critical phases in adolescence which are universally—but variously—dealt with: (1) occupational recruitment and training; (2) the patterning of sex behavior, marriage, and reproduction; (3) emancipation from parental control, (4) and the means of inculcating cultural norms. Davis is principally concerned with adolescence in American society, and he is especially vocal in his criticism of the public school's failure to come to effective grips with "youth culture." He is critical, too, of the ill-defined system of roles, obligations, and functions which are assigned adolescents in our society.[6]

"The Acquisition of Personality: a Sociological Perspective" examines the way in which raw "original nature" is translated into human nature. The relative roles of heredity and culture, Harold M. Hodges' article affirms, cannot be accurately conceptualized in simple black-and-white terms, nor is there a clearly discernible juncture when the infant becomes more a human than a mere animal. Yet gradual and imperceptible as it is, this transition cannot be bypassed by any one who would know the fundamental dynamics of personality growth. Hodges examines the transition in terms of "drive" theory—in terms of those universal biological needs, which not only permit socialization, but require it. But to realize that the hunger or thirst drives are reshaped by cultural pressures, is only a first step in comprehending the mechanics

---

[6] The turbulence which accompanies American adolescence is discussed with clarity and insight by Ruth Benedict in "Continuities and Discontinuities in Cultural Conditioning," *Psychiatry* (May, 1939), pp. 161-167.

of socialization. It is here that social role theory once more comes into play. And in order to understand how the child acquires his role repertoire, we must learn how his sense of "self" evolves in the course of interaction with other human beings: how he acquires a whole series of "selves" by engaging in such processes as "taking the role of others." After re-examining the nature of social roles, the author analyzes a series of concepts which further clarify the intricate nature of personality and the socialization process which shapes it. The membership-reference group distinction is particularly relevant in our age, as are the questions of "peer-group" socialization and "basic personality."

THE INDIVIDUAL, CULTURE AND SOCIETY*

by Ralph Linton

Studies of the individual, culture and society, and of their manifold interrelations are a response to the old admonition, "Man, know thyself." Most of the phenomena with which such studies deal have been tacitly recognized since time immemorial, but their investigation has been left largely to the philosopher and theologian. It is only within the last two or three generations that they have come to be considered an appropriate field for scientific research. Even now, such research is fraught with great difficulty. Although scientific attitudes are being invoked with increasing success, many of the recognized scientific techniques simply are not applicable to phenomena of these orders. Thus the very nature of the materials precludes, in large part, the use of experimental methods. The intrinsic qualities of cultures and societies are such that it is impossible to produce them to order or to study them under rigid control conditions. The individual is more amenable to experimental techniques, but even he leaves much to be desired. Even as a small child he comes to the investigator with his own distinctive configuration of experience. and innate, biologically determined potentialities. These constitute an unsolved X in all equations; one which cannot be solved by any of the techniques now available to us. In theory, it might be possible to take care of the innate factors by developing, through controlled breeding, human strains of nearly uniform heredity. Given these, it might then be possible to observe the sorts of personality produced by various environmental conditions created by the investigator. However, such human guinea pigs belong to a future as remote as it is depressing in terms of all that we have been taught to value. Even the first step, that of developing pure strains, will have to await such an improbable event as the disappearance of incest taboos.

These limitations on the use of the experimental method are by no means the only difficulties which confront the investigator. Personalities, cultures and societies are all configurations in which the patterning and organization of the whole is more important than any of the component parts. Until very recent times the scientific trend has been toward the increasingly minute analysis of such configurations and the study of the parts rather than the whole. Even today, when the importance of configurations as such is generally recognized, there is a notable lack of techniques for dealing with them. Lastly, the lack of exact and demonstrable units for the measurement of most social and cultural phenomena is still a severe handicap. Until such units have been established, it will be impossible to apply many of the mathematical techniques which have proved so valuable in other fields of research.

The greatest technological advance within the general area under discussion has been made in connection with psychological studies. Here a long series of tests has been developed. Many of these tests serve to reveal only certain aspects of personality content, not the personality configurations as a whole. On the basis of their results a series of individuals can be ranged with respect to a single quality, as intelligence, but such series will bear little relation to the order in which the same individuals can be ranged with respect to some other quality, as aggressiveness. The most recent and, from certain points of view most promising, advances in this field are the development of tests directed toward the personality configuration as a whole. These are still in their infancy, but such tests as the Rorschach and the Murray thematic aperception have already proved their value and promise well for the future.

Even when formal tests shall have been brought to the highest point of perfection they will not provide an answer to some of the most significant problems connected with the study of personality. Any test can throw light on the personality only as it exists at the time the test is given. Personalities are dynamic continuums, and although it is important to discover their content, organization and performance at a given point in time, it is still more important to discover the processes by which they develop, grow and change. With regard to these processes, formal tests can do no more than to give us a series of datum points along the individual's life trajectory. Very few records of this sort are now available. Until they become so, the best approach to the problems of personality development must remain the study and comparison of life histories as these can be obtained from the individuals themselves. Important work along this line has been done by the psychoanalysts, but even here much remains to be done in the development of objective techniques. In spite of the apparent validity of many of the psycho-analytic conclusions, most of these conclusions have been arrived at on the basis of subjective judgments and are not susceptible to the sort of proof required by workers in the exact sciences.

Many of the difficulties just enumerated will probably disappear with time. Pending the development of new techniques suited to the particular qualities of personality, culture, and society, investigators must arrive at their conclusions through the simple observation and comparison of their materials. Such an approach is comparable to that of the old-style naturalist rather than that of the modern student of animal behavior. However, it must not be forgotten that without the orientations provided by the naturalists' work many of the later developments would have been impossible. Students of human behavior, whether at the individual or the social level, have developed adequate descriptive techniques and a considerable understanding of the phenomena with which they have to deal. They have also developed an increasing awareness of the complexity of this material and of the close functional interdependence of the individual, society and culture. Following the earlier atomistic trends of scientific research, each of these has been treated as a separate field of investigation and made the subject of a distinct discipline. The individual has been assigned to Psychology, society to Sociology and culture to Cultural Anthropology, although the last two sciences have shown a constant tendency to overlap in their investigations. It is now becoming apparent that the integration between the individual, society and culture is so close and their interaction so continuous that the investigator who tries to work with any one of them without reference to the other two soon comes to a dead end. There is still room for specialists and there are still vested interests which profit by keeping the various disciplines separate. However, it seems safe to say that the next few years will witness the emergence of a science of human behavior which will synthesize the findings of Psychology, Sociology and Anthropology. To this trinity Biology will probably be added in due course of time, but the relation between biological phenomena and psychological, social and cultural ones is still so poorly understood that it seems safest to omit it for the present.

In spite of the functional interrelations of the individual, society and culture, these three entities may, and indeed must, be differentiated for descriptive purposes. Although any particular individual is rarely of great importance to the survival and functioning of the society to which he belongs or the culture in which he participates, *the individual,* his needs and potentialities, lies at the foundation of all social and cultural phenomena. Societies are organized groups of individuals, and cultures are, in the last analysis, nothing more than the organized repetitive responses of a society's members. For this reason the individual is the logical starting point for any investigation of the larger configuration.

It may be assumed that it is the needs of the individual which provide the motivations for his behavior and which are, through this, responsible for the operation of society and culture. The needs of human beings appear to be more numerous and more varied than those of any other species. In addition to those which can be traced directly to physiological tensions, as the needs for food, for sleep, for escape from pain and for sexual satisfaction, man has a whole series of other needs whose connection with such tensions cannot be clearly demonstrated. These, for lack of a better term, we may call the *psychic needs*. Although the physiologically determined needs of the individual are usually called primary and the psychic ones secondary, such a distinction is justifiable mainly in terms of a genetic approach. The physiologically determined needs unquestionably appear first in the general course of evolution and are the first to manifest themselves in the individual life cycle. However, as motivations of adult behavior, physical and psychic needs seem to stand very much on a par. Perhaps in any long-continued conflict between the two the odds are on the physical needs, but the victory of the body's demands is never assured. Hunger strikers do persist to the end, and, as in Europe today, men die under torture rather than betray a friend or even give up an opinion. In the less violent exigencies of daily life we find the psychic needs again and again given precedence over the physical ones. Everyone knows the old proverb, "One must suffer to be beautiful."

In spite of the importance of psychic needs as motivations of behavior, we still know very little about them. Their genesis is obscure, and they have not even been adequately described or classified. Psychological states are tenuous things exceedingly difficult to deal with by exact objective methods. The nature and even the presence of psychic needs can only be deduced from the behavior to which they give rise. This behavior is so varied that it becomes largely a matter of choice whether it is to be referred to a small number of general motivations or a great number of specific ones. If the latter method is followed, the psychic needs can be expanded almost to infinity and most of the value inherent in taxonomic systems is thereby lost. A further difficulty in the development of an adequate classification of psychic needs arises from the fact that any human need, whether physical or psychic, rarely stands in a clear-cut one-to-one relationship with any pattern of overt behavior. When people act, especially if they do so in accordance with an established culture pattern, the action usually contributes toward satisfying several different needs simultaneously. Thus when we dress we do so partly to protect the body and partly to satisfy vanity or at least avoid censure. Under the circumstances it seems safest not to try to set up any classification of psychic needs, contenting ourselves with a brief discussion of a few of those which seem to be most general and most significant for the understanding of human behavior.

Perhaps the most outstanding and most continuously operative of man's psychic needs is that for emotional response from other individuals. The term emotional response is used advisedly, since the eliciting of mere behavioral responses may leave this need quite unsatisfied. Thus in a modern city it is quite possible for the individual to interact in formal, culturally established terms with a great number of other individuals and to obtain necessary services from them without eliciting any emotional responses. Under such circumstances his psychic need for response remains unsatisfied and he suffers from feelings of loneliness and isolation which are almost as acute as though no one else were present. In fact the experience tends to be more frustrating than genuine solitude. We all know what it means to be alone in a crowd. It is this need for response, and especially for favorable response, which provides the individual with his main stimulus to socially acceptable behavior. People abide by the mores of their societies quite as much because they desire approval as because they fear punishment.

This need for emotional response from others is so universal and so strong that many social scientists have regarded it as instinctive in the sense of being inborn. Whether it actually is so or whether it is a product of conditioning is a problem which may never be solved. The individual is so completely dependent upon others during infancy that he cannot survive without eliciting response from them. Such response would, therefore, come to be associated with the satisfaction of even his most elementary needs, and the desire for it might well survive even when he had developed techniques for satisfying them without assistance. On the other hand, there is good evidence that even young infants require a certain amount of emotional response for their well-being. Lack of it seems to be the only explanation for the high infant death-rate in even the best-run and most sanitary institutions, which far exceeds that under even unsanitary conditions of home life. As a leading psychoanalyst has succinctly phrased it in his lectures: "Babies who aren't loved don't live." Since all individuals go through the experiences of infancy, the question of whether this need is innate or acquired is really an academic one. In either case its presence is universal.

A second and equally universal psychic need is that for security of the long-term sort. Thanks to the human ability to perceive time as a continuum extending beyond past and present into the future, present satisfactions are not enough as long as future ones remain uncertain. We are in constant need of reassurance, although the same time sense which makes it possible for us to worry about what may happen also makes it possible for us to postpone the satisfaction of present needs and put up with current discomforts in the expectation of future rewards. This need for security and for reassurance is reflected in innumerable forms of culturally patterned behavior. It leads the primitive craftsman to mingle magic with his technology and men at all levels of culture to imagine heavens in which the proper behavior of the present will be properly rewarded. In the light of our present very limited knowledge of psychological processes it seems idle to speculate as to the origins of this need. It is enough to recognize its importance as a motivation of forward-looking behavior.

The third and last psychic need which deserves mention at this time is that for novelty of experience. This is probably less compulsive than the needs which have just been discussed; at least it rarely seems to come into play until most other needs have been satisfied. It finds its expression in the familiar phenomenon of boredom and leads to all sorts of experimental behavior. Just as in the case of the need for response, there is a possible explanation for it in terms of early conditioning. During early childhood the individual is constantly having new experiences, and, since many of these are pleasurable, the qualities of novelty and of pleasureableness may very well come to be linked in anticipation. On the other hand, the roots of this need may lie deeper. Even very small children show experimental tendencies, and Pavlov has recognized what he calls the exploratory reflex in animals.

The role of both physical and psychological needs in human behavior is strictly that of first causes. Without the spur which they provide, the individual would remain quiescent. He acts to relieve tensions, and this applies equally to overt actions and to such covert ones as learning and thinking. However, the forms which behavior assumes can never be explained in terms of the motivating needs alone. Such needs are forces whose expression is shaped by a multitude of other factors. The behavior which will suffice to satisfy any need or combination of needs must be organized with constant reference to the milieu in which the individual has to operate. This milieu includes factors of both environment and experience. Thus the behavior which will serve to meet the need for food is quite different in a modern city and in the wilderness. Moreover, the techniques which the individual will employ in each case will vary with his past experience. In the wilderness one who is accustomed to hunt will go about getting food in a quite different way from one who is not.

If the forms of human behavior cannot be explained in terms of the individual's needs, it is equally impossible to explain them in terms of his innate potentialities for action. These potentialities set ultimate limits to the forms which behavior can assume, but they leave an exceedingly wide range of possibilities. The choice of any one of these possibilities is determined by still other factors. The individual's behavior is immediately determined by his experience, and this, in turn, is derived from his contacts with his environment. It follows that an understanding of this environment is indispensable for the understanding both of individual personalities and of personality in general.

Although no two individuals, even identical twins reared in the same family, ever have identical environments, all human environments have certain features in common. We are prone to think of environment in terms of natural phenomena such as temperature, terrain or available food supply, factors which inevitably vary with the time and place. Although these things are reflected in the individual's experience and through this in his personality, they seem to be of rather minor importance in personality formation. Between the natural environment and the individual there is always interposed a human environment which is vastly more significant. This human environment consists of an organized group of other individuals, that is, a society, and of a particular way of life which is characteristic of this group, that is, a culture. It is the individual's interaction with these which is responsible for the formation of most of his behavior patterns, even his deep-seated emotional responses.

Unpleasant as the realization may be to egotists, very few individuals can be considered as more than incidents in the life histories of the societies to which they belong. Our species long ago reached the point where organized groups rather than their individual members became the functional units in its struggle for survival. Social living is as characteristic of *homo sapiens* as his mixed dentition or opposable thumb. However, in view of man's antecedents and nature, the most surprising thing about human societies is that they should have been developed at all. Our species is by no means the first to make the experiment of organized group living, but the gap which separates our societies from those of even our closest sub-human relatives is enormous. To find any real parallels to the human situation we must turn to the members of another phylum, the insects. These have developed societies only a shade less complicated than our own, but they have developed them by methods impossible to us. Insects have elaborated their instincts at the expense of their inventiveness. Their whole evolutionary trend has been toward the production of elaborate, living automatons adjusted to fixed environments. They are beings in which a maximum of efficiency is combined with a minimum of individuality. Insects learn with difficulty and forget readily, but in most cases they can complete their brief life cycles without having to learn at all, still less to solve new problems. The adjustment of such automatons to functioning as members of an intricately organized society is only one step beyond their adjustment to functioning in a limited, stable natural environment and involves no new principle. Each ant or bee is fitted to his place in the community by a combination of structural specialization and instincts. He is organized both physically and psychologically to be a worker or soldier and cannot function in any other capacity. He has a minimum of individual needs and none which might bring him into conflict with other members of the same community. Unless singled out for a reproductive role, he (or she) has even been divested of those sexual drives which are such a fertile source of conflict among most vertebrates. In short, the social insects are less individuals than standardized, interchangeable units. From the time they are hatched they are so accurately fitted to their predestined social functions that they are incapable of departing from them. The class struggle could never develop in an anthill. Such units provide the perfect building blocks for a homogeneous, closely integrated and completely static social structure. The ant is born with everything that the most exacting dictator might wish his subjects to have.

In contrast to the social insects, man is the end product of an evolutionary process whose whole trend has been toward increasing individualization. Mammals have specialized in the ability to learn and, in the higher stages of their development, to think. By the time our ancestors reached the human level they had lost most of their automatic responses, and those which did survive were of the simplest sort. Man has no instincts, at least in the sense in which we use that term when we talk about insect behavior. He has to learn or invent practically everything that he does. Thus every individual not only can but must develop his own patterns of behavior. Moreover, in spite of the partial fixation of such patterns through the process of habit formation, they never become set and unalterable in the way that instincts are. Coupled with the human ability to learn and form habits there is an equally important ability to forget, to recognize new situations for what they are and to invent new behavior to meet them. The possibilities for individual variation in behavior are thus almost infinite. When several persons react in the same way to a particular situation, the cause must be sought in the experience which such individuals have in common. Obviously this fund of common experience will be much greater for the members of a single society than for members of different societies. However, there are certain sorts of experience which are common to all mankind. For example, every adult has been an infant dependent for his very survival on the care accorded him by other individuals. It is these common experiences and the common needs and abilities of mankind which are responsible for such uniformities of behavior as we can discern among mankind as a whole.

Intrinsically, the members of our species seem to have greater potentialities for differentiation and individualization than have the members of any other. The whole trend of our evolution has been away from the production of those standardized units which are the ideal building blocks for complex social structures. How we became socialized must remain a puzzle. Our subhuman relatives, who share our psychological qualities with differences of degree rather than of kind, are generally gregarious, but even anthropoid societies lack most of the specialization and differentiation of social functions which is so characteristic of our own. The gap between such societies and the simplest human ones is so wide that the development of our own patterns of social living must be regarded as an evolutionary tour de force. We are anthropoid apes trying to live like termites while lacking most of the termite equipment. One wonders whether we could not do it better with instincts.

Whatever the genesis of human societies may have been, all of them have certain features in common. The first and perhaps most important of these is that the society, rather than the individual, has become the significant unit in our species struggle for survival. Except by some unhappy accident, like that of Robinson Crusoe, all human beings live as members of organized groups and have their fate inextricably bound up with that of the group to which they belong. They cannot survive the hazards of infancy or satisfy their adult needs without the aid and cooperation of other individuals. Human life has passed long since from the stage of the individual workman to that of the assembly line in which each person makes his small, specific contribution to the finished product.

A second characteristic of societies is that they normally persist far beyond the life span of any one individual. Each of us is brought, by the accident of birth, into an organization which is already a going concern. Although new societies may come into being under certain conditions, most people are born, live and die as members of old ones. Their problem as individuals is not to assist in the organization of a new society but to adjust themselves to a pattern of group living which has long since crystallized. It may seem hardly necessary to point this out, but one finds in many writings a confusion between the genesis of social forms and the genesis of social behavior in the individual. How such an institution as the family originated is a problem of quite a different sort from that of how the individual becomes a functional, fully integrated member of a family.

Third, societies are functional, operative units. In spite of the fact that they are made up of individuals, they work as wholes. The interests of each of their component members are subordinated to those of the entire group. Societies do not even hesitate to eliminate some of these members when this is to the advantage of the society as a whole. Men go to war and are killed in war that the society may be protected or enriched, and the criminal is destroyed or segregated because he is a disturbing factor. Less obvious but more continuous are the daily sacrifices of inclinations and desires which social living requires of those who participate in it. Such sacrifices are rewarded in many ways, perhaps most of all by the favorable responses of others. Nevertheless, to belong to a society is to sacrifice some measure of individual liberty, no matter how slight the restraints which the society consciously imposes. The so-called free societies are not really free. They are merely those societies which encourage their members to express their individuality along a few minor and socially acceptable lines. At the same time they condition their members to abide by innumerable rules and regulations, doing this so subtly and completely that these members are largely unconscious that the rules exist. If a society has done its work of shaping the individual properly, he is no more conscious of most of the restrictions it has imposed than he is of the restraints which his habitual clothing imposes on his movements.

Fourth, in every society the activities necessary to the survival of the whole are divided and apportioned to the various members. There is no society so simple that it does not distinguish at least between men's and women's work, while most of them also set aside certain persons as intermediaries between man and the supernatural and as leaders to organize and direct the group's activities along certain lines. Such a division represents the absolute minimum, and in most societies we find it carried far beyond that point, with an assignment of various crafts to specialists and the appointment of social functionaries. This formal division of activities serves to give the society structure, organization and cohesion. It transforms the group of individuals who constitute the society from a mere amorphous mass into an organism. With each step in the differentiation of functions the individuals who perform these functions become increasingly dependent upon the whole. The merchant cannot exist without customers or the priest without a congregation.

It is the presence of such a system of organization which makes it possible for the society to persist through time. The mere biological processes of reproduction suffice to perpetuate the group, but not the society. Societies are like those historic structures, say our own frigate *Constitution,* which are replaced bit by bit while preserving the original pattern in its entirety. The simile is not quite satisfactory, since the structures of societies also change through time in response to the needs imposed by changing conditions. However, such changes are, for the most part, gradual, and patterning persists in spite of them. Societies perpetuate themselves as distinct entities by training the individuals who are born into the group to occupy particular places within the society's structure. In order to survive they must have not merely members but specialists, people who are able to do certain things superlatively well while leaving other things to other people. Seen from the standpoint of the individual, the process of socialization is thus one of learning what he should do for other people and what he is entitled to expect from them.

Both laboratory experiments and common sense tell us that the essence of successful learning lies in consistent reward or punishment. The behavior which always brings a desired result is learned much more quickly and readily than that which only brings it now and then. The successful training of the individual for a particular place in society depends upon the standardization of the behavior of the society's members. The boy who can learn to act like a man and to be a successful man when the time comes does so because everybody in his society agrees on how men should behave and rewards or punishes him in terms of how closely he adheres to or how far he departs from this standard. Such standards of behavior are called *culture patterns* by the anthropologist. Without them it would be impossible for any society either to function or to survive.

The concept of culture is so important that it will have to be dealt with in a separate chapter. For the present it is sufficient to define a culture as the way of life of any society. This way of life includes in-numerable details of behavior but all of these have certain factors in common. They all represent the normal, anticipated response of any of the society's members to a particular situation. Thus, in spite of the infinite number of minor variations which can be found in the responses of various individuals, or even in those of the same individual at different times, it will be found that most of the people in a society will respond to a given situation in much the same way. In our own society, for example, nearly everybody eats three times a day and takes one of these meals approximately at noon. Moreover, individuals who do not follow this routine are regarded as queer. Such a consensus of behavior and opinion constitutes a culture pattern; the culture as a whole is a more or less organized aggregate of such patterns.

The culture as a whole provides the members of any society with an indispensable guide in all the affairs of life. It would be impossible either for them or for the society to function effectively without it. The fact that most members of the society will react to a given situation in a given way makes it possible for anyone to predict their behavior with a high degree of probability, even though never with absolute certainty. This predictability is a prerequisite for any sort of organized social living. If the individual is going to do things for others, he must have assurance that he will get a return. The presence of culture patterns, with their background of social approval and consequent potentialities for social pressure upon those who do not adhere to them, provides him with that assurance. Moreover, through long experience and largely by the use of the trial-and-error method, the culture patterns which are characteristic of any society have usually come to be closely adjusted to one another. The individual can get good results if he adheres to them, poor or even negative ones if he does not. The old proverb, "When in Rome do as the Romans do," is based on sound observation. In Rome or in any other society things are organized in terms of the local culture patterns and make few provisions for departure from them. The difficulties of an Englishman in quest of his tea in a small middle western town would be a case in point.

If the presence of culture patterns is necessary to the functioning of any society, it is equally necessary to its perpetuation. The structure, that is, system of organization, of a society is itself a matter of culture. Although for purposes of description we can turn to spatial analogies and plot such a system in terms of positions, such positions cannot be defined adequately except in terms of the behavior expected of their occupants. Certain characteristics of age, sex or biological relationship may be prerequisites for the occupation of particular positions by the individual, but even the designation of such prerequisites is a cultural matter. Thus the positions of father and son in our own social system cannot be made clear by any statement of the biological relationship existing between the two. It is necessary to give an account of the culturally patterned behavior of the occupants of these positions toward each other. When it comes to such positions as those of employer and employee, we find it impossible to define them except in terms of what the occupants of these two positions are expected to do for (or possibly to) each other. A position in a social system, as distinct from the individual or individuals who may occupy it at a particular point in time, is actually a configuration of culture patterns. This configuration provides the individual with techniques for group living and social interaction in much the same way that other pattern configurations, also within the total culture, provide him with techniques for exploiting the natural environment or protecting himself from supernatural dangers. Societies perpetuate themselves by teaching the individuals in each generation the culture patterns which belong with the positions in the society which they are expected to occupy. The new recruits to the society learn how to behave as husbands or chiefs or craftsmen and by so doing perpetuate these positions and with them the social system as a whole. Without culture there could be neither social systems of the human sort nor the possibility of adjusting new members of the group to them.

I realize that in the foregoing discussion of society and culture emphasis has been laid mainly upon the passive role of the individual and upon the way in which he is shaped by cultural and social factors. It is time now to present the other side of the picture. No matter how carefully the individual has been trained nor how successful his conditioning has been, he remains a distinct organism with his own needs and with capacities for independent thought, feeling and action. Moreover, he retains a considerable degree of individuality. His integration into society and culture goes no deeper than his learned responses, and although in the adult these include the greater part of what we call the personality, there is still a good deal of the individual left over. Even in the most clearly integrated societies and cultures no two people are ever exactly alike.

Actually, the role of the individual with respect to society is a double one. Under ordinary circumstances, the more perfect his conditioning and consequent integration into the social structure, the more effective his contribution to the smooth functioning of the whole and the surer his rewards. However, societies have to exist and function in an ever changing world. The unparalleled ability of our species to adjust to changing conditions and to develop ever more effective responses to familiar ones rests upon the residue of individuality which survives in every one of us after society and culture have done their utmost. As a simple unit in the social organism, the individual perpetuates the status quo. As an individual he helps to change the status quo when the need arises. Since no environment is ever completely static, no society can survive without the occasional inventor and his ability to find solutions for new problems. Although he frequently invents in response to pressures which he shares with other members of his society, it is his own needs which spur him on to invention. The first man who wrapped a skin about him or fed a fire did this not because he was conscious that his society needed these innovations but because he felt cold. To pass to a higher level of culture complexity, no matter how injurious an existing institution may be to a society in the face of changing conditions, the stimulus to change or abandon it never comes from the individual upon whom it entails no hardship. New social inventions are made by those who suffer from the current conditions, not by those who profit from them.

An understanding of the double role of individuals as individuals and as units in society will provide a key to many of the problems which trouble students of human behavior. In order to function successfully as a unit in society, the individual must assume certain stereotyped forms of behavior, that is, culture patterns. A great many of these culture patterns are oriented toward the maintenance of society rather than the satisfaction of individual needs. Societies are organisms of a sort, and it has become common practice to speak of their having needs of their own as distinct from those of the individuals who compose them. Such usage carries unfortunate implications, since the qualities of societies are quite different from those of living organisms. It is safer to express the necessities implicit in the social situation by saying that a society can neither endure through time nor function successfully at any point in time unless the associated culture fulfills certain conditions. It must include techniques for indoctrinating new individuals in the society's system of values and for training them to occupy particular places in its structure. It must also include techniques for rewarding socially desirable behavior and discouraging that which is socially undesirable. Lastly, the behavior patterns which compose the culture must be adjusted to one another in such a way as to avoid conflict and prevent the results of one pattern of behavior from negating those of another. All societies have developed cultures which fulfill these conditions, although the processes involved in their development are still obscure.

The culture patterns upon which any society depends for its survival must be established as patterns of habitual response on the part of its members. This is rendered possible by man's extraordinary ability to absorb teaching. Teaching is used advisedly since something more than mere learning from accidental and organized experience is involved. All human beings receive deliberate and purposeful instruction from their elders. Complex patterns of behavior are transferred from generation to generation in this way. The individual's incentive for assuming these patterns lies in the satisfaction which they afford to his personal needs, especially his need for favorable response from others. However, from the point of view of his society such satisfactions are important mainly as bait. He learns the patterns as wholes, and these wholes subtend the necessities of social living quite as much as they subtend his own needs. He takes the bait of immediate personal satisfaction and is caught upon the hook of socialization. He would learn to eat in response to his own hunger drive, but his elders teach him to "eat like a gentleman." Thus, in later years, his hunger drive elicits a response which will not only satisfy it but do so in a way acceptable to his society and compatible with its other culture patterns. Through instruction and imitation the individual develops habits which cause him to perform his social role not only effectively but largely unconsciously. This ability to integrate into a single configuration elements of behavior some of which serve to meet individual needs, others to satisfy social necessities, and to learn and transmit such configurations as wholes is the thing that makes human societies possible. By assuming such configurations and establishing them as habits the individual is adjusted to occupy a particular position in society and to perform the role associated with that position.

The fact that most human behavior is taught in the form of organized configurations rather than simply developed by the individual on the basis of experience, is of the utmost importance to personality studies. It means that the way in which a person responds to a particular situation often provides a better clue to what his teaching has been than to what his personality is. In general, all the individuals who occupy a given position in the structure of a particular society will respond to many situations in very much the same way. That any one individual of such a group manifests this response proves nothing about his personality except that he has normal learning ability. His personal predispositions will be revealed not by his culturally patterned responses but by his deviations from the culture pattern. It is not the main theme of his behavior but the overtones which are significant for understanding him as an individual. In this fact lies the great importance of cultural studies for personality psychology. Until the psychologist knows what the norms of behavior imposed by a particular society are and can discount them as indicators of personality he will be unable to penetrate behind the facade of social conformity and cultural uniformity to reach the authentic individual.

PERSONALITY FORMATION: THE DETERMINANTS*

by Clyde Kluckhohn and Henry A. Murray

Every man is in certain respects
  a. like all other men,
  b. like some other men,
  c. like no other man.

He is like all other men because some of the determinants of his personality are universal to the species. That is to say, there are common features in the biological endowments of all men, in the physical environments they inhabit, and in the societies and cultures in which they develop. It is the very obviousness of this fact which makes restatements of it expedient, since, like other people, we students of personality are naturally disposed to be attracted by what is unusual, by the qualities which distinguish individuals, environments, and societies, and so to overlook the common heritage and lot of man. It is possible that the most important of the undiscovered determinants of personality and culture are only to be revealed by close attention to the commonplace. Every man experiences birth and must learn to move about and explore his environment, to protect himself against extremes of temperature and to avoid serious injuries; every man experiences sexual tensions and other importunate needs and must learn to find ways of appeasing them; every man grows in stature, matures, and dies; and he does all this and much more, from first to last, as a member of a society. These characteristics he shares with the majority of herd animals, but others are unique to him. Only with those of his own kind does he enjoy an

*Reprinted from *Personality in Nature, Society, and Culture—Second Edition* by Clyde Kluckhohn and Henry A. Murray with the collaboration of David M. Schneider (eds.) by permission of Alfred A. Knopf, Inc. Copyright 1948, 1953 by Alfred A. Knopf, Inc., pp. 53-67.

erect posture, hands that grasp, three-dimensional and color vision, and a nervous system that permits elaborate speech and learning processes of the highest order.

Any one personality is like all others, also, because, as social animals, men must adjust to a condition of interdependence with other members of their society and of groups within it, and, as cultural animals, they must adjust to traditionally defined expectations. All men are born helpless into an inanimate and impersonal world which presents count-less threats to survival; the human species would die out if social life were abandoned. Human adaptation to the external environment de-pends upon that mutual support which is social life; and, in addition, it depends upon culture. Many types of insects live socially yet have no culture. Their capacity to survive resides in action patterns which are inherited via the germ plasm. Higher organisms have less rigid habits and can learn more from experience. Human beings, however, learn not only from experience but also from each other. All human societies rely greatly for their survival upon accumulated learning (culture). Culture is a great storehouse of ready-made solutions to problems which human animals are wont to encounter. This storehouse is man's sub-stitute for instinct. It is filled not merely with the pooled learning of the living members of the society, but also with the learning of men long dead and of men belonging to other societies.

Human personalities are similar, furthermore, insofar as they all experience both gratifications and deprivations. They are frustrated by the impersonal environment (weather, physical obstacles, etc.) and by physiological conditions within their own bodies (physical incapacities, illnesses, etc.). Likewise, social life means some sacrifice of autonomy, subordination, and the responsibilities of superordination. The pleasure and pain men experience depend also upon what culture has taught them to expect from one another. Anticipation of pain and pleasure are internalized through punishment and reward.

These universalities of human life produce comparable effects upon the developing personalities of men of all times, places, and races. But they are seldom explicitly observed or commented upon. They tend to remain background phenomena—taken for granted like the air we breathe.

Frequently remarked, however, are the similarities in personality traits among members of groups or in specific individuals from different groups. In certain features of personality, most men are "like some other men." The similarity may be to other members of the same socio-cultural unit. The statistical prediction can safely be made that a hundred Americans, for example, will display certain defined characteristics more frequently than will a hundred Englishmen comparably distributed as to age, sex, social class, and vocation.

But being "like some men" is by no means limited to members of social units like nations, tribes, and classes. Seafaring people, regardless of the communities from which they come, tend to manifest similar qualities. The same may be said for desert folk. Intellectuals and athletes the world over have something in common; so have those who were born to wealth or poverty. Persons who have exercised authority over large groups for many years develop parallel reaction systems, in spite of culturally tailored differences in the details of their behaviors. Probably tyrannical fathers leave a detectably similar imprint upon their children, though the uniformity may be superficially obscured by local manners. Certainly the hyperpituitary type is equally recognizable among Europeans, African Negroes, and American Indians. Also, even where organic causes are unknown or doubtful, certain neurotic and psychotic syndromes in persons of one society remind us of other individuals belonging to very different societies.

Finally, there is the inescapable fact that a man is in many respects like no other man. Each individual's modes of perceiving, feeling, needing, and behaving have characteristic patterns which are not precisely duplicated by those of any other individual. This is traceable, in part, to the unique combination of biological materials which the person has received from his parents. More exactly, the ultimate uniqueness of each personality is the produce of countless and successive interactions between the maturing constitution and different environing situations from birth onward. An identical sequence of such determining influences is never reproduced. In this connection it is necessary to emphasize the importance of "accidents," that is, of events that are not predictable for any given individual on the basis of generalized knowledge of his physical, social, and cultural environments. A child gets lost in the woods and suffers from exposure and hunger. Another child is nearly drowned by a sudden flood in a canyon. Another loses his mother and is reared by an aged grandmother with a psychopathic personality. Although the personalities of children who have experienced a trauma of the same type will often resemble each other in certain respects, the differences between them may be even more apparent, partly because the traumatic situation in each case had certain unique features, and partly because at the time of the trauma the personality of each child, being already unique, responded in a unique manner. Thus there is uniqueness in each inheritance and uniqueness in each environment, but, more particularly, uniqueness in the number, kinds, and temporal order of critically determining situations encountered in the course of life.

In personal relations, in psychotherapy, and in the arts, this uniqueness of personality usually is, and should be, accented. But for general scientific purposes the observation of uniformities, uniformities of elements and uniformities of patterns, is of first importance. This is so because without the discovery of uniformities there can be no concepts, no classifications, no formulations, no principles, no laws; and without these no science can exist.

The writers suggest that clear and orderly thinking about personality formation will be facilitated if four classes of determinants (and their interactions) are distinguished: constitutional, group-membership, role, and situational. These will help us to understand in what ways every man is "like all other men," "like some other men," "like no other man."

1. CONSTITUTIONAL DETERMINANTS

The old problem of "heredity *or* environment" is essentially meaningless. The two sets of determinants can rarely be completely disentangled once the environment has begun to operate. All geneticists are agreed today that traits are not inherited in any simple sense. The observed characters of organisms are, at any given point in time, the product of a long series of complex interactions between biologically-inherited potentialities and environmental forces. The outcome of each interaction is a modification of the personality. The only pertinent questions therefore are: (1) which of the various genetic potentialities will be actualized as a consequence of a particular series of life-events in a given physical, social, and cultural environment? and (2) what limits to the development of this personality are set by genetic constitution?

Because there are only a few extreme cases in which an individual is definitely committed by his germ plasm to particular personality traits, we use the term "constitutional" rather than "hereditary." "Constitution" refers to the total physiological make-up of an individual at a given time. This is a product of influences emanating from the germ plasm and influences derived from the environment (diet, drugs, etc.).

Since most human beings (including scientists) crave simple solutions and tend to feel that because simple questions can be asked there must be simple answers, there are numberless examples both of overestimation and of underestimation of constitutional factors in theories of personality formation. Under the spell of the spectacular success of Darwinian biology and the medicine of the last hundred years, it has often been assumed that personality was no less definitely "given" at birth than was physique. At most, it was granted that a personality "unfolded" as the result of a strictly biological process of maturation.

On the other hand, certain psychiatrists, sociologists, and anthropologists have recently tended to neglect constitutional factors almost completely. Their assumptions are understandable in terms of common human motivations. Excited by discovering the effectiveness of certain determinants, people are inclined to make these explain everything instead of something. Moreover, it is much more cheerful and reassuring to believe that environmental factors (which can be manipulated) are all important, and that hereditary factors (which can't be changed) are comparatively inconsequential. Finally, the psychiatrists, one suspects, are consciously or unconsciously defending their livelihood when they minimize the constitutional side of personality.

The writers recognize the enormous importance of biological events and event patterns in molding the different forms which personalities assume. In fact, in the last chapter personality was defined as "the entire sequence of organized governmental processes in the brain from birth to death." They also insist that biological inheritance provides the stuff from which personality is fashioned and, as manifested in the physique at a given time-point, determines trends and sets limits within which variation is constrained. There are substantial reasons for believing that different genetic structures carry with them varying potentialities for learning, for reaction time, for energy level, for frustration tolerance. Different people appear to have different biological rhythms: of growth, of menstrual cycle, of activity, of depression and exaltation. The various biologically inherited malfunctions certainly have implications for personality development, though there are wide variations among those who share the same physical handicap (deafness, for example).

Sex and age must be regarded as among the more striking constitutional determinants of personality. Personality is also shaped through such traits of physique as stature, pigmentation, strength, conformity of features to the culturally fashionable type, etc. Such characteristics influence a man's needs and expectations. The kind of world he finds about him is to a considerable extent determined by the way other people react to his appearance and physical capacities. Occasionally a physically weak youth, such as Theodore Roosevelt was, may be driven to achieve feats of physical prowess as a form of over-compensation, but usually a man will learn to accept the fact that his physical makeup excludes him from certain types of vocational and social activities, although some concealed resentment may remain as an appreciable ingredient of his total personality. Conversely, special physical fitnesses make certain other types of adjustment particularly congenial.

2. GROUP MEMBERSHIP DETERMINANTS

The members of any organized enduring group tend to manifest certain personality traits more frequently than do members of other groups. How large or how small are the groupings one compares depends on the problem at hand. By and large, the motivational structures and action patterns of West Europeans seem similar when contrasted to those of Mohammedans of the Near East or to Eastern Asiatics. Most white citizens of the United States, in spite of regional, ethnic, and class differences, have features of personality which distinquish them from Englishmen, Australians, or New Zealanders. In distinguishing group-membership determinants, one must usually take account of a concentric order of social groups to which the individual belongs, ranging from large national or international groups down to small local units. One must also know the hierarchical class, political or social, to which he belongs within each of these groups. How inclusive a unit one considers in speaking of group-membership determinants is purely a function of the level of abstraction at which one is operating at a given time.

Some of the personality traits which tend to distinguish the members of a given group from humanity as a whole derive from a distinctive biological heritage. Persons who live together are more likely to have the same genes than are persons who live far apart. If the physical vitality is typically low for one group as contrasted with other groups, or if certain types of endocrine imbalance are unusually frequent, the personalities of the members of that group will probably have distinctive qualities.

In the greatest number of cases, however, the similarities of character within a group are traceable less to constitutional factors than to formative influences of the environment to which all members of the group have been subjected. Of these group-membership determinants, culture is with little doubt the most significant. To say that "culture determines" is, of course, a highly abstract way of speaking. What one actually observes is the interaction of people. One never sees "culture" any more than one sees "gravity." But "culture" is a very convenient construct which helps in understanding certain regularities in human events, just as "gravity" represents one type of regularity in physical events. Those who have been trained in childhood along traditional lines, and even those who have as adults adopted some new design for living, will be apt to behave predictably in many contexts because of a prevailing tendency to conform to group standards. As Edward Sapir has said:

> All cultural behavior is patterned. This is merely a way of saying that many things that an individual does and thinks and feels may be looked upon not merely from the standpoint of the forms of behavior that are proper to himself as a biological organism but from the standpoint of a generalized mode of conduct that is imputed to society rather than to the individual, though the personal genesis of conduct is of precisely the same nature, whether we choose to call the conduct "individual" or "social." It is impossible to say what an individual is doing unless we have tacitly accepted the essentially arbitrary modes of interpretation that social tradition is constantly suggesting to us from the very moment of our birth.

Not only the action patterns but also the motivational systems of individuals are influenced by culture. Certain needs are biologically given, but many others are not. All human beings get hungry, but no gene in any chromosome predisposes a person to work for a radio or new car or a shell necklace or "success." Sometimes biologically-given drives, such as sex, are for longer or shorter periods subordinated to culturally acquired drives, such as the pursuit of money or religious asceticism. And the means by which needs are satisfied are ordinarily defined by cultural habits and fashions. Most Americans would go hungry rather than eat a snake, but this is not true of tribes that consider snake meat a delicacy.

Those aspects of the personality that are not inherited but learned all have—at least in their more superficial and peripheral aspects—a cultural tinge. The skills that are acquired, the factual knowledge, the basic assumptions, the values, and the tastes, are largely determined by culture. Culture likewise structures the conditions under which each kind of learning takes place: whether transmitted by parents or parental substitutes, or by brothers and sisters, or by the learner's own age mates; whether gradually or quickly; whether renunciations are harshly imposed or reassuringly rewarded.

Of course we are speaking here of general tendencies rather than invariable facts. If there were no variations in the conceptions and applications of cultural standards, personalities formed in a given society would be more nearly alike than they actually are. Culture determines only what an individual learns as a member of a group—not so much what he learns as a private individual and as a member of a particular family. Because of these special experiences and particular constitutional endowments, each person's selection from and reaction to cultural teachings have an individual quality. What is learned is almost never symmetrical and coherent, and only occasionally is it fully integrated. Deviation from cultural norms is inevitable and endless, for variability appears to be a property of all biological organisms. But variation is also perpetuated because those who have learned later become teachers. Even the most conventional teachers will give culture a certain personal flavor in accord with their constitution and peculiar life-experiences. The culture may prescribe that the training of the child shall be gradual and gentle, but there will always be some abrupt and severe personalities who are temperamentally disposed to act otherwise. Nor is it in the concrete just a matter of individuality in the strict sense. There are family patterns resultant upon the habitual ways in which a number of individuals have come to adjust to each other.

Some types of variation, however, are more predictable. For example, certain differences in the personalities of Americans are referable to the fact that they have grown up in various sub-cultures. Jones is not only an American; he is also a member of the middle class, an Easterner, and has lived all his life in a small Vermont community. This kind of variation falls within the framework of the group determinants.

The values imbedded in a culture have special weight among the group membership determinants. A value is a conception, explicit or implicit, distinctive of an individual or characteristic of a group, of the desirable which influences the selection from available modes, means, and ends of action. It is thus not just a preferences, a desire, but a formulation of the *desirable,* the "ought" and "should" standards which influence action.

The component elements of a culture must, up to a point, be either logically consistent or meaningfully congruous. Otherwise the culture carriers feel uncomfortably adrift in a capricious, chaotic world. In a personality system, behavior must be reasonably regular or predictable, or the individual will not get expectable and needed responses from others because they will feel that they cannot "depend" on him. In other words, a social life and living in a social world both require standards "within" the individual and standards roughly agreed upon by individuals who live and work together in a group. There can be no personal security and no stability of social organization unless random carelessness, irresponsibility, and purely impulsive behavior are restrained in terms of private and group codes. If one asks the question, "Why are there values?" the reply must be: "Because social life would be impossible without them; the functioning of the social system could not continue to achieve group goals; individuals could not get what they want and need from other individuals in personal and emotional terms, nor could they feel within themselves a requisite measure of order and unified purpose." Above all, values add an element of predictability to social life.

Culture is not the only influence that bears with approximate constancy upon all the members of a relatively stable, organized group. But we know almost nothing of the effects upon personality of the continued press of the impersonal environment. Does living in a constantly rainy climate tend to make people glum and passive, living in a sunny, arid country tend to make them cheerful and lively? What are the differential effects of dwelling in a walled-in mountain valley, on a flat plain, or upon a high plateau studded with wide-sculptured red buttes? Thus far we can only speculate, for we lack adequate data. The effects of climate and even of scenery and topography may be greater than is generally supposed.

Membership in a group also carries with it exposure to a social environment. Although the social and cultural are inextricably intermingled in an individual's observable behavior, there is a social dimension to group membership that is not culturally defined. The individual must adjust to the presence or absence of other human beings in specified numbers and of specified age and sex. The density of population affects the actual or potential number of face-to-face relationships available to the individual. Patterns for human adjustment which would be suitable to a group of five hundred would not work equally well in a group of five thousand, and vice versa. The size of a society, the density of its population, its age and sex ratio are not entirely culturally prescribed, although often conditioned by the interaction between the technological level of the culture and the exigencies of the physical environment. The quality and type of social interaction that is determined by this social dimension of group membership has, likewise, its consequences for personality formation.

Before leaving the group-membership determinants, we must remind the reader once more that this conception is merely a useful abstraction. In the concrete, the individual personality is never directly affected by the group as a physical totality. Rather, his personality is molded by the particular members of the group with whom he has personal contact and by his conceptions of the group as a whole. Some traits of group members are predictable—in a statistical sense—from knowledge of the biological, social, and cultural properties of the group. But no single person is ever completely representative of all the characteristics imputed to the group as a whole. Concretely, not the group but group agents with their own peculiar traits determine personality formation. Of these group agents, the most important are the parents and other members of the individual's family. They, we repeat, act as individuals, as members of a group, and as members of a sub-group with special characteristics (the family itself).

3. ROLE DETERMINANTS

The culture defines how the different functions, or roles, necessary to group life are to be performed—such roles, for example, as those assigned on the basis of sex and age, or on the basis of membership in a caste, class, or occupational group. In a sense, the role determinants of personality are a special class of group-membership determinants; they apply to strata that cross-cut most kinds of group membership. The long-continued playing of a distinctive role, however, appears to be so potent in differentiating personalities within a group that it is useful to treat these determinants separately.

Moreover, if one is aware of the role determinants, one will less often be misled in interpreting various manifestations of personality. In this connection it is worth recalling that, in early Latin, *persona* means "a mask"—*dramatis personae* are the masks which actors wear in a play, that is, the characters that are represented. Etymologically and historically, then, the personality is the character that is manifested in public. In modern psychology and sociology this corresponds rather closely to the role behavior of a differentiated person. From one point of view, this constitutes a disguise. Just as the outer body shields the viscera from view, and clothing the genitals, so the public personality shields the private personality from the curious and censorious world. It also operates to conceal underlying motivations from the individual's own consciousness. The person who has painfully achieved some sort of integration, and who knows what is expected of him in a particular social situation, will usually produce the appropriate responses with only a little personal coloring. This explains, in part, why the attitudes and action patterns produced by the group-membership and role determinants constitute a screen which in the case of normal individuals, can be penetrated only by the intensive, lengthy, and oblique procedures of depth psychology.

The disposition to accept a person's behavior in a given situation as representative of his total personality is almost universal. Very often he is merely conforming, very acceptably, to the cultural definition of his role. One visits a doctor in his office, and his behavior fits the stereotype of the physician so perfectly that one says, often mistakenly, "There indeed is a well-adjusted person." But a scientist must train himself to get behind a man's cultivated surface, because he will not be able to understand much if he limits his data to the action patterns perfected through the repeated performance of the roles as physician, as middle-aged man, as physician dealing with an older male patient, etc.

4. SITUATIONAL DETERMINANTS

Besides the constitutional determinants and the forces which will more or less inevitably confront individuals who live in the same physical environment, who are members of a society of a certain size and of a certain culture, and who play the same roles, there are things which "just happen" to people. Even casual contacts of brief duration ("accidental"—i.e., not forcordained by the cultural patterns for social inter-relations) are often crucial, it seems, in determining whether a person's life will proceed along one or another of various possible paths. A student, say, who is undecided as to his career, or who is about equally drawn to several different vocations, happens to sit down in a railroad car next to a journalist who is an engaging and persuasive advocate of his profession. This event does not, of course, immediately and directly change the young man's personality, but it may set in motion a chain of events which put him into situations that are decisive in molding his personality.

The situational determinants include things that happen a thousand times as well as those that happen only once — provided they are not standard for a whole group. For example, it is generally agreed that the family constellation in which a person grows up is a primary source of personality styling. These domestic influences are conditioned by the cultural prescriptions for the roles of parents and children. But a divorce, a father who is much older than the mother, a father whose occupation keeps him away from home much of the time, the fact of being an only child or the eldest or youngest in a series—these are situational determinants.

Contact with a group involves determinants which are classified as group-membership or situational, depending on the individual's sense of belongingness or commitment to the group. The congeries of persons among whom a man accidentally finds himself one or more times may affect his personality development but not in the same manner as those social units with which the individual feels himself allied as a result of shared experiences or of imaginative identification.

5. INTERDEPENDENCE OF THE DETERMINANTS

"Culture and personality" is one of the fashionable slogans of contemporary social science and, by present usage, denotes a range of problems on the borderline between anthropology and sociology, on the one hand, and psychology and psychiatry, on the other. However, the phrase has unfortunate implications. A dualism is implied, whereas "culture *in* personality" and "personality *in* culture" would suggest conceptual models more in accord with the facts. Moreover, the slogan favors a dangerous simplification of the problems of personality formation. Recognition of culture as one of the determinants of personality is a great gain, but there are some indications that this theoretical advance has tended to obscure the significance of other types of determinants. "Culture and personality" is as lopsided as "biology and personality." To avoid perpetuation of an over-emphasis upon culture, the writers have treated cultural forces as but one variety of the press to which personalities are subjected as a consequence of their membership in an organized group.

A balanced consideration of "personality in nature, society, and culture" must be carried on within the framework of a complex conceptual scheme which explicitly recognizes, instead of tacitly excluding, a number of types of determinants. But it must also not be forgotten that any classification of personality determinants is, at best, a convenient abstraction.

A few illustrations of the intricate linkage of the determinants will clarify this point. For example, we may instance a network of cultural, role and constitutional determinants. In every society the child is differently socialized according to sex. Also, in every society different behavior is expected of individuals in different age groups, although each culture makes it own prescriptions as to where these lines are drawn and what behavioral variations are to be anticipated. Thus, the personalities of men and women, of the old and young, are differentiated, in part, by the experience of playing these various roles in conformity with cultural standards. But, since age and sex are biological facts, they also operate throughout life as constitutional determinants of personality. A woman's motivations and action patterns are modified by the facts of her physique as a woman.

Some factors that one is likely to pigeonhole all too complacently as biological often turn out, on careful examination, to be the product of complicated interactions. Illness may result from group as well as from individual constitutional factors. And illness, in turn, may be considered a situational determinant. The illness—with all of its effects upon personality formation—is an "accident" in that one could predict only that the betting odds were relatively high that this individual would fall victim to this illness. However, when the person does become a patient, one can see that both a constitutional predisposition and membership in a caste or class group where sanitation and medical care were substandard are causative factors in this "accidental" event. Similarly, a constitutional tendency towards corpulence certainly has implications for personality when it is characteristic of a group as well as when it distinguishes an individual within a group. But the resources of the physical environment as exploited by the culturally-transmitted technology are major determinants in the production and utilization of nutritional substances of various sorts and these have patent consequences for corpulence, stature, and energy potential. Tuberculosis or pellagra may be endemic. If hookworm is endemic in a population, one will hardly expect vigor to be a striking feature of the majority of people. Yet hookworm is not an unavoidable "given," either constitutionally or environmentally: The prevalence and effects of hookworm are dependent upon culturally enjoined types of sanitary control.

Complicated interrelations of the same sort may be noted between the environmental and cultural forces which constitute the group membership determinants. On the one hand, the physical environment imposes certain limitations upon the cultural forms which man creates, or it constrains toward change and readjustment in the culture he brings into an ecological area. There is always a large portion of the impersonal environment to which men can adjust but not control; there is another portion which is man-made and cultural. Most cultures provide technologies which permit some alterations in the physical world (for example, methods of cutting irrigation ditches or of terracing hillsides). There are also those artifacts (houses, furniture, tools, vehicles) which serve as instruments for the gratification of needs, and, not infrequently, for their incitement and frustration. Most important of all, perhaps, culture directs and often distorts man's perceptions of the external world. What effects social suggestion may have in setting frames of reference for perception has been shown experimentally. Culture acts as a set of blinders, or series of lenses, through which men view their environments.

Among group-membership determinants, the social and cultural factors are interdependent, yet analytically distinct. Man, of course, is only one of many social animals, but the way in which social, as opposed to solitary, life modifies his behavior are especially numerous and varied. The fact that human beings are mammals and reproduce bi-sexually creates a basic predisposition toward at least the rudiments of social living. And the prolonged helplessness of human infants conduces to the formation of a family group. Also, certain universal social processes (such as conflict, competition, and accommodation) are given distinct forms through cultural transmission. Thus, while the physically strong tend to dominate the weak, this tendency may be checked and even to some extent reversed by a tradition which rewards chivalry, compassion, and humility. Attitudes towards women, towards infants, towards the old, towards the weak will be affected by the age and sex ratios and the birth and death rates prevalent at a particular time.

The social and cultural press likewise interlock with the situational determinants. There are many forces involved in social interaction which influence personality formation and yet are in no sense culturally prescribed. All children (unless multiple births) are born at different points in their parents' careers, which means that they have, psychologically speaking, somewhat different parents. Likewise, whether a child is wanted or unwanted and whether it is of the desired sex will make a difference in the ways in which it will be treated, even though the culture says that all children are wanted and defines the two sexes as of equal value.

A final example will link the constitutional with both the group-membership and situational determinants. Even though identical twins may differ remarkably little from a biological standpoint, and participate in group activities which are apparently similar, a situational factor may intrude as a result of which their experiences in social interaction will be quite different. If, for instance, one twin is injured in an automobile accident and the other is not, and if the injured twin has to spend a year in bed, as the special object of her mother's solicitations, noticeable personality differences will probably develop. The extent to which these differences endure will depend surely upon many other factors, but it is unlikely that they will be entirely counteracted. The variations in treatment which a bed-ridden child receives is partly determined by culture (the extent to which the ideal patterns permit a sick child to be petted, etc.), and partly by extra-cultural factors (the mother's need for nurturance, the father's idiomatic performance of his culturally patterned role in these circumstances, etc.).

6. SIMILARITIES AND DIFFERENCES IN PERSONALITY

In conclusion, let us return for a moment to the observed fact that every man is "like all other men, like some other men, like no other man." In the beginning there is (1) the organism and (2) the environment. Using this division as the starting point in thinking about personality formation, one might say that the *differences* observed in the personalities of human beings are due to variations in their biological equipment and in the total environment to which they must adjust, while the *similarities* are ascribable to biological and environmental regularities. Although the organism and the environment have a kind of wholeness in the concrete behavioral world which the student loses sight of at his peril, this generalization is substantially correct. However, the formulation can be put more neatly in terms of field. There is (1) the organism moving through a field which is (2) structured both by culture and by the physical and social world in a relatively uniform manner, but which is (3) subject to endless variation within the general patterning due to the organism's constitutionally-determined peculiarities of reaction and to the occurence of special situations.

In certain circumstances, one reacts to men and women, not as unique organizations of experience, but as representatives of a group. In other circumstances, one reacts to men and women primarily as fulfilling certain roles. If one is unfamiliar with the Chinese, one is likely to react to them first as Chinese rather than as individuals. When one meets new people at a social gathering, one is often able to predict correctly: "That man is a doctor." "That man certainly isn't a businessman, he acts like a professor." "That fellow over there looks like a government official, surely not an artist, a writer, or an actor." Similarities in personality created by the role and group-membership determinants are genuine enough. A man is likely to resemble other men from his home town, other members of his vocation, other members of his class, as well as the majority of his countrymen as contrasted to foreigners.

But the variations are equally common. Smith is stubborn in his office as well as at home and on the golf course. Probably he would have been stubborn in all social contexts if he had been taken to England from America at an early age and his socialization had been completed there. The playing of roles is always tinged by the uniqueness of the personality. Such differences may be distinguished by saying, "Yes, Brown and Jones are both forty-five-year-old Americans, both small-businessmen with about the same responsibilities, family ties, and prestige—but somehow they are different." Such dissimilarities may be traced to the interactions of the constitutional and situational determinants, which have been different for each man, with the common group-membership and role determinants to which both have been subjected.

Another type of resemblance between personalities cuts across the boundaries of groups and roles but is equally understandable within this framework of thinking about personality formation. In general, one observes quite different personality manifestations in Hopi Indians and in white Americans—save for those common to all humanity. But occasionally one meets a Hopi whose behavior, as a whole or in part, reminds one very strongly of a certain type of white man. Such parallels can arise from similar constitutional or situational detriments or a combination of these. A Hopi and a white man might both have an unusual endocrine condition. Or both Hopi and white might have had several long childhood illnesses which brought them an exceptional amount of maternal care. While an over-abundance of motherly devotion would have had somewhat different effects upon the two personalities, a striking segmental resemblance might have been produced which persisted throughout life.

In most cases the observed similarities, as well as the differences, between groups of people are largely attributable to fairly uniform social and cultural processes. When one says, "Smith reminds me of Brown," a biologically inherited determinant may be completely responsible for the observed resemblance. But when one notes that American businessmen, for example, have certain typical characteristics which identify them as a group and distinguish them from American farmers and teachers it can hardly be a question of genetic constitution. Likewise, the similarities of personality between Americans in general as contrasted with Germans in general must be traced primarily to common press which produces resemblances in spite of wide variations in individual constitutions.

To summarize the content of this chapter in other terms: The personality of an individual is the product of inherited dispositions and environmental experiences. These experiences occur within the field of his physical, biological, and social environment, all of which are modified by the culture of his group. Similarities of life experiences and heredity will tend to produce similar personality characteristics in different individuals, whether in the same society or in different societies.

Although the distinction will not always be perfectly clear-cut, the readings which follow will be organized according to this scheme of constitutional, group-membership, role, and situational determinants, and the interactions between them. It is believed that this will assist the reader in keeping steadily in mind the variety of forces operative in personality formation and the firm but subtle nexus that links them.

STATUS AND ROLE*

by Ralph Linton

In the preceding chapter we discussed the nature of society and pointed out that the functioning of societies depends upon the presence of patterns for reciprocal behavior between individuals or groups of individuals. The polar positions in such patterns of reciprocal behavior are technically known as *statuses.* The term *status,* like the term *culture,* has come to be used with a double significance. A *status,* in the abstract, is a position in a particular pattern. It is thus quite correct to speak of each individual as having many statuses, since each individual participates in the expression of a number of patterns. However, unless the term is qualified in some way, *the status* of any individual means the sum total of all the statuses which he occupies. It represents his position with relation to the total society. Thus the status of Mr. Jones as a member of his community derives from a combination of all the statuses which he holds as a citizen, as an attorney, as a Mason, as a Methodist, as Mrs. Jones's husband, and so on.

A status, as distinct from the individual who may occupy it, is simply a collection of rights and duties. Since these rights and duties can find expression only through the medium of individuals, it is extremely

*From *The Study of Man,* by Ralph Linton, pp. 113-121. Copyright 1936, D. Appleton-Century Co., Inc. Reprinted by permission of the publishers, Appleton-Century-Crofts, Inc.

hard for us to maintain a distinction in our thinking between statuses and the people who hold them and exercise the rights and duties which constitute them. The relation between any individual and any status he holds is somewhat like that between the driver of an automobile and the driver's place in the machine. The driver's seat with its steering wheel, accelerator, and other controls is a constant with ever-present potentialities for action and control, while the driver may be any member of the family and may exercise these potentialities very well or very badly.

A *role* represents the dynamic aspect of a status. The individual is socially assigned to a status and occupies it with relation to other statuses. When he puts the rights and duties which constitute the status into effect, he is performing a role. Role and status are quite inseparable, and the distinction between them is of only academic interest. There are no roles without statuses or statuses without roles. Just as in the case of *status,* the term *role* is used with a double significance. Every individual has a series of roles deriving from the various patterns in which he participates and at the same time a *role,* general, which represents the sum total of these roles and determines what he does for his society and what he can expect from it.

Although all statuses and roles derive from social patterns and are integral parts of patterns, they have an independent function with relation to the individuals who occupy particular statuses and exercise their roles. To such individuals the combined status and role represent the minimum of attitudes and behavior which he must assume if he is to participate in the overt expression of the pattern. Status and role serve to reduce the ideal patterns for social life to individual terms. They become models for organizing the attitudes and behavior of the individual so that these will be congruous with those of the other individuals participating in the expression of the pattern. Thus if we are studying football teams in the abstract, the position of quarterback is meaningless except in relation to the other positions. From the point of view of the quarterback himself it is a distinct and important entity. It determines where he shall take his place in the line-up and what he shall do in various plays. His assignment to this position at once limits and defines his activities and establishes a minimum of things which he must learn. Similarly, in a social pattern such as that for the employer-employee relationship the statuses of employer and employee define what each has to know and do to put the pattern into operation. The employer does not need to know the techniques involved in the employee's labor, and the employee does not need to know the techniques for marketing or accounting.

It is obvious that, as long as there is no interference from external sources, the more perfectly the members of any society are adjusted to their statuses and roles the more smoothly the society will function. In its attempts to bring about such adjustments every society finds itself caught on the horns of a dilemma. The individual's formation of habits and attitudes begins at birth, and, other things being equal, the earlier his training for a status can begin the more successful it is likely to be. At the same time, no two individuals are alike, and a status which will be congenial to one may be quite uncongenial to another. Also, there are in all social systems certain roles which require more than training for their successful performance. Perfect technique does not make a great violinist, nor a thorough book of knowledge of tactics an efficient general. The utilization of the special gifts of individuals may be highly important to society, as in the case of the general, yet these gifts usually show themselves rather late, and to wait upon their manifestation for the assignment of statuses would be to forfeit the advantages to be derived from commencing training early.

Fortunately, human beings are so mutable that almost any normal individual can be trained to the adequate performance of almost any role. Most of the business of living can be conducted on a basis of habit, with little need for intelligence and none for special gifts. Societies have met the dilemma by developing two types of statuses, the *ascribed* and the *achieved*. *Ascribed* statuses are those which are assigned to individuals without reference to their innate differences or abilities. They can be predicted and trained for from the moment of birth. The *achieved* statuses, are, as a minimum, those requiring special qualities, although they are not necessarily limited to these. They are not assigned to individuals from birth but are left open to be filled through competition and individual effort. The majority of the statuses in all social systems are of the ascribed type and those which take care of the ordinary day-to-day business of living are practically always of this type.

In all societies certain things are selected as reference points for the ascription of status. The things chosen for this purpose are always of such a nature that they are ascertainable at birth, making it possible to begin the training of the individual for his potential statuses and roles at once. The simplest and most universally used of these reference points is sex. Age is used with nearly equal frequency, since all individuals pass through the same cycle of growth, maturity, and decline, and the statuses whose occupation will be determined by age can be forecast and trained for with accuracy. Family relationships, the simplest and most obvious being that of the child to its mother, are also used in all societies as reference points for the establishment of a whole series of statuses. Lastly, there is the matter of birth into a particular socially established group, such as a class or caste. The use of this type of reference is common but not universal. In all societies the actual ascription of statuses to the individual is controlled by a series of these reference points which together serve to delimit the field of his future participation in the life of the group.

The division and ascription of statuses with relation to sex seems to be basic in all social systems. All societies prescribe different attitudes and activities to men and to women. Most of them try to rationalize these prescriptions in terms of the physiological differences between the sexes or their different roles in reproduction. However, a comparative study of the statuses ascribed to women and men in different cultures seems to show that while such factors may have served as a starting point for the development of a division the actual ascriptions are almost entirely determined by culture. Even the psychological characteristics ascribed to men and women in different societies vary so much that they can have little physiological basis. Our own idea of women as ministering angels contrasts sharply with the ingenuity of women as torturers among the Iroquois and the sadistic delight they took in the process. Even the last two generations have seen a sharp change in the psychological patterns for women in our own society. The delicate, fainting lady of the middle eighteen-hundreds is as extinct as the dodo.

When it comes to the ascription of occupations, which is after all an integral part of status, we find the differences in various societies even more marked. Arapesh women regularly carry heavier loads then men "because their heads are so much harder and stronger." In some societies women do most of the manual labor; in others, as in the Marquesas, even cooking, housekeeping, and baby-tending are proper male occupations, and women spend most of their time primping. Even the general rule that women's handicap through pregnancy and nursing indicates the more active occupations as male and the less active ones as female has many exceptions. Thus among the Tasmanians seal-hunting was women's work. They swam out to the seal rocks, stalked the animals, and clubbed them. Tasmanian women also hunted oppossums, which required the climbing of large trees.

Although the actual ascription of occupations along sex lines is highly variable, the pattern of sex division is constant. There are very few societies in which every important activity has not been definitely assigned to men or to women. Even when the two sexes cooperate in a particular occupation, the field of each is usually clearly delimited. Thus in Madagascar rice culture the men make the seed beds and terraces and prepare the fields for transplanting. The women do the work of transplanting, which is hard and back-breaking. The women weed the crop, but the men harvest it. The women then carry it to the threshing floors, where the men thresh it while the women winnow it. Lastly, the women pound the grain in mortars and cook it.

When a society takes over a new industry, there is often a period of uncertainty during which the work may be done by either sex, but it soon falls into the province of one or the other. In Madagascar, pottery is made by men in some tribes and by women in others. The only tribe in which it is made by both men and women is one into which the art has been introduced within the last sixty years. I was told that during the fifteen years preceding my visit there had been a marked decrease in the number of male potters, many men who had once practised the art having given it up. The factor of lowered wages, usually advanced as the reason for men leaving one of our own occupations when women enter it in force, certainly was not operative here. The field was not overcrowded, and the prices for men's and women's products were the same. Most of the men who had given up the trade were vague as to their reasons, but a few said frankly that they did not like to compete with women. Apparently the entry of women into the occupation had robbed it of a certain amount of prestige. It was no longer quite the thing for a man to be a potter, even though he was a very good one.

The use of age as a reference point for establishing status is as universal as the use of sex. All societies recognize three age groupings as a minimum: child, adult and old. Certain societies have emphasized age as a basis for assigning status and have greatly amplified the divisions. Thus in certain African tribes the whole male population is divided into units composed of those born in the same years or within two- or three-year intervals. However, such extreme attention to age is unusual, and we need not discuss it here.

The physical differences between child and adult are easily recognizable, and the passage from childhood to maturity is marked by physiological events which make it possible to date it exactly for girls and within a few weeks or months for boys. However, the physical passage from childhood to maturity does not necessarily coincide with the social transfer of the individual from one category to the other. Thus in our own society both men and women remain legally children long after they are physically adult. In most societies this difference between the physical and social transfer is more clearly marked than in our own. The child becomes a man not when he is physically mature but when he is formally recognized as a man by his society. This recognition is almost always given ceremonial expression in what are technically known as puberty rites. The most important element in these rites is not the determination of physical maturity but that of social maturity. Whether a boy is able to breed is less vital to his society than whether he is able to do a man's work and has a man's knowledge. Actually, most puberty ceremonies include tests of the boy's learning and fortitude, and if the aspirants are unable to pass these they are left in the child status until they can. For those who pass the tests, the ceremonies usually culminate in the transfer to them of certain secrets which the men guard from women and children.

The passage of individuals from adult to aged is harder to perceive. There is no clear physiological line for men, while even women may retain their full physical vigor and their ability to carry on all the activities of the adult status for several years after the menopause. The social transfer of men from the adult to the aged group is given ceremonial recognition in a few cultures, as when a father formally surrenders his official position and titles to his son, but such recognition is rare. As for women, there appears to be no society in which the menopause is given ceremonial recognition, although there are a few societies in which it does alter the individual's status. Thus Comanche women, after the menopause, were released from their disabilities with regard to the supernatural. They could handle sacred objects, obtain power through dreams and practice as shamans, all things forbidden to women of bearing age.

The general tendency for societies to emphasize the individual's first change in age status and largely ignore the second is no doubt due in part to the difficulty of determining the onset of old age. However, there are also psychological factors involved. The boy or girl is usually anxious to grow up, and this eagerness is heightened by the exclusion of children from certain activities and knowledge. Also, society welcomes new additions to the most active division of the group, that which contributes most to its perpetuation and well-being. Conversely, the individual who enjoys the thought of growing old is atypical in all societies. Even when age brings respect and a new measure of influence, it means the relinquishment of much that is pleasant. We can see among ourselves that the aging usually refuse to recognize the change until long after it has happened.

In the case of age, as in that of sex, the biological factors involved appear to be secondary to the cultural ones in determining the content of status. There are certain activities which cannot be ascribed to children because children either lack the necessary strength or have not had time to acquire the necessary technical skills. However, the attitudes between parent and child and the importance given to the child in the family structure vary enormously from one culture to another. The status of the child among our Puritan ancestors, where he was seen and not heard and ate at the second table, represents one extreme. At the other might be placed the status of the eldest son of a Polynesian chief. All the *mana* (supernatural power) of the royal line converged upon such a child. He was socially superior to his own father and mother, and any attempt to discipline him would have been little short of sacrilege. I once visited the hereditary chief of a Marquesan tribe and found the whole family camping uncomfortably in their own front yard, although they had a good house built on European lines. Their eldest son, aged nine, had had a dispute with his father a few days before and had tabooed the house by naming it after his head. The family had thus been compelled to move out and could not use it again until he relented and lifted the taboo. As he could use the house himself and eat anywhere in the village, he was getting along quite well and seemed to enjoy the situation thoroughly.

The statuses ascribed to the old in various societies vary even more than those ascribed to children. In some cases they are relieved of all heavy labor and can settle back comfortably to live off their children. In others they perform most of the hard and monotonous tasks which do not require great physical strength, such as the gathering of firewood. In many societies the old women, in particular, take over most of the care of the younger children, leaving the younger women free to enjoy themselves. In some places the old are treated with consideration and respect; in others they are considered a useless incumbrance and removed as soon as they are incapable of heavy labor. In most societies their advice is sought even when little attention is paid to their wishes. This custom has a sound practical basis, for the individual who contrives to live to old age in an uncivilized group has usually been a person of ability and his memory constitutes a sort of reference library to which one can turn for help under all sorts of circumstances.

In certain societies the change from the adult to the old status is made more difficult for the individual by the fact that the patterns for these statuses ascribe different types of personality to each. This was the case among the Comanche, as it seems to have been among most of the Plains tribes. The adult male was a warrior, vigorous, self-reliant, and pushing. Most of his social relationships were phrased in terms of competition. He took what he could get and held what he had without regard to any abstract rights of those weaker than himself. Any willingness to arbitrate differences or to ignore slights was a sign of weakness resulting in loss of prestige. The old man, on the other hand, was expected to be wise and gentle, willing to overlook slights and, if need be, to endure abuse. It was his task to work for the welfare of the tribe, giving sound advice, settling feuds between the warriors, and even preventing his tribe from making new enemies. Young men strove for war and honor, old men strove for peace and tranquillity. There is abundant evidence that among the Comanche the transition was often a difficult one for the individual. Warriors did not prepare for old age, thinking it a better fate to be killed in action. When waning physical powers forced them to assume the new role, many of them did so grudgingly, and those who had strong magic would go on trying to enforce the rights which belonged to the younger status. Such bad old men were a peril to young ones beginning their careers, for they were jealous of them simply because they were young and strong and admired by the women. The medicine power of these young men was still weak, and the old men could and did kill them by malevolent magic. It is significant that although benevolent medicine men might be of any age in Comanche folklore, malevolent ones were always old.

THE SOCIOLOGY OF PARENT-YOUTH CONFLICT*

by Kingsley Davis

Whether recognized as a separate status or not, the adolescent period seemingly has one outstanding peculiarity — namely, that it is a time when the individual is attaining physical maturity without necessarily attaining social maturity. In terms of growth, strength, fecundity, and mental capacity, full maturity tends to be attained only a short time after puberty; but socially the adolescent still has a long way to go, in most cases, before full status is reached.

This tendency for the adolescent to be more mature physically than socially is most pronounced in settled and traditionalized, and also modern, societies, but it is a condition that is to some extent inherent in the nature of all human society. Evolving through uncounted millennia, culture has developed a complexity of principle and a fullness of content

* From Kingsley Davis, "The Psychology of Adolescence," *Annals of the American Academy of Political and Social Science,* Volume 236 (November 1944), pp. 8-16. Reprinted by permission.

that require a long time for the individual to master. At the same time it has made possible a type of social organization in which power and advantage are dependent on social position, knowledge, experience, and reputation, rather than brute strength or innate cunning. In so far as these things have anything to do with age, they are more likely to come with middle age, or even old age, than with adolescence. There has grown up, therefore, a situation in which the adolescent, despite his physical equality with or even superiority to the older person, is, nevertheless placed in a socially subordinate position. The result is a sort of disharmony which, in times of social disorganization, *sometimes* expresses itself in conflict between the generations.

If mental and physical maturity came between 30 and 35 years of age, instead of between 15 and 20, there would be a much longer period of youthful plasticity during which an enormously enhanced amount of culture could be absorbed. As it is, especially in modern society, the individual must keep on learning after his capacity to do so has already begun to decline. Even though his mental capacity has reached its peak during adolescence, his acquired knowledge, judgment, insight, and self-reliance are generally far from their peak.

The great extension of the average length of life in modern times, while it has afforded more scope and rationale to post-adolescent learning, has not lengthened the adolescent period itself. Instead, it has prolonged the duration of adulthood, and has consequently made adolescence a smaller fraction of the average life span.

Also helping to make the complex heritage of modern culture possible is specialization. Each individual is not required to learn the entire culture, but only that part of it which concerns him. The mechanism, however, like the extension of the length of life, has its limitations, as one can readily see by imagining a society with no general language but merely a separate language for every occupational group.

Societies of course differ as to how freely they permit young people to accumulate knowledge and experience. Frequently in order to transmit first the ideal elements of the culture, the elders select the cultural content that is given to children and protect them from contrary experiences. To the extent that this happens, it postpones social maturity to some stage beyond adolescence. In modern society, because of this protectiveness as well as other factors, even middle-aged people are commonly accused of being emotionally immature.

In addition to the increasing complexity of culture and the consequent length of time required for socialization, social evolution has progressed to the point where power does not ordinarily depend on physical prowess. Even an army, which presumably depends par excellence on physical skill and strength, is controlled by elderly generals and colonels. The adolescent, despite his achievements in battles, sports, and tests, has long been forced to defer to older persons whose biological capacities are less than his. The latter, by virtue of having held a position early in life, are able, in a stable society, to continue to hold it later in life, and by virtue of it to acquire other positions of even greater influence. Furthermore, because of the endlessness of the educational process, they are in a way better qualified for responsible positions. Their qualification, however, is a socially acquired and not a biologically maturing qualification. It is based on knowledge and experience, both necessary for successful political and administrative decisions.

Thus in a sense (the physical sense) the community does not utilize its great men until they are already past their prime; but in another sense (the social sense) it utilizes them at the peak of their greatness—in what one might call their administrative or sociological maturity. The principle of seniority, therefore, is no accident, no empty form. The charge is frequently made that the old hang onto their positions as vested interests, and that this is the explanation of the subordination of youth to age. That older persons seek to hold what power they have is generally true, but their desire does not explain the fact that they *can* do so. They are able to hold their power because they have a kind of superiority—a superiority developed and buttressed by an organized society, but a superiority nonetheless.

If our hypothesis is true, then adolescence is ordinarily the time when the lag of social development behind physical development first becomes pronounced. As society grows more complex the lag becomes greater, and adolescence, as socially defined, extends farther into organic adulthood.

MAJOR POINTS OF ARTICULATION

Sociologically, it is necessary to get behind the kaleidoscopic array of customs in different societies and to examine the alternative principles which *any* human society, as a functional and structural system, has at its disposal in utilizing the adolescent generation. Between the adolescent stratum and the rest of the social structure there are numerous points of articulation where alternative principles may be employed. Indeed, anyone unfamiliar with the anthropological literature is likely to be surprised at the number of junctures in which adolescence must somehow be handled but in which the mode of handling is open to several divergent possibilities. In what follows, only four such points of articulation will be discussed, viz., occupational placement, reproductive control, authoritarian organization, and cultural acquisition. These correspond to four major foci of institutional organization, namely the economic, the familial, the political, and the educational. In each case the alternative employed by any given society depends primarily on that society's total structure.

OCCUPATIONAL PLACEMENT

Since every society involves some specialization of function, an important matter is the selection of individuals for various occupations. This selection may be made by ascription or by choice. If by choice, it can be made at any time, but if much training is required, it needs to be made by the time of adolescence at the latest, because this period represents the last stage of rapid learning. The earlier the choice is made, the more intensive can be the training. On the other hand, the later it is made, the more it may rest on a true evaluation of personal talent and preference.

It is probably no accident, therefore, that the most complex societies (i.e., modern Occidental ones) on the whole defer the final decision until adolescence and provide most of the specialized training during that period. Less complex societies, such as that of classical India, may decide the matter at birth and provide what training is necessary during the entire childhood. In simpler societies the division of labor may be so slight that the question, except perhaps as regards the positions of chief and shaman, may be unimportant. In a complex but changing society the decision as to occupation tends to be deferred until late adolescence or early adulthood, because occupational possibilities are altering so fast that decisions made earlier may be subsequently rendered inadvisable; yet it is precisely in such a society that an elaborate training, and hence an early decision, are necessary.

The handling of occupational placement plays a significant role in determining the status of the adolescent. If in a simple and stable society the occupation is ascribed or chosen early in life, if the training extends through childhood or is relatively simple in character, adolescence does not stand out occupationally as a period of any particular importance. By the time he reaches adolescence the individual may in fact be practicing his occupation, and may be looked upon in this regard as an adult. If on the other hand the society is complex and changing, adolescence tends to become a time of difficult choosing and intensive training, and hence to acquire a pronounced importance as a socially recognized, eventful period of life. If there is a gradation within each occupation, the adolescent generally starts at the bottom rung. This tends to give him a distinct subordinate status. If the element of competition is introduced, it acts as an individualizing force that makes of adolescence a period of strain and perhaps of deprivation, at the same time that it raises the level of general achievement.

REPRODUCTIVE CONTROL

In its determinization of the adolescent status, every society must somehow recognize the fact that the reproductive capacity first appears at the inception of adolescence. One crucial question is whether the adolescent shall be permitted to gratify his sexual desires through normal heterosexual intercourse or whether such gratification must be postponed. A second is whether the gratification, if permitted, shall be in marriage or in premartial relations; and if the latter, whether the illegitimate children shall be killed, disposed of to relatives, or kept by the girl. Finally, there is the question of whether marital choice is free or is controlled by others, and whether marriage establishes a separate household or merely an extension of the parental menage.

Among most peoples of the world, at least until recently, there was some variation of a recurrent pattern. Either marriage occurred shortly after puberty or premarital intercourse prevailed. The choice of marital partner was generally in the hands of parents or kinsmen, though the right of veto, in theory at least, supposedly belonged to the parties to the marriage. Wedlock did not usually imply a separate household, and did not convey full emancipation from the parents. Although there were countless variations on this generalized pattern, the underlying theme was extremely widespread. Its main characteristic was that it gave a sexual and reproductive function to the adolescent but carefully controlled the exercise of this function.

By way of contrast, American society is unusual, though not entirely unique, in the following ways: It maintains the ideal of premarital chastity in the face of a long period of postponement of marriage after puberty. In with this it upholds the freedom of marital choice and fosters competition and the doctrine of *caveat emptor* in courtship. Finally, it emphasizes the independence and separateness of the wedded couple. As a consequence, the adolescent period becomes one of considerable strain. The young person is permitted to associate closely with the opposite sex but is put on his honor to remain virtuous, is supposed to choose his own mate independently but is in many ways still under the authority of the parents, and is forced to compete for love in a rating and dating system that interferes and gets entangled with his fortunes in that other competitive system, the occupational. The strains are somewhat different for boys and for girls, but only as two different sides of the same situation.

AUTHORITARIAN ORGANIZATION

Whereas American youth think that getting a job and getting married entitle them to independence, the case is quite different in many other societies. In old India, Ireland, China, and Japan, for example, the authority of the parent tended to continue until death. The end of adolescence did not mean a significant change in authority, and hence the adolescent phase, for that reason at least, did not stand apart as a separate period. In addition, there was little conflict over authority, not only because complete emancipation did not occur, but also because such emancipation as did occur developed by well-grooved, mutually accepted, publicly ritualized steps.

In modern society, by contrast, the child is supposed to become completely emancipated from the parental power, but the exact time, manner, and cause of such emancipation remain uncertain, a subject of dispute, recrimination, and remorse. The individual may become a full-fledged wage earner as early as childhood or as late as adulthood. Marriage is often postponed so long that there tends to arise a distinction between the adolescent and the unmarried adult. Neither employment nor matrimony, therefore, may be accepted as a standard criterion of emancipation. There is no such standard criterion. Each family must virtually settle the matter for itself as a result of private interaction. This in spite of the fact that the emancipation, once it does come, is relatively more complete than in most societies.

In Peter Blos's book, *The Adolescent Personality,* one of the three major goals of adolescence is claimed to be "emancipation from the family." Achieving this goal is viewed as a long and hard psychic struggle. Yet in most societies it either comes in the normal course of affairs or never comes at all. Among us, it comes as a struggle because the adolescent needs the protection of his family at the same time that he rebels against its authority, because he dreads to leave the glamorous irresponsibility of youth for the humdrum cares of adulthood, and because he has no standardized steps by which emancipation can be automatically and publicly achieved.

In relation to older persons outside his family, the adolescent, if he has a separate status at all, usually has a subordinate one, because of the sociological reasons for the senority principle already discussed. The adolescent boy is most likely to be accorded full adult status in simple, mobile, warlike societies, where physical prowess is emphasized as a societal necessity. Even so, it is only during the latter part of the adolescent period, say between the ages of 18 and 22, that he achieves virtual parity. The Comanche culture, for example, prior to the coming of the whites placed considerable emphasis on youth but the older men nevertheless retained a superiority in magic which partially compensated them for their loss of prestige due to physical decline.

In our society, even apart from the family, the adolescent finds an absence of definitely recognized, consistent patterns of authority. Because of the compartmentalization of the culture he is defined at times as an adult, at other times as a child. Furthermore, he is subjected to a confusing array of competing authorities, of which the school is the principal but not the happiest one.

CULTURAL ACQUISITION

In most social systems the child acquires the rudiments of the culture informally. Any definite instruction by parents or elders is of short duration and limited scope. Only the highly civilized societies possess specialized educational establishments professionaly staffed and forming a separate phase of life, and even they until recently reserved these establishments primarily for the upper social ranks (as in most of Latin America today).

For inculcating modern culture, the universal and specialized school system is a necessity. Its concentrated and abstract curriculum, professional staff, physical separateness, and internal organization all give a rapid and systematic grounding in the principles of the civilization, and remarkably facilitate the educational process. But by virture of the very qualities that make it efficient in teaching abstractions, it tends to divorce itself from the facts and experiences of everyday life. For years the pupil is drilled in principles, on the assumption that he will subsequently apply them in actual life. His childhood is thus treated as the preparation for life, not as real life itself.

The difficulty, of course, is that not everything can be taught in school. The person often emerges with a hoard of abstract knowledge, but with little knowledge of the concrete situations he must negotiate in order to get along. The harder he studies, the more unfit he becomes for ordinary day-to-day existence. Above all, there is such a long interval between learning and application that the incentive to learn often flags and must be bolstered by an amazing system of planned competition and artificial rewards.

Out of ennui and practical necessity the average pupil finally begins to participate in a more vivid world, the world of youth culture. This, in its adolescent phase, is characterized by irresponsibility, "having a good time," athletics, sex attraction, and the repudiation of adult control. One reason it takes this form is that it is "denied status by society at large, and is regarded primarily as destructive and undesirable, a foolish and queer expression of the impulses of young people." It has, in other words, no avowed function in the institutional structure, but is interstitial, officially purposeless, a phenomenon seldom found in other societies.

No wonder the cry of unreality is raised against the school system, and reforms are proposed which have in view the reintegration of education and life. Some of the reforms, however, have missed the point. They have overlooked the efficiency of systematic instruction and have attempted to make education "grow out of real life situations," not realizing that since modern culture rests on abstract knowledge, to confine all instruction to the applied and the concrete would soon produce stagnation.

The root of the difficulty apparently lies in the fact that while the young person is going to school he is doing little else of a responsible and productive nature. Therefore, the remedy is, perhaps, to give him an essential function in the world outside of school—i.e., to let him work—and to relate his schooling to this function. He could then receive his reward not solely in terms of grades, diplomas, honors, and degrees, but also in terms of wages and things accomplished. Thus the learning of principles would be attached to actual situations, not by the radical method of reducing all learning to the clumsy empiricism and thereby bankrupting the culture, but by making the young person a citizen who produces to the limit of his natural and acquired capacities.

The objection that a thorough grounding in basic principles leaves little time for participation in economic and political activity is valid.

But there are three directions in which this obstacle may be overcome: first, the invention of new educational technology; second, the elimination of irrelevancies from the curriculum; and third, the overhauling of the incentive mechanism. New educational technology, such as the recent methods of improving reading habits, may make possible the absorption of the same amount of knowledge in a much shorter time. As to irrelevancies in the curriculum, it seems clear that they are there because the purpose of schooling, both for the society and for the individual, is not clear. One way of eliminating them would be to define more clearly the fundamentals in our culture and thus reduce the number and the variety of "liberal arts" subjects, such as manual training and shorthand, except in so far as they relate to the pupil's known vocation. This would require specialization earlier in the school career than is now in fashion, and would have the disadvantage of requiring the choice of an occupation when the individual is still young and hence incapable of choosing wisely; although under a planned economy, vocational guidance by experts would be required in any case. Early specialization would allow the school work to be tied to actual life, because the child would enter the first stages of his occupation while already going to school. This, in turn, would help to solve the incentive problem. If a child were already launched on the first stages of his occupation, if his school subjects had specific application to his job, so that his wages, advancement, and so forth, depended on them, he would be more disposed to study.

THE ACQUISITION OF PERSONALITY: A SOCIOLOGICAL PERSPECTIVE

by Harold M. Hodges, Jr.

Thanks to the converging interests and the increasingly cooperative endeavors of the social sciences—most notably cultural anthropology, social and clinical psychology, social psychiatry, and sociology —man's historic quest for insights into the meaning, growth, and dynamics of personality is at last within sight of its long-sought goal. We still have a long path to tread; but we have begun to solve the more baffling of the mysterious components which blend to fashion what we call "personality makeup."

The explanations advanced here are frankly eclectic in nature; we have borrowed freely from the basic contributions of a variety of disciplines. But we have re-woven this welter of information into a sociological frame of reference. Thus our main concern will be with the personality—or, more properly, the "self"—as it is shaped by cultural and societal forces.

Space limitations will not allow us to delve into man's biological heritage—the genetic factor. We shall recall, however, that the carriers of heredity are the genes—the minute units which are believed to carry the potentialities for future growth and development.

But we must not make the mistake of assuming that each physical trait is due to a single gene—or that each trait is the automatic product of such a gene. We do inherit genes carrying fixed potentials—but these can and do combine into an infinite cluster of combinations; indeed, it is probable that no two individuals in mankind's history have ever been biologically identical.

ORIGINAL NATURE: THE CONSTITUTIONAL COMPONENTS

It is through his genes (roughly one half of his characteristics are inherited from his mother and father combined) that the infant receives his basic physical structure and his capacities. Bypassing the intriguing but dubiously supported assertion—advanced by Sheldon—that personality make-up is in large part a product of body build, we shall concentrate for the moment on three critical constitutional (inherited) facets of personality: capacities, biogenic drives, and temperament.[1] These organic foundations of personality are important to us primarily because they *limit* the larger role enacted by interpersonal, idiosyncratic and cultural pressures. Where, one might ask, do "instincts" fit into this picture? If we define instincts as *complex,* inherited patterns of behavior which predetermine man's social behavior, they simply do not exist in the human species; or, if they should (by some stretch of the imagination) exist at birth, they are so quickly submerged by cultural forces that they will never again enact a detectable role in the individual

---

[1] Less meaningful—from the standpoint of personality growth—are another trio of constitutional variables: (1) mass movement, (2) reflexes, and (3) physical and skeletal structure.

human's life span. Above the level of mechanical and simple reflexes (which in turn are reshaped by cultural conditioning), *no* pattern of human behavior is the automatic expression of inborn dispositions. The organism contains a myriad of individual response *possibilities* capable of an infinite number of combinations, but the combinations are not predetermined.

(1) *Capacities*. These may be defined as a sort of inherited *potentiality* or adaptability which *enables*—but will not guarantee—the organism to *acquire* the ability to perform certain tasks. Abilities or aptitudes, in contrast, are the developed, *learned* skills based on, and limited by, the inherited potentials which we label capacities. Thus a person born with a finely developed digital dexterity (hand-and-finger coordination) *could* become a skilled surgeon *or* a skilled mechanic *or* a skilled weaver; but, in order to become one of these things, his unique capacity must blend with other, cultural forces: intelligence, motivation, social-class conditioning, for example. Other examples of capacities—the uses of which will be largely determined by the culture milieu: eye-hand-foot coordination and intelligence.

(2) *Biogenic drives* connote the undefined character of inner deep-seated tensions, needs and urges. These are vague and vaguely understood. But lacking them, the human being could not live. Such drives may be visceral (originating in the tensions of the endocrine glands and unstriped muscles)—such as the hunger, thirst, oxygen-want, excretion and sexual drives. They may be activity drives, originating in striped-muscle tensions, such as the exercise and sleep-rest drives. Or they may be drives that can be satisfied by sensory stimulation—such as tones, colors, textures, smells, tastes. Each of these drives is (1) *unlearned* (or innate) and (2) *universal* (in the sense that each exists in every living member of the human species). In a while, we shall see how these biogenic drives *are* strictly biogenic for only a few weeks, or perhaps a few hours—how shortly after birth they are reshaped by the press of cultural experience—into what we shall label "sociogenic" drives.

(3) *Temperament* is an ill-defined term. Nor is it certain, as will become apparent when we examine prenatal influences, that temperament is indisputably a constitutional factor. Basically, the term refers to the general mode of the individual's response, to his characteristic mood, to his mental-emotional set. Thus we might define a person as lethargic or excitable, vivacious or dull, melancholic or gay, sluggish or hair-triggered. A whole theory of psychology—trait psychology—premises its worth on the assumption that temperament is the key, in-

tegral aspect of personality configuration. Little is known about the specific functions of the endocrine glands; but it is generally recognized that the hormones secreted by such glands as the thyroid, gonads, pancreas, and pituitary play a critical part in determining temperamental reactions. And studies such as Gessel's and Ilg's point to the conclusion that distinctive—and largely permanent—temperamental proclivities are present in the newly born child before learning has had much chance to modify behavior. Studies have demonstrated that the jolly or solemn infant tends to remain jolly or solemn throughout his life.

THE PRENATAL ENVIRONMENT

Until recently, until the pioneering experiments conducted by Lester Sontag at Johns Hopkins, the expectant mother's womb was believed to be "environmental" only in the physical sense. But Sontag's work has re-aligned thinking and has posed baffling and as-yet-untapped vistas for personality theory. In essence, what the Johns Hopkins researchers discovered amounted to this: pregnant mothers, when exposed to prolonged emotional turmoil during the first months of their child-bearing, almost inevitably gave birth to babies who differed significantly from babies born to mothers who had experienced less strainful pregnancies. Because the "emotional" and "non-emotional" mothers were carefully matched in terms of personality variables prior to the experiment, hereditary propensities were believed to be almost totally minimized. The emotional strain during pregnancy was in each case attributable to such temporary external factors as fatigue, financial strains, and short-lived crises. Nonetheless, infants born to the "emotional" mothers were almost without exception marked at birth by excessive motor activity, irritability, and attention-getting, extrovertive behavior syndromes. Significantly, too, children born to these same mothers after later, normal pregnancies, were characterized as "normal" infants at birth. How can these prenatal influences be explained? There are, of course, no communicating fibres between the mother's and fetus' nervous systems; hence the fetus cannot experience an emotional episode of the mother in the *usual* sense. The explanation advanced (hypothetically) by Sontag was basically this: to the degree that the mother's anxieties or fears modify the function of her *endocrine* glands, and therefore change the composition of the blood, the fetus *is* able to experience this emotional state. Such "blood-borne" anxieties or stimulations seemingly prove irritating to the fetus, as evidence by his immediate increase in bodily activity. The significant factor in this research is the doubt it sheds on the role of inherent, constitutional components of temperament. But the mystery attaching to the question of temperament is, in essence, still unsolved.

The neonatal phase refers to the first ten days or two weeks of postnatal life. Although the vast bulk of the child's physiological tools—his brain, organs, muscles, nervous system and endocrine glands—were developed in the intrauterine environment (the "embryo" during his first two months in the womb, the "fetus" during the seven months preceding birth), his adjustment to the harshness of the postnatal environment is at first much more on the physical than the social-psychological level. His earliest acts do not derive—cannot derive—from attitudes, but from his biological tensions and biogenic drives. Although the newborn infant is not, as we know, 100 per cent original nature, the human organism at this point is heavily weighted by heredity factors. He is born a cultural blank, totally lacking a self or personality. Dominated during this neonatal phase by mass, uncoordinated, often haphazard movements, his reactions to his environment are diffused, random, and "global." Only gradually will his bodily movements become specific, coordinated, self-controlled, and goal-directed. But the *maturation process*[2] (a purely physiological phenomenon not dependent on the social environment—a predetermined unfolding of such feats as sitting, crawling, walking, pubescense, the menopause) sees a rapid development of increasingly complex coordination among eyes, hands, and brain. At the age of two months, his eyes follow a moving person; at three months, he can look at his own hand which is now opening; at four months he can pick up a tiny object with his eyes but not yet with his hands. "He has made," Arnold Gesell notes, "neurological advance toward adult levels of skill." And he continues to advance from one "development level" to another —"not altogether because of specific training or instruction, but primarily because he is richly endowed with natural powers of growth . . ." But heavily weighted as the maturation process is by heredity, it is not exclusively so: for diet can partially determine when teeth will appear, and emotional experiences may even influence the functioning of the endocrine glands. The baby, however, cannot be *trained* to walk or manipulate blocks or swim before he is maturationally *ready* to.

---

[2] Not to be confused with *social* maturation"—the gradual, *learned* quality of social maturity, the attainment of adult qualities.

THE LEARNING PROCESS

The beginning of self-growth. At first his lack of neural organization is a handicap to the human being, but later it becomes his greatest asset. *Because* he is incapable of dealing with the physical environment on his own as soon as are lower (less complex) species of animals, because his physical and cultural incubation period is lengthier, he *is* dependent upon *other* humans for the *learning* which will eventually make him human. Because he is equipped with a larger and more complex brain, because he can symbolize, engage in abstract reasoning and learn and *transmit* culture (this latter is what differentiates him from the "highest" species of non-human animal—the chimpanzee)—because he can, in other words, *communicate,* he will eventually become an adult human being. "Unlike the chick," Ogburn and Nimkoff point out, "the baby cannot shift for himself at birth, but because his actions are less rigid and predetermined, his learning is much more extensive." The infant does *learn*—can only learn—to become human (i.e., to acquire a personality) because he is at first dependent upon other human beings for the satisfaction of his organic, biogenic needs. Because of these and other satisfactions bestowed by humans, the child as he grows older becomes increasingly identified with other persons and comes to crave social relations.[3] This process of self growth will be described after a brief consideration of the learning process which accounts for the fusion of sociogenic with biogenic drives.

Such biogenic tensions as hunger, thirst, activity-sleep-rest, defecation, and sex do not remain at the subliminal, reflexive level for long. Almost at birth, certainly as the neonatal phase draws to a close, the infant's biogenic drives commence to be reshaped by cultural forces. He learns these culturally defined ways of satisfying his various drives because these are the only modes of satisfaction taught him. At this juncture it will be germane to consider the learning process which enacts so decisive a role in the patterning of his inherent drives. This process can best be delineated in terms of four factors—each of which must be present if learning is to occur: drive, cue, response, and reward (reinforcement). The *drive* is a strong stimulus resulting from some unpleasant disequilibrium in the organism (we shall take hunger pangs or tensions as a graphic example); this stimulus impels the organism to react or respond in some way in order to lessen this tension. The *cue* is a stimulus that determines *how* the particular response will occur (when,

---

[3] There is no sound evidence that the neonate "instinctively" craves love and affection—nor is there evidence of a "maternal instinct."

where, and in which way); it may be visual, tactual, auditory, etc. An example: food (say apricots) on a table, in a bowl, at noon. The *response* in this case will consist of eating these apricots in the culturally prescribed manner. The *reward* will be the satisfaction of this hunger drive—the abating of the hunger tensions. In other words, for learning to occur, some sort of strengthening reward *must* be present. In this way—according to the folkways of his society—the Frenchman will learn to crave wine, the German beer, the American milk. None of these tastes is "natural." Each is learned by dint of being reared in a particular society or subculture. And thus the infant's biogenic drives almost immediately become sociogenic.[4] It becomes readily apparent, too, why the old-hat debates about "nature *vs.* nurture" or heredity *vs.* environment are now passé. The shift and blending from hereditary into environmental responses is so subtly fused that no clear demarcating point remains. This applies with equal force to, say, intellectual or athletic or occupational performance. Thus the biological, potentially human animal *becomes* human. Lacking others to mediate and direct this transition, the child would remain (if he survived) at the feral or animal level. Dramatic illustration of this latter point is afforded by studies of social isolates—children reared in isolation from other humans; when discovered, such children have inevitably been rudimentary humans fixated at a level perhaps equal to that of the chimpanzee. But, once exposed to human culture in the person of other people, most of them have rapidly become recognizably human.

SELF-GROWTH: THE ACQUISITION OF PERSONALITY

"By the self," wrote Charles Horton Cooley, "is meant that which is designated in common speech as 'I,' 'me,' and 'myself.' " Self in this sense does not refer to any clearcut entity such as one's body. Rather, it refers (in Gardner Murphy's words) to "the individual as known to the individual." No matter what a person objectively "is," his "self" is what *he* consciously and unconsciously *conceives* himself to be. His self, then, consists of the sum total of *his* perceptions of himself and, especially, his attitudes toward himself.

The infant, remember, is not born with a concept of self. The idea of self develops only out of interaction with other persons in his environment. In order to satisfy his biogenic needs, the infant learns to make responses to other's behavior. First in imitating and then in antici-

---

[4] This is known as the *tension-reduction* theory of self growth.

pating another person's response to his behavior, he is identifying himself with the other person or, as we shall see presently, "taking the role of the other." Not, then, until the individual experiences other "selves" and becomes conscious that they have attitudes toward him, can his idea of self have any concrete meaning. And since *language* is the chief medium by which others' attitudes can be communicated the growth of self is markedly limited until the child acquires a language.

This process whereby personality is acquired through social interaction is known as *socialization*. In Francis Merrill's words, "every society is faced with the necessity of making a responsible member out of each child born into it. The child must learn the expectations of the society so that his behavior can be relied upon." Socialization is both conscious and unconscious. The group may deliberately instill the appropriate expectations in the child, so that he will act in a responsible manner throughout his life. An example: the mother teaching her child how to talk, walk, and eat his spinach. But even more numerous and critical are the unconscious aspects of socialization. Most of the child's values, aspirations, skills, and roles are learned without his realizing what he is doing.

A unique characteristic of the self is that it may be an object to itself (i.e., self conscious). From infancy throughout life the central element in the world of the individual is himself; every man spends his life in a prolonged love-affair with himself. But this "love-affair" is not so selfish as it is natural. It *is* true, though, that one measure of social maturation—of the shedding of childhood dependency for adult autonomy—is the gradual transition from infantile egocentrism to adult "sociocentrism." The infant, necessarily for survival at first, is a blind, unthinking, demanding little tyrant. But he gradually learns that others won't respond to his every wish, won't continually wait on him hand-and-foot. And because he has learned to crave affection, response, and approval from others, he quickly learns to take the wishes of others into account, to give as well as receive. This egocentrism-to-sociocentrism trend is accentuated by an increasing facility in communication and a consequent recognition of the more subtle nuances of others' needs and wishes. Thus, as his interpersonal contacts increase, his personality constantly changes. And as his vocabulary and verbal facility grow, he increasingly acquires the values and norms of his society.

The mother (and, to a lesser extent, the father and siblings) is the chief mediator of the social norms of his group. She imparts to him many of the basic folkways and mores and he "incorporates" them into the central fabric of his personality. At first, in order to make the child obey these norms, the mother's physical presence is required. But, as they become pushed into his subconscious or "interiorized," these "do's" and "don'ts" become a central feature of his personality. They become, in other words, his *conscience* (in Freudian language, his "superego"). Later, when he does something which his conscience tells him is "wrong," he is plagued by pangs of remorse and guilt. But fighting a constant and intermittent battle with his conscience are a host of pleasure-sating, hedonistic urges (in Sigmund Freud's terminology, his 'id" forces). The socialization process gradually *represses* these "naughty" tendencies, pushing them into his subconscious.

George Herbert Mead, a pioneering sociological student of personality growth, noted three basic stages in the development of the self: the stage of meaningless imitative acts, the play stage, and the game stage. During the first, occurring around his second year of life, the child imitates others without understanding the meaning of his or other's actions. Later, about his third year, he takes the place of mother, father, postman, fireman, grocer in a vast variety of roles in play activities. In "taking the role of others" (a critical phase of self growth), he is in a position to act toward himself as others do. In this way, the child gets outside himself and gains perspective of himself. And since the child takes many roles, he acquires what amounts to a *series* of selves. Because his power of integration is ill-developed, there is little consistency in his behavior. The unified self, according to Mead, emerges in the game stage when the child commences to act toward himself from the viewpoint of the whole group—rather than from the standpoint of one particular individual. As a member of a team, he must anticipate the behavior of *all* the other members; he accordingly plays a number of roles simultaneously. We thus *derive* our self-attitudes by projecting ourselves into the minds of others. The ability to take the role of the other corresponds roughly to what is known in psychological circles as "empathy"—the emotional identification of one person with another. These empathic responses vary hugely from one individual to another. Some have the ability to participate fully in the emotions of others; they are warm, expressive, out-going, optimistic. Others lacking such a degree of empathic ability, are correspondingly rigid, indifferent and inhibited. They keep to themselves because they cannot participate in the responses of others. They do not make friends easily and their social relationships are limited and formal.[5]

According to Cooley, self-ideas or self-attitudes develop by a

---

[5] There is also an apparent relation between such extrovertive-introvertive propensities and one's temperamental (glandular) makeup.

process of imagining what others think of us, by what he labeled "the looking-glass process." "A self-idea of this sort," he contended, "seems to have three principal elements: (1) the imagination of our appearance to others, (2) the imagination of his judgment of that (imagined) appearance, and (3) some sort of self-feeling, such as pride or mortification."

The most enduring and deep-lying (deeply interiorized) components of self are acquired during the first four or five or six years of life—the so-called *"formative years."* And they are largely acquired through interaction in *"primary groups"*—groups, such as the family or play group, characterized by warmth, intimacy and face-to-face association. Later in life, though playing a less significant role (for the core self or personality is already firmly embedded) other quasi- or semi-primary groups will play a similar role: the college fraternity, for example, or buddies in the Army or intimate friends. The family, of course, is the "Number One" primary group, for it is the most *intimate* of all, and it is the *first* with which we come into contact. As he takes the role of the other, we know, the child begins to hold internal conversations with himself. These conversations, launched within the context of his primary groups, involve the *"significant others"* in his milieu—the persons who matter most to him. Ordinarily the most significant other in his early experience is the child's mother—with father and others supplementing her. The child learns to anticipate the responses of these significant others by putting himself in their places. Thus the core self—that complex of largely subconscious attitudes and concepts of right and wrong, proper and improper—is primarily derived from the significant others in our development. The next and more complex stage in the growth of the social self arises when the individual begins to take the role of society as a whole toward himself. This is what Mead called "taking the role of the *generalized* other." But the generalized other—the norms and values of his larger society are not the same for all persons—will be warped, colored, distorted and mediated in terms of his parents and playmates and teachers (each, in turn, influenced by his own unique personality makeup). And his growing conceptions of values will be further interpreted in terms of his social-class level and, perhaps, his regional (southern, New England, or Texan) subculture and his ethnic (Negro or Italian) and religious (Catholic, Unitarian, fundamental Baptist) subcultural memberships.

So an American is a product of American culture only in the *broadest* sense. His eventual personality (which is never finally fixed, but is in a constant state of flux) represents a subtle *fusion* of many forces: his *heredity* (constitution), perhaps his *prenatal environment,* his *culture* and more narrowly his subcultures as mediated to him by unique individuals, and, finally, his own *unique experiences.* In reference to the latter component, no two individuals, even identical twins, experience their environment in identical ways. So within the framework of "sameness" imposed by cultural pressures exist individuals who are above all individuals—each in some distinguishing way unique and different.

Social roles constitute another crucial determinant of personality — a determinant which must be comprehended before we can gain a basic grasp of "why people act that way." A social role is an expected pattern of behavior that goes with a certain position in the social order. It is a system of rights and obligations expected of a person who occupies the position, for example, of a mother, a father, a husband, a wife, a child, a professor, a doctor, a citizen, a basketball forward, or the president of the United States. Thus, the American adult male has a pattern of culturally stamped and determined behavior ascribed to him merely because he is an adult, a male, an American. This role is defined by society, and he has little to say regarding the privileges or responsibilities attaching to it. From earliest infancy, he is given, in the words of Ralph Linton, a progressively changing set of roles appropriate to his age and sex—and he is expected to play them with reasonable persistence and accuracy.

Such a tightly patterned organization of social roles makes it *possible* for the group to function as an efficient unit. It is a vital aspect of *all* societies; without social roles—and the statuses to which they are linked—behavior would be an unpredictable welter of chaos and anarchy. Social life (society) *must,* in other words, *be* ordered and structured; and the roles prescribed for its individual members are a chief means of insuring such stability and predictability.

What we said earlier of the internalization into the self of the attitudes of others accounts for the learning by which the individual defines his roles appropriately. At first, when he is new to the group, his role is external to him; he only gradually, through the process of socialization (or by sensing the norms of a new group—such as the Marines or a fraternity or his corporation or his gang) incorporates these role expectations into his personality configuration. Self, then, consists in part of an interlocking *web* of roles.

From the perspective of personality, each role consists of a network of attitudes—predispositions to act according to the expected pattern (given the physical assets, a good halfback will have incorporated into his personality the attitudes which predispose him to play the halfback role in standardized fashion). With this in mind, we can further define a role as a pattern of attitudes predisposing a person to act according to the expectations of others.

In large part, then, the growth of the self involves the incorporation of an increasing number of roles. As a boy Morcomb Malheart will gradually interiorize the role requirements of Hawthorne School first grader, member of the Crescent Drive gang, Trailfinder, Boy Scout, rock collector, Willy Davis fan, and so on as he moves through the school years. These roles are overlayed, of course, on the more intimate, deep-seated roles he learned in interaction with the "significant others" of his home environment. Eventually he will play a series of adult roles. At every stage, his personality is an organization or fusion of roles.

Virtually every role is a "me-you" or, in sociological parlance, a "self-other" role. They are, in other words, reciprocal. Thus we find parent-child, husband-wife, boss-employee, officer-noncom, doctor-patient, teacher-pupil, and boy-girl roles typifying everyday life. Each person, then, acts out a set of expected roles and looks at other persons in terms of them. Because of this, he knows what to expect in the way of response from others.

In a relatively simple, homogeneous, stable "folk" type society, social roles—like all norms, values and cultural paraphernalia, are tightly interlocking; each is in a state of harmonious balance with the others. But in a complex, heterogeneous, rapidly changing urban or industrial society, roles—like other aspects of culture, are often in conflict. Designed in earlier ages or in other cultures, they frequently fit different and contradictory values and expectations. Thus, in our society, the Christian concept of brotherly love and turning the other cheek clashes sharply with qualities demanded in such competitive spheres of life as business enterprise. Or the second-generation immigrant might struggle between roles calling for support of his parents in the name of familial loyalty and the urban, middle-class role calling for independence and freedom from family ties.[6] Such instances of role conflict approximate one aspect of what Emile Durkheim meant by *anomie*. They also relate to the concept of the "marginal man"—the person caught between two contrasting sets of cultural loyalties. Contradictory social roles, finally, are believed by many students of per-

---

[6] On a more personal, typical level, witness the meek bank clerk at work, but the fiendish horn-honker and cusser in his car—and then, at home, the lovable father and efficient do-it-yourself home repairman.

sonality disorganization—notably Karen Horney and Erich Fromm—
to be cataclysmic agents in the process of neurotic reaction.

When we state that age roles or husband-wife roles or sex roles
are universal—that they exist in every known society—we do not
intend to imply that such roles are identical in all societies. Age and
sex roles—virtually all social roles—vary hugely from one culture or
knowledge of subculture to another. We need only recall our cultural
variability to realize how culturally patterned such roles are. Behavior
that we in America define as masculine will find its almost exact
counterpart in approved female behavior roles in some other society.
Even within American society, definitions of appropriate sex or age
behavior will vary strikingly between, say, middle-class and lower-
class subcultures. Maleness or femaleness, Margaret Mead has pointed
out, is far more a matter of a role definition that it is a biological
definition.

Roles, finally, may be *ascribed* or *achieved* in character—although
this dichotomy is an artificial one, and many roles are in part ascribed,
in part achieved. Ascribed roles are those concerning which the individual has no choice; it is established at birth, for instance, that an
individual is a male or female, that he is a member of a certain race.
One is *born* into an ascribed role. Achieved roles, as the name connotes,
are those which involve an element of choice; these often prescribe special abilities or talents and are often filled by competition. Occupational
roles afford a prime example; so do husband and wife roles and parental
roles. The bulk of ascribed statuses in all societies, Ralph Linton points
out, are parceled out to the individual on the basis of sex, age, and family relationships. But, he adds, practically every possible arrangement in
each of these spheres is represented in one society or another. Ascribed
roles comprise the majority of roles in all societies—but they are much
more likely to typify static folk cultures than they are urban cultures
which are geared to mobility, change, and competition. Less relevant to
personality, but intricately related to the concept of role is the concept
of *status*. A status, as distinct from the individual who may occupy it,
is in essence a collection of rights and duties. A role, in Linton's words,
is ". . . the dynamic aspect of a status; the individual is socially assigned
to a status. When he puts the rights and duties which constitute the status
into effect, he is performing a role." In other words, status is the position a person occupies in society by dint of his sex, occupation, age,
marriage, or achievement. The role is the part he is expected to play in
each of these statuses. Role and status are, then, reciprocal and inseparable. There are no roles without statuses or statuses without roles.

Membership groups and reference groups are concepts recently introduced by the social psychologists. They shed considerable light on the relationship between culture and personality.

One's *membership* group is the group—family, race, nation, social class, etc.—to which he actually belongs. A person's *reference* groups are those he identifies with, consciously or unconsciously. Thus a person may belong to a group without sentimentally identifying himself with it and accepting its values. An individual, for example, may have been born into a lower-lower class Hebrew family. But he may at the same time be "upward-mobile"—aspiring to middle-class membership. Knowingly or not—more often the latter—he incorporates middle-class norms and values into his personality makeup. He increasingly thinks and talks and dresses and behaves like the middle-class people about him. He might even abandon the Jewish faith and adopt the Methodist faith in this process.[7]

The membership-reference group concept has particular relevance for modern, complex, rapidly changing urban cultures. With their high rates of spatial and social-class mobility, a large proportion of their citizens will be members of one set of groups—perhaps immigrant, lower-class-subcultures—but will aspire to membership in others. Keeping in mind what we have read about the incorporation of group values, we can easily see the significance of the concept in relation to personality growth. The agrarian folk society, in contrast to the industrialized urban, is typically marked by social units which are simultaneously peoples' membership *and* reference groups. Gaps between the two are virtually nonexistent. But in a society as mobile as the United States, where second-generation immigrants or farmers' sons are poles apart from parental values, the rift between persons' membership and reference group allegiances is of striking import.

Basic personality type represents another recently introduced concept—a cooperative brainchild of the cultural anthropologist and the social psychiatrist. The basic personality concept is, as a matter of fact, one of the central focuses of the newly emergent academic area generally known as "culture and personality." And before proceeding further, it is worth while reminding ourselves that culture and personality are not two separate, distinct and independent entities, but are in reality two aspects of the same thing. Neither, like role or status, can exist without

---

[7] Take another graphic example—the private who is rejected by his squad mates because he won't play the private's role; in reality, his reference group—the officers—might represent the goal he aspires to. His membership group does not effectively control his behavior.

the other. As Melford Spiro remarks, personality and culture ". . . are part and parcel of the same process of interaction. Both personality and culture reside in the individual or, to put it differently, they *are* the individual as modified by learning." When we additionally recall that each society is unique in its own right—with unique patterns of statuses, role expectations, institutions, and values, it will be readily apparent that each society's socialization and child-rearing practices will also be unique. We know that personality is the *product* of socialization; so we may infer that a given society—especially a homogeneous, folk-type society—will tend to produce in its members something akin to a core or modal or basic personality which will differ from personality types produced by other societies.

Modal (or basic) personality, then, refers to those elements of personality that are relatively frequent or *typical* in a social group. We must disregard the suggestion of statistical accuracy inherent in the term "modal." Modal in the sense utilized here refers only to the *roughly* most frequent or typical personality characteristics. Related to this concept is the term "national character."

The basic premise underlying the modal personality concept is that the *way* children are *reared* in the *family* is an important personality determinant. "A society," as Merrill comments, "that enforces a general code of severity will produce one type of personality, whereas one where the parents spoil the child will produce another." And the basic personality type is a product of socialization as it is conducted in a *particular* society. The central forum of this process is, of course, the family. The cluster of roles making up the family are perhaps the most powerful that the individual will encounter during his life. His own personality, we shall remember, is at its most plastic during his formative years. This combination of demanding roles and infant plasticity gives rise to the similarities implicit in the modal personality concept. In the words of Talcott Parsons, modal personality is "a function of socialization in a particular type of system of role relationships with particular values."

The modal personality type must not be construed as a rigid norm, but rather as a general pattern of behaviors and beliefs toward which members of a society tend to gravitate. Thus the "typical" German, American, Britisher, and Frenchman will differ from one another in terms of the fundamental values, roles and norms which they have incorporated into their personality configurations. Similar *sub-cultural* differences exist within any given society—differences related to ethnic, religious, class and economic levels. Such differences are especially likely to typify a society which, like the U.S., is composed of a heterogeneous welter of such diverse segments. It is apparent, then, why the simpler and more homogeneous the society, the more similar and uniform are its inhabitants' personalities.

Acceptance of the notion of shared elements of personality does *not* require us to reject the common-sense observation that in any community there exist differences in individual personality; the concept does not imply that all members of a given society have uniform personalities. Finally, the modal personality structure is not a mere conglomeration of traits but consists of a certain patterning derived from the values and institutions to which the individual is exposed.

LATER SOCIALIZATION:
THE ADOLESCENT AND HIS PEER GROUP

All societies recognize the transition from childhood to adult maturity. In some, this is highly structured and carefully controlled; in others it is diffuse and ill-defined. In any case, there is almost universal recognition that the so-called teen-age years are those which give preparation for adulthood. But considerable confusion and misinformation marks the layman's conception of the problems relating to adolescence. Many of these erroneous beliefs derive from the turn-of-the-century pronouncements of G. Stanley Hall. Adolescence to Hall and the many social scientists who for several decades accepted his views was believed to be a period when marked and rapid changes occurred in *all* aspects of personality. Rather suddenly, it was contended, the child became a new being and developed a totally new outlook. Some even spoke of something akin to a "new birth." Furthermore, these developments were thought to be *biologically* generated; they were presumably prompted by the maturation of certain instincts which resulted in the "flowering of new and curiously wonderful behavior patterns." A child was thus "predestined" to experience adolescent change by his very biological makeup. Finally, it was asserted that the period of adolescence was essentially erratic, vacillating, unpredictable, and stressful. The German term, *"Sturm und Drang"* (storm and strain) epitomized this contention. But in the late 1920s Margaret Mead, reporting on the growing-up process in Samoa, stressed the role of culture rather than biology; simultaneously, Leta Hollingworth was emphasizing the *gradualness* of change and the essential continuity of growth during adolescence. Since then, buttressed by the works of cultural anthropologists which chronicled societies in which adolescence was *not* a strainful epoch, most social scientists have come to abandon their earlier belief that adolescence is a biologically predetermined period of strain and confusion.

Nonetheless, the cross-cultural viewpoint espoused by such observers as Mead and Ruth Benedict does lend credence to the belief that adolescence *is* more strainful for the typical American child than for his counterparts in many other societies. In a classic paper, Benedict pointed out the effects of "discontinuity" in personality development. All societies prepare individuals for adult responsibilities, for dominance in certain social relationships, and for adequate execution of sexual roles. Sometimes, however (notably in America), earlier learning is not directly relevant to adult responsibilities, dominance, or sexual obligations. Our society, for example, places a blanket restriction on sex in childhood and later expects the individual to *unlearn* a virtually total inhibition if he is to adjust satisfactorily to his marriage role. Again, we demand submission of children and then expect them to manifest patterns of adult self-assertion and dominance. Finally, our children are typically first denied responsibility and later faced with the problem of acquiring an adult's sense of responsibility. *Discontinuous* describes this style of learning. Writes Benedict, ". . . the adolescent period of *Sturm und Drang* with which we are so familiar becomes intelligible in terms of our discontinuous cultural institutions and dogmas." In a large proportion of nonliterate societies the child is trained through a progressively greater participation in adult activities. His "coming of age" is sudden only in a ceremonial sense, when he is formally inducted into the adult community by *"rites de passage"* or puberty rituals which designate his attainment of adult status. In such societies, the child becomes a man, not when he is *physically* mature, but when he is formally recognized as a man by his society.

In societies which recognize adolescents as a distinct category and ascribe activities to them suited to their level of physiological development, the period passes with little or no stress; the transition from the roles of childhood to those of adult life is accomplished with little shock to the personality. But in our own society we tend to leave the social role of adolescents in doubt. We alternately demand from them the obedience and submission of children and the initiative and acceptance of personal responsibilities which go with adult status. It is possible, however, to generalize too glibly about the "American adolescent" in general; we are in danger of overlooking the multiplicity of subcultural forces which socialize Americans. There is evidence, for example, that

the pubescent son or daughter of the immigrant (particularly the southern and central European immigrant) finds the discontinuity of urban
American adolescence compounded by what often amounts to a revolt
or rejection in the face of their parents' "old-fashioned" old-world
values. Again, there is evidence that the upper-middle-class adolescent—
though shielded longer from the economic demands of adulthood—is
less likely to revolt against parental standards than is the lower or lower-
middle-class adolescent.

Before closing our discussion of adolescence, one more point is relevant. Adolescence is a culturally defined *social* categorization; puberty
is its *physiological* correlate. Puberty connotes the time—not the specific
point of sexual maturation. Although it occurs approximately two years
earlier in girls, and is more clearly marked by bodily and glandular
changes, in neither sex can a single event or a given point of time be
taken as *the* criterion of sexual maturity. The shift in endocrine makeup
and external and internal bodily dimensions occupies at least one year.

The American adolescent's concept of his self—his configuration of
attitudes and values—does not ungerdo a sudden transformation at
puberty. It is true that such factors as his sudden attainment of sexual
maturity and his bodily and voice changes often occasion self-consciousness and a sense of awkwardness. But his core self (or attitudinal configuration) is at too deep-seated a level to realign itself radically. Thus
his adolescent self is essentially a continuation of his childhood self.
This is not to deny, however, that the self is not marked by important
"surface" changes during this period. And perhaps the most critical impact upon such surface changes is exercised by the *peer group*.

Although elaborated at greater length in Albert K. Cohen's interpretation of delinquent behavior, a few comments about the role of the
peer group are especially pertinent at this juncture. The pattern of
"socialization by peers," although certainly not confined to American
culture, perhaps achieves its apogee in our society. This, at least, is the
impression to be gained from such astute observers of the world's cultures as Linton, Mead, Benedict, and Goeffrey Gorer.

The peer group—the child's "age-grade" mates who adhere to
similar basic attitudes—and, who, according to August Hollingshead
and others, occupy identical or adjacent social-class levels—is vitally
important in defining and incorporating the version of the generalized
other to which the individual ultimately responds. In the development
of his social self, the child is continually interacting with a succession
of such groups, and they provide an important part of his environment.
In certain respects the peer group is even more important than the

parents in establishing the version of the generalized other to which the adolescent responds. And whether the child is accepted or rejected by his peers enacts a critical role in the conception of his self which he will carry over into adulthood.

One of the most frequently hypothesized explanations for the impact of the peer group is that the growing child comes to depend more and more on his peers for the achievement of status and less on his parents—and hence values more highly the opinions of his contemporaries. For one thing, his status in his home is generally more secure; but status in the peer group has to be won and validated by being one of the group, which means subscribing to the group values. And in a rapidly changing society such as America's, an appreciable number of the values of youth significantly differ from the values cherished by elders. In his quest for autonomy and the independence of adulthood, the adolescent in our society typically tends to reject parental norms and to adopt those of his peers. What we said earlier about reference groups applies with special force in this context.

It is suggested by such clinical studies as those of D. M. Levy that the child who is dominated and overprotected by his parents tends to become a submissive child, whereas the child who is over-protected but indulged often becomes rebellious. The play group of peers, on the other hand, emphasizes give-and-take. As a consequence, the child usually gets from others in his play group a more realistic judgment of himself than he does from his parents. The play group of peers may accordingly serve as a corrective for the errors of parents in dealing with their children.

David Riesman, particularly in *The Lonely Crowd,* has had much to say about the phenomenon of peer-group socialization. Parents, Riesman contends, are no longer able to inculcate in their children the clearly defined values, behavior patterns, and goals which formerly made for success. "Parents in our era," he writes, "can only equip the child to do his best, whatever that may turn out to be. What is best is not in their control but in the hands of the school and peer group . . ." Ours is increasingly the era, claims Riesman, of "other-direction." The other-directed person is by definition highly conformistic to the norms and values of *others*. And much of this overriding concern for the opinions of others arises, he believes, when young children learn to be sensitive to their peers rather than to their parents. Such other-directed individuals are those who are preoccupied by a desire for popularity and whose contemporaries are their reference groups and principal source of direction. "Inner-directed" souls, Riesman thinks, are those who test their behavior by specific ethical principles rather than by what others think. Such inner-directed persons have derived their goals from their parents—not from their peers—and have internalized these clear-cut values at an early age. But today's inner-directed personality, who possesses a relatively flexible "gyroscropic" standard for judging success, goodness and morality, often finds himself in a diversified social milieu that calls for something else. Fashioned in a Horatio Alger, rags-to-riches era when the Carnegies, Rockefellers, and Fords plowed to the top embued with the philosophy "full speed ahead, others be damned!" he is simply not designed for an era which calls for togetherness, backslapping gregariousness, and an amiable concern for others.

The other-directed person came into being in response to the demands presented by a corporation-dominated society. If the inner-directed's control is gyroscopic-like, the other-directed individual possesses something like a radar system—tuned to the subtlest currents of popular vogues, expressions, heroes, and fads. He has been socialized not so much to rely upon his own rigorous standards and values but is trained to respond flexibly and with finesse to the standards of whatever group he finds himself in. Parents who are inner-directed run the risk of failing to train their children for successful cultural participation. "Under the new conditions of social and economic life," observes Riesman, "parents who try, in inner-directed fashion, to complete the internalization of disciplined pursuit of clear goals run the risk of having their children styled clear out of the personality market." Riesman also posited a third character type—the tradition-directed; but, a correlate of agrarian, folk-type societies, he is rarer in today's American world than the inner and other-directed types. Riesman has been accused of generalizing too broadly on the basic of scanty empirical data; but his trichotomy of character-logical types has been met with guardedly enthusiastic reception on the part of many students of personality—particularly those in the culture and personality field.

Correlative with Riesman's theories has been the increasingly voiced assertion that America has entered an era of "mass culture"—an era marked by a leveling of excellence and an unparalleled degree of conformism. The mass media in particular—and notably the television and advertising industries—have been singled out as the prime culprits. But other critics of American society proffer the rebuttal that we are entering a cultural renascence; witness, they say, the groundswell of interest in ballet, classical music and the paperbound classics. The evidence offered by both sides is, however, both subjective and poorly documented. The jury is still out.

Chapter Four

THE FAMILY

If there is one key cultural unit which assures human survival, it is the family. No known culture, living or dead, has existed without it. It has survived war, pestilence, migration, and the breakup of empires because, of all the cultural devices man has evolved, nothing else has so effectively held societies intact, has provided them with a cement both firm enough and pliable enough to weather the impact of social change.

The family's biological role is obvious; but beyond insuring reproduction of the species, it is the most critical agent in the whole socialization process. As such, it is the most basic of all primary groups and the central matrix of personality. It should be far from surprising, then, that of the whole catalogue of social problems that plague today's Americans, none has aroused more widespread concern than marital discord and divorce; none of our social ills—including delinquency, crime, mental illness, racial conflict, alcoholism, opiate addiction, and suicide—have been experienced, directly or indirectly, by so many. For virtually every adult American can count at least one couple among his acquaintances whose marriage is either strife-ridden or broken.

The multifold hazards which confront today's American families can only make sense, and perhaps afford some degree of encouragement, when they are appraised in their historical context. For the family that we know in the mid-twentieth century differs radically from the characteristic nineteenth-century American family. The reader has already reviewed, in the first selection by Harold M. Hodges, the telling

143

consequences of the industrial—and social—revolution that witnessed the disintegration of the "folk" way of life that had historically prevailed in America. He will realize, too, that when the social fabric of a society is virtually rewoven within the span of a single century, it is axiomatic that its family system will undergo a similar mutation. Ernest W. Burgess assesses these changes and predicts the shape of things to come in "The Family in a Changing Society."

Yesterday's American family was male-dominated, parent-centered, tradition-bound, self-sufficient, and fertile. The individual happiness of its members was subservient to family welfare; life was family-centered. Women were almost totally subordinate to men; their spheres of activity were sharply differentiated from infancy on. Girls were trained only in the house-wifely arts, and they learned their roles by confining their activities to the kitchen, housekeeping, and waiting on brothers and fathers. Only males enjoyed relative freedom of action and opportunity. The sacred connotations of the marital vows were taken more literally. There were variations of the traditional American family of course, but these, at least, were the dominant features. There are still sporadic survivals of such family forms, especially in the more rural areas of the country and in big-city ethnic islands. But on the whole, as Burgess makes clear in "The Family in a Changing Society," the "institutional" family type has inevitably given way to the emergent "companionship" form, for the latter has evolved in response to the changing dynamics of America's social, economic, and ideological structures. Burgess details why and how so drastic a permutation has taken place.

His essay focuses on the decreasing centrality of the family within the larger social system and the correlative dissipation of its former functions. But to those who would take alarm at the high rates of marital discord (rates which, by the way, appear to have leveled off since Burgess wrote his article), the author suggests that the American family is not in a state of decline but is, instead, in the midst of a transition that will ultimately add to its strength. If the family of the past was stable, its stability—like the stability that kept the other basic institutions intact—inhered in its unyielding rigidity. If today's family is strong, it is strong for different reasons. Like other contemporary institutions such as the economic, governmental, religious, educational, and military, its survival is based upon its flexibility and its readiness to change as conditions change.[1]

---

[1] For a particularly lucid account of the courtship system which is evolving within America's teen-age subculture, see E. E. LeMasters, *Modern Courtship and Marriage* (N. Y.: The Macmillan Co., 1957).

Talcott Parsons examines another, equally provocative aspect of family organization in "Age and Sex in the Social Structure of the United States." Like Burgess, he explores the changing structure of the urban, middle-class American family. Parsons, however, is interested less in the evolution of new family forms than in the roles assigned to its members on the basis of their age and sex. Children in our society, he observes, are assigned highly similar sex roles.[2] Yet almost from the beginning, girls are presented with sex-role models—in the persons of their mothers—that are unavailable to boys who are gradually initiated into the dynamics of the adult male role. It is our society's adult roles which evoke Parson's major interest.

The author asserts that there are elements of strain attached to the roles of both husband and wife; however, while the success of the former is generally assessed in well-defined occupational and economic terms, wifely accomplishment is a more ambiguous matter. Because her housewife role is being increasingly shorn of its traditional obligations, its utility, and its correlative well-entrenched status, the married American woman is faced with the choice of several alternative—but conflicting—role options: career woman, glamour girl, civic worker, or good companion. All but the latter involve some degree of emancipation from domesticity and disengagement from the husband's role; none of them is easily played and each involves some degree of insecurity, conflict, and uncertainty. The final portion of Parsons' article examines the American inclination to idealize youth—a consequence, he hypothesizes, of the strain that characterizes adulthood. A corollary of our romantic adulation of youth culture, Parsons notes, is a native tendency to isolate the elderly.

In "Socialization and Social Class Through Time and Space", Urie Bronfenbrenner pieces together the disparate segments of a "jig-saw" puzzle that has perplexed students of personality and social class alike: a puzzle that has existed ever since 1954 when Eleanor E. Maccoby and P. K. Gibbs sharply challenged Allison Davis and Robert J Havighurst in their earlier conclusion that middle-class parents "place their

---

[2] What is more, Parsons observes, such sex-linked differences as dress and play patterns are tending to diminish—particularly among urban upper-middle class children. "Sex-role convergence," it would seem, has been under way in our society at least since the turn of the century. The double standard (broadly interpreted) has increasingly become more a single standard as American women have achieved more and more *equal rights* in employment, suffrage, marriage, and in the less tangible (but perhaps more significant) realms of folkways and values. Witness, for example, the ever-larger proportion of women who engage in such *unfeminine* (by nineteenth-century standards) activities as sports, smoking, and drinking.

children under a stricter regimen, with more frustration of their impulses, than do lower-class parents." Although the selection from Bronfenbrenner's article does not do his definitive presentation full justice (only his summary statements are reproduced here), his central contention is readily clear: neither the Davis-Havighurst nor the Maccoby-Gibbs conclusions wholly explain the long-term (1) national and (2) class-linked trends in infant care and child training. Bronfenbrenner's analysis, in fact, was the first to systematically integrate and interpret the numerous studies of social-class differences in child rearing that had been published since 1932.

The extensive concern with infant-training procedures is derived in large part from the Freudian contention that frustrations encountered in infancy, as a consequence of weaning and toilet-training experiences, are of crucial importance in determining basic personality characteristics. Yet efforts to assess the adequacy and validity of such a widely disseminated psychoanalytic assumption—most notably the cautious studies conducted by Orlansky[3] and Sewell[4]—cast considerable doubt on the worth of Freud's contention. Orlansky and Sewall suggest, instead, that the *over-all tone* of the mother-child relationship, and the total situation in home and family, are far more consequential than some specific practice such as early or late weaning. Another study, conducted by Wolfenstein, assesses the consistency of the child-rearing advice offered American parents since 1914. She concludes that child-rearing advice and practice seem to change as rapidly as do fashions in women's clothes. "Each method of rearing," one critic observes, "—breast or bottle feeding, self-demand or scheduled feeding, self or forced toilet training—is claimed to have special psychological significance in the development and growth of a stable personality."[5] Although analyzing class-linked differences in feeding, weaning, and toilet training, Bronfenbrenner appears to agree with Wolfenstein's counsel. His major conclusions relate to the broader variations and trends in socialization practices: differences in expectations, permissiveness, and disciplining. His conclusion that the long-standing gap distinguishing the middle and lower-class child-training systems may be narrowing is of special consequence for those who will work with a cross-section of American children.

---

[3] Harold Orlansky, "Infant Care and Personality," *Psychological Bulletin,* 46 (1949), pp. 1-48.

[4] William H. Sewell, "Infant Training and the Personality of the Child," *American Journal of Sociology,* 58 (1952), pp. 150-159.

[5] Martha Wolfenstein, "Trends in Infant Care," *American Journal of Orthopsychiatry,* 33 (1953), pp. 120-130.

"Socialization," Robert J. Havighurst and Hilda Taba remind us, continues well beyond the child's formative years. Although recognizing the fact that the family retains its role as the chief agent in this never-ending process, the authors of "Adolescent Character and Development" call special attention to the roles enacted by the community, the school, and the adolescent peer culture in instilling and re-inforcing "moral" values among teen-agers. Each influence—especially the latter adolescent peer culture—is potent and pervasive. Yet, the authors conclude, the most compelling force of all in forging, as well as sustaining basic value orientations, is the social class level into which each child is born.

That the intimate yet subtle relationship among the community, school, and family milieus should evoke such concern is symptomatic of a deeply rooted, long-run trend: the American family is not the all-encompassing institution it once was. Although circumstances have inevitably forced it to default much of its historical centrality as a socio-economic unit—and if its offspring are increasingly influenced by such other mediators of societal norms as the school, the peer culture, and the mass media—the American family still remains the major agent of socialization. Its network of social ties and emotional attachments are the most intense and enduring of all.[6]

---

[6] For a succinct analysis of the role of the teacher and the school in the socialization process, see Elkin *op. cit.*, pp. 56-62.

THE FAMILY IN A CHANGING SOCIETY*

by Ernest W. Burgess

The American family presents an external picture of diversity and instability. When viewed in the context of the social change from rural to urban conditions of life, a trend is revealed to the companionship type of family, adapted to urbanization and exemplifying the American ideals of democracy, freedom, and self-expression. The seeming instability of the family is largely a symptom of this transition which may be regarded as a vast social experiment in which adaptability becomes more significant for success in marriage and family living than a rigid stability. This experiment provides a favorable condition for studies on marriage and the family and for the utilization of their findings by their public.

The title of this symposium, "The American Family," may seem a misnomer. In this country the patterns of family life are so numerous and varied that it appears more appropriate to speak of American families rather than of any homogeneous entity, as implied by the term *"the* American family."

Never before in human history has any society been composed of so many divergent types of families. Families differ by sections of the country, by communities within the city, by ethnic and religious groups, by economic and social classes, and by vocations. They are different ac-

---

*Reprinted from "The Family in a Changing Society," *American Journal of Sociology* by Ernest W. Burgess by permission of the University of Chicago Press. Copyright 1948, the University of Chicago Press. Volume 53 (May 1948), pp. 417-422.

cording to the family life-cycle and by number and role of family members. They vary by the locus of authority within the family and by widely different styles of life. There are the families of the Hopi Indian (primitive maternal), of the old Amish of Pennsylvania (patriarchal), of the Ozark mountaineers (kinship control), of the Italian immigrant (semipatriarchal), the rooming-house (emancipated), the lower middle class (patricentric), the apartment house (equalitarian), and the suburban (matricentric).

Unity in Diversity

With due recognition of all the diversity in American families, it is still possible and desirable to posit the concept of *the* American family. In a sense it is an ideal construction in that it attempts to concentrate attention upon what is distinctive of families in the United States in comparison with those of other countries. These differential characteristics are largely in terms of process rather than of structure and represent relative, rather than absolute, differences from families in other cultures. Chief among these distinctive trends are the following:

1. *Modifiability and adaptability* in response to conditions of rapid social change.

2. *Urbanization,* not merely in the sense that the proportion of families living in cities is increasing but that rural, as well as urban, families are adopting the urban way of life.

3. *Secularization,* with the declining control of religion and with the increasing role of material comforts, labor-saving devices, and other mechanical contrivances like the automobile, the radio, and television.

4. *Instability,* as evidenced by the continuing increase in divorce, reaching in 1945 the proportion of one for every three marriages.

5. *Specialization,* on the functions of the giving and receiving of affection, bearing and rearing of children, and personality development, which followed the loss of extrinsic functions, such as economic production, education, religious training, and protection.

6. *The trend to companionship,* with emphasis upon consensus, common interests, democratic relations, and personal
happiness of family members.

These distinctive trends in the American family will not be
elaborated. Certain of them, however, will receive additional
comment at appropriate places in this paper.

THE FAMILY AND SOCIETY

With all the variations in American families, it is apparent that they
are all in greater or less degree in a process of change toward an emerging type of family that is perhaps most aptly described as the "companionship" form. This term emphasizes the point that the essential
bonds in the family are now found more and more in the interpersonal
relationship of its members, as compared with those of law, custom,
public opinion, and duty in the older institutional forms of the family.

The point is not that companionship, affection, and happiness are
absent from the institutional family. They exist there in greater or less
degree, but they are not its primary aims. The central objectives of the
institutional family are children, status, and the fulfilment of its social
and economic function in society.

The distinctive characteristics of the American family, as of the
family in any society, are a resultant of (1) survivals from earlier forms
of the family, developing under prior or different economic and social
conditions; (2) the existing social and economic situation; and (3)
the prevailing and evolving ideology of the society.

I. *Survivals*

The American family has had a rich and varied historical heritage,
with strands going back to all European countries and to the religious
ideologies of the Catholic, Jewish, and Protestant faiths. What is distinctive in the American family, however, has resulted from its role,
first, in the early rural situation of the pioneer period, and, second, in
the modern urban environment.

The growth of democracy in the family proceeded in interaction with the development of democracy in society. Pioneer conditions promoted the emancipation both of women and of youth from subordination to the family and to the community. Arrangements for marriage passed from the supervision of parents into the control of young people.

The rural family of the United States before World War I, however, had progressed toward, but had not achieved, democratic relations among its members. Control was centered in the father and husband as the head of the farm economy, with strict discipline and with familistic objectives still tending to be dominant over its members. Children were appraised in terms of their value for farm activities, and land tenure and farm operations were closely interrelated with family organization and objectives.

2. The Evolving Urban Environment

The modern city, growing up around the factory and serving as a trade center for a wide area, provided the necessary conditions for the development of the distinctive characteristics of the American family. It still further promoted the equality of family members and their democratic interrelationships, initiated and fostered to a certain degree by the rural pioneer environment. In the urban community the family lost the extrinsic functions which it had possessed from time immemorial and which continued, although in steadily diminishing degrees, in the rural family. The urban family ceased to be, to any appreciable extent, a unity of economic production. This change made possible a relaxation of authority and regimentation by the family head. Then, too, the actual or potential employment of wife and children outside the home signified their economic independence and created a new basis for family relations. In the city the members of the family tended to engage in recreational activities separately, in their appropriate sex and age groups. Each generation witnessed a decline of parental control over children.

This increased freedom and individualization of family members and their release from the strict supervision of the rural neighborhood was naturally reflected in the instability of the family. The divorce rate has averaged a 3 per cent increase each year since the Civil War.

Urbanization involves much more than the concentration and growth of population. It includes commercialization of activities, particularly recreation; specialization of vocations and interests; the development of new devices of communication: telephone, telegraph, motion picture, radio, the daily newspaper, and magazines of mass circulation. All these still further promote the urbanization and secularization of families residing not only in cities but even in remote rural settlements.

3. *The Ideology of American Society*

Democracy, freedom, and opportunity for self-expression are central concepts of the American ideology. The frontier situation favored their expression in the social, economic, and political life of the people. As they found articulation in the American creed, they reinforced existing tendencies toward democracy and companionship within the family.

Urban life in its economic aspects provided less opportunity than did the rural environment for the exemplification of the American ideology. For example, the development of big business and enormous industries decreased the opportunities for the husband and father to run his own business. But the city greatly increased the economic freedom and independence of the wife and children by providing employment outside the home. The social conditions of the modern city led to the emancipation of family members from the institutional controls of the rural family. The urban family tended to become an affectional and cultural group, united by the interpersonal relations of its members.

THE FAMILY IN PROCESS

The paradox between the unity and the diversity of the American family can be understood in large part by the conception of the family in process. This means, first of all, that it is in transition from earlier and existing divergent forms to an emergent generic type and, second, that it is in experimentation and is developing a variety of patterns corresponding to the subcultures in American society.

1. *The Family in Transition*

Much of what is termed the "instability" of the American family arises from the shift to the democratic companionship type from the old-time rural family of this country and the transplanted old-world family forms of immigrant groups.

Many of the current problems within the family are to be explained by the resulting conflicting conceptions in expectations and roles of husbands and wives and of parents and children. The husband may expect his wife to be a devoted household slave like his mother, while she aspires to a career or to social or civic activities outside the home. Immigrant parents attempt to enforce old-world standards of behavior upon their children, who are determined to be American in appearance, behavior, and ideas.

2. The Family in Experimentation

The changes taking place in the family have constituted a vast experiment in democracy. Hundreds of thousands of husbands and wives, parents and children, have participated in it. Couples have refused to follow the pattern of the marriages of their parents and are engaged in working out new designs of family living more or less of their own devising. This behavior has been fully in accord with the ideals and practices of democracy and has exemplified the American ideology of individual initiative and opportunity for self-expression.

This experiment in family formation, while apparently proceeding by individual couples, has been essentially collectivistic rather than pluralistic behavior. Each couple has naturally cherished the illusion that it was acting on its own. To be sure, individual initiative and risk-taking were involved. Many individual ventures have ended in disaster. But actually it has been a collective experiment in the sense that the couples were acting under the stimulus of current criticisms of family life and were attempting to realize in their marriage the new conceptions of family living disseminated by the current literature, presented by the marriages of friends, or developed in discussion by groups of young people.

ADAPTABILITY VERSUS STABILITY

In the past, stability has been the great value exemplified by the family and expected of it by society. This was true because the family was the basic institution in a static society. American society, however, is not static but dynamic. The virtue of its institutions do not inhere in their rigid stability but in their adaptability to a rapid tempo of social change.

The findings of two recent studies underscore the significance of adaptability for the American family. Angell began his study of the family in the depression with the hypothesis that its degree of integration would determine its success or failure in adjustment to this crisis. He found, however, that he needed to introduce the concept of adaptability to explain why certain families, highly integrated, and stable before the depression, failed, and why some moderately integrated families succeeded in adjusting to the crisis. A restudy of these cases indicated that adaptability was more significant than integration in enabling families to adjust to the depression.

Another study arrived at a similar conclusion. In predicting success and failure in marriage, data were secured from couples during the engagement period. Certain couples with low prediction scores were later found to be well adjusted in their marriage. The explanation seemed to lie in the adaptability of one or both members of the couple, which enabled them to meet and solve successfully difficult problems as they developed in the marriage.

Adaptability as a personal characteristic has three components. One is psychogenic and represents the degree of flexibility in the emotional reaction of a person to a shift from an accustomed to a different situation. The second component is the tendency of the person as culturally or educationally determined to act in an appropriate way when entering a new situation. The third component of adaptability is the possession of knowledge and skills which make for successful adjustments to a new condition.

Successful marriage in modern society with its divergent personalities, diversity of cultural backgrounds, and changing conditions depends more and more upon the adaptability of husbands and wives and parents and children. The crucial matter, then, becomes the question of the adaptability of the family as a group, which may be something different from the adaptability of its members.

The growing adaptability of the companionship family makes for its stability in the long run. But it is a stability of a different kind from that of family organization in the past, which was in large part due to the external social pressures of public opinion, the mores, and law. The stability of the companionship family arises from the strength of the interpersonal relations of its members, as manifested in affection, rapport, common interests and objectives.

Flexibility of personality is not sufficient to insure adaptability of the family to a changing society. Its members should also be culturally and educationally oriented to the necessity for making adjustments. For example, the prospects of successful marriage would be greatly improved if husbands on entering wedded life were as predisposed in attitudes as are wives to be adjustable in the marital relation. Finally, adaptability in marriage and family living demands knowledge and skills on the part of family members. These are no longer transmitted adequately by tradition in the family. They can be acquired, of course, the hard way by experience. They can best be obtained through education and counseling based upon the findings of social science research.

THE FAMILY AND SOCIAL SCIENCE RESEARCH

The instability of the American family as evidenced by its rising divorce rate is, in general, incidental to the trial-and-error method by which divorced persons ultimately find happiness in a successful remarriage. But trial and error is a wasteful procedure. It involves tragic losses both to husbands and wives and to their children. So far as possible, it should be replaced by a more rational and less risk-taking planning.

The solutions, however, do not lie fundamentally in legislation. Laws, within limits, may be helpful as in the insuring of economic and social security, the improvement of housing and nutrition, in the exemptions from income taxes for wives and children, and in family allowances for children.

The state and federal governments have taken steps to undergird the economic basis of the family and are likely to be called upon for further aid. But assistance to young people entering marriage and to the family in attaining its cultural objectives is coming from other institutions and agencies.

The school and the church have for some time shown a growing interest in assuming responsibility for education for marriage and family life. This is most marked in colleges and universities, a large majority of which, upon demand of the student body, now offer one or more courses in the family, family relations, marriage and the family, and preparation for marriage. High schools are experimenting with different types of courses in human relations and in family relations or with the introduction of family-life educational material in existing course. Churches, through Sunday school classes, young peoples' societies, young married couples' clubs, and Sunday evening forums, have promoted programs in family-life education. Community programs have been organized under the auspices of the Y.M.C.A., the Y.W.C.A., settlements, social centers, associations for family living, parent-child study associations, and other agencies.

Marriage and family counseling are developing under both older and newer auspices. The public still turns to the minister, the physician, and the lawyer for assistance upon spiritual, physical, and legal aspects of marriage. Theological, medical, and law schools are beginning to realize their responsibilities for training their students for this activity. The family social case workers, particularly those with psychiatric training, are at present the persons best trained professionally for marriage and family counseling. The identification in the public mind of family-service societies with relief-giving has largely limited this service to dependent families, although in some cities special provision has been made to extend marriage and family counseling on a fee basis to middle-class clientele.

Beginning with the Institute of Family Relations in Los Angeles, established in 1930, and the Marriage Council of Philadelphia two years later, marriage-counseling centers under independent auspices are now functioning in an increasing number of our largest cities, in some smaller communities, and in a growing number of colleges and universities.

The growing disposition of young people is, as we have seen, to make their own plans for marriage and family living. They are, at the same time, interested in the resources available in education, in counseling, and in the findings of research in the psychological and social sciences. Leaders in the family-life educational and counseling movement are also looking to research to provide the knowledge which they may use in giving more efficient service.

Later in this symposium Dr. Nimkoff summarizes recent research trends in the study of the family and points the way to further studies.

This paper attempts only to state the role of research in relation to the solution of the problems of the family in our modern society. Its role is to provide the knowledge which an increasing number of young people are desirous of using in planning marriage and parenthood.

The outstanding evidence of this attitude and expectation is the reliance upon science of upper- and middle-class parents in the rearing of children. Their diet is determined upon the advice of a pediatrician, and their rearing is guided by the latest book on child psychology. This is a wide and significant departure from the older policy of bringing up the child according to methods carried down by tradition in the family.

A second illustration is the growing interest of young people in the factors making for the wise selection of a mate and for success or failure in marriage as derived from psychological and sociological studies.

A third significant fact is the widespread public interest in A. C. Kinsey's book, *Sexual Behavior in the Human Male,* containing the first report of sex behavior of 5,300 male Americans, based upon a very complete schedule and a carefully organized interview.

These are but three of the indications of the receptivity of intelligent young people to the findings of the psychological and social sciences and of their willingness to utilize them in planning for marriage and parenthood. In short, these activities are being taken out of the realm of the mores and are being transferred to the domain of science.

The findings of research do not, in and of themselves, provide the data for a design for marriage and family life. It is, however, the function of social science research to collect and to analyze the fund of experience of young people in their various experiments in achieving happiness in marriage and family life. Therefore, these findings of research should be made available to them through books, magazines, and newspapers; through motion pictures and radio; and through marriage counseling and programs of family-life education.

In conclusion, the main points of this paper may be briefly summarized. The American family, both in its apparent variety and in its essential unity, needs to be viewed in the perspective of social change. It is in transition from older rural institutional forms to a democratic companionship type of family relations adapted to an urban environment. This great change in the mores is a vast social experiment, participated in by hundreds of thousands of families under the collective stimulation of the American ideology of democracy, freedom, and self-expression. This experimental situation places the emphasis upon the adaptability

rather than upon the rigid stability of the family. This experiment provides an unusual opportunity for the study of the family in transition.
Moreover, participants in the experiment are demonstrating an increasing
interest in utilizing research findings in designing their own patterns for
marriage and family life.

AGE AND SEX IN THE SOCIAL STRUCTURE OF THE UNITED STATES*

by Talcott Parsons

In our society age grading does not to any great extent, except for
the educational system, involve formal age categorization, but is interwoven with other structural elements. In relation to these, however, it
constitutes an important connecting link and an organizing point of
reference in many respects. The most important of these for present
purposes are kinship structure, formal education, occupation, and
community participation. In most cases the age lines are not rigidly
specific, but approximate; this does not, however, necessarily lessen
their structural significance.

In all societies the initial status of every normal individual is that
of child in a given kinship unit. In our society, however, this universal
starting point is used in distinctive ways. Although in early childhood
the sexes are not usually sharply differentiated, in many kinship systems
a relatively sharp segregation of children begins very early. Our own
society is conspicuous for the extent to which children of both sexes are
in many fundamental respects treated alike. This is particularly true of
both privileges and responsibilities. The primary distinctions within the
group of dependent siblings are those of age. Birth order as such is
notably neglected as a basis of discrimination; a child of eight and a
child of five have essentially the privileges and responsibilities appropriate
to their respective age levels without regard to what older, intermediate,
or younger siblings there may be. The preferential treatment of an older
child is not to any significant extent differentiated if and because he
happens to be the first born.

*From Talcott Parsons, "Age and Sex in the Social Structure of the United
States," *American Sociological Review,* Volume 7 (October 1942), pp. 604-616.
Reprinted by permission of author and publisher.

There are, of course, important sex differences in dress and in approved play interest and the like, but if anything, it may be surmised that in the urban upper-middle classes these are tending to diminish. Thus, for instance, play overalls are essentially similar for both sexes. What is perhaps the most important sex discrimination is more than anything else a reflection of the differentiation of adult sex roles. It seems to be a definite fact that girls are more apt to be relatively docile, to conform in general according to adult expectations, to be "good," whereas boys are more apt to be recalcitrant to discipline and defiant of adult authority and expectations. There is really no feminine equivalent of the expression "bad boy." It may be suggested that this is at least partially explained by the fact that it is possible from an early age to initiate girls directly into many important aspects of the adult feminine role. Their mothers are continually about the house and the meaning of many of the things they are doing is relatively tangible and easily understandable to a child. It is also possible for the daughter to participate actively and usefully in many of these activities. Especially in the urban middle classes, however, the father does not work in the home and his son is not able to observe his work or to participate in it from an early age. Furthermore, many of the masculine functions are of a relatively abstract and intangible character, such that their meaning must remain almost wholly inaccessible to a child. This leaves the boy without a tangible meaningful model to emulate and without the possibility of a gradual initiation into the activities of the adult male role. An important verification of this analysis could be provided through the study in our own society of the rural situation. It is my impression that farm boys tend to be "good" in a sense which is not typical of their urban brothers.

The equality of privileges and responsibilities, graded only by age but not by birth order, is extended to a certain degree throughout the whole range of the life cycle. In full adult status, however, it is seriously modified by the asymmetrical relation of the sexes to the occupational structure. One of the most conspicuous expressions and symbols of the underlying equality, however, is the lack of sex differentiation in the process of formal education, so far, at least, as it is not explicitly vocational. Up through college, differentiation seems to be primarily a matter on the one hand of individual ability, on the other hand of class status, and only to a secondary degree of sex differentiation. One can certainly speak of a strongly established pattern that all children of the family have a "right" to a good education, rights which are graduated according to the class status of the family but also to individual ability. It is only in post-graduate professional education, with its direct connection with future occupational careers, that sex discrimination becomes conspicuous. It is particularly important that this equality of treatment exists in the sphere of liberal education since throughout the social structure of our society there is a strong tendency to segregate the occupational sphere from one in which certain more generally human patterns and values are dominant, particularly in informal social life and the real, of what will here be called community participation.

Although this pattern of equality of treatment is present in certain fundamental respects at all age levels, at the transition from childhood to adolescence new features appear which disturb the symmetry of sex roles while still a second set of factors appears with marriage and the acquisition of full adult status and responsibilities.

An indication of the change is the practice of chaperonage, through which girls are given a kind of protection and supervision by adults to which boys of the same age group are not subjected. Boys, that is, are chaperoned only in their relations with girls of their own class. This modification of equality of treatment has been extended to the control of the private lives of women students in boarding schools and colleges. Of undoubted significance is the fact that it has been rapidly declining not only in actual effectiveness but as an ideal pattern. Its prominence in our recent past, however, is an important manifestation of the importance of sex role differentiation. Important light might be thrown upon its functions by systematic comparison with the related phenomena in Latin countries where this type of asymmetry has been far more sharply accentuated than in this country in the more modern period.

It is at the point of emergence into adolescence that a set of patterns and behavior phenomena which involve a highly complex combination of age grading and sex role elements begins to develop. These may be referred to together as the phenomena of the "youth culture." Certain of its elements are present in pre-adolescence and others in the adult culture. But the peculiar combination in connection with this particular age level is unique and highly distinctive of American society.

Perhaps the best single point of reference for characterizing the youth culture lies in its contrast with the dominant pattern of the adult male role. By contrast with the emphasis on responsibility in this role, the orientation of the youth culture is more or less specifically irresponsible. One of its dominant notes is "having a good time" in relation to which there is a particularly strong emphasis on social activities in company with the opposite sex. A second predominant characteristic on the male side lies in the prominence of athletics, which is an avenue of achievement and competition which stands in sharp contrast to the primary standards of adult achievement in professional and executive capacities. Negatively, there is a strong tendency to repudiate interest in adult things and to feel at least a certain recalcitrance to the pressure of adult expectations and discipline. In addition to, but including, athletic prowess, the typical pattern of the male youth culture seems to emphasize the value of certain qualities of attractiveness, especially in relation to the opposite sex. It is very definitely a rounded humanistic pattern rather than one of competence in the performance of specified functions. Such stereotypes as the "swell guy" are significant of this. On the feminine side there is correspondingly a strong tendency to accentuate sexual attractiveness in terms of various versions of what may be called the "glamour girl" pattern. Although these patterns defining roles tend to polarize sexually — for instance, as between star athlete and socially popular girl — yet on a certain level they are complementary, both emphasizing certain features of a total personality in terms of the direct expression of certain values rather than of instrumental significance.

One further feature of this situation is the extent to which it is crystallized about the system of formal education. One might say that the principal centers of prestige dissemination are the colleges, but that many of the most distinctive phenomena are to be found in high schools throughout the country. It is of course of great importance that liberal education is not primarily a matter of vocational training in the United States. The individual status on the curricular side of formal education, is, however, in fundamental ways linked up with adult expectations, and doing "good work" is one of the most important sources of parental approval. Because of secondary institutionalization this approval is extended into various spheres distinctive of the youth culture. But it is notable that the youth culture has a strong tendency to develop in directions which are either on the borderline of parental approval or beyond the pale, in such matters as sex behavior, drinking, and various forms of frivolous and irresponsible behavior. The fact that adults have attitudes to these things which are often deeply ambivalent and that on such occasions as college reunions they may outdo the younger generation, as, for instance, in drinking, is of great significance, but probably structurally secondary to the youth-versus-adult differential aspect. Thus, the youth culture is not only, as is true of the curricular aspect of formal education, a matter of age status as such but also shows strong signs of being a product of tensions in the relationship of younger people and adults.

From the point of view of age grading, perhaps the most notable fact about this situation is the existence of definite pattern distinctions from the periods coming both before and after. At the line between childhood and adolescence "growing up" consists precisely in ability to participate in youth culture patterns, which are not for either sex the same as the adult patterns practiced by the parental generation. In both sexes the transition to full adulthood means loss of a certain "glamorous" element. From being the athletic hero or the lion of college dances, the young man becomes a prosaic business executive or lawyer. The more successful adults participate in an important order of prestige symbols but these are of a very different order from those of the youth culture. The contrast in the case of the feminine role is perhaps equally sharp, with at least a strong tendency to take on a "domestic" pattern with marriage and the arrival of young children.

The symmetry in this respect must, however, not be exaggerated. It is of fundamental significance to the sex role structure of the adult age levels that the normal man has a "job" which is fundamental to his social status in general. It is perhaps not too much to say that only in very exceptional cases can an adult man be genuinely self-respecting and enjoy a respected status in the eyes of others if he does not "earn a living" in an approved occupational role. Not only is this a matter of his own economic support but, generally speaking, his occupational status is the primary source of the income and class status of his wife and children.

In the case of the feminine role the situation is radically different. The majority of married women, of course, are not employed, but even of those that are a very large proportion do not have jobs which are in basic competition for status with those of their husbands. The majority of "career" women whose occupational status is comparable with that of men in their own class, at least in the upper-middle and upper classes, are unmarried, and in the small proportion of cases where they are married the result is a profound alteration in family structure.

This pattern, which is central to the urban middle classes, should not be misunderstood. In rural society, for instance, the operation of the farm and the attendant status in the community may be said to be a matter of the joint status of both parties to a marriage. Whereas a farm is operated by a family, an urban job is held by an individual and does not involve other members of the family in a comparable sense. One convenient expression of the difference lies in the question of what would happen in case of death. In the case of a farm it would at least be not at all unusual for the widow to continue operating the farm with the help of a son or even of hired men. In the urban situation the widow would cease to have any connection with the organization which had employed her husband and he would be replaced by another man without reference to family affiliations.

In this urban situation the primary status-carrying role is in a sense that of housewife. The woman's fundamental status is that of her husband's wife, the mother of his children, and traditionally the person responsible for a complex of activities in connection with the management of the household, care of children, etc.

For the structuring of sex roles in the adult phase the most fundamental considerations seem to be those involved in the interrelations of the occupational system and the conjugal family. In a certain sense the most fundamental basis of the family's status is the occupational status of the husband and father. As has been pointed out, this is a status occupied by an individual by virtue of his individual qualities and achievements. But both directly and indirectly, more than any other single factor, it determines the status of the family in the social structure, directly because of the symbolic significance of the office or occupation as a symbol of prestige, indirectly because as the principal source of family income it determines the standard of living of the family. From one point of view the emergence of occupational status into this primary position can be regarded as the principal source of strain in the sex role structure of our society since it deprives the wife of her role as a partner in a common enterprise. The common enterprise is reduced to the life of the family itself and to the informal social activities in which husband and wife participate together. This leaves the wife a set of utilitarian functions in the management of the household which may be considered a kind of "pseudo-" occupation. Since the present interest is primarily in the middle classes, the relatively unstable character of the role of housewife as the principal content of the feminine role is strongly illustrated by the tendency to employ domestic servants wherever financially possible. It is true that there is an American tendency to accept tasks of drudgery with relative willingness, but it is notable that in middle-class families there tends to be a dissociation of the essential personality from the performance of these tasks. Thus, advertising continually appeals to such desires as to have hands which one could never tell had washed dishes or scrubbed floors. Organization about the function of housewife, however, with the addition of strong affectional devotion to husband and children, is the primary focus of one of the principal patterns governing the adult feminine role—what may be called the "domestic" pattern. It is, however, a conspicuous fact that strict adherence to this pattern has become progressively less common and has a strong tendency to a residual status—that is, to be followed most closely by those who are unsuccessful in competition for prestige in other directions.

It is, of course, possible for the adult woman to follow the masculine pattern and seek a career in fields of occupational achievement in direct competition with men of her own class. It is, however, notable that in spite of the very great progress of the emancipation of women from the traditional domestic pattern only a very small fraction have gone very far in this direction. It is also clear that its generalization would only be possible with profound alterations in the structure of the family.

Hence, it seems that concomitant with the alteration in the basic masculine role in the direction of occupation there have appeared two important tendencies in the feminine role which are alternative to that of simple domesticity on the one hand and to a full-fledged career on the other. In the older situation there tended to be a very rigid distinction between respectable married women and those who were "no better than they should be." The rigidity of this line has progressively broken down through the infiltration into the respectable sphere of elements of what may be called again the glamour pattern, with the emphasis on a specifically feminine form of attractiveness which on occasion involves directly sexual patterns of appeal. One important expression of this trend lies in the fact that many of the symbols of feminine attractiveness have been taken over directly from the practices of social types previously beyond the pale of respectable society. This would seem to be substantially true of the practice of women smoking and of at least the modern version of the use of cosmetics. The same would seem to be true of many of the modern versions of women's dress. "Emancipation" in this connection means primarily emancipation from traditional and conventional restrictions on the free expression of sexual attraction and impulses, but in a direction which tends to segregate the element of sexual interest and attraction from the total personality and in so doing tends to emphasize the segregation of sex roles. It is particularly notable that there has been no corresponding tendency to emphasize masculine attraction in terms of dress and other such aids. One might perhaps say that in a situation which strongly inhibits competition between the sexes on the same plane the feminine glamour pattern has appeared as an offset to masculine occupational status and to its attendant symbols of prestige. It is perhaps significant that there is a common stereotype of the association of physically beautiful, expensively and elaborately dressed women with physically unattractive but rich and powerful men.

The other principal direction of emancipation from domesticity seems to lie in emphasis on what has been called the common humanistic element. This takes a wide variety of forms. One of them lies in a relatively mature appreciation and systematic cultivation of cultural interests and educated tastes, extending all the way from the intellectual sphere to matters of art, music, and house furnishings. A second consists in cultivation of serious interests and humanitarian obligations in community welfare situations and the like. It is understandable that many of these orientations are most conspicuous in fields where through some kind of tradition there is an element of particular suitability for feminine participation. Thus, a woman who takes obligations to social welfare particularly seriously will find opportunities in various forms of activity which traditionally tie up with women's relation to children, to sickness and so on. But this may be regarded as secondary to the underlying orientation which would seek an outlet in work useful to the community following the most favorable opportunities which happen to be available.

This pattern, which with reference to the character of relationship to men may be called that of the "good companion," is distinguished from the others in that it lays far less stress on the exploitation of sex role as such and more on that which is essentially common to both sexes. There are reasons, however, why cultural interests and interest in social welfare and community activities are particularly prominent in the activities of women in our urban communities. On the one side, the masculine occupational role tends to absorb a very large proportion of the man's time and energy and to leave him relatively little for other interests. Furthermore, unless his position is such as to make him particularly prominent his primary orientation is to those elements of the social structure which divide the community into occupational groups rather than those which unite it in common interests and activities. The utilitarian aspect of the role of housewife, on the other hand, has declined in importance to the point where it scarcely approaches a full-time occupation for a vigorous person. Hence the resort to other interests to fill up the gap. In addition, women being more closely tied to the local residential community are more apt to be involved in matters of common concern to the members of that community. This peculiar role of women becomes particularly conspicuous in middle age. The younger married woman is apt to be relatively highly absorbed in the care of young children. With their growing up, however, her absorption in the household is greatly lessened, often just at the time when the husband is approaching the apex of his career and is most heavily involved in its obligations. Since to a high degree this humanistic aspect of the feminine role is only partially institutionalized it is not surprising that its patterns often bear the marks of strain and insecurity, as perhaps has been classically depicted by Helen Hokinson's cartoons of women's clubs.

The adult roles of both sexes involve important elements of strain which are involved in certain dynamic relationships, especially to the youth culture. In the case of the feminine role marriage is the single event toward which a selective process, in which personal qualities and effort can play a decisive role, has pointed up. This determines a woman's fundamental status, and after that her role patterning is not so much status-determining as a matter of living up to expectations and finding satisfying interests and activities. In a society where such strong emphasis is placed upon individual achievement it is not surprising that there should be a certain romantic nostalgia for the time when the fundamental choices were still open. This element of strain is added to by the lack of clear-cut definition of the adult feminine role. Once the possibility of a career has been eliminated there still tends to be a rather unstable oscillation between emphasis in the direction of domesticity or glamour or good companionship. According to situational pressures and individual character the tendency will be to emphasize one or another of these more strongly. But it is a situation likely to produce a rather high level of insecurity. In this state the pattern of domesticity must be ranked lowest in terms of prestige but also, because of the strong emphasis in community sentiment on the virtues of fidelity and devotion to husband and children, it offers perhaps the highest level of a certain kind of security. It is no wonder that such an important symbol as Whistler's mother concentrates primarily on this pattern.

The glamour pattern has certain obvious attractions since to the woman who is excluded from the struggle for power and prestige in the occupational sphere it is the most direct path to a sense of superiority and importance. It has, however, two obvious limitations. In the first place, many of its manifestations encounter the resistance of patterns of moral conduct and engender conflicts not only with community opinion but also with the individual's own moral standards. In the second place, the highest manifestations of its pattern are inevitably associated with a rather early age level — in fact, overwhelmingly with the courtship period. Hence, if strongly entered upon, serious strains result from the problem of adaptation to increasing age.

The one pattern which would seem to offer the greatest possibilities for able, intelligent, and emotionally mature women is the third — the good companion pattern. This, however, suffers from a lack of fully institutionalized status and from the multiplicity of choices of channels of expression. It is only those with the strongest initiative and intelligence who achieve fully satisfactory adaptations in this direction. It is quite clear that in the adult feminine role there is quite sufficient strain and insecurity so that widespread manifestations are to be expected in the form of neurotic behavior.

The masculine role at the same time is itself by no means devoid of corresponding elements of strain. It carries with it to be sure the primary prestige of achievement, responsibility, and authority. By comparison with the role of the youth culture, however, there are at least two important types of limitations. In the first place, the modern job absorbs an extraordinarily large proportion of the individual's energy and emotional interests in a role which often has relatively narrow content. This in particular restricts the area within which he can share common interests and experiences with others not in the same occupational specialty. It is perhaps of considerable significance that so many of the highest prestige statuses of our society are of this specialized character. There is in the definition of roles little to bind the individual to others in his community on a comparable status level. By contrast with this situation, it is notable that in the youth culture common human elements are far more strongly emphasized. Leadership and eminence are more in the role of total individuals and less of competent specialists. This perhaps has something to do with the significant tendency in our society for all age levels to idealize youth and for the older age groups to attempt to imitate the patterns of youth behavior.

It is perhaps as one phase of this situation that the relation of the adult man to persons of the opposite sex should be treated. The effect of the specialization of occupational role is to narrow the range in which the sharing of common human interests can play a large part. In relation to his wife the tendency of this narrowness would seem to be to encourage on her part either the domestic or the glamorous role, or community participation somewhat unrelated to the marriage relationship. This relationship between sex roles presumably introduces a certain amount of strain into the marriage relationship itself since this is of such overwhelming importance to the family and hence to a human companionship. Outside the marriage relationship, however, there seems to be a notable inhibition against easy social intercourse, particularly in mixed company. The man's close personal intimacy with other women is checked by the danger of the situation being defined as one of rivalry with the wife, and easy friendship without sexual-emotional involvement seems to be inhibited by the specialization of interests in the occupational sphere. It is notable that brilliance of conversation of the "salon" type

seems to be associated with aristocratic society and is not prominent
in ours.

Along with all this goes a certain tendency for middle-aged men, as
symbolized by the "bald-headed row," to be interested in the physical
aspect of sex — that is, in women precisely as dissociated from those
personal considerations which are important to relationships of companionship or friendship, to say nothing of marriage. In so far as it
does not take this physical form, however, there seems to be a strong
tendency for middle-aged men to idealize youth patterns—that is, to
think of the ideal inter-sex friendship as that of their pre-marital period.

In so far as the idealization of the youth culture by adults is an
expression of elements of strain and insecurity in the adult roles it would
be expected that the patterns thus idealized would contain an element
of romantic unrealism. The patterns of youthful behavior thus idealized
are not those of actual youth so much as those which older people wish
their own youth might have been. This romantic element seems to
coalesce with a similar element derived from certain strains in the
situation of young people themselves.

The period of youth in our society is one of considerable strain and
insecurity. Above all, it means turning one's back on the security both
of status and of emotional attachment which is engaged in the family
of orientation. It is structurally essential to transfer one's primary emotional attachment to a marriage partner who is entirely unrelated to the
previous family situation. In a system of free marriage choice this applies
to women as well as men. For the man there is in addition the necessity
to face the hazards of occupational competition in the determination
of a career. There is reason to believe that the youth culture has
important positive functions in easing the transition from the security
of childhood in the family of orientation to that of full adult in marriage
and occupational status. But precisely because the transition is a period
of strain it is to be expected that it involves elements of unrealistic
romanticism. Thus, significant features in the status of youth patterns
in our society would seem to derive from the coincidence of the emotional
needs of adolescents with those derived from the strains of the situation
of adults.

A tendency to the romantic idealization of youth patterns seems in
different ways to be characteristic of modern Western society as a whole.
It is not possible in the present context to enter into any extended comparative analysis, but it may be illuminating to call attention to a striking
difference between the patterns associated with this phenomenon in
Germany and in the United States. The German "youth movement,"

starting before World War I, has occasioned a great deal of comment and has in various respects been treated as the most notable instance of the revolt of youth. It is generally believed that the youth movement has an important relation to the background of National Socialism, and this fact as much as any suggests the important difference. While in Germany as everywhere there has been a generalized revolt against convention and restrictions on individual freedom as embodied in the traditional adult culture, in Germany particular emphasis has appeared on the community of male youth. "Comradeship," in a sense which strongly suggests that of soldiers in the field, has from the beginning been strongly emphasized as the ideal social relationship. By contrast with this, in the American youth culture and its adult romantization a much stronger emphasis has been placed on the cross-sex relationship. It would seem that this fact, with the structural factors which underlie it, has much to do with the failure of the youth culture to develop any considerable political significance in this country. Its predominant pattern has been that of the idealization of the isolated couple in romantic love. There have, to be sure, been certain tendencies among radical youth to a political orientation but in this case there has been a notable absence of emphasis on the solidarity of the members of one sex. The tendency has been rather to ignore the relevance of sex difference in the interest of common ideals.

The importance of youth patterns in contemporary American culture throws into particularly strong relief the status in our social structure of the most advanced age groups. By comparison with other societies the United States assumes an extreme position in the isolation of old age from participation in the most important social structures and interests. Structurally speaking, there seem to be two primary bases of this situation. In the first place, the most important single distinctive feature of our family structure is the isolation of the individual conjugal family. It is impossible to say that with us it is "natural" for any other group than husband and wife and their dependent children to maintain a common household. Hence, when the children of a couple have become independent through marriage and occupational status the parental couple is left without attachment to any continuous kinship group. It is, of course, common for other relatives to share a household with the conjugal family but this scarcely ever occurs without some important elements of strain. For independence is certainly the preferred pattern for an elderly couple, particularly from the point of view of the children.

The second basis of the situation lies in the occupational structure. In such fields as farming and the maintenance of small independent enterprises there is frequently no such thing as abrupt "retirement," rather a gradual relinquishment of the main responsibilities and functions with advancing age. So far, however, as an individual's occupational status centers in a specific "job," he either holds the job or does not, and the tendency is to maintain the full level of functions up to a given point and then abruptly to retire. In view of the very great significance of occupational status and its psychological correlates, retirement leaves the older man in a peculiarly functionless situation, cut off from participation in the most important interests and activities of the society. There is a further important aspect of this situation. Not only status in the community but actual place of residence is to a very high degree a function of the specific job held. Retirement not only cuts the ties to the job itself but also greatly loosens those to the community of residence. Perhaps in no other society is there observable a phenomenon corresponding to the accumulation of retired elderly people in such areas as Florida and Southern California in the winter. It may be surmised that this structural isolation from kinship, occupational, and community ties is the fundamental basis of the recent political agitation for help to the old. It is suggested that it is far less the financial hardship of the position of elderly people than their social isolation which makes old age a "problem." As in other connections we are here very prone to rationalize generalized insecurity in financial and economic terms. The problem is obviously of particularly great significance in view of the changing age distribution of the population with the prospect of a far greater proportion in the older age groups than in previous generations. It may also be suggested, that through well-known psychosomatic mechanisms, the increased incidence of the disabilities of older people, such as heart disease, cancer, etc., may be at least in part attributed to this structural situation.

SOCIALIZATION AND SOCIAL CLASS
THROUGH TIME AND SPACE*

by Urie Bronfenbrenner

OVER-ALL CHARACTER OF THE
PARENT-CHILD RELATIONSHIP

The material considered so far has focused on specific practices employed by the parent. A number of researches document class differences as well in variables of a more molar sort—for example, the emotional quality of the parent-child relationship as a whole. These investigations have the additional advantage of reaching somewhat further back in time, but they also have their shortcomings. First of all, the results are not usually reported in the conventional form of percentages or means for specific social-class levels. In some studies the findings are given in terms of correlation coefficients. In others, social status can only be estimated from educational level. In others still, the data are presented in the form of graphs from which no significance tests can be computed. Partly to compensate for this lack of precision and comparability, partly to complete the picture of available data on class differences in child rearing, we cite in Table 11 not only the results from these additional studies of molar variables but also all other statistically significant findings from researches considered previously which might have bearing on the problem at hand. In this way, we hope as well to avoid the bias which occasionally arises from looking only at those variables in which one has a direct theoretical interest.

The data of Table 11 are noteworthy in a number of respects. First, we have clear confirmation that, over the entire 25-year period, middle-class parents have had a more acceptant, equalitarian relationship with their children. In many ways, the contrast is epitomized in Duvall's distinction between the "developmental" and "traditional" conceptions of mother and child. Duvall asked the mothers in her

---

*From Urie Bronfenbrenner, "Socialization and Social Class Through Time and Space, *Readings in Social Psychology, Third Edition,* pp. 420-425. Reprinted by permission from *Readings In Social Psychology,* Third Edition. Edited by Maccoby, Newcomb, and Hartley, copyright © 1947, 1952, 1958, Holt, Rinehart and Winston, Inc.

sample to list the "five things that a good mother does" and the "five things that a good child does." Middle-class mothers tended to emphasize such themes as "guiding and understanding," "relating herself lovingly to the child," and making sure that he "is happy and contented," "shares and cooperates with others," and "is eager to learn." In contrast, working-class mothers stressed the importance of keeping house and child "neat and clean," "training the child to regularity," and getting the child "to obey and respect adults."

What is more, this polarity in the value orientation of the two social classes appears to have endured. In data secured as recently as 1957, Kohn reports that working-class mothers differ from those of the middle class in their choice of characteristics most desired in a child; the former emphasize "neatness, cleanliness and obedience," while the latter stress "happiness, considerateness, and self-control."

Yet, once again, it would be a mistake to conclude that the middle-class parent is exerting less pressure on his children. As the data of Table 11 also show, a higher percentage of middle-class children are punished in some manner, and there is more "necessary" discipline to prevent injury or danger. In addition, though the middle-class father typically has a warmer relationship with the child, he is also likely to have more authority and status in family affairs.

Although shifts over time are difficult to appraise when the data are so variable in specific content, one trend is sufficiently salient to deserve comment. In the early Berkeley data the working-class parent is more expressive of affection than his middle-class counterpart. But in the follow-up study of the same children eight years later the trend is reversed. Perhaps the same mothers behave differently toward younger and older children. Still, the item "Baby picked up when cries" yields a significant difference in favor of the working-class mother in 1932 and a reliable shift in the opposite direction in 1953. *Sic transit gloria Watsoniensis!*

Especially with terms as heavily value laden as those which appear in Table 11, one must be concerned with the possibility that the data in the studies examined document primarily not actual behavior but the middle-class mother's superior knowledge of the socially acceptable response. Undoubtedly, this factor operates to inflate the reported relationships. But there are several reassuring considerations. First, although the items investigated vary widely in the intensity of their value connotations, all show substantially the same trends. Second, four of the studies reported in Table 11 (Berkeley I and II, Yellow Springs, and New

Haven II) are based not on the mother's responses to an interview but on observation of actual interaction among family members. It seems highly unlikely, therefore, that the conclusions we have reached apply only to professed opinions and not to real behavior as well.

Retrospect and Prospect

It is interesting to compare the results of our analysis with the traditional view of the differences between the middle- and lower-class styles of life, as documented in the classic descriptions of Warner, Davis, Dollard, and the more recent accounts of Sprinley, Clausen, and Miller and Swanson. In all these sources the working class is typically characterized as impulsive and uninhibited, the middle class as more rational, controlled, and guided by a broader perspective in time. Thus Clausen writes:

The lower class pattern of life . . . puts a high premium on physical gratification, on free expression of aggression, on spending and sharing. Cleanliness, respect for property, sexual control, educational achievement—all are highly valued by middle class Americans—are of less importance to the lower class family or are phrased differently.

To the extent that our data even approach this picture, it is for the period before World War II rather than for the present day. The modern middle class has, if anything, extended its time perspective so that the tasks of child training are now accomplished on a more leisurely schedule. As for the lower class the fit is far better for the actual behavior of parents rather than for the values they seek to instill in their children. As reflected in the data of Tables 10 and 11, the lower-class parent—though he demands compliance and control in his child—is himself more aggressive, expressive, and impulsive than his middle-class counterpart. Even so, the picture is a far cry from the traditional image of the casual and carefree lower class. Perhaps the classic portrait is yet to be seen along the skid rows and Tobacco Roads of the nation, but these do not lie along the well-trodden paths of the survey researcher. He is busy ringing doorbells, no less, in the main section of the lower-class district, where most of the husbands have steady jobs and, what is more important, the wife is willing to answer the door and the interviewer's questions. In this modern working-class world there may be greater freedom of emotional expression, but there is no laxity or vagueness with respect to goals of child training. Consistently over the past 25 years, the parent in this group has emphasized what are usually regarded as the traditional middle-class virtues of cleanliness, conformity, and control, and although his methods are not so effective as those of his middle-class neighbors, they are perhaps more desperate.

Perhaps this very desperation, enhanced by early exposure to impulse and aggression leads working-class parents to pursue new goals with the old techniques of discipline. While accepting middle-class levels of aspiration he has not yet internalized sufficiently the modes of response which make these standards readily achievable for himself or his children. He has still to learn to wait, to explain, and to give and withhold his affection as the reward and price of performance.

As of 1957, there are suggestions that the cultural gap may be narrowing. Spock has joined the Bible on the working-class shelf. If we wish to see the shape of the future, we can perhaps do no better than to look at the pages of the newly revised edition of this ubiquitous guidebook. Here is a typical example of the new look—a passage not found in the earlier version:

> If the parent can determine in which respects she may be too permissive and can firm up her discipline, she may, if she is on the right track, be delighted to find that her child becomes not only better behaved but much happier. Then she can really love him better, and he in turn responds to this.

Apparently "love" and "limits" are both watchwords for the coming generation of parents. As Mrs. Johnson, down in the flats, puts away the hairbrush and decides to have a talk with her unruly youngster "like the book says," Mrs. Thomas, on the hill, is dutifully striving to overcome her guilt at the thought of giving John the punishment she now admits he deserves. If both ladies are successful, the social scientest may eventually have to look elsewhere in his search for ever larger F's and t's.

Such speculations carry us beyond the territory yet surveyed by the social scientist. Perhaps the most important implication for the future from our present analysis lies in the sphere of method rather than substance. Our attempt to compare the work of a score of investigators over a score of years will have been worth the labor if it but convinces future researchers of the wastefulness of such uncoordinated efforts. Our best hope for an understanding of the differences in child rearing in various segments of our society and the effects of these differences on personality formation lies in the development of a systematic long-range plan for gathering comparable data at regular intervals on large samples of families at different positions in the social structure. We now have survey organizations with the scientific competence and adequate technical facilities to perform the task. With such hopes in mind, the author looks ahead to the day when the present analysis becomes obsolete, in method as well as substance.

RECAPITULATION AND CODA

A comparative analysis of the results of studies of social-class differences in child rearing over a 25-year period points to the following conclusions.

A. *Trends in Infant Care*

1. Over the past quarter of a century, American mothers at all social-class levels have become more flexible with respect to infant feeding and weaning. Although fewer infants may be breast fed, especially over long periods of time, mothers are increasingly more likely to feed their children on demand and to wean them later from the bottle.

2. Class differences in feeding, weaning, and toilet training show a clear and consistent trend. From about 1930 till the end of World War II, working-class mothers were uniformly more permissive than those of the middle-class. They were more likely to breast feed, to follow a self-demand schedule, to wean the child later both from breast and bottle, and to begin and complete both bowel and bladder training at a later age. After World War II, however, there has been a definite reversal in direction; now it is the middle-class mother who is the more permissive in each of the above areas.

3. Shifts in the pattern of infant care—especially on the part of middle-class mothers—show a striking correspondence to the changes in practices advocated in successive editions of U.S. Children's Bureau bulletins and similar sources of expert opinion.

4. In addition to varying with social-class level, methods of infant care appear to differ as a function of cultural background, urban vs. rural upbringing, and exposure to particular ideologies of child rearing.

5. Taken together, the findings on changes in infant care lead to the generalization that socialization practices are most likely to be altered in those segments of society which have most ready access to the agencies or agents of change (e.g., books, pamphlets, physicians, and counselors).

B. *Trends in Child Training*

6. The data on the training of the young child show middle-class mothers, especially in the postwar period, to be consistently more permissive toward the child's expressed needs and wishes. The generalization applies in such diverse areas as oral behavior, toilet accidents, dependency, sex, aggressiveness, and freedom of movement outside the home.

7. Though more tolerant of expressed impulses and desires, the middle-class parent, throughout the period covered by this survey, has higher expectations for the child. The middle-class youngster is expected to learn to take care of himself earlier, to accept more responsibility about the home, and—above all—to progress further in school.

8. In matters of discipline, working-class parents are consistently more likely to employ physical punishment, while middle-class families rely more on reasoning, isolation, appeals to guilt, and other methods involving the threat of loss of life. At least two independent lines of evidence suggest that the techniques preferred by middle-class parents are more likely to bring about the development of internalized values and controls. Moreover, the effectiveness of such methods should, at least on theoretical grounds, be enhanced by the more acceptant atmosphere experienced by middle-class children in their early years.

9. Over the entire 25-year period studied, parent-child relationships in the middle-class are consistently reported as more acceptant and equalitarian, while those in the working class are oriented toward maintaining order and obedience. Within this context, the middle-class has shown a shift away from emotional control toward freer expression of affection and greater tolerance of the child's impulses and desires.

In the past few years, there have been indications that the gap between the social classes may be narrowing. Whatever trend the future holds in store, let us hope that the social scientist will no longer be content to look at them piecemeal but will utilize all the technical resources now at his command to obtain a systematic picture of the changes, through still more extended space and time, in the way in which humanity brings up its children.

TABLE 11
OVERALL CHARACTER OF PARENT-CHILD RELATIONSHIP

Sample	Approx. date of practice	No. of cases reported	Age	Middle-class trend	Working-class trend
Berkeley I	1928-32	31	1-3	Grants autonomy Cooperative Equalitarian	Expresses affection Excessive contact Intrusive Irritable Punitive Ignores child
National I	1932	494	0-1		Baby picked up when cries †
National IV	1932	3239	1-12	Higher percentage of children punished †	Nothing done to allay child's fears †
Yellow Springs, Ohio	1940	124	3-12	Acceptant-democratic	Indulgent Active-rejectant
Berkeley II	1939-42	31	9-11	Grants autonomy Cooperative Equalitarian Expresses affection	Excessive contact Intrusive Irritable Punitive Ignores child
Chicago I	1943	100	5		Father plays with child more †
Chicago II	1943-44	433	1-5	"Developmental" conception of "good mother" and "good child." †	"Traditional" conception of "good mother" and "good child." †
New Haven I	1949-50	219	1	More necessary discipline to prevent injury or danger. †	More prohibitive discipline beyond risk of danger or injury.
Boston	1951-52	372	5	Mother warmer toward child † Father warmer toward child * Father exercises more authority * Mother has higher esteem for father † Mother delighted about pregnancy † Both parents more often share authority *	Father demands instant obedience † Child ridiculed † Greater rejection of child † Emphasis on neatness, cleanliness, and order † Parents disagree more on child-rearing policy †
New Haven II	1951-53	48	14-17	Fathers have more power in family decisions † Parents agree in value orientations †	
Palo Alto	1953	73	2½-5½	Baby picked up when cries †	Mother carries through demands rather than dropping the subject †
Eugene	1955-56	206	0-18	Better relationship between father and child †	
Washington, D.C.	1956-57	400	10-11	Desirable qualities are happiness,* considerateness,* curiosity,* self-control *	Desirable qualities are neatness, cleanliness,* obedience *

* Trend significant at 5-percent level or better.

† The difference between percentages is not significant but the difference between mean ratings is significant at the 5-percent level or better.

ADOLESCENT CHARACTER AND PERSONALITY*

by Robert J. Havighurst and Hilda Taba

VALUES OF VARIOUS GROUPS IN THE COMMUNITY

The child learns values from two general sources: from the adults
who have prestige in his eyes and from his own age group. Some of the
values which the boy or girl learns are community-wide. They are held
by all persons, regardless of social or economic status. Such variations
as occur in these values are individual and not the result of systematic
group differences. Other values learned by children are characteristic of
smaller groups within the community, such as social classes, churches,
ethnic groups, and the age group to which the boy or girl belongs.

VALUES OF THE COMMUNITY AS A WHOLE

The community values the general moral virtues of honesty, responsibility, loyalty, and kindliness, though these virtues are interpreted
differently by different groups in the community. For example, loyalty
to one's own family is valued by everybody, but loyalty to the community is a value limited largely to middle-class people. Projects for
community betterment, for making Prairie City "the finest little city in
the Corn Belt," enlist the active support of middle-class people but fail
to stir the interest of the lower classes.

Prairie City is socially and politically conservative. It changes its
mind slowly and holds to the ideals that have served it in the past. Above
all, it holds to the doctrine that the individual should be responsible for
his own economic security.

At the same time one of the traditional American ideals seems to
be losing ground in Prairie City. This is the ideal of progress—the goal
of making the community bigger and bigger. Instead of working toward
this goal, most people in Prairie City feel that inscrutable external forces
will have their way, regardless of what individuals do. Consequently,

*From Robert J. Havighurst and Hilda Taba, *Adolescent Character and
Personality,* 1949, John Wiley and Sons, Inc., pp. 28-46. Reprinted with permission.

the community makes no effort to expand. For example, when all the vacant houses in Prairie City were filled as a result of a war boom in a neighboring town, it was proposed that Prairie City apply for federal funds to construct several hundred new houses. But there was very little public sentiment for the proposal. None but a few merchants pushed the idea actively. Some people feared that a post-war business recession would leave houses empty and that an increase of population would leave just so many more families to "go on relief" when the boom was over.

People are not optimistic about life growing better in Prairie City. The memory of the depression of the 1930's is vivid, and World War II created a pessimistic uncertainty about the future. Thus, while the individual is expected to make the most of his abilities, the people doubt that this will result in better economic and social conditions.

Nevertheless, people do not let their uncertainty about the future mar their enjoyment of the present. They prefer present comfort to the promise of future wealth and power. They want the joys of this world, the solid joys, and they are more interested in the comfort that material wealth can provide than in the power it can bestow upon its owner. For this reason they value leisure. When the duck-hunting season opens, for example, men of all economic levels leave their businesses and their work and go hunting for a few days. Fishing is popular too, and men and boys will take a day off any time to fish in near-by lakes and rivers.

We see this desire for material comfort and stability reflected in the following excerpts from essays written by sixteen-year-olds on the subject, "The Person I Would Like to Be Like."

> I would like to be about 23 years old. At that age I would probably know something about what my future occupation would be. I would be more or less settled in life as an adult and my worries and anticipation of what I was to do for a living would be over. I would like to do manual labor on a project of my own or for someone else. I like work where I would be able to decide things for myself. If I wanted to go somewhere, I would like to go without my work always hampering me from doing it.

> When I become an adult I would like very much to own a little business of some kind, grocery store, sporting store, something on that order. After I have established a good profitable business I would like to settle down and get married. Have two or three children. Then spend the rest of my days making my family happy.

These boys at sixteen want security rather than adventure. They will be content with modest achievements. The following two essays, written by middle-class boys who expect to be engineers, show a surprising lack of the youthful enthusiasm and the aggressive drive for achievement which have long been considered American characteristics.

The clothes I have would be good and not worn out. I would not be fat. My profession would be such as to provide me with enough money for a home of my own, a car, a wife, etc. My profession would probably be electrical engineering or some other sort of engineering. The town I live in would not be too big, and not too small. I would travel quite a bit. I would do some hunting, play golf, probably gamble some. I would know how to fly if at all possible, and I'd own my own plane.

Suppose I am thirty-five years old. I would like to be an engineer at some plant. I would be making a good income, enough to have a small home of my own, in a town of about 5,000 population, and enough to support a small family and be able to save enough to go on a vacation every year and to have some of the things I have always looked forward to having. I should like to be very healthy and have an electric tool shop in the basement as well as a boat in the river and short enough hours at work so I could use some of these privileges. Maybe I would be more satisfied if I owned a business of my own, small or large; it makes no difference.

The following essays, written by girls, express similar values. All three girls are thinking of settling down in Prairie City to a comfortable, industrious, but not ambitious, life.

When I become an adult I would like to be an understanding person, also a very patient one. I would like to be a person that gets up in the morning at regular hours and that gets her housework done in the morning without fooling around and stopping to monkey with every little thing. Also I would like to be respected enough to have discipline in the home among the children. I also would like to be able to cook good meals and know quite a little about sewing, canning and other things useful in the home. I want to be a person that people like if I want to have many friends. I also want a home where religion is stressed and where everyone works for the good of each other.

I would like to be a combination of several people I know. I would like to be a beauty operator when I get out of school. I would like to have the appearance of someone "neat" all of the time. I would like to have character like that of Greer Garson in her pictures. She is a movie actress but I would like to be the character that she usually plays in her pictures, kind-hearted, always smiling, and helpful to others when they need help. For recreation I would like to do things around the home or to do any kind of recreation with other people if it were at all possible.

> When I am 21 I would like to be well liked by everyone. Have a nice disposition and be easy to get along with. I would like to have a nice complexion, straight teeth, and nice hair. I want to be a typist or a secretary, make a good salary and live comfortably. I want to be able to dance well, play tennis and all sorts of sports. I would like to know about the world of today and of tomorrow, so I will be an interesting person to talk to.

The impression one obtains from all the essays is that their authors are down-to-earth and unimaginative—none of these young people wants to save the world or to set it on fire.

Religion is a basic element of Prairie City culture although many people do not take active part in the churches. When a Prairie City resident says he lives in "God's country," he believes he is speaking the literal truth. The general attitude is that the churches are good for the community. For the churchgoers, religion nearly always takes an active form—the churches exist for service. Contemplative religion does not flourish.

Human nature is considered rational and responsible. A person is responsible for using his will power to control his impulses; if he behaves immorally, it is his own fault. Moral character, therefore, is generally thought to be the responsibility of the individual and of his family. Most people in Prairie City would say for instance that delinquency is a sign that something is wrong with the delinquent individual. Few persons would stop to question whether or not juvenile delinquency is also a sign that something is wrong with the community. On the other hand, the leaders in the community are beginning to think of the social environment of boys and girls as having something to do with their character development. An indication of this is the fact that a recreation center for young people was recently established under the sponsorship of the Rotary and Lions clubs.

VALUES HELD BY THE VARIOUS SOCIAL CLASSES

The various social classes of Prairie City have somewhat different sets of values.

Members of the *upper class* place importance on their family's past history. They like to talk about the preceding generations. They like to spend money on things which will not produce a profit, such as objects of art, fine horses, fine houses, and philanthropy. Prairie City's upper class is not so clearly marked off from the upper-middle class as is the case in older cities in the East and South. Hence the characteristic upper-class values are not much in evidence, and the community is dominated more by the values of the upper-middle class.

The *upper-middle* class set great store by civic virtue. For them a man's duty to God is his duty to the community. They may even let their responsibilities as parents be subordinated to their responsibilities as citizens, by giving time to community affairs which they might otherwise give to their children. They are great believers in education and in education as the solution of social problems. Their children are leaders in the high school and nearly all go to college.

A leading upper-class man defined the virtues of the upper-middle class when, in speaking about the father of one of the sixteen-year-olds, he said:

He is one of the finest men we have in town. He has an excellent community attitude. Of course, maybe I judge people too much by their community attitudes, but if people are really interested in their children and interested in the community institutions and working together, I don't give a damn about their social standing.

The values which the upper-middle class instill in their children are self-reliance, initiative, loyalty, good manners, and responsibility to the community. The vices against which they train their children are stealing and destruction of property, sexual immorality, bad manners, and carelessness in dress and speech.

In the upper-middle class certain of the general moral virtues held as values by the entire community have taken on specific forms which differentiate them from the same moral virtues in other social classes. For example, honesty is accepted as a virtue by all classes, but in the upper-middle class it is a generalized virtue. One is expected to be honest toward all people; and honest in matters of property, of truth telling, and of keeping promises. In the lower class, honesty is limited to dealings within the family and within a small neighborhood group. The average lower-class person does not feel compelled to tell the truth to everybody, to be careful of the property of everyone, or to keep his promises to everyone.

The *lower-middle* and *upper-lower* classes are very much alike in their values. They stress respectability, thrift, loyalty, responsibility to family and church, and fidelity in marriage. The church is important in the lives of these people. It is, for them, what the community is for the upper-middle class. It is the scene of most of their social life and the theater of their efforts toward moral improvement of society. The lower-middle people are the most active and faithful church workers, while the upper-lower group follow their lead.

Moral and religious beliefs vary somewhat from one church to another within the lower-middle and upper-lower classes. The Lutherans, for example, teach against dancing, smoking, card playing, and movie going. Their argument against these practices is that, although they are not sins in themselves, they lead to sin.

The lower-class members of a church tend more toward other-worldliness—the belief that they will be rewarded in the next life for good works and sacrifice and suffering in this life. They also set great store by personal religious conversion and the personal experience of salvation.

Education has a different value for this group than it has for the upper-middle class. The majority accept school simply as a means of getting children ready for adulthood. Education, for them, is necessary for individual vocational success. The socially mobile minority of this group—those who are trying to "improve their station in life"—look on college as a means for getting their children ahead in the world, but the majority think of high-school graduation as the highest educational goal. In contrast to these attitudes, the upper middle class thinks of college as necessary to give their children their own status, and they put great trust in education and research as a means of solving social and economic problems.

The *lower-lower* class are thought to be immoral by those above them on the social scale. The members of this class are arrested more frequently than those of any other group. Their violations of the code of sexual morality are, if not more frequent, at least more widely known and more flagrant than those of other groups. On the other hand, there are some thoroughly respectable families in this social group who, because of being "foreigners" or because of poverty, are placed in the lowest class.

The principal values held by the lower-lower class center about food, leisure, and family solidarity. The moral virtues of honesty, responsibility, and loyalty are restricted to a small sphere of action that includes the family and a few neighbors or friends.

It seems probable that at least some of the moral ideals held up to children of the lower-lower class are different from those taught to children in the other classes. Stealing is more apt to be overlooked or condoned. Church influence is absent or weak. The moral teaching of the school is not so strongly reinforced by the home, and children of this class tend to drop out of school at an earlier age than children of other social classes. Lower-class children are taught to fight. They experience more open exhibition of aggression in their homes, where the father may beat the mother, the children are whipped frequently, and the child's own aggressive impulses are not much restrained by his parents.

Similarly, lower-class children suffer less restraint on sex play and sex exploration than do middle-class children.

As a generalization it might be said that lower-class children have fewer and less rigid controls on the free play of their impulses, while middle-class children are made to inhibit their impulses through the watchfulness of their parents and the ever-present question in their own minds, "What will people think?"

Lower-class life in Prairie City differs in one important way from lower-class life in a metropolis. The great city presents the disturbing phenomenon of "disorganized areas" in which, from the middle-class viewpoint, social values have gone awry. In these areas it is normal for a child to steal, to lie to the authorities, and to be sexually delinquent. In fact, delinquency is normal, and only those children who deviate from the normal have a chance of adopting middle-class values. This phenomenon of a "delinquency culture" is possible because of the geographical fragmentation of the city, which forces thousands of lower-class people to live together, with their own schools and places of recreation, and which effectively prevents their children from having contact with children from other social classes.

In Prairie City there is very little segregation by social class, and there is no "disorganized area." The people of the lower-lower class live in a fringe around the town, as well as in the poorer parts of the business district. Their children are found in all the elementary schools. Thus they are exposed in the school and on the playground to middle-class influences among their own age group. There are no delinquent groups in Prairie City, though of course some groups of young people have lower reputations than others. Among the sixteen-year-old group there was no history of gang delinquency.

The differences in moral values among the various social classes are probably greater in practice than in words. People all up and down the social scale in Prairie City tend to agree verbally with an official moral ideology, from which their actual moral behavior departs in various ways. For example, upper-class parents undoubtedly tell their children that gambling is wrong, although adults in this class do gamble. Parents of the lower-lower class tell their children that stealing is wrong but do not punish stealing consistently and may themselves set an example of stealing.

The official value system and moral ideology of Prairie City is that of the middle class. This was found to be true when boys and girls were given a test called the Moral Ideology Test in which they were asked to name examples of good behavior and bad behavior. There were few differences between children of the different social classes.

VALUES OF THE ADOLESCENT CULTURE

Recent studies of adolescents have emphasized the fact that boys and girls in their teens have a culture of their own with moral standards and with moral pressures behind those standards. This culture has been called the "adolescent peer culture." Boys and girls, desiring the approval of their age mates, follow the fashions of the peer culture in morals, dress, and speech, and the moral standards and practices of the adolescent peer culture are probably an important factor in character formation.

The principal values of the adolescent peer culture in Prairie City are social participation, group loyalty, and individual achievement and responsibility. As a means of social participation, such social skills as dancing are desirable, as well as a supply of spending money and good clothes. Group loyalty takes the form principally of loyalty to the high school and its activities, but church youth groups and the informal cliques of the adolescent social world also command loyalty. Individual achievement and responsibility mean, for most young people, doing well in school, getting a part-time job, and being a responsible member of several clubs or other organizations.

The high school is the principal locus of the adolescent peer culture. School dances, athletic contests, hay rides, and club activities, as well as study halls and classrooms, are the places where boys and girls learn how to behave socially and morally as young men and women. When a community recreation center was opened for the use of the young people, it was placed under the supervision of the high-school Student Council and became an adjunct of the school program.

The moral standards of the adolescent peer culture are largely middle-class standards set by the high school which is, in turn, run by people with middle-class values. The teachers are nearly all middle-class people and so are the parents who are most active in school affairs. Finally, the dominant adolescent group in the high school is composed mainly of middle-class boys and girls.

During the period of these studies, the adolescent peer culture of Prairie City was dominated by one clique of girls, who formed themselves into a secret society. This clique was composed of girls from upper-middle-class families and the few upper-class girls in school, together with a few popular girls from lower-status families. These girls elected their candidates to school offices and also set the social pace. There was no comparable group of boys. The leaders among the boys tended to cooperate with this group of girls. The teachers gave this girls' clique their tacit support, since it included the "best" girls in the school.

Thus the two most powerful groups in the school, the teachers and the leading clique among the adolescents, worked pretty much together in setting standards. Most of the students followed their lead. Only in the sphere of relations between boys and girls was there any considerable conflict between teachers and parents, on the one hand, and adolescents, on the other hand.

To achieve success in the adolescent peer culture, a boy or girl must stay in school, be a reasonably good student, take part in school activities, and go to the school dances and parties. In the process of adjusting successfully in these ways, he would be learning middle-class morality. The majority of young people attempted to fit themselves into this situation.

There were three groups which did not adjust well to the dominant adolescent peer culture as it operated in the high school. Failure to adjust meant for each group that it adopted a code of morals which deviated from the accepted code of the school.

One of these groups was the Lutherans. As will be explained in a later chapter, the Lutherans are largely a Norwegian group who try to keep themselves apart from the rest of the community. Since they oppose dancing and motion pictures, their young people cannot participate freely with the dominant group. The Lutheran Church has an extensive young people's program, including parties at the church on the nights when the school holds dances. Thus a rival peer culture has been established by the Lutherans, with a somewhat different set of moral standards from that of the group that centers in the high school. This does not work out as well as the leaders of the Norwegian group would like, for it causes a good deal of conflict in the lives of the young people as they feel the pressure of the dominant peer culture. Some of them leave the church, at least temporarily.

One of the young people who had dropped out of the Lutheran social group had this to say:

> Those Lutherans kids gang together, except for me. They stick together just like glue. I was ostracized from them because I danced and went to shows and played bridge. They're against everything. In fact, every time we had a dance at the high school, they threw some kind of a party at the church and tried to make the kids come. Those that didn't were ostracized.

The character reputation of the Norwegian group does not suffer from their lack of adjustment to the dominant peer culture. This is easily understood, for they deviate from the accepted pattern toward the side of more rigorous morality. Furthermore, their academic adjustment in the school is satisfactory, and they participate freely in athletics and other activities which are not frowned on by the church. If anything, membership in the Norwegian group is an advantage, as far as moral reputation is concerned.

The second deviant group consisted of a number of high-school students who felt that they were "out of things" socially. They came mostly from upper-lower-class families. Perhaps because the dominant social group consisted of girls, the most vocal of this deviant group also were girls. They openly flouted school regulations, made no effort in their studies, refused to attend the school dances, and went with boys who had dropped out of school or lived out of town.

One of the leaders of this group was a girl who will be called Esther. She was the third child in a large family. Her father was a factory worker with a good reputation. Esther had been an inconspicuous student in school and seemed to be getting along all right until her junior year, when she was sixteen. About this time a number of things went wrong for her. During the summer she had begun to go out at night with boys. She had a job at this time in a soda fountain which was a favorite meeting place for boys and girls of lower-class families and also for young men who lived in the surrounding country. Her parents became alarmed at reports they heard about her and ruled that she must be home by ten o'clock in the evening and that she was not to go automobile riding with boys. She resented these restrictions and complained that she was being treated like a baby.

When school started for her junior year, Esther made an attempt to win social prestige by competing for the post of cheer leader. There were three girls to be chosen. The ruling clique put up three candidates who practiced together and learned from each other. Esther and another girl who tried out for the position were left alone, without aid and encouragement from anyone. The three who had the backing of the ruling clique won the positions, and Esther became bitter about it. Shortly afterward she and some of her friends began "skipping school," which was a serious offense in Prairie City. After one flagrant case of "skipping," the mothers of several of the girls were called to the school. These mothers were worried about their daughters but were inclined to blame the school for what they called "playing favorites" and discriminating against their daughters.

Interviews by a field worker with Esther at about this time showed something of her situation and her reactions to it. The field worker, in this case a man, said to her:

> "Well now, Esther, could you tell me how you feel about school cutting, and why you did it? I just want to have some idea of how you feel about the school situation, the cutting, and so on."

> "Well, I'll tell you, Mr. S————," she said, "the way a lot of us girls are treated here, you can't blame us for the way we feel. Frankly, for a lot of us, there's nothing here but just coming to classes, and listening to the teacher, and reciting our lessons, and studying, and going home again. We're just pushed out of things. There are a group of girls here who think they're higher than us, and they look down on us. I won't mention any names, but they're a group of girls from the wealthier families. They have a club that's supposed to be outside the school, but it's really in the school. They can do things that we can't afford, and they hog all the offices and are in all the activities. They just won't pay any attention to us. I've almost quit going to church because some of this same group go to ·the church I used to go to, and there's only one girl besides myself who goes there that's not in that group. They snub us, and they won't talk to us. Now I know that we're not rich. Dad's only a factory worker, and we can't afford to do a lot of things, but we'd like to be in the school activities and the school games, go to the dances, and things like that. But they just make us feel like we're not wanted. I went to some of the activities when I first started high school, but they just ignored us. Last year I was in two clubs, but this year I'm not in anything. If we go to the high-school dances, nobody will dance with us. They just dance among themselves and have a good time, and we're just nobody. Well, why come to school? We're made to feel out of place, and that's just the way it is."

> "Well," said S————, "do you go with boys in the high school?"

> "No, I don't go with boys in the high school. I just don't care to. I'd like to go with some of them, but most of the boys that I'd

want to go with, they wouldn't ask me. I guess they just don't want to go with me. This year I've been going with a boy that works over at the ammunition plant (in a nearby town)."

"What's his last name?"

"Well, I don't know just how to spell it. I know it starts with K-r-a-k-o, but I don't know the rest of it."

"Did he go to Prairie City High?"

"No, he never went to high school. His family just moved over into the neighborhood last year."

"I've been in the doghouse so long now I don't know whether I'll ever get out." Esther changed the subject.

"Well, what would you like to do in school?" asked S_____.

"I'd like to have an office, just a secretary of a club, or some-thing like that. I like to do things, and I just want to have fun like the rest of these girls do."

Esther is one of a group of about ten girls in her class who feel this way about the social life of the school and have said so in inter-views with field workers. Several boys have made similar comments, though somewhat less articulate.

Esther and her friends are caught in a vicious circle. Since they are not accepted in the social life of the adolescent peer culture, they make a life for themselves with other adolescents who are not accepted. This gives them a bad reputation, and they have more difficulty than ever in their relations with their schoolmates. School becomes a prison, and, when they try to escape from it, the school authorities come down on them heavily and bring their parents into the situation. The parents alternately punish their children and accuse the school authorities of favoritism.

The character reputations of Esther and others in this group are low—probably lower than their behavior actually warrants. But their situation is a bad one and may influence their characters negatively. They need, obviously, a more wholesome situation, one which offers greater possibilities for satisfaction of their social needs.

The feelings of the majority of high-school students toward this deviant group and the resultant attitudes of the deviant group are brought out in a study by Neugarten. She studied how high-school students were rated by their fellow students on popularity and other personality traits. The dominant clique of girls all came out with high favorable scores though they were rated unfavorably by members of the deviant group. On the other hand, Esther and her friends were mentioned frequently on unfavorable items. With a few exceptions, the upper- and upper-middle-class boys and girls received the most favorable ratings; the upper-lower- and lower-lower-class youth received unfavorable ratings.

The third deviant group consisted of those who had dropped out of school. These boys and girls were almost completely outside the dominant adolescent peer culture, except for a few who participated in the young-people's organizations of the churches. This group had a loose, ill-organized culture of their own, with its locus in certain recreational places of questionable repute, such as a skating rink, the bowling alley, and two or three small eating places. Here they came in contact with the unadjusted high-school students who hovered between the two cultures.

The out-of-school group had poor reputations among the teachers and students in the high school, as well as in the community at large. The values of this group were quite different from the values of the school group. They did not care about education. They had no desire for social participation outside their own group. Their vocational expectations were lower. Their moral standards were said to be lower, by the dominant group. They probably were somewhat freer in their sexual behavior than would be approved by middle-class standards.

There were several out-of-school youth with very good reputations, and everybody recognized that they did not belong to this out-of-school peer culture. They had to stop school for economic reasons or because they were needed to care for invalid persons at home. They tended to seek association with other adolescents in church groups.

To summarize what has been found about the social life of Prairie City adolescents as a factor in character formation, the dominant peer culture encourages conformity to middle-class values and morals; boys and girls who do not adjust well to the dominant peer culture are subject to somewhat deviate character-forming influences. The Norwegian Lutheran group has a peer culture which encourages a rigorous, puritanical morality. The out-of-school group has a peer culture which encourages a moral code that is undesirable judged by middle-class standards. Within the school, but on the fringe of the dominant peer culture, is an unadjusted group which is hostile to the school and the things the school stands for and which leans toward the peer culture of the out-of-school group.

MORAL QUALITY OF HOME LIFE

Undoubtedly the most important single influence on character is the home. Consequently, it is necessary in a study of character formation to evaluate the moral influence of the home upon different individuals and different groups of individuals.

The following description of home life in Prairie City is based on the observations of field workers; it needs to be supplemented by more detailed information and analysis in subsequent work in Prairie City.

There is something of a contrast between middle- and lower-class family life. The middle-class family has allies in the school, church, and youth organizations. The lower-class family takes a relatively greater responsibility for training its children and relies less upon the assistance of outside institutions.

The child of a middle-class family spends relatively more time than does the lower-class child in activities of the Boy and Girl Scouts, in school activities, in the public library, and in the church (with the exception, in the last instance, of the lower-class Lutheran child). The child of a lower-class family spends more time with his parents. His parents do not belong to many associations, nor do they have many things to do in their leisure time that take them out of their homes. Furthermore, since families are larger in the lower classes, there is more chance for a lower-class child to find playmates in his own home. This does not necessarily mean that the lower-class parent plays a more important role in the character formation of the child than does the middle-class parent. It may be that middle-class parents give more thought to the training of their children, and, with fewer children in the family, they may be able to give more attention to the individual child. Lower-class parents may be too busy or too careless to put forth much effort on the moral training of their children, even though they spend much of their time in the company of their children. The lower-class parent transmits his moral values to his child in an effective manner; but this is probably due to the fact that the lower-class child is subjected to a minimum of pressure from the dominant middle-class, child-caring institutions in the community.

The middle-class family is supplemented by the school, church, and character-building organizations which reinforce middle-class values. Thus the middle-class child finds little or no conflict between the standards of his home and the expectations of his teachers, Sunday school, and club leaders. The lower-class child faces such a conflict but usually resolves it by participating in a few activities outside the home.

CHARACTER-FORMING ORGANIZATIONS

Prairie City has a full complement of organizations designed to improve the character of boys and girls. For the most part Prairie City residents regard the influence of these agencies as good, although enthusiasm is frequently tempered by awareness of factors that limit the influence of a given organization.

The Boy Scouts, Girl Scouts, and Camp Fire Girls are generally approved. However, these organizations tend to draw very largely from middle-class families when perhaps the lower-class children need them more. For example, the following comments by people in the community were made about the Boy Scouts: "Unfortunately, that group doesn't reach the children that need it most." . . . "It has the weakness that it reaches those who would be reached in the home anyway."

Concerning the girls' organizations, one person said: "Probably the Girl Scouts have done pretty well as a character-building agency, but both the Girl Scouts and the Camp Fire Girls have drawn social and religious lines a little close, and that has hampered their work somewhat."

While extracurricular school activities in general are considered good influences for high-school people, the activity that has attracted most attention is music. The high-school band is a very popular organization. The following are typical comments by Prairie City people: "That is a very fine influence, and the director is a splendid influence, too." . . . "The music program touches a lot of young people in Prairie City, and there is a fine spirit of good fellowship and working together."

One person spoke approvingly of the extracurricular activities themselves but critically of the fact that participation was limited to too small a number: "Those things are good, but I criticize them from the standpoint that they don't reach a lot of the youngsters. They are quite selective."

The men's service clubs are interested in character formation. They have tried to accomplish something in the way of dealing with the problem of juvenile delinquency. One club has a special committee for boys' work. The other club has been responsible for the recreation center.

The recreation center was established during the course of these studies. Its purpose was to provide under good auspices a social center for teen-age youth. Though financed by adults, the operation of the center was a responsibility of the high-school Student Council. The boys and girls who frequented the recreation center tended to be the ones who were best adjusted to the social life of the high school. Relatively few out-of-school youth attended. One local resident commented as follows: "Well, it's done a fairly good job, but it doesn't reach the ones that you want to reach." The center was closed after less than a year of operation.

Recreation Places Frequented by Young People

Perhaps fully as effective in character formation as the so-called "character-building" organizations are the commercial recreational places frequented by young people. These are the swimming pool, the pool hall, the roller-skating rink, the bowling alley, the movies, and the taverns.

The public swimming pool is generally approved. This is an open-air pool, available only during the summer. "I think our swimming pool provides the right kind of recreation and guidance." ... "It is very valuable for young people, well supervised and well directed."

It is interesting to note the attitudes of Prairie City people toward the pool hall in their town. In most towns a pool hall has a poor reputation as a "hangout" for young men; but such is not the case here. People will not go so far as to say that the pool hall is a good influence, but they almost invariably point out that it is not a harmful influence and that it is well supervised. The following comment is a typical one: "I don't think that the pool hall is a bad influence here. It certainly has a very good reputation. The boys think a great deal of the man who operates the place, and, the way it is run, I don't think it is a bad influence at all."

There are mixed feelings about the skating rinks. There are two rinks: one in the municipal park and one over a store downtown. People agree that skating is a desirable form of entertainment, but some are skeptical of the way in which the rinks are run: "That's probably a combination of both good and bad. Skating itself, under the right supervision, is certainly good recreation. They have well-supervised high-school parties at the rink downtown, and I think that is a good social function. But the general run of youngsters who hang around there night after night do considerable drinking, I know." ... "The rink in the park is a grand place, very clean and well run. They don't allow any drinking there." ... "I guess the rink downtown is not very good. People speak of it as a 'hole.' "

The bowling alley has a variable reputation also. "In some ways it is fine, and in other ways it is not, but I think it is pretty well run. They don't permit drinking on the premises, and that is a considerable help." ... "I don't believe they serve alcoholic drinks there so probably that wouldn't be a bad influence. It may even be a good one." ... "I enjoy bowling, but I'm not inclined to think too well of our bowling alley here."

Motion pictures are a pervasive influence. Except for those whose parents forbid movie going on religious grounds, nearly every boy and girl goes regularly, and averages about two shows a week. There is no question that the movies play an important role in determining superficial behavior patterns of adolescents such as choice of clothes and hair styles. To what extent the movies influence character development remains a moot question.

The middle-class people of Prairie City deplore undesirable movies but do little to influence the type of pictures shown. "In this community they are decidedly bad, just decidedly. So many of the young people go regardless of what's being shown, and it seems to me they must waste a lot of good time. I enjoy good movies, but we don't get many of them here." ... "Some of the shows are simply terrible. I think we are cursed with poor pictures here in this community." ... "Movies may be both good and bad in their influence, but here we are likely to get about ten bad ones to one good one." ... "It's partly the parents' fault. Parents appear to be complacent rather than critical, and it seems to me that any mother would have to be critical of some of the things that are brought in to be shown to children." ... "I wouldn't say that movies are an absolutely negative influence, but I don't think they have much to contribute by and large. At best perhaps they are a neutral influence, but certainly they have contributed to poor living standards. They have tended to give people an idea of money as the chief value in life, and I think our young people definitely reflect that fact."

The people who were interviewed were unanimous in their opinion that the taverns had a definitely harmful influence on the young people who frequent them, but judgments varied as to how many young people were actually affected. One person said: "Taverns are not a problem here in town. Kids are afraid to go into them here. When they go to places of that kind they stay away from this town and go where they won't be recognized." Another person said: "There is some drinking. No question about that, I know. Some of the tavern keepers are no help. There are some that 'cheat,' and there are various ways in which it is done." Another said: "I know that a great many high-school people go to taverns. The law is certainly not very well enforced so far as age is concerned." Still another person made this comment: "I hear people say that very many of our young people do go to these places, but as far as I'm concerned it is just hearsay. I think quite probably some of the girls have tried it out, and personally I think that's rather a natural situation. They want to see what it is like."

CONCLUSION

Through the home, school, church, youth organizations, recreational agencies, and the informal "peer culture" of the children's own world, values and moral standards are taught to boys and girls by their parents, teachers and other adults in positions of prestige, and by leaders of their own age groups. In Prairie City some values are community wide, and some are held mainly by members of a particular social class or of a particular church group.

Boys and girls tend to learn the values and standards of their own homes, churches, and social classes. But the adolescent peer culture of the high school is a pervasive middle-class influence, affecting all boys and girls who go to high school. In general, the school teaches middle-class values.

There are three deviant groups of adolescents in Prairie City who are learning values and standards which deviate from the middle-class forms. The Lutherans are learning a more rigorous, puritanical morality. Most of the out-of-school group are learning a morality which is generally stigmatized as "lower class," and some of the lower-class boys and girls who are in high school but not well adjusted to its social life are becoming discontented and hostile toward middle-class values.

The "character-building" youth organizations teach middle-class values and appeal mainly to middle-class youth, though they also succeed in serving a minority of lower-class youth.

The commercial recreation places vary in their moral influence. Several are very well managed from the point of view of middle-class people and are quite generally approved. Others are less well managed, and their owners are indifferent to their character-forming influence.

Chapter Five

THE CULTURE OF THE SCHOOL

There is no doubt that each school has a culture of its own. These cultures can range from the comparatively homogeneous culture of the rural, one-room schoolhouse (now disappearing), with perhaps a teacher from that same community, to the diverse patterns of an urban secondary school of three thousand or more students.

As can be seen, each of these cultures has a hierarchy of statuses with their own respective roles, some assigned and some assumed; a system of rules, some formal, some informal (and these not always easily compatible); an in-group feeling, and, very probably, a jargon.

Why should teachers and others know about the *culture* of the school? For one thing, as Howard S. Becker points out in "Social-Class Variations in the Teacher-Pupil Relationship," if your expectations of pupil behaviors fit fairly closely to what actually occurs, you will not suffer from what some have described as "reality (or cultural) shock." You are not expected to adopt the attitudes and patterns of behavior of the pupils, but foreknowledge of these will facilitate your role as educational leader.

The most comprehensive definitions today of what good teaching should be are stated in terms of teaching roles and the specific behaviors to be achieved within each role. If teachers, administrators, pupils, parents, school board members, and college professors could generally agree upon what represents the good school and good teaching, more effort could be given to working toward the common goals rather than to disputing one against the other—or all the others. Major policy-making groups have attempted to state our national purpose and our major goals in education; individual writers have given their own views on these topics and accounts of some of these appear in Chapter Nine. In California, the teaching profession has developed a set of standards describing the various roles of the competent teacher.[1] The relationships between competent teaching and the achievement of our major educational objectives have yet to be demonstrated, but the actual statement of these educational standards is a major step forward.

The first reading, "The Sociology of the School," by the late Willard Waller, still stands as a classic description of school culture although written over a generation ago. Some portions, for example, the section on the formal relations between teachers and students, seem to be less applicable today, especially in suburban schools; but many parts, for example, the discussion on athletics, are still meaningful.

There is almost universal agreement that teachers present middle class values in their relations with pupils, although not all teachers come from the middle class. In her article, "Class Biases in the Teaching of Values," Celia Burns Stendler urges teachers to place less emphasis upon the secondary values (mores)—speech patterns, manners, dress—which differ from one social group to another, and to stress instead the moral qualities of honesty, loyalty, kindness, and courage, which are very nearly universal.

Some of our teachers and many of our textbooks, albeit in subtle ways, serve to reinforce biased images of certain minority groups and the desirability of being a white, Anglo-Saxon, fair-haired (to the extent of *every* person in one book being fair-haired) member of a carefree middle-class family. In "Intergroup Relations in the Elementary School," Anne Phillips McCreary, of the University of British Columbia, carefully documents the need for teachers to be aware and effective in the area of intercultural relations.

In "Social-Class Variations in the Teacher-Pupil Relationship," Howard S. Becker presents contrasts of teacher-pupil relationships in a large metropolitan school system; he gives vivid, anecdotal accounts of teachers' likes and dislikes of certain forms of pupil behavior and of the pupils themselves. The article focuses on the ways in which the middle-class teacher's reactions to class differences perpetuate the existing inequities.

Major attention is being given to ameliorating our urban area and urban school problems. Robert J. Havighurst, Chairman of the Commit-

---

[1] The Teacher Education Commission, *Teacher Competence: Its Nature and Scope*. Burlingame, California: California Teachers Association, 1957.

tee on Human Development, the University of Chicago, is a leader in this field. In his two contributions, "Metropolitan Development and the Educational System" and "National Policy for Alienated Youth," Havighurst maintains that the approach to the solution of the problems must be a multiple one. While the school must take a primary role as a key socializing agency, it cannot be expected to work alone on the problems.

Elementary and secondary teachers are urged to exemplify the democratic process in their teaching; the same must be equally true for their colleagues in the colleges and universities.

The selection, "Social Class in a Teachers College," by Durlyn E. Wade, is included to give insight into the reader's own college schooling, whether current or previous. It should be most worthwhile to test the implications of social class bias that the Wade study exposes at other teacher education institutions.

THE SOCIOLOGY OF THE SCHOOL*

by Willard Waller

The school is a closed system of social interaction. Without pedantry, we may point out that this fact is of importance, for if we are to study the school as a social entity, we must be able to distinguish clearly between school and not-school. The school is in fact clearly differentiated from its social milieu. The existence of a school is established by the emergence of a characteristic mode of social interaction. A school exists wherever and whenever teachers and students meet for the purpose of giving and receiving instruction. The instruction which is given is usually formal classroom instruction, but this need not be true. The giving and receiving of instruction constitutes the nucleus of the school as we now think of it. About this nucleus are clustered a great many less relevant activities.

When we analyze existing schools, we find that they have the following characteristics which enable us to set them apart and study them as social unities:

1. They have a definite population.
2. They have a clearly defined political structure, arising from the mode of social interaction characteristic of the school, and influenced by numerous minor processes of interaction.
3. They represent the nexus of a compact network of social relationships.
4. They are pervaded by a we-feeling.
5. They have a culture that is definitely their own.

The school has, as we have said, a definite population, composed of those who are engaged in the giving or receiving of instruction, who "teach" or "are in school." It is a relatively stable population and one whose depletion and replacement occur slowly. Population movements go according to plan and can be predicted and charted in advance. A bimodal age distribution marks off teachers from students. This is the most significant cleavage in the school.

---

*From Willard Waller, *The Sociology of Teaching,* 1932, John Wiley and Sons, Inc., pp. 6-13. Reprinted with permission.

The young in the school population are likely to have been subjected to some sifting and sorting according to the economic status and social classification of their parents. The private schools select out a certain group, and there are specializations within the private schools, some being in fact reformatories for the children of the well-to-do, and some being very exacting as to the character and scholastic qualifications of their students. The public schools of the exclusive residence district are usually peopled by students of a limited range of social types. Slum schools are for slum children. Country schools serve the children of farmers. In undifferentiated residence districts and in small towns which have but one school the student population is least homogeneous and most representative of the entire community.

The teaching population is probably less differentiated. In part, this is because the variation from the teacher type must be limited if one is to teach successfully. There is nevertheless considerable variation in the training and ability of teachers from one school to another and one part of the country to another. Teachers the country over and in all schools tend to be predominantly selected from the rural districts and from the sons and daughters of the lower middle classes. The teaching population is in some schools more permanent than the student population. There is nevertheless a large turnover among teachers.

The characteristic mode of social interaction of the school, an interaction centered about the giving and receiving of instruction, determines the political order of the school. The instruction which is given consists largely of facts and skills, and of other matter for which the spontaneous interests of students do not usually furnish a sufficient motivation. Yet teachers wish students to attain a certain mastery of these subjects, a much higher degree of mastery than they would attain, it is thought, if they were quite free in their choices. And teachers are responsible to the community for the mastery of these subjects by their students. The political organization of the school, therefore, is one which makes the teacher dominant, and it is the business of the teacher to use his dominance to further the process of teaching and learning which is central in the social interaction of the school.

Typically the school is organized on some variant of the autocratic principle. Details of organization show the greatest diversity. Intrafaculty relations greatly affect the relations between teachers and students. Where there is a favorable rapport between the teachers and the administrative authorities, this autocracy becomes an oligarchy with the teacher group as a solid and well-organized ruling class. It appears that the best practice extends the membership in this oligarchy as much as possible without making it unwieldy or losing control of it. In the most happily conducted institutions all the teachers and some of the leading students feel that they have a very real voice in the conduct of school affairs.

Where there is not a cordial rapport between school executives and teachers, control becomes more autocratic. A despotic system apparently becomes necessary when the teaching staff has increased in size beyond a certain limit. Weakness of the school executive may lead him to become arbitrary, or it may in the extreme case lead some other person to assume his authority. The relationship between students and teachers is in part determined by intra-faculty relationships; the social necessity of subordination as a condition of student achievement, and the general tradition governing the attitudes of students and teachers toward each other, set the limits of variation. But this variation is never sufficient to destroy the fact that the schools are organized on the authority principle, with power theoretically vested in the school superintendent and radiating from him down to the lowest substitute teacher in the system. This authority which pervades the school furnishes the best practical means of distinguishing school from not-school. Where the authority of the faculty and school board extends is the school. If it covers children on the way to and from school, at school parties, and on trips, then those children are in school at such times.

The generalization that the schools have a despotic political structure seems to hold true for nearly all types of schools, and for all about equally, without very much difference in fact to correspond to radical differences in theory. Self-government is rarely real. Usually it is but a mask for the rule of the teacher oligarchy, in its most liberal form the rule of a student oligarchy carefully selected and supervised by the faculty. The experimental school which wishes to do away with authority continually finds that in order to maintain requisite standards of achievement in imparting certain basic skills it has to influence some variant of the authority principle, or it finds that it must select and employ teachers who can be in fact despotic without seeming to be so. Experimental schools, too, have great difficulty in finding teachers who are quite free from the authoritarian bias of other schools and able to treat children as independent human beings. Military schools, standing apparently at the most rigid pole of authority, may learn to conceal their despotism, or, discipline established, may furnish moments of relaxation and intimate association between faculty and students, and they may delegate much power and responsibility to student officers; thus they may be not very much more arbitrary than schools quite differently organized, and sometimes they are very much less arbitrary than schools with a less rigid formal structure. The manifestations of the authority principle vary somewhat. The one-room country school must have a different social structure from the city high school with five thousand students, but the basic fact of authority, of dominance and subordination, remains a fact in both.

It is not enough to point out that the school is a despotism. It is a despotism in a state of perilous equilibrium. It is a despotism threatened from within and exposed to regulation and interference from without. It is a despotism capable of being overturned in a moment, exposed to the instant loss of its stability and its prestige. It is a despotism demanded by the community of parents, but specially limited by them as to the techniques which it may use for the maintenance of a stable social order. It is a despotism resting upon children, at once the most tractable and the most unstable members of the community.

There may be some who, seeing the solid brick of school buildings, the rows of nicely regimented children sitting stiff and well behaved in the classroom or marching briskly through the halls, will doubt that the school is in a state of unstable equilibrium. A school may in fact maintain a high morale through a period of years, so that its record in the eyes of the community is marred by no untoward incident. But how many schools are there with a teaching body of more than—let us say— ten teachers, in which there is not one teacher who is in imminent danger of losing his position because of poor discipline? How many such schools in which no teacher's discipline has broken down within the last three years? How many school executives would dare to plan a great mass meeting of students at which no teachers would be present or easily available in case of disorder?

To understand the political structure of the school we must know that the school is organized on the authority principle and that that authority is constantly threatened. The authority of the school executives and the teachers is in unremitting danger from: (1) The students. (2) Parents. (3) The school board. (4) Each other. (5) Hangers-on and marginal members of the group. (6) Alumni. The members of these groups, since they threaten his authority, are to some extent the natural enemies of the person who represents and lives by authority. The difficulties of the teacher or school executive in maintaining authority are greatly increased by the low social standing of the teaching profession and its general disrepute in the community at large. There is a constant interaction between the elements of the authoritative system; the school is continually threatened because it is autocratic, and it has to be autocratic because it is threatened. The antagonistic forces are balanced in that ever-fickle equilibrium which is discipline.

Within the larger political order of the school are many subsidiary institutions designed to supplement, correct, or support the parent institution, drawing their life from it and contributing in turn to its continued existence. These institutions are less definitely a part of the political structure, and they mitigate somewhat the rigidity of that structure by furnishing to students an opportunity for a freer sort of social expression. These ancillary institutions are organizations of extra-curricular activities, and comprise such groups as debating societies, glee clubs, choral societies, literary societies, theatrical groups, athletic teams, the staff of a school paper, social clubs, honorary societies, fraternities, etc. They are never entirely spontaneous social groupings but have rather the character of planned organizations for which the major impetus comes from the faculty, generally from some one member of the faculty delegated to act as "faculty adviser." These "activities" are part of that culture which springs up in the school from the life of students or is created by teachers for the edification of students. Such groups are often hardly less pervaded by faculty control than classroom activities, and there seems a tendency for the work of such institutions to be taken over by the larger social structure, made into courses and incorporated into the curriculum. Perhaps the worst that can happen to such organizations, if they are viewed as opportunities for the spontaneous self-expression of students, is that they shall be made over into classes. But the school administrator often thinks differently; from his point of view, the worst that can happen to such groups is that they shall become live and spontaneous groups, for such groups have a way of declaring their independence, much to the detriment of school discipline.

The school is the meeting-point of a large number of intertangled social relationships. These social relationships are the paths pursued by social interaction, the channels in which social influences run. The criss-crossing and interaction of these groups make the school what it is. The social relationships centering in the school may be analyzed in terms of the interacting groups in the school. The two most important groups are the teacher-group and the pupil-group, each of which has its own moral and ethical code and its customary attitudes toward members of the other groups. There is a marked tendency for these groups to turn into conflict groups. Within the teacher group are divisions according to rank and position, schismatic and conspiral groups, congenial groups, and cliques centering around different personalities. Within the student groups are various divisions representing groups in the larger community, unplanned primary groups stair-stepped according to age, cliques, political organizations, and specialized groups such as teams and gangs. The social influence of the school is a result of the action of such groups upon the individual and of the organization of individual lives out of the materials furnished by such groups.

The school is further marked off from the world that surrounds it by the spirit which pervades it. Feeling makes the school a social unity. The we-feeling of the school is in part a spontaneous creation in the minds of those who identify themselves with the school and in part a carefully nurtured and sensitive growth. In this latter aspect it is regarded as more or less the property of the department of athletics. Certainly the spirit of the group reaches its highest point in those ecstatic ceremonials which attend athletic spectacles. The group spirit extends itself also to parents and alumni.

A separate culture, we have indicated, grows up within the school. This is a culture which is in part the creation of children of different age levels, arising from the breakdown of adult culture into simpler configurations or from the survival of an older culture in the play group of children, and in part devised by teachers in order to canalize the activities of children passing through certain ages. The whole complex set of ceremonies centering around the school may be considered a part of the culture indigenous to the school. "Activities," which many youngsters consider by far the most important part of school life, are culture patterns. The specialized culture of the young is very real and satisfying for those who live within it. And this specialized culture is perhaps the agency most effective in binding personalities together to form a school.

INTERNAL CULTURE OF THE SCHOOL

Teachers have always known that it was not necessary for the students of strange customs to cross the seas to find material. Folklore and myth, tradition, taboo, magic rites, ceremonials of all sorts, collective representations, participation mystique, all abound in the front yard of every school, and occasionally they creep upstairs and are incorporated into the more formal portions of school life.

There are, in the school, complex rituals of personal relationships, a set of folkways, mores, and irrational sanctions, a moral code based upon them. There are games, which are sublimated wars, teams, and an elaborate set of ceremonies concerning them. There are traditions, and traditionalists waging their world-old battle against innovators. There are laws, and there is the problem of enforcing them. There is Sittlichkeit. There are specialized societies with a rigid structure and a limited membership. There are no reproductive groups, but there are customs regulating the relations of the sexes. All these things make up a world that is different from the world of adults. It is this separate culture of the young, having its locus in the school, which we propose to study. To work out all the details of this culture would be a task long and difficult, and, for our purpose, not altogether necessary. We shall be content to mark out the main lines of the cultural background of school life.

Certain cultural conflicts are at the center of the life of the school. These conflicts are of two sorts. The first and most obvious is that which arises from the peculiar function of the school in the process of cultural diffusion. A conflict arises between teachers and students because teachers represent the culture of the wider group and students are impregnated with the culture of the local community. Where the differences concern matters of religion or of fundamental morality, the struggle which then ensues may become quite sharp and may seriously affect the relation of the school to the community. A second and more universal conflict between students and teachers arises from the fact that teachers are adult and students are not, so that teachers are the bearers of the culture of the society of adults, and try to impose that culture upon students, whereas students represent the indigenous culture of the group of children.

The special culture of the young grows up in the play world of childhood. It is worth while to note that it arises in the interstices of the adult social world. Thrasher's "The Gang" is a study of the conflict between the established social order and the interstitial group which has sprung up and grown strong in the sections of society where the adult order does not hold. But this is by no means a complete explanation of the behavior norms of childhood groups. Another fact of importance is that the child does not experience the world in the same manner as does the adult. The child perceives the world differently from the adult in part because he sees it in smaller and simpler configurations. The adult sees social situations as falling into certain highly complex configurations; the child, with a simpler mental organization, does not see these, but breaks up his sensory data into different wholes. The sensory patterns of childhood, then, arise in part from imperfectly experienced adult situations. What the child appropriates from the cultural patterns around him must always be something which it is within his power to comprehend. This is usually one of the simpler and more elementary forms of adult behavior, as the criminal behavior followed out by the gang, or it is a split-off part of a more complex whole common in the culture of adults.

Though an enlightened pedagogy may ameliorate the conflict of adults and children, it can never remove it altogether. In the most humane school some tension appears between teacher and students, result, apparently, from the role which the situation imposes upon the teacher in relation to his students. There are two items of the teacher's duty which make it especially likely that he will have to bring some pressure to bear upon students: he must see to it that there is no retrogression from the complexity of the social world worked out for students of a certain age level, and he must strive gradually to increase that complexity as the child grows in age and approximates adult understanding and experience. Activities may reduce conflict, but not destroy it.

Children have something which can be regarded as a culture of their own. Its most important loci are the unsupervised play group and the school. The unsupervised group presents this culture in a much purer form than does the school, for the childish culture of the school is partly produced by adults, is sifted and selected by adults, and is always subject to a certain amount of control by teachers. The culture of the school is a curious melange of the work of young artisans making culture for themselves and old artisans making culture for the young; it is also mingled with such bits of the greater culture as children have been able to appropriate. In turning to more concrete materials, we may note certain aspects of tradition in the school. It will illustrate well this mingling of cultures if we divide the tradition which clusters about the school into three classes: tradition which comes entirely, or almost entirely, from the outside; tradition which is in part from outside the school and in part indigenous; and tradition which is almost entirely indigenous. It is roughly true that tradition of the first class exists in the community at large, that of the second class among teachers, and that of the third class among students.

Tradition of the first class, that which for the particular school comes altogether from the outside, is a manifestation of a culture complex diffused throughout the whole of Western European culture. The historic school has of course had a part in the formation of this complex, but any particular school is largely the creation of it. Tradition of this sort governs the very existence of schools, for without such a culture complex, schools would not exist at all. This traditional culture complex governs also the general nature of the life in the schools. It determines that the old shall teach the young, and not that the young shall ever teach the old, which would be at least equally justifiable in a world that changes so rapidly that an education twenty years old is out of date. Tradition governs what is taught and it holds a firm control upon the manner in which it is taught. Tradition determines who shall teach; we have already discussed some of the traditional requirements for teaching. It is this same sort of tradition also which largely determines how students and teachers shall think of each other.

The best example of a mingled tradition in part absorbed from the general culture of the group and in part produced in the particular institution is the tradition of teachers. In so far as this tradition of teachers is derived from outside a particular school, it is drawn by teachers from the general culture, and from association with members of the teaching profession everywhere. In so far as it is a purely local product, it is produced by the teachers in the institution and is passed on from one teacher to another. We may mention some cardinal points of the teacher tradition as it is usually encountered, making due allowance for local variations. There is a teacher morality, and this morality regulates minutely the teacher's relations with his students and with other teachers; it affects his relations with other teachers especially where the standing of those teachers with students might be affected. There is a character ideal of the teacher; nearly every group which lives long in one stereotyped relation with other groups produces its character ideal, and this ideal for teachers is clearly observable. When teachers say of a colleague, "He's a school teacher," they mean that he conforms to this local character idea. (It usually implies that the individual puts academic above other considerations, is conscientious in his duties, and exacting in the demands he makes upon himself and others.) There is a taboo on seeking popularity among students, and this taboo operates with dreadful force if it is thought that popularity seeking is complicated by disloyalty to the teacher group. There is a traditional attitude toward students; this attitude requires that a certain distance be kept between teachers and students. The desire to be fair is very likely not the strongest motive that teachers have for keeping students at a distance, but it is certainly one of the consequences of the policy, and it has in its own right the compelling value of an article of faith. None may violate the code of equality with impunity. Teachers have likewise a certain traditional attitude toward each other. The most obvious manifestation of this traditional attitude is the ceremoniousness of teachers toward each other and toward the administration of the school. It seems clear that this is the ceremoniousness of a fighting group which does not care to endanger its prestige with underlings by allowing any informality to arise within itself. Another interesting observation that has often been made about particular groups of teachers is that they discriminate markedly between veterans and new men. This distinction is in the folkways. Occasionally there is a more or less definite ceremony of initiation, more rarely, actual hazing.

The indigenous tradition of the school is found in its purest form among students. This tradition, when it has been originated on the spot, is passed on, largely by word of mouth, from one student to another. Some of the indigenous tradition has been originated by the faculty, and then imposed upon the students; once it has been accepted by students, however, it may be passed on by student groups. Some of the traditional observances which students follow are not home-grown; there is a great literature of school life, and students occasionally appear who are obviously playing the parts of story-book heroes. Besides, there exists in the culture of any community a set of traditional attitudes toward school and school life, varying from one social class to another, and from family to family; these attitudes influence profoundly the attitudes which students have toward school life. Nevertheless the tradition of students is very largely indigenous within the particular school. Although this sort of tradition varies much in detail from one school to another, we may mention certain characteristics of the fundamental patterns.

Like teacher morality, student morality is the morality of a fighting group, but the differences appear in that the student group is subordinate, and its morality is relevant to that situation. Social distance between student and teacher seems as definitely a part of the student code as of the teacher code. The student must not like the teacher too much, for that is naivete. There is the well-known schoolboy code, the rule that students must never give information to teachers which may lead to the punishment of another student. Certain folkways grow up in every group of school children, as the folkway of riding to grade school on a bicycle or of not riding to high school on a bicycle, and these folkways have a great influence over the behavior of all members of the group. These groups of children are arranged in stair-steps. Membership in the older group implies repudiation of the folkways of the younger group. No one more foolish than the high-school boy on a bicycle, or the college boy wearing a high-school letter! Interlocking groups look forward only, each group aping its elders and despising its juniors. In modern schools, there is a whole complex of traditions pertaining to activities; it seems that all activities are meritorious, that they are in some way connected with the dignity and honor of the school, that some activities are more meritorious than the others.

Sometimes a whole social system is carried in the tradition of students, and such social systems are very resistant to change. The fagging system, or a system of any sort of hazing, may persist

for decades against the best efforts of highly efficient teachers
and administrators to change them. A collegiate institution comes to
mind which has conducted such a struggle for upwards of a hundred
years. We are led to believe that hazing, at least, having its roots in the
desire of those already in the group to dominate new members (and
having its parallel on the faculty), would be destined to have some
place in the culture which the young work out for themselves even if it
had no sanction in tradition. In other words, the manner in which the
young experience the universe recreates a hazing problem in every generation of students.

The cultural anthropologists have taught us to analyze the actions
of human beings living in a certain culture into culture patterns. Those
partially formalized structures of behavior known as "activities" will
serve as excellent examples of culture patterns existing in the school.
Among the "activities" to be found in most public schools may be
mentioned athletics, work on the school paper, oratory and debating,
glee club work, Hi-Y work, dramatics, participation in social clubs, de-
partmental clubs, literary societies, fraternities, etc. Each of these activities may be thought of as representing a more or less ritualized form
of behavior carried out by the individual as a member of a group and,
often, a representative of the larger group. There is a set form for these
activities. There is merit in these activities, and that merit seems to rest
ultimately upon the notion that group welfare and group prestige are
involved in them; the honor of the high school is damaged if the team
loses. ("Our team is our frame-protector. On, boys, for we expect a
touchdown from you—" is unpoetic, but explicit on this point.) But
there is intrinsic, irrational merit in them, too, as in the trading of the
Trobiand Islanders. There is distinction in these activities for upon the
prominence which participation in them gives the individual in the eyes
of the school at large, and in part upon the recognition which the adult
group accords them. The variety of activities is almost endless, for each
of the activities mentioned above has many subdivisions; these subdivisions are sometimes arranged in something of a hierarchy as in athletics, where the greatest distinction attaches to football, a little less to
basketball, less yet to baseball and track. These activities are commonly
justified on the grounds that they actually prepare for life, since they
present actual life situations; their justification for the faculty is in their
value as a means of control over restless students. It is noteworthy that
a competitive spirit prevails in nearly all activities. Not all activities are
really competitive, but the struggle for places may make them so, and
the desirability of having some place in some school activity makes the

competition for places keen. One "makes" the school orchestra or glee club quite as truly as one makes the football team.

These culture patterns of activities are partly artificial and faculty-determined, and partly spontaneous. In so far as they have been evolved by the faculty, they have been intended as means of control, as outlets for adolescent energies or substitutes for tabooed activities. They represent also the faculty's attempt to make school life interesting and to extend the influence of the school. Any activity, however, which is to affect the life of students at all deeply, any activity, then, which aspires to a greater influence than is exerted by the Latin Club or the Cercle Francais, must have a spontaneous basis, and must appeal to students by presenting to them behavior patterns of considerable intrinsic interest. Each activity usually has some sort of faculty connection, and the status of the faculty adviser is thought to rise or fall with the prosperity or unprosperity of the activity which he promotes. Activities, then, increase in importance and gain recognition from the faculty through the efforts of interested faculty members, as well as through their own intrinsic appeal to students. (A change is taking place in our teacher idiom. The young teacher now refers to himself not as the teacher of a certain subject, but as the coach of a certain activity.)

Of all activities athletics is the chief and the most satisfactory. It is the most flourishing and the most revered culture pattern. It has been elaborated in more detail than any other culture pattern. Competitive athletics has many forms. At the head of the list stands football, still regarded as the most diagnostic test of the athletic prowess of any school. Then come basketball, baseball, track, lightweight football, lightweight basketball, girls' basketball, girls' track, etc. Each of these activities has importance because the particular school and its rivals are immersed in a culture stream of which competitive athletics is an important part. Each school has its traditional rivals, and a greater psychic weighting is attached to the games with traditional rivals than to those with other schools. Schools are arranged in a hierarchy, and may therefore win moral victories while actually suffering defeats. Pennsylvania wins, but Swarthmore triumphs.

The code of sportsmanship becomes a very important ethical principle, one almost says the very source and spring of all ethics, for youngsters and for those adults who hold to the conflict theory of human life. There are men who insist that they learned the most important lessons of life upon the football field. They learned to struggle there and to hold on, and they learned to respect the rights of others and to play according to the rules. It may be surmised that men who have such a conception of life do not live in a very complex world. It is difficult to generalize about the effect of athletics upon the personalities of those participating. One might guess that it is in general favorable, and that its favorable effects are in the line of a growing into such roles as those mentioned above. Part of the technique, indeed, of schools and teachers who handle difficult cases consists in getting those persons interested in some form of athletics. This constitutes a wholesome interest, opens the way to a normal growth of personality, and inhibits abnormal interests and undesirable channels of growth.

The author would be inclined to account for the favorable influence of athletics upon school life in terms of changes effected in group alignments and the individual attitudes that go with them. It is perhaps as a means of unifying the entire school group that athletics seem most useful from the sociological point of view. There is a tendency for the school population to split up into its hostile segments of teachers and students and to be fragmented by cliques among both groups. The division of students into groups prevents a collective morale from arising and thereby complicates administration; the split between students and teachers is even more serious, for these two groups tend to become definite conflict groups, and conflict group tensions are the very antithesis of discipline. This condition athletics alleviates. Athletic games furnish a dramatic spectacle of the struggle of picked men against the common enemy, and this is a powerful factor in building up a group spirit which includes students of all kinds and degrees and unifies the teachers and the taught. In adult life we find the analogue of athletics in war; patriotism runs high when the country is attacked. Likewise we find the most certain value of punishment to be the unification of the group which punishes. Athletic sports use exactly the same mechanism in a controlled way for the attainment of a more limited end.

By furnishing all the members of the school population with an enemy outside the group, and by giving them an opportunity to observe and participate in the struggle against that enemy, athletics may prevent a conflict group tension from arising between students and teachers. The organization of the student body for the support of athletics, though it is certainly not without its ultimate disadvantages, may bring with it certain benefits for those who are interested in the immediate problems of administration. It is a powerful machine which is organized to whip all students into line for the support of athletic teams, and adroit school administrators learn to use it for the dissemination of other attitudes favorable to the faculty and the faculty policy.

In yet another way an enlightened use of athletics may simplify the problem of police work in the school. The group of athletes may be made to furnish a very useful extension of the faculty-controlled social order. Athletes have obtained favorable status by following out one faculty-determined culture pattern; they may be induced to adopt for themselves and to popularize other patterns of a similar nature. Athletes, too, in nearly any group of youngsters, are the natural leaders, and they are leaders who can be controlled and manipulated through the medium of athletics. Those who are fortunate enough to be on the squad of a major sport occupy a favored social position; they are at or near the center of their little universe; they belong to the small but important group of men who are doing things. They have much to lose by misconduct, and it is usually not difficult to make them see it. They have, too, by virtue of their favored position, the inevitable conservatism of the privileged classes, and they can be brought to take a stand for the established order. In addition, the athletes stand in a very close and personal relationship to at least one faculty member, the coach, who has, if he is an intelligent man or a disciplinarian, an opportunity to exert a great influence upon the members of the team. The coach has prestige, he has favors to give, and he is in intimate rapport with his players. Ordinarily he uses his opportunities well. As the system usually works out, the members of the major teams form a nucleus of natural leaders among the student body, and their influence is more or less conservative and more or less on the side of what the faculty would call decent school citizenship.

There are other activities. Their effects upon the school group, and upon the personalities of the individuals who participate in them, differ widely.

The most important consideration affecting our judgment of any particular activity is its effect upon the personality of the participant, and this effect is usually beneficial in proportion as the activity gives to the individual opportunities for wholesome self-expression and growth through interested self-activity. A further value of activities is that they may often give a sense of solidarity to a wide group, which is an essential part of the training of the young; it is a part which is doubtless overdone at present, but it would be very regrettable if it were to be omitted altogether. From the faculty point of view, activities have a very great value in facilitating faculty control of school life. The growth of school activities in recent years, and not the development of new theories of education, would seem to have been chiefly instrumental in making school interesting for the student, and undoubtedly helps to account for the recent success of the public schools in holding their students through the years of high school. There is added the fact that most of the activities carried on in the schools would probably exist in one form or another whether the faculty fostered them or not. If the faculty is able to foster and control them, there is at least a greater likelihood that they will subserve ends acceptable to the faculty than there would be if activities were quite spontaneous.

CLASS BIASES IN THE TEACHING OF VALUES*

by Celia Burns Stendler

The process of socialization, by which the child is brought under control of society, has been of considerable interest to psychiatrists and child guidance experts for many years. It is also a process which concerns teachers, for bringing the child under control of society is part and parcel of sound character and wholesome personality development, long accepted as ends toward which the schools should work. Because they are implicated in the socialization of the child it is important for teachers to be informed concerning the factors which affect the process. One of these factors which is being increasingly recognized as significant is that of social class. How social class may influence the socialization of the child will be discussed in this article.

It is generally recognized that the years from two to six constitute an important part of the socialization process. In the infant and young baby stage, the child is regarded as "cute" and "darling" regardless of what he does. But once he begins to walk, to go outside the home, perhaps to mingle with other children, he is made subject to pressures designed to make him conform to the mores of our society. He receives instruction, deliberate or incidental, from adults and from peer groups, which builds up in him certain attitudes toward property, authority, aggression, sex, achievement, and his role in his peer group. This instruction is enforced by rewards and punishments so that the child gradually builds inside himself a system of values which guides his choice of conduct even when adults are not present. At three he may refrain from hitting a playmate over the head because Mother is looking

*From Celia B. Stendler, "Class Biases in the Teaching of Values," *Progressive Education,* Volume 27 (February 1950), pp. 123-126. Reprinted by permission.

and he knows he will be punished for his aggression; the socialization process is much farther along when he wants to hit but refrains, even when no adults are near, because he has taken inside himself the warning voice of his parents and society.

HOW THE CHILD LEARNS VALUES

A consideration of how the child learns values, of how socialization takes place, is necessary at this point. While much light still needs to be shed on the process, it seems clear that socialization in the preschool years is facilitated by two factors: (1) a consistent discipline, and (2) the child's desire to be like his parents. Through identification with his parents, the child takes inside himself their values and begins to acquire a conscience which will guide him in doing good or bad regardless of whether he is observed or not. Two conditions are proposed by Davis as necessary if socialization is going to take place.

"First, the child should receive complete love from his parents or from his parent substitutes; second, he should receive socially appropriate prohibitions from them. The love relationship seems to be necessary as a basis of the best type of identification. The prohibitions are necessary in order that the child may take into himself a warning and punishing voice. Thus, parents who never punish their children (either by corporal punishment or by withdrawing affection from them) would not be able to instill a warning, punishing conscience in them. On the other hand, parents who never show affection to their children would not instill a conscience in them, either, no matter how much they punish them, because their children would not love them enough to want to be good. (There is some evidence that some children can identify with cruel repressive parents on the basis of fear. But this identification probably leads to pathological results.)[1]

But socialization is not necessarily completed by six years of age. Even after the child enters public school the process continues, with the teacher becoming an important socializing agent. In addition to reading, writing and arithmetic, she also teaches, directly or indirectly, a system of values which may or may not become a part of the character structure of her pupils.

It is at this point that a consideration of social class becomes important. As some sociologists have pointed out, we live in a society

---

[1] Allison Davis and Robert Havighurst, *Father of the Man.* Houghton Mifflin Company, Boston 1947, pp. 177-178.

which is stratified into social classes, distinguished one from the other by such factors as income, ancestors, housing, occupation, social activities, and mores. But even more fundamental as far as this particular problem goes is the possibility that social classes may also differ among each other in the values which each class cherishes. This may have particular significance for teachers of lower and upper class children, for such teachers, as members of a middle class, may be trying to impart their class values to the children of other social classes.

WHOSE VALUES DOES THE SCHOOL RECOGNIZE?

Perhaps a look at what values the school does attempt to teach is in order here. While there is no research which bears directly on this question, some light on the subject is shed by two studies primarily designed to answer other questions. These studies have been concerned with the kinds of child behavior which teachers regard as serious. From the results, it would appear that children who answer back, who fight, who are tardy, who swear or use toilet talk, who are dirty, who do not respect property, who bully, are the problem children as far as the school is concerned. One might infer from these findings that the teachers hold in high esteem such values as respect for authority and property, work, non-aggression, promptness, cleanliness, and sexlessness.

But while the middle-class teacher may teach her group that "nice" people don't swear, a lower-class pupil (or an upper-class) in her room may not accept her judgment; indeed, his parents may have a rich and varied vocabulary and still be "nice" people in his eyes. The middle-class teacher may teach, "We don't fight" to children who are taught at home that we do, and that they had better fight to stick up for their rights. Respect for authority may be drilled into the middle-class child, whereas the lower-class may suspect the respectful child as an apple polisher. In "Father of the Man" the conflict in values is well illustrated in the case studies of the two Washington children.

"Mary, who is praised by her middle-class teacher for being quiet and anxious to please, is criticized by most of her family for the same behavior. Her softness and compliancy are regarded by Hazel and all her sisters as traits of a schemer and of an apple polisher. Most of her family believe that she is designing . . .

"Paulette's aggression, on the other hand, seems to her mother and Hazel to prove her honesty . . . In her slum community, where a curse and a blow—a readiness to 'tell people off' and let them 'like it or lump it'—are highly admired, Paulette is popular."

What happens when the school attempts to teach values which run counter to those of its pupils?

Several possibilities suggest themselves. For one, the pupil may learn two or more patterns for behaving. He may learn that in school one talks and acts in a particular way but that outside of school one acts in a different way. He may discontinue fighting on the playgrounds but fight when a block away from the school; or he may refrain from cursing in the boys' locker room because someone may squeal but continue to do so when playing in his neighborhood. Children who adopt this pattern have not taken within themselves the values the school is teaching; they are actually rejecting these values. They are like the three-year-old in that they are learning a method of adjustment in order to avoid punishment.

A second possible outcome of a conflict in values is that the pupil may reject the values of the school openly as well as privately. Such pupils will continue to exhibit in school the kinds of behavior based upon values learned outside the school. They fight and swear; they are disrespectful of people and property. They are the pupils who are continually in trouble with school authorities and who drop out of school when they reach the legal leaving age. However, in their out-of-school life, they may be the Paulette Washington, accepted and liked by their own social class, and secure in their feelings of belonging to such a group.

A third possibility is that the pupil may accept the values which the school is teaching, and may substitute these for the values of his own sub-culture group. These are the pupils who become socially mobile; who will eventually leave their own social class and move on to the middle class as they become more and more like the middle class in their ways of thinking, speaking and acting. But such children in accepting middle-class values wholeheartedly may find themselves rejected and regarded with suspicion by those in their own culture. The case of Mary Washington, to which reference has already been made, illustrates the point. While moving into the middle class may bring with it the advantages that go with middle-class membership, it also imposes a penalty, the penalty of growing up without a feeling of belongingness. The socially mobile child may find himself an outcast from his own class before he has made the grade with a higher social class group.

How To Teach Values Which Are in Conflict
With the Pupil's Values

If the schools are going to be effective agents in building sound character and wholesome personality, the last choice mentioned in the above paragraph where the child accepts the values of the school is obviously the goal toward which we should be working. But in order to build values effectively, and with less cost to the socially mobile, several important steps need to be taken. First it would seem necessary for schools to re-examine the values which they are attempting to teach. While middle-class values of cleanliness, respect for authority and property, and others already indicated are important to a degree, one might question the compulsiveness of the middle-class adherence to them and also the extent to which they are advocated. While a certain standard of cleanliness is necessary for health reasons, one might raise questions about making a fetish out of clean finger nails. While a certain amount of respect for authority is necessary, one might question the teacher who holds this value so rigidly that she becomes emotionally upset when a youngster threatens her authority or her control of the group. Again, while proper use of school materials is something schools should be teaching, one might question the extreme emphasis teachers place on the use of two paper towels to dry the hands instead of one. What we are arguing for here is that teachers develop more insight into the origin of their own values. When a teacher finds herself unduly disturbed by pupil conduct—that is, disturbed out of proportion to the actual deed when she stands off and looks at herself objectively, she might well see if the misdeed is one which grates upon her middle-class personality. The next step for the teacher to take is to see whether the particular value being violated by the pupil deserves the prestige she has placed upon it.

Not only the extent to which middle class values are advocated, but also the choice of values to be emphasized needs to be examined critically. In *Adolescent Character and Personality,* the authors point out, "The influence of the school affects primarily the sense of responsibility and honesty; it is less effective as far as loyalty, moral courage and friendliness are concerned." A recommendation from the author is to the effect that "They (boys and girls) should learn to make distinctions between the lesser mores of eating, drinking, amusement, clothing, and marriage customs, which differ from one social group to another, and the more basic moral qualities such as honesty, loyalty, kindness, and courage, which are very nearly universal." Readers, too, will no doubt be in agreement that these basic qualities are more important than saying "Excuse me" when one walks in front of the teacher, yet they are receiving far less attention in our schools than the lesser mores. Such a re-evaluation of our teaching of values may result in a program which will make better sense to lower class children and therefore stand a better chance of being accepted by them.

A third step necessary for schools to take if they are to be effective in teaching values is to establish a warm emotional climate in the classroom. This means that teachers must accept all pupils regardless of social class background, for the child who feels himself rejected by the teacher will not accept the values for which she stands. This means that teachers must watch their own emotional reactions to child behavior to see to what extent these may be class conditioned. For a horrible example of class-biased attitudes towards pupils, the reader is referred to *Elmtown's Youth*. Here we have an account of how a superintendent of schools and a high school principal excuse upper-class youngsters who evade staying after school for being late. This is contrasted with their shocking treatment of "Boney" Johnson, a lower-class member who is also tardy:

> When school was out that afternoon, the Superintendent stood in the hall near the side exit, Mr. White, a teacher, watched the front door, while the principal patrolled the building. Mr. Garner, another teacher, was in the detention room. After the building was cleared of students and most of the teachers had gone home, the Superintendent walked back to his office, but the principal stood outside the front door. Suddenly the door was thrown open from the outside, and angry voices were heard. The Superintendent rushed out of his office and stood at the head of the stairs. The principal pushed and shoved "Boney" up the stairs as he repeated, "You can't get away with that stuff." As they neared the top, "Boney" broke from his grasp and started down the hall toward the side door. The Superintendent leaped and grabbed him by the coat collar with his left hand. "Boney" turned and started to fight. The principal spun him around, seized the visor of his cap with his right hand and yanked it down over his eyes. While "Boney" was fighting to get the cap off his face, the principal hit him three times with the heel of his hand on the back of the neck near the base of the skull. "Boney" cursed, struggled, and hit in all directions. Soon he broke free and ran toward the Superintendent, who shook and slapped him three or four times. Both men then grabbed

him by the arms and shook him vigorously. The Superintendent angrily screeched, "You're going out of this building. You're never coming back until you bring your father and we talk this over." By this time, the three had reached the front door. "Boney" was shoved outside. He stood there, cursing and threatening both men with violence. In a few minutes he composed himself, straightened his clothes, and walked away, muttering to himself.

Obviously, teachers and administrators who are hoping to build the basic moral qualities of honesty, kindliness, loyalty and courage cannot do so in such a fashion. If we want children to accept the values we are attempting to teach, it is necessary for children to feel that we like them and accept them.

Still a fourth step for teachers to take in facilitating the socialization process is to work on group structures in the classroom. In addition to being liked and accepted, children should have a feeling of belonging in order to accept more readily the values that the school is attempting to teach. By the use of socio-metric measures the teacher can discover which children are isolates and then work to bring those youngsters into the group. She can also find out about the cliques operating in her room, and through the use of projects give children in school at least the opportunity to know intimately and to work with different social classes.

The measures that have been suggested so far have been in line with current thinking on the problem. The fifth suggestion, however, goes much deeper. It suggests that teacher should carefully open up the problem of social class with older children and help them see class differences in values in so far as we know them. Research has shown that by the time the children reach the eighth grade (indeed, in some cases, the sixth) they are pretty well aware of the fact that a class structure exists in their particular community. Perhaps then, at the junior high school level teachers could profitably explore this issue with their pupils. There is no beaten path for teachers to follow in this connection, but experimentally-minded teachers might cull from some of the case studies in the numerous volumes on social class, materials to be presented in social studies, or English, or problems of living classes. Pupils might analyze and discuss the case studies and in so doing, develop keener insight into their own value systems. It is to be hoped also, that with their new insights, pupils will be helped to build a system of values that will contribute to the moral fibre of our democracy.

INTERGROUP RELATIONS IN THE ELEMENTARY SCHOOL*

by Anne Phillips McCreary

Prejudice is not only a world-wide problem but also a crucial factor in world stability. At a recent conference sponsored by UNESCO a five-nation research program was set up to study prejudice in young people. Those attending the conference noted that group prejudices held by youth are a serious deterrent to both internal and international harmony and understanding. They pointed out, however, that these feelings and attitudes are learned, not inborn, and that the climate of opinion which prevails in national institutions has a strong influence on the development of prejudices. In light of this, the conference suggested that a statement be sent to teacher education centers emphasizing the value of helping teachers to learn ways to combat prejudice and to promote non-prejudiced attitudes.

This is a commendable suggestion. However, before teachers can learn ways to combat prejudice, an awareness of its presence and a sensitivity to its signs are essential. With this in mind, an attempt has been made to examine intergroup relations in the elementary school. The discussion will be limited to the teacher, the child, and the elementary school system as they appear in upstate New York. Those aspects which could foster prejudice will be selected, and suggestions for teachers will be presented.

THE CHILD

The child enters the elementary school with many attitudes already formed through interaction as a member of various groups, both within

*From Anne Phillips McCreary, "Intergroup Relations in the Elementary School," *The Journal of Teacher Education,* Volume XIV, No. 1 (March, 1963), pp. 74-79. Copyright, 1963, National Education Association of the United States. Reprinted by permission.

and outside the family circle. These attitudes reflect the values of our society. In this informal, educative process the child learns acceptable ways of conforming, identifying, and displaying aggression. He forms definite ideas of certain things that are good or bad, right or wrong, clean or dirty. These ideas extend to people also. For example, studies of prejudice in pre-school children reveal that both Negro and white children see the Negro as inferior; Jewish children are rejected most often; [1], [2] and at the age of four, systems of race-related values are well formed. [3]

Before he enters school, the child has already formed a stereotype of the family, based on his family, and of the good child, based on standards set up by his parents. Within the family group, parents condition the attitudes of their children, sometimes unknowingly. Trager and Yarrow,[4] interviewing parents, found that they didn't understand their own feelings of prejudice; that they often communicated prejudice and misconceptions to children through inadequate or imprecise explanations; and that they created for their children a negative set which might have been positive. The child, then, as he enters school, is much like a mirror, reflecting the attitudes which are important in the groups in which he functions as a member.

Research also reveals that prejudice increases from kindergarten to grade two.[5] Certain factors within the elementary schools themselves increase intergroup tension and attitudes of prejudice and discrimination. In the public school system, a degree of segregation is produced by (1) school zoning which restricts the choice of a school; (2) residential living which is segregated; (3) transfer, transportation, and school boundaries; and (4) school holidays which are scheduled to conform only to the Christian religion. In addition, schools often follow community patterns of segregation, prestige, and leadership.

---

[1] Marion Radke Yarrow; Helen G. Trager; and Hadassah Davis. "Social Perceptions and Attitudes of Children." *Genetic Psychology Monographs* 40:327-47; 1949.

[2] Helen G. Trager and Marion Radke Yarrow. *They Learn What They Live.* New York: Harper, 1952.

[3] Mary Ellen Goodman. *Race Awareness in Young Children.* Cambridge, Massachusetts: Addison-Wesley Press, 1952.

[4] *Op. cit.*

[5] *Ibid.*

THE COMMUNITY

At the community level, leadership comes from the local school board. Members usually belong to the upper-middle or upper socioeconomic classes. These citizens have been shaped by our culture and reflect, to some degree, the wishes and values of the community members. Administrative policies followed by these members are often discriminatory with respect to (1) committees for the planning of educational procedure; (2) salary and promotions; and (3) the manner of carrying out administrative procedures.[6] Discrimination is also evident in the hiring of teachers. According to Cook, "A white Protestant applicant has the best chance for job placement."[7]

Discrimination continues after the teacher is hired. Brookover[8] outlines the community expectations for many teachers as follows: In general, the teacher is supposed to be dominant, maintain order, keep social distance, live in the community but take part in only certain activities such as religion and the PTA, live by a special code, and satisfy all groups. Not only do community rules discriminate against teachers; salaries are also discriminatory. In many schools, teachers are paid less than the school janitor.

THE SCHOOL

Certain procedures within some school systems tend to perpetuate the concept of the teacher as an underpaid drudge with little freedom or status. For example, teachers' salaries sometimes depend upon a rating which is based on inspection. Attendance at professional meetings is closely checked: no attendance, no pay. Among the teachers there may be segregation by age, sex, interest, length of service, and religion.[9]

Within the school system, goals, organization, curriculum, and textbooks all influence intergroup relations. Although the goals of education are stated in broad general terms, the basic aim is to help each child to

---

[6] Clyde B. Moore, and William E. Cole. *Sociology in Educational Practice.* Cambridge, Massachusetts: Riverside Press, 1952, p. 259.

[7] Lloyd A. Cook, and Elaine F. Cook. "Community Expectations of the Teacher." In B. N. Melter (ed.), *Education in Society: Readings.* New York: Thomas Y. Crowell, 1958, pp. 254-60.

[8] Wilbur B. Brookover. *A Sociology of Education.* New York: American Book Company, 1955.

[9] *Ibid.*

develop attitudes and understandings and to acquire the skills and knowledge necessary to live in a democracy. Individual difference is the keynote, and teaching is aimed at changing behavior and not primarily at instilling facts. Thus, the goals of education would appear to favor intergroup relations which are desirable.

With this increasing emphasis on the importance of the individual, curricular and organizational changes were necessary. These led to a type of discrimination and segregation. In order to meet individual needs, variety and choice entered the program. Children were grouped according to ability and achievement. Under this system, teaching tends to be geared to the average student. Also, standard tests used for measuring intelligence and achievement are discriminatory in that they depend chiefly upon language ability. In addition, as Dodson so aptly warns, "A vast reservoir of potential creativeness is lost in each generation because educational leadership isn't competent to hurdle gaps of social class and motivate children of all classes to develop latent talents."[10] Simpson and Yinger[11] focus the effect of this discrimination at the national level where education is of political, social, and economic importance in a free society.

Not only do tests and grouping procedures discriminate in the ways which have been mentioned. Warner[12] feels that the American school system selects a minority and trains them for social mobility. His Yankee City Study revealed that the class system exercises control over both the curriculum and the pupils' choice of subjects. Upper and middle class children took courses which would move them up so that they would fit into a higher status group. The lower class children took courses which would help them adjust to the socio-economic class into which they were born.

While this type of segregation is not so openly labeled in the elementary school, slow learners are often segregated. Children may also be assigned to the low, high, or average sections of a specific grade on the basis of ability or achievement. Within the classroom, groups are formed in different subject areas, and even though the children in a particular group are given the innocuous name, "Robin," they still know the Robins are the "dumb ones" who can't read yet.

---

[10] Don W. Dodson. "The Impact of Sociology Upon Education." In B. N. Meltzer *et al.* (eds.), *Education in Society: Readings.* New York: Thomas Y. Crowell, 1958, pp. 7-11.

[11] George Simpson, and J. Yinger. *Racial and Cultural Minorities.* New York: Harper, 1953.

[12] W. Lloyd Warner; Robert J. Havighurst; and Martin B. Loeb. *Who Shall Be Educated?* New York: Harper, 1944, p. 61.

In most curriculums there is no mention of intergroup relations, and it is assumed that the topic will be introduced incidentally. Allport[13] found in a study of college students that only 8 percent of the subjects recalled having learned scientific facts about race. What, then, might a survey of upper elementary grades reveal? Race, religion, prejudice, and discrimination are almost taboo subjects at this level.

Stepchildren of the curriculum are the so-called extracurricular activities within the school. These activities often exclude such minorities as the lower income group, students who must ride to school by bus, and below-average students. Even if there are activities which are open to minority groups, these are likely to be low in prestige. All organizations within a school seldom have equal dignity and status.

Within the school, then, the organizational pattern of having groups formed on a variety of bases forces a form of segregation. Tests used for selecting group members are discriminatory. Nonacademic activities also discriminate unjustly. Finally, intergroup relations is not included in most courses of study in the elementary school.

If, as the case seems to be, most teaching of intergroup relations is supposed to be carried on incidentally with other subjects, it is appropriate to examine textbooks used in other areas. In many cases, teachers have no choice of textbooks but must use those which are provided. If the teacher does have a choice, he is rarely primarily concerned with implications for intergroup relations. When this is a consideration, the task is a discouraging one. Either references to the problem are missing or they are of an indirect nature and are more destructive than helpful.

An appraisal of textbooks conducted by a committee of the American Council on Education pointed to the worst errors in the area of intergroup relations as: (1) omission of pertinent basic information; (2) undue simplification; (3) unwarranted generalization; (4) failure to come to grips with basic issues.[14] Placing part of the responsibility upon the curriculum makers, whose plans guide the textbook writers, this committee said:

They have failed to think through the implications of cultural democracy. They emphasize the success of individual persons rather than cultural patterns.

---

[13] Gordon W. Allport. "Resolving Intergroup Tensions: An Appraisal of Methods." In Lloyd A. Cooke (ed.), *Toward Better Human Relations*. Detroit, Michigan: Wayne University, 1952, pp. 37-72.

[14] *Intergroup Relations in Teaching Materials*. Washington, D.C.: the Council, 1949.

Specific information pertaining to prejudice in textbooks is reported by Stewart[15] in a comprehensive survey. Many of his points apply not only to intergroup relations but to the evaluation of any textbook.

Even at the primary level, prejudice is revealed in textbooks. In primers and pre-primers the family depicted is always one which is white, Protestant Anglo-Saxon. It consists of two or three children, a dog, and a cat. The father works in an office. The family lives in a suburban home and visits grandparents who live on a farm. Parents and friends are white. If a Negro is introduced, he is the porter on a train; if an Oriental appears, he is a laundryman. Authors of children's books for supplementary reading are presenting a more realistic picture. Several lists are available, two of which are *Reading Ladders for Human Relations*[16] and *About 100 Books.*[17] The National Film Board of Canada provides material for intergroup education in a series of fine films which present both sides of cultural groups. A list of these appears in *One America.*[18]

In curricular areas where textbooks do not play a prominent role, teachers lean heavily toward stereotyped ideas. In art, music, drama, and crafts at the elementary level the Mexican is pictured asleep under the cactus plant; the Indian with feathered head-dress and tomahawk in hand; the Negro picking cotton, playing a banjo, or eating watermelon.

In summary, textbooks and teaching materials are not, at present, very helpful in the teaching of intergroup relations, and teachers should be critical and careful in their choices and in their presentation of facts in this area.

SUGGESTIONS FOR TEACHERS

The school, the teacher, the books, and the child have been examined for factors which may lead to prejudice and discrimination. When the child enters school these factors combine, and a multiplicity of new opportunities for interaction arises. Whether this will result in increased understanding and tolerance for others or in a reinforcement of already established roots of prejudice will depend upon several things. The discussion of these will focus first on the teacher and the child in the schoolroom. With this as background, suggestions for a more specific program in education for intergroup relations will be presented.

---

[15] Maxwell S. Stewart. *Prejudice in Textbooks.* Public Affairs Pamphlet No. 160. New York: National Conference on Christians and Jews.

[16] Margaret M. Heaton, and Helen B. Lewis, Washington, D. C.: American Council on Education, 1955.

[17] New York: American Jewish Committee, 1951.

[18] Francis J. Brown and Joseph E. Roucek. Englewood Cliffs, New Jersey: Prentice-Hall, 1952.

Taba[19] lists school factors which affect interpersonal relations. Although these reflect school policy, it is still possible for the teacher, within her own classroom, to exert a personal influence (except in Area B). These factors are as follows:

A. Homogeneous Grouping.
   1. Reduced chance for interrelating.
   2. Narrowness of mind and feeling.
   3. Lowered self-expectations.
   4. Low economic group and minority racial groups are placed together where they have no opportunity to learn the common culture.
   5. The stigma of the group destroys motivation and self-respect.
   6. There is no feeling of groupness.
B. Opportunities for Interaction.
   1. Seats fastened down.
   2. Rigid routine in large schools.
   3. Large classes.
   4. School work is geared to the individual, not to the group.
C. Standards and Rewards.
   1. Uniform standards with each person responsible for himself.
D. Opportunities to Function as a Group Member.
E. Teacher's Attitudes.

The most important of these factors is the teacher. She must work within the organizational pattern, restricted by curriculum and textbooks and inhibited by the community's expectations. However, within her own classroom she can be effective, since atmosphere and method are more important than organization and material. It is the teacher who sets the tone and who decides upon the best method for establishing and reaching goals. One goal of education is to develop attitudes and values which will lead to a democratic type of behavior. Trager and Yarrow[20] suggest that this be done by focusing education on people and human relations so that intercultural education is "the curriculum permeated throughout by democratic values."

Conclusions based on the Lewin, Lippitt, and White study indicate that authoritarian procedures in the classroom impair independence and initiative and give rise to hostility and aggression.[21] There are varying

[19] Hilda Taba. *Elementary Curriculum in Intergroup Relations.* Washington, D. C.: American Council on Education, 1949.

[20] *Op. cit.,* p. 362.

[21] K. Lewin; R. Lippitt; and R. K. White. "Patterns of Aggressive Behavior in Experimentally Created 'Social Climate.' " *Journal of Social Psychology* 10:271-99; 1939.

degrees of authoritarianism and of democracy in the organization and management of a classroom. Many teachers would describe themselves as giving democratic leadership, but in reality the choices which they offer may be of the either/or type and the planning which the pupils do may amount to no more than the carrying out of plans which the teacher has previously made and skillfully edged the children into.

The teacher may set the tone for democratic behavior by establishing an informal classroom where children are free to move around and to work in small groups or individually. Psychological freedom, mutual respect for each individual, and freedom to express ideas should be present. Competitive activities should be minimal and talent in diverse areas recognized. Gitler[22] emphasizes the fact that differences do not create problems. The ways in which we regard and react to these differences and the degree to which we respect and accept them create the problem. Most teachers have difficulty in accepting differences in feelings of what is right and wrong.[23] They demand absolute conformity.

The teacher sets the tone and establishes the definition of the "right" attitudes for the pupils. This is no easy task. The basic nature of the learning process presents a dilemma for the teaching of intergroup relations. MacIver[24] states that all education is a learning of distinctions. As the child distinguishes, he evaluates. This evaluation is often not on a continuum but is of the either/or type. Children are encouraged to classify and to generalize, and though these skills are necessary in organizing knowledge, they are destructive to intergroup relations. A democratic, valid basis for such classification and generalization in areas of race relations needs to be established by the teacher. It can be as simple as classifying according to likenesses rather than differences and generalizing on the basis of proved scientific facts. Children should be taught that, within each classification, each person should still be treated as a unique individual with distinguishing characteristics.

The child must realize that there is no rigid classification into which each person can be permanently placed within the school situation. Children should have membership in several different groups so that this becomes a real situation for them. In considering the area of think-

---

[22] Joseph B. Gitler (ed.). *Understanding Minority Groups.* New York: John Wiley, 1956, p. 136.

[23] Taba, *op. cit.*

[24] R. M. MacIver. *The More Perfect Union.* New York: Macmillan, 1948, p. 190.

ing, Taba[25] suggests another type of flexibility. Children can be taught that judgments are situational and relative. In order to teach this, the teacher must first believe it.

The teacher, then, plays a very important role in providing the proper atmosphere and in developing certain basic attitudes. If these functions are not carried out, education in intergroup relations will be practically impossible.

The importance of the teacher has been established. However, she cannot carry out a successful program in intergroup relations alone. Authorities agree that education by itself is not enough, that action is necessary. Attitudes and behavior must be transferred from the school situation to all other aspects of living. Thus, the community, family, school, and students should all be involved. Several methods have been suggested for promoting such a program.

The "contact" theory, which supposes that if persons come into contact with one another they will grow to understand, respect, and like one another, has received some support. An early report on the Philadelphia study stated that stereotype and prejudice do not arise primarily from interpersonal contacts and that contact will not change stereotype and prejudice. Children tend to regard the good contacts as exceptions.[26] A later study[27] showed that carefully planned contacts with factual information allayed suspicions and fears for young children. In his review of studies, Stember[28] found education more effective than contact in reducing prejudiced beliefs. Allport says,

> Truth and facts will, in the long run, weaken the prejudice of intelligent people.[29]

An effective program of intergroup relations will not be an "either/or" program but rather a constant, concentrated combination of any of the possible methods and approaches which are usable in the specific situation and at the particular time. For four-year-olds, for example, Goodman[30] suggests that a sensible, matter-of-fact explanation be given when children mention color. This information should be accurate; not black but brown. Color should be thought of on a continuum. The child

---

[25] Hilda Taba; E. H. Brady; and John T. Robinson. *Intergroup Education in Public Schools.* Washington, D. C.: American Council on Education, 1952.

[26] Yarrow; Trager; and Davis, *op. cit.*

[27] Trager and Yarrow, *op. cit.*

[28] Charles H. Stember. *The Effect of Education on Prejudice Against Minority Groups.* New York: the American Jewish Committee, 1960.

[29] Gordon W. Allport, *op. cit.,* p. 47.

[30] *Op. cit.*

should be taught to think that variety is attractive and that tastes in looks are not absolutes. Personality is important, too. Help the child to see that the unqualified generalization, "I don't like," doesn't make sense and must be backed up. Children should be helped to understand the power of hurtful words.

At the five-year-old level, the approach, the concepts, and the specific teaching will differ. This will be true throughout the elementary grades. But at any grade level, the goals of intercultural education as set forth by Kilpatrick and Van Til[31] will be reached by each pupil:

1. All pupils shall live together in mutual respect and appreciation based on personal merit.
2. Pupils shall build a clear understanding of what democracy means and learn to live it personally.
3. They shall learn techniques of group discussion and decision.
4. Pupils shall learn that freedom in a democracy is limited by the requirements of equal regard for others.
5. They shall learn to act on the basis of thinking, not habit or custom.
6. They shall build the habit of acting on the best that they find.
7. They shall know and respect cultural contributions of other groups.
8. They shall understand and appreciate the composite character of the American population and its advantages to us.
9. They shall study the causes and supporting statements of group prejudice.

SOCIAL-CLASS VARIATIONS IN THE TEACHER-PUPIL RELATIONSHIP*

by Howard S. Becker

The major problems of workers in the service occupations are likely to be a function of their relationship to their clients or customers, those for whom or on whom the occupational service is performed. Members of such occupations typically have some image of the "ideal" client, and it is in terms of this fiction that they fashion their conceptions of how their work ought to be performed, and their actual work tech-

[31] William Heard Kilpatrick and William Van Til. *Intercultural Attitudes in the Making.* New York: Harper, 1947, p. 5.

*From Howard S. Becker, "Social-Class Variations in the Teacher-Pupil Relationship," *Journal of Educational Sociology,* Volume 25 (1952), pp. 451-465. Reprinted by permission.

niques. To the degree that actual clients approximate this ideal the worker will have no "client problem."

In a highly differentiated urban society, however, clients will vary greatly, and ordinarily only some fraction of the total of potential clients will be "good" ones. Workers tend to classify clients in terms of the way in which they vary from this ideal. The fact of client variation from the occupational ideal emphasizes the intimate relation of the institution in which work is carried on to its environing society. If that society does not prepare people to play their client roles in the manner desired by the occupation's members there will be conflicts, and problems for the workers in the performance of their work. One of the major factors affecting the production of suitable clients is the cultural diversity of various social classes in the society. The cultures of particular social-class groups may operate to produce clients who make the worker's position extremely difficult.

We deal here with this problem as it appears in the experience of the functionaries of a large urban educational institution, the Chicago public school system, discussing the way in which teachers in this system observe, classify and react to class-typed differences in the behavior of the children with whom they work. The material to be presented is thus relevant not only to problems of occupational organization but also to the problem of differences in the educational opportunities available to children of various social-classes. Warner, Havighurst and Loeb and Hollingshead have demonstrated the manner in which the schools tend to favor and select out children of the middle classes. Allison Davis has pointed to those factors in the class cultures involved which make lower-class children less and middle-class children more adaptable to the work and behavioral standards of the school. This paper will contribute to the knowledge in this area by analyzing the manner in which the public school teacher reacts to these cultural differences and, in so doing, perpetuates the discrimination of our educational system against the lower-class child.

The analysis is based on sixty interviews with teachers in the Chicago system. The interviews were oriented around the general question of the problems of being a teacher and were not specifically directed toward discovering feelings about social-class differences among students. Since these differences created some of the teachers' most pressing problems they were continually brought up by the interviewees themselves. They typically distinguished three social-class groups with which they, as teachers, came in contact: (1) a bottom stratum, probably equivalent to the lower-lower and parts of the upper-lower class; (2) an upper stratum, probably equivalent to the upper-middle class; and (3) a middle stratum, probably equivalent to the lower-middle and parts of the upper-lower class. We will adopt the convention of referring to these groups as lower, upper and middle groups, but it should be understood that this terminology refers to the teachers' classification of students and not to the ordinary sociological description.

We will proceed by taking up the three problems that loomed largest in the teachers' discussion of adjustment to their students: (1) the problem of *teaching* itself, (2) the problem of *discipline,* and (3) the problem of the *moral acceptability* of the students. In each case the variation in the form of and adjustment to the problem by the characteristics of the children of the various class groups distinguished by teachers is discussed.

I

A basic problem in any occupation is that of performing one's given task successfully, and where this involves working with human beings their qualities are a major variable affecting the ease with which the work can be done. The teacher considers that she has done her job adequately when she has brought about an observable change in the children's skills and knowledge which she can attribute to her own efforts:

> Well, I would say that a teacher is successful when she is putting the material across to the children, when she is getting some response from them. I'll tell you something, teaching is a very rewarding line of work, because you can see those children grow under your hands. You can see the difference in them after you've had them for five months. You can see where they've started and where they've got to. And it's all yours. It really is rewarding in that way, you can see results and know that it's your work that brought those results about. She feels that she has a better chance of success in this area when her pupils are interested in attending and working hard in school, and are trained at home in such a way that they are bright and quick at school work. Her problems arise in teaching those groups who do not meet these specifications, for in these cases her teaching techniques, tailored to the "perfect" student, are inadequate to cope with the reality, and she is left with a feeling of having failed in performing her basic task.

Davis has described the orientations toward education in general, and schoolwork in particular, of the lower and middle classes:

Thus, our educational system, which next to the family is the most effective agency in teaching good work habits to middle class people, is largely ineffective and unrealistic with underprivileged groups. Education fails to motivate such workers because our schools and our society both lack *real rewards* to offer under-privileged groups. Neither lower class children or adults will work hard in school or on the job just to please the teacher or boss. They are not going to learn to be ambitious, to be conscientious, and to study hard, as if school and work were a fine character-building game, which one plays just for the sake of playing. They can see, indeed, that those who work hard at school usually have families that already have the occupations, homes, and social acceptance that the school holds up as the rewards of education. The underprivileged workers can see also that the chances of their getting enough education to make their attainment of these rewards in the future at all probable is very slight. Since they can win the rewards of prestige and social acceptance in their own slum groups without much education, they do not take very seriously the motivation taught by the school.

As these cultural differences produce variations from the image of the "ideal" student, teachers tend to use class terms in describing the children with whom they work.

Children of the lowest group, from slum areas, are characterized as the most difficult group to teach successfully, lacking in interest in school, learning ability, and outside training:

They don't have the right kind of study habits. They can't seem to apply themselves as well. Of course, it's not their fault; they aren't brought up right. After all, the parents in a neighborhood like that really aren't interested. . . . But, as I say, those children don't learn very quickly. A great many of them don't seem to be really interested in getting an education. I don't think they are. It's hard to get anything done with children like that. They simply don't respond.

In definite contrast are the terms used to describe children of the upper group:

In a neighborhood like this there's something about the children, you just feel like you're accomplishing so much more. You throw an idea out and you can see that it takes hold. The children know what you're talking about and they think about it. Then they come in with projects and pictures and additional information, and it just makes you feel good to see it. They go places and see things, and they know what you're talking about. For instance, you might be teaching social studies or geography. . . . You bring something up and a child says, "Oh, my parents took me to see that in the museum." You can just do more with material like that.

Ambivalent feelings are aroused by children of the middle group. While motivated to work hard in school they lack the proper out-of-school training:

> Well, they're very nice here, very nice. They're not hard to handle. You see, they're taught respect in the home and they're respectful to the teacher. They want to work and do well. . . . Of course, they're not too brilliant. You know what I mean. But they are very nice children and very easy to work with.

In short, the differences between groups make it possible for the teacher to feel successful at her job only with the top group; with the other groups she feels, in greater or lesser measure, that she has failed.

These differences in ability to do schoolwork, as perceived by teachers, have important consequences. They lead, in the first place, to differences in actual teaching techniques. A young high school teacher contrasted the techniques used in "slum" schools with those used in "better" schools:

> At S............, there were a lot of guys who were just waiting till they were sixteen so they could get out of school. L..............., everybody—well, a very large percentage, I'll say—was going on to secondary school, to college. That certainly made a difference in their classroom work. You had to teach differently at the different schools. For instance, at S..............., if you had demonstrations in chemistry they had to be pretty flashy, lots of noise and smoke, before they'd get interested in it. That wasn't necessary at L.............. Or at S.............. if you were having electricity or something like that you had to get the static electricity machine out and have them all stand around and hold hands so that they'd all get a little jolt.

Further, the teacher feels that where these differences are recognized by her superiors there will be a corresponding variation in the amount of work she is expected to accomplish. She expects that the amount of work and effort required of her will vary inversely with the social status of her pupils. This teacher compared schools from the extremes of the class range:

> So you have to be on your toes and keep up to where you're supposed to be in the course of study. Now, in a school like the D.............. slum school you're just not expected to complete all that work. It's almost impossible. For instance, in the second grade we're supposed to cover nine spelling words a week. Well, I can do that up here at the K.............. "better" school, they can take nine new words a week. But the best class I ever had at the D.............. was only able to achieve six words a week and they had to work

pretty hard to get that. So I never finished the year's work in spelling. I couldn't and I really wasn't expected to.

One resultant of this situation—in which less is expected of those teachers whose students are more difficult to teach—is that the problem becomes more aggravated in each grade, as the gap between what the children should know and what they actually do know becomes wider and wider. A principal of such a school describes the degeneration there of the teaching problem into a struggle to get a few basic skills across, in a situation where this cumulative effect makes following the normal program of study impossible:

The children come into our upper grades with very poor reading ability. That means that all the way through our school everybody is concentrating on reading. It's not like at a school like S.............. middle group where they have science and history and so on. At a school like that they figure that from first to fourth you learn to read and from fifth to eighth you read to learn. You use your reading to learn other material. Well, these children don't reach that second stage while they're with us. We have to plug along getting them to learn to read. Our teachers are pretty well satisfied if the children can read and do simple number work when they leave here. You'll find that they don't think very much of subjects like science, and so on. They haven't got any time for that. They're just trying to get these basic things over. . . . That's why our school is different from one like the S..............

Such consequences of teachers' differential reaction to various class groups obviously operate to further perpetuate those characteristics to which they object in the first place.

II

Discipline is the second of the teacher's major problems with her students. Willard Waller pointed to its basis when he wrote that "Teacher and pupil confront each other in the school with an original conflict of desires, and however much that conflict may be reduced in amount, or however much it may be hidden, it still remains." We must recognize that conflict, either actual or potential, is ever present in the teacher-pupil relationship, the teacher attempting to maintain her control against the children's efforts to break it. This conflict is felt even with those children who present least difficulty; a teacher who considered her pupils models of good behavior nevertheless said:

But there's that tension all the time. Between you and the students. It's hard on your nerves. Teaching is fun, if you enjoy your subject, but it's the discipline that keeps your nerves on edge, you know what I mean. There's always that tension. Sometimes people say, "Oh, you teach school. That's an easy job, just sitting around all day long." They don't know what it's really like. It's hard on your nerves.

The teacher is tense because she fears that she will lose control, which she tends to define in terms of some line beyond which she will not allow the children to go. Wherever she may draw this line (and there is considerable variation), the teacher feels that she has a "discipline" problem when the children attempt to push beyond it. The form and intensity of this problem are felt to vary from one social-class group to another, as might be expected from Davis' description of class emphases on aggression:

> In general, middle-class aggression is taught to adolescents in the form of social and economic skills which will enable them to compete effectively at that level. . . . In lower-class families, physical aggression is as much a normal, socially approved and socially inculcated type of behavior as it is in frontier communities.

These differences in child training are matched by variation in the teachers' reactions.

Children in "slum" schools are considered most difficult to control, being given to unrestrained behavior and physical violence. The interviews are filled with descriptions of such difficulties. Mirian Wagenschein, in a parallel study of the beginning school teacher, gave this summary of the experiences of these younger teachers in lower-class schools:

> The reports which these teachers give of what *can* be done by a group of children are nothing short of amazing. A young white teacher walked into her new classroom and was greeted with the comment, "Another damn white one." Another was "rushed" at her desk by the entire class when she tried to be extremely strict with them. Teachers report having been bitten, tripped and pushed on the stairs. Another gave an account of a second grader throwing a milk bottle at the teacher and of a first grader having such a temper tantrum that it took the principal and two policemen to get him out of the room. In another school following a fight on the playground, the principal took thirty-two razor blades from children in a first grade room. Some teachers indicated fear that they might be attacked by irate persons in the neighborhood in which they teach. Other teachers report that their pupils carry long pieces of glass and have been known to threaten other pupils with them, while others jab each other with hypodermic needles. One boy got angry with his teacher and knocked in the fender of her car."

In these schools a major part of teacher's time must be devoted to discipline; as one said: "It's just a question of keeping them in line." This emphasis on discipline detracts from the school's primary function of teaching, thus discriminating, in terms of available educational opportunity, against the children of these schools.

Children of the middle group are thought of as docile, and with them the teacher has least difficulty with discipline:

> Those children were much quieter, easier to work with. When we'd play our little games there was never any commotion. That was a very nice school to work in. Everything was quite nice about it. The children were easy to work with. . . .

Children of the middle group are felt hard to handle in some respects, and are often termed "spoiled," "overindulged," or "neurotic"; they do not play the role of the child in the submissive manner teachers consider appropriate. One interviewee, speaking of this group, said:

> I think most teachers prefer not to teach in that type of school. The children are more pampered and, as we say, more inclined to run the school for themselves. The parents are very much at fault. The children are not used to taking orders at home and naturally they won't take them at school either.

Teachers develop methods of dealing with these discipline problems, and these tend to vary between social-class groups as do the problems themselves. The basic device used by successful disciplinarians is to establish authority clearly on the first meeting with the class:

> You can't ever let them get the upper hand on you or you're through. So I start out tough. The first day I get a new class in, I let them know who's boss. . . . You've got to start off tough, then you can ease up as you go along. If you start out easy-going, when you try to get tough they'll just look at you and laugh.

Having once established such a relation, it is considered important that the teacher be consistent in her behavior so that the children will continue to respect and obey her:

> I let them know I mean business. That's one thing you must do. Say nothing that you won't follow through on. Some teachers will say anything to keep kids quiet, they'll threaten anything. Then they can't or won't carry out their threats. Naturally, the children won't pay any attention to them after that. You must never say anything that you won't back up.

In the difficult "slum" schools, teachers feel the necessity of using stern measures, up to and including physical violence (nominally outlawed):

> Technically you're not supposed to lay a hand on a kid. Well,

they don't—technically. But there are a lot of ways of handling a
kid so that it doesn't show—and then it's the teacher's word
against the kid's, so the kid hasn't got a chance. Like dear Mrs.
.... She gets mad at a kid, she takes him out in the hall.
She gets him stood up against the wall. Then she's got a way of
chucking the kid under the chin, only hard, so that it knocks his
head back against the wall. It doesn't leave a mark on him. But
when he comes back in that room he can hardly see straight,
he's so knocked out. It's really rough. There's a lot of little tricks
like that that you learn about.

Where such devices are not used, there is recourse to violent punishment, "tongue lashing." All teachers, however, are not emotionally
equipped for such behavior and must find other means:

The worst thing I can do is lose my temper and start raving
... You've got to believe in that kind of thing in order for it to
work ... If you don't honestly believe it it shows up and the children know you don't mean it and it doesn't do any good anyway
... I try a different approach myself. Whenever they get too
rowdy I go to the piano and ... play something and we have
rhythms or something until they sort of settle down ... That's
what we call "softsoaping" them. It seems to work for me. It's
about the only thing I can do.

Some teachers may also resort to calling in the parents, a device
whose usefulness is limited by the fact that such summonses are most
frequently ignored. The teacher's disciplinary power in such a school is
also limited by her fear of retaliation by the student: "Those fellows are
pretty big, and I just think it would take a bigger person than me to
handle them. I certainly wouldn't like to try."

In the school with children of the middle group no strong sanctions
are required, mild reprimands sufficing:

Now the children at Z............ here are quite nice to teach.
They're pliable, yes, that's the word, they're pliable. They will
go along with you on things and not fight you. You can take them
any place and say to them, "I'm counting on you not to disgrace
your school. Let's see that Z .... spirit." And they'll behave
for you ... They can be frightened, they have fear in them.
They're pliable, flexible, you can do things with them. They're
afraid of their parents and what they'll do to them if they get into
trouble at school. And they're afraid of the administration.
They're afraid of being sent down to the principal. So that they
can be handled.

Children of the upper group often act in a way which may be interpreted as "misbehavior" but which does not represent a conscious at-

tack on the teacher's authority. Many teachers are able to disregard such
activity by interpreting it as a natural concomitant of the "brightness"
and "intelligence" of such children. Where such an interpretation is not
possible the teachers feel hampered by a lack of effective sanctions:

> I try different things like keeping them out of a gym period
> or a recess period. But that doesn't always work. I have this one
> little boy who just didn't care when I used those punishments.
> He said he didn't like gym anyway. I don't know what I'm going
> to do with him.

The teacher's power in such schools is further limited by the fact
that the children are able to mobilize their influential parents so as to
exert a large degree of control over the actions of school personnel.

It should be noted, finally, that discipline problems tend to become
less important as the length of the teacher's stay in a particular school
makes it possible for her to build a reputation which coerces the children
into behaving without attempting any test of strength:

> I have no trouble with the children. Once you establish a
> reputation and they know what to expect, they respect you and
> you have no trouble. Of course, that's different for a new teacher,
> but when you're established that's no problem at all.

III

The third area of problems has been termed that of *moral acceptability,* and arises from the fact that some actions of one's potential
clients may be offensive in terms of some deeply felt set of moral standards; these clients are thus morally unacceptable. Teachers find that some
of their pupils act in such a way as to make themselves unacceptable
in terms of the moral values centered around health and cleanliness, sex
and aggression, ambition and work, and the relation of age groups.

Children of the middle group present no problem at this level, being
universally described as clean, well dressed, moderate in their behavior,
and hard working. Children from the "better" neighborhoods are considered deficient in the important moral traits of politeness and respect
for elders:

> Where the children come from wealthy homes. That's not so
> good either. They're not used to doing work at home. They have
> maids and servants of all kinds and they're used to having things
> done for them, instead of doing them themselves . . . They won't
> do anything. For instance, if they drop a piece of cloth on the
> floor, they'll just let it lay, they wouldn't think of bending over
> to pick it up. That's janitor's work to them. As a matter of fact,

one of them said to me once: "If I pick that up there wouldn't be any work for the janitor to do." Well, it's pretty difficult to deal with children like that.

Further, they are regarded as likely to transgress what the teachers define as moral boundaries in the matter of smoking and drinking; it is particularly shocking that such "nice" children should have such vices.

It is, however, the "slum" child who most deeply offends the teacher's moral sensibilities; in almost every area mentioned above these children, by word, action or appearance, manage to give teachers the feeling that they are immoral and not respectable. In terms of physical appearance and condition they disgust and depress the middle-class teacher. Even this young woman, whose emancipation from conventional morality is symbolized in her habitual use of the argot of the jazz musician, was horrified by the absence of the toothbrush from the lives of her lower-class students:

> It's just horribly depressing, you know. I mean, it just gets you down. I'll give you an example. A kid complained of a toothache one day. Well, I thought I could take a look and see if I could help him or something so I told him to open his mouth. I almost wigged when I saw his mouth. His teeth were all rotten, every one of them. Just filthy and rotten. Man, I mean, I was really shocked, you know. I said, "Don't you have a toothbrush?" He said no, they were only his baby teeth and Ma said he didn't need a toothbrush for that. So I really got upset and looked in all their mouths. Man, I never saw anything like it. They were all like that, practically. I asked how many had toothbrushes, and about a quarter of them had them. Boy, that's terrible. And I don't dig that crap about baby teeth either, because they start getting molars when they're six, I know that. So I gave them a talking to, but what good does it do? The kid's mouth was just rotten. They never heard of a toothbrush or going to a dentist.

These children, too, are more apt than the other groups to be dishonest in some way that will get them into trouble with law enforcement officials. The early (by middle-class standards) sexual maturity of such children is quite upsetting to the teacher:

> One thing about these girls is, well, some of them are not very nice girls. One girl in my class I've had two years now. She makes her money on the side as a prostitute. She's had several children . . . This was a disturbing influence on the rest of the class.

Many teachers reported great shock on finding that words which were innocent to them had obscene meanings for their lower-class students:

I decided to read them a story one day. I started reading them "Puss in Boots" and they just burst out laughing. I couldn't understand what I had said that had made them burst out like that. I went back over the story and tried to find out what it might be. I couldn't see anything that would make them laugh. I couldn't see anything at all in the story. Later one of the other teachers asked me what had happened. She was one of the older teachers. I told her that I didn't know; that I was just reading them a story and they thought it was extremely funny. She asked me what story I read them and I told her "Puss in Boots." She said, "Oh, I should have warned you not to read that one." It seems that Puss means something else to them. It means something awful —I wouldn't even tell you what. It doesn't mean a thing to us.

Warner, Havighurst and Loeb note that "unless the middle-class values change in America, we must expect the influence of the schools to favor the values of material success, individual striving, thrift, and social mobility." Here again, the "slum" child violates the teacher's moral sense by failing to display these virtues:

Many of these children don't realize the worth of an education. They have no desire to improve themselves. And they don't care much about school and schoolwork as a result. That makes it very difficult to teach them.

That kind of problem is particularly bad in a school like .... That's not a very privileged school. It's very under-privileged, as a matter of fact. So we have a pretty tough element there, a bunch of bums, I might as well say it. That kind you can't reach at all. They don't want to be there at all, and so you can't do anything with them. And even many of the others— they're simply indifferent to the advantages of education. So they're indifferent, they don't care about their homework.

This behavior of the lower-class child is all the more repellent to the teacher because she finds it incomprehensible; she cannot conceive that any normal human being would act in such a way. This teacher stresses the anxiety aroused in the inexperienced teacher by her inability to provide herself with a rational explanation for her pupils' behavior:

We had one of the girls who just came to the school last year and she used to come and talk to me quite a bit. I know that it was just terrible for her. You know, I don't think she'd ever had anything to do with Negroes before she got there and she was just mystified, didn't know what to do. She was bewildered. She came to me one day almost in tears and said, "But they don't want to learn, they don't even want to learn. Why is that?" Well, she had me there.

It is worth noting that the behavior of the "better" children, even when morally unacceptable, is less distressing to the teacher, who feels that, in this case, she can produce a reasonable explanation for the behavior. An example of such an explanation is the following:

> I mean, they're spoiled, you know. A great many of them are only children. Naturally, they're used to having their own way, and they don't like to be told what to do. Well, if a child is in a room that I'm teaching he's going to be told what to do, that's all there is to it. Or if they're not spoiled that way, they're the second child and they never got the affection the first one did, not that their mother didn't love them, but they didn't get as much affection, so they're not easy to handle either.

IV

We have shown that school teachers experience problems in working with their students to the degree that those students fail to exhibit in reality the qualities of the image of the ideal pupil which teachers hold. In a stratified urban society there are many groups whose life-style and culture produce children who do not meet the standards of this image, and who are thus impossible for teachers like these to work with effectively. Programs of action intended to increase the educational opportunities of the underprivileged in our society should take account of the manner in which teachers interpret and react to the cultural traits of this group, and the institutional consequences of their behavior. Such programs might profitably aim at producing teachers who can cope effectively with the problems of teaching this group and not, by their reactions to class differences, perpetuate the existing inequities.

A more general statement of the findings is now in order. Professionals depend on their environing society to provide them with clients who meet the standards of their image of the ideal client. Social class cultures, among other factors, may operate to produce many clients who, in one way or another, fail to meet these specifications and therefore aggravate one or another of the basic problems of the worker-client relation (three were considered in this paper).

In attacking this problem we touch on one of the basic elements of the relation between institutions and society, for the differences between ideal and reality place in high relief the implicit assumptions which institutions, through their functionaries, make about the society around them. All institutions have embedded in them some set of assumptions about the nature of the society and the individuals with whom they deal, and we must get at these assumptions, and their embodiment in actual social interaction, in order fully to understand these organizations. We can, perhaps, best begin our work on this problem by studying those institutions which, like the school, make assumptions which have high visibility because of their variation from reality.

METROPOLITAN DEVELOPMENT AND THE EDUCATIONAL SYSTEM*

by Robert J. Havighurst

According to census reports, in 1960 more than half the population of the United States was living in metropolitan areas. That year these areas accounted for 61 per cent of the population. If these areas, which are growing faster than the remainder of the country, continue to grow at their present rate, by 1980 they will account for between 70 and 75 per cent of the total population. Chains of urban-industrial communities will stretch along the principal axes of communication—from Boston to Washington, from Chicago to Detroit to Toledo to Cleveland to Pittsburgh, from Los Angeles to San Diego.

In the past, urban evolution has on the whole been advantageous. But it has had some disadvantages that are now forcing massive and costly urban renewal programs aimed at making metropolitan areas more fit for human living and more conducive to human values.

Metropolitan growth presents two major concerns. First, it has led to increased segregation on the basis of income and race. This segregation is a threat to democratic unity and educational opportunity, for slums or gray areas of the central cities breed political and social devisiveness and discontent. Second, space is not used properly. The location of industry, business, and dwellings has made the daily journey to work longer and more difficult than is really necessary for a large part of the population. The distance from residential areas to centers of leisure and cultural activity—theaters, museums, concert halls—is too great. Open space for recreation and for the enjoyment of nature has not been distributed so as to be available to the majority of the people.

*From Robert J. Havighurst, "Metropolitan Development and the Educational System," *The School Review*, Volume 69, Number 3 (Autumn 1961), pp. 251-267. Copyright 1961 by the University of Chicago. Reprinted by permission of the author and the University of Chicago Press.

Metropolitan developments have produced or intensified many social problems most of which have had repercussions in education. The net effect has been to make the educational system less efficient and less effective in achieving its democratic goals. We shall call the complex of a central city and its surrounding suburbs a megalopolis and analyze some of its problems.

One major problem is increased socioeconomic and racial segregation of the population. As the total population of a megalopolis grows, the slum belt around the central business district becomes thicker. This is a result not only of the growth in total population but also of the concentration of lower-class people in areas of poorest housing, which are usually in the oldest parts of the city. Those who can afford to do so move away from the inner city as their economic circumstances improve. In general, working-class people whose income permits it move out of the slum district and take up residence farther from the center of the city, while people in middle-class districts of the central city move out to middle-class suburbs. Thus the ever growing total population divides itself into a lower class conglomerate at the center, with successively higher socioeconomic groups at greater distances and the upper-middle class and the upper class largely in the suburbs.

Data from the Detroit area illustrate this generalization, which applies to most, if not all, of the other great cities. In the Detroit Area Study of the University of Michigan, information was collected on the incomes of families in Detroit and its suburbs (1). According to a report on this research, which covered family income from 1951 to 1959, the median income per family in the Detroit metropolitan area was related to the distance the family lived from the central business district. For families living within six miles of the central business district, the median income rose 3 per cent between 1951 and 1959, while the cost of living rose 12 per cent; thus during this period the median family in this area lost real income. Families living farther out, between the six-mile radius and the city limits, gained 5 per cent in median real income. Meanwhile, families in the Detroit suburban area gained 37 per cent in median real income. Thus, during the years the people in the central part of the city grew poorer, while the people in the suburbs grew richer. In other words, the central part of the city became more solidly lower class in composition, while the suburbs became more middle class.

This process can be seen in detail by looking at what happened between 1955 and 1960 in Leibnitz School, an elementary school in another northern industrial city. The district served by the school was located about seven miles from the center of the city and close to transportation lines. Parents of some of the pupils had attended the same school.

In 1955, enrolment totaled 1,250 pupils, most of them from lower middle-class and upper middle-class families of German, Dutch, and Swedish origin. Then came a period of rapid change. The owners of some of the three-story apartment buildings cut them up into smaller units and rented to southern white and Negro families. By 1960 enrolment at Leibnitz had climbed to twenty-four hundred, and the school had two shifts. One group of pupils came for four and a half hours in the morning, and another group came for four and a half hours in the afternoon to a new shift of teachers. To accommodate the hundreds of pupils who arrive at noon and mill around waiting for their shift to begin, the campus of the school, once beautifully landscaped, was covered with gravel.

Transiency is calculated at about 70 per cent. From September, 1960, to June, 1961, nineteen hundred pupils transferred in or out of the school. During times of heavy turnover, the children who are waiting to transfer sit in the auditorium, some of them with their parents and some unaccompanied. Two clerks work at desks on the stage. The clerk at one side of the stage processes transfers and records for incoming children, while the clerk at the opposite side processes papers for outgoing children. The records of pupils transferred out during the past several years show that most of these children have gone to schools farther from the center of the city or to schools in the suburbs.

There is not only increased economic stratification in the schools, but there is also increased racial and ethnic segregation. In northern cities Negro ghettos have come into being, and the schools reflect this fact. In New York City the superintendent of schools in his report for 1958 showed a net loss of fifteen thousand white pupils a year for the preceding five years (2). These pupils had moved out of New York City to the suburbs. In 1958 Negroes formed 20 per cent of the school enrolment, and Puerto Ricans 15 per cent. In one of New York City's five boroughs, Negroes and Puerto Ricans outnumbered other pupils in the public schools. In 1958, of 704 public schools, 455 had enrolments in which 90 per cent or more of the pupils were Negroes, Puerto Ricans, or other whites (3). Thus about two-thirds of the schools were segregated in the sense that less than 10 per cent of the pupils did not belong to the majority group of the school.

While this process goes on in the central city, the suburbs themselves become stratified into communities that are predominantly upper-middle class or lower-middle class, or upper-lower class. The city dweller who aspires to a house in the suburbs will find that the amount of money he can pay for a house determines the type of suburb he will live in. If he is employed as a manual worker in an auto assembly plant or an electronics factory fifteen miles out of the city, he is likely to make a payment on a two-bedroom bungalow in a real estate development that has hundreds of similar houses, all variants of one basic design, all on small lots with a plot of grass in front, a garage and a clothesline in the rear. He will live in a working-class suburb. If he is a lawyer with an office in the city, he will buy a ranch-type house on a large lot in an area where all the other houses are of similar type and cost, in a new section of a well-established upper-middle-class suburb with a reputation for good schools and a good country club.

One result of the segregation of lower-class boys and girls into elementary and secondary schools where they are exposed only to other young people of similar socioeconomic status is to deny them the stimulation of associating with middle-class youth in the school and the classroom. If lower-class boys and girls are in classes where a third or more of the pupils are from a middle-class family, they will be stimulated to keep up with the middle-class children in schoolwork, and they will also be in a position to form friendships and thus learn some of the social behavior and social values of middle-class children. But when lower-class youth are segregated in slum schools, they may lose these advantages.

A study made by Patricia Sexton in Detroit shows how the socioeconomic characteristics of schools are related to important educational factors (4). She obtained the average incomes of the families living in the various school districts and then grouped the 243 schools by income rank. The schools in a given income group tended to be located at about the same distance from the central business district. The schools that had children from highest-income families were farthest from the center of the city. The schools in the lower-income areas had poorer records of achievement, intelligence, and behavior, and a higher dropout rate. The schools in the higher-income areas had more pupils who were chosen in elementary and junior high school to take part in programs for gifted children and more students from senior high school who were going to college. Also the schools closer to the center of the city had a higher proportion of families with mothers working and with mothers receiving aid for dependent children. The assistance indicated that there was no father in the home.

Another problem in megalopolis is the weakening of civic and social relations between the various socioeconomic groups. While it has always been a principle of American democracy that all kinds of people should participate in the same schools and churches and political organizations, the growing segregation in megalopolis lessens the opportunity for this kind of interrelationship. Middle-class boys and girls grow up in antiseptic suburbs. Slum children grow up with no contact with middle-class children, with whom they might learn the art of co-operative citizenship.

Poverty in the central city is another problem. The central city suffers from a progressive economic downgrading of its population but must maintain increasingly expensive urban services—expressways, subways, schools, hospitals, many of which serve the entire population of megalopolis.

With the polarization of megalopolis into lower-class urban areas and middle-class suburbs comes a chronic state of cold war between the two sets of interests, with no authority in a position to bring about co-operation for the common welfare.

Problems of megalopolitan housekeeping become critical. Certain essential services are not readily available to some areas. New suburbs may have difficulty in getting fire protection, a water supply, and sewage disposal. The various police departments in a metropolitan area may not co-operate, and law enforcement may become lax. Transportation and traffic problems arise, and people have increasing difficulty in getting to places of work and recreation. The daily journey to work becomes more and more time-consuming, eating up the time gained by shorter working hours. Distances and difficulties of transport cut down freedom of movement.

Suburban slums arise in the unincorporated areas outside the central city. People living in these areas may have primitive sanitary facilities, insufficient water, inadequate fire protection, inadequate schools and other cultural facilities. Absence of a strong county or metropolitan government permits this kind of haphazard development.

Finally, there is the problem of the rustication of suburban dwellers. Middle-class suburban dwellers become almost parochial in their outlook and attitudes. Because of transportation difficulties they lose contact with the vigorous and variegated culture of the central city. Their children grow up in isolation from many of the educational influences of a great city.

Because of the many problems associated with metropolitan growth and megalopolitan complexity, it might be supposed that people would cease fleeing from the central city to the suburbs and instead remake slum areas into middle-class residential areas. This course is being urged, and urban renewal plans are under way to make the central city attractive for middle-class living. However, these efforts at urban renewal are meeting with difficulty, and the schools are at the heart of the difficulty.

People who have a choice as to where they will live in a metropolitan area look first at the schools if they have children. They generally want schools that have good standards of schoolwork and behavior. They also like schools that have new buildings and wide play spaces. Some who are prejudiced against non-whites, or fearful that the presence of non-whites will cause the neighborhood and the school to deteriorate, look for schools that have a mixture of races and economic levels, because they believe that such schools can teach their children democracy.

As more and more people, including working-class people, can choose among various places to live, they become more aware of and interested in school policies and school performance. Among other things, they try to sense the spirit, or ethos, of the school. Does it stimulate children to do well academically? Does it encourage children to want to finish high school and go to college? Does it have a program that is useful and interesting for children from all kinds of families? Does it provide a social life they like for their children?

There is a crude quantitative index, called the status ratio, which is useful for studying the ethos of a school. The status ratio is simply the ratio of the number of pupils from middle-class families to the number of pupils from working-class families. The ratio is $[2 \ (U+UM) + LM] \div UL + 2LL$. The number of pupils from the upper class and the upper-middle class is weighted twice as heavily as the number of pupils from the upper-lower class.

The reason for weighting the number of pupils from the upper-middle class and the lower-lower class more heavily in the formula is that pupils from the upper-middle class are about twice as likely to go to college and to exhibit other forms of academic interest and achievement as youth from the lower-middle class are, while youth from the lower-lower class are only about half as likely as pupils from the upper-lower class to show these characteristics.

The race index is also an important indicator of the desire of middle-class families to send their children to a particular school. The race index is a ratio that shows the proportions of white and Negro children in a school. Middle-class parents are likely to favor an index of 1.5 or higher, or a proportion of 60 per cent or more of whites. Negro middle-class parents might accept a lower ratio, but they generally favor a mixed or integrated school over a segregated one. Some white middle-class parents favor complete segregation, but most middle-class whites in northern cities would accept a school for their children that was stabilized at a race index of 1.5 and a status ratio of .6 or higher.

The most powerful factor in determining whether a family that can choose among places to live will stay in the central city or move to a suburb is the nature of the school to which its children will go. If the status ratio is close to a critical point, middle-class parents become anxious and start to think of moving away. This critical point depends on the attitudes and the experience of a particular parent and therefore is a subjective thing. The critical point also depends on the race index, the tradition of the school, the type of curriculum, and the quality of the teachers. However, among middle-class parents there is substantial agreement on the critical point—enough agreement to cause them to stream out of a school district as if by common agreement when the status ratio reaches a certain point.

That is what happened in the Leibnitz School. In 1955 this school had a status ratio of about 1. Then as apartments were subdivided and rented to working-class families with large numbers of children, the ratio dropped. The crowding of the school, the introduction of a double-shift program, and the appearance of Negro children all combined to cause some people to move out of the district. As a result the status ratio dropped past the critical point, which by 1960 was $7 \div 117$ or .06.

Secondary schools are more vulnerable than primary schools to desertion by middle-class parents when the status ratio reaches the critical point. In a community where the residents represent a cross section of the American population in socioeconomic status the high school has a status ratio of about 1.0. The ratio is higher than that of an elementary school in the same type of community because a number of boys and girls from families of the lower class drop out of high school. In an upper-middle-class suburb the status ratio is very high. But in the central city the slums continually encroach upon high schools in formerly middle-class areas and reduce the status ratio. When the critical point is reached, there is a rapid flight of middle-class families that have children of high-school age.

In spite of these difficulties and problems that stand in the way of the improvement of life in metropolitan areas, the coming decade will see various programs aimed at achieving the following goals:

Maximum freedom of choice for the people. All kinds of people should have as much choice as possible on such matters as where to live, where and how to spend free time, where to work, with whom to associate, where to educate their children.

Maximum opportunity for people to better themselves through employment, education, recreation, and use of libraries, museums, theaters.

Maximum use of the city as an educative experience for all kinds of people. People of all ages should be in a position to learn through experience with the whole city—its rich variety of ethnic groups and its wide range of work and cultural opportunities.

There are two alternative approaches to the realization of these goals. One is adaptation to the trends of megalopolitan evolution; the other is a bold effort to reverse the trends and design and build a new megalopolis for the future. Both approaches require co-operation by the schools, and both involve much change in school programs and school organization. The twin functions of the school—to mirror the present community and to aid the community in achieving its goals—are both called into action.

The policy of adaptation to existing metropolitan trends assumes that the future structure of megalopolis will follow present trends. The belt of the lower-class residential area around the center of the city will expand and grow thicker. The flight of middle-class families to the suburbs will continue. Suburbs will increase in number, size, and variety. Low-cost public housing will gradually make a physical improvement in the gray areas and result in physical renewal of slums. Expressways will give automobile owners quicker and more comfortable access to all parts of megalopolis. The present trend toward residential segregation by socioeconomic status will continue, together with at least as much racial segregation as now exists. Only a few small countertrends will be seen, such as the growth of working-class suburbs and the construction of expensive apartment houses near the center of the city for well-to-do people with few school-age children.

The major education adaptations will consist of attempts to provide educational stimulation and opportunity for children in slum areas and programs for the identification and the separation of the abler children in special classes and groups in the school.

A multitrack system will be introduced to separate children into groups formed on the basis of learning ability and social status. In schools in slum areas or areas threatened by encroaching slums, the system will have the effect of maintaining at least one subgroup that has a fairly strong academic motivation. The children of higher social status tend to be placed in the superior group, an arrangement that makes the school more tolerable for their parents. Whatever the value of homogeneous grouping in helping children achieve according to their intelligence, and the alleged benefits are repeatedly questioned by research studies, there is no doubt that most teachers and parents favor a multitrack system in a school where the status ratio has fallen below the critical point. The multitrack organization gives middle-class parents and working-class parents who seriously want their children to get the most out of school some assurance that they will be given special help and special consideration.

Enrichment programs will be set up for working-class children who achieve fairly well. These programs will supplement the multitrack program. The more promising children will be placed in smaller classes and given special counseling and guidance, and their parents will be encouraged to take more interest in their education. The children will be given access to museums, libraries, theaters, and concerts. One widely known example of such an approach is the Higher Horizons Program of Junior High School 43 and the George Washington High School in New York City. This program has stimulated a considerable number of boys and girls to graduate from high school and to enter college who would not have done so if they had not received special attention. Financial assistance for college attendance is a necessary part of such a program.

Enrichment programs will be set up for culturally deprived children at the kindergarten-primary level. Several large cities are already trying programs that give special assistance in the primary grades of slum schools on the theory that many of these children lack stimulation from parents to read and to achieve well in school. If these boys and girls are not given special attention, they may fail to master the task of reading. For the first few years in school, they will stumble along. In time they will become confirmed non-learners and during adolescence, social misfits. These children can get a better start in school and thus a better start in life. The school can give these boys and girls the better start they need by assigning specially trained teachers to small classes, by using social workers or visiting teachers to bring home and school into contact, and by giving the children the enrichment that middle-class children are likely to get in their homes.

Work-study programs will be introduced for youth who are failing in school. Under present conditions about 15 per cent of all boys and girls fail to grow up successfully through the avenue the school provides. At about seventh grade they react to school with apathy or hostility and aggression. In slum areas this group is likely to make up 25 or 30 per cent of the young people. These boys and girls are alienated from the value of the school and the other middle-class institutions. It is these boys and girls who make teaching difficult in seventh, eighth, and ninth grades, and who make junior high school and the early years of senior high school difficult for academically motivated youth in schools where the status ratio is below the critical point. For alienated youth, especially for the boys, a good deal of experimentation with work-study programs is now going on. The aim is to give the young people who take part a chance to grow up satisfactorily through the avenue of work. Most such programs commence with young people at the age of sixteen, when they may drop out of school if they wish. The programs appear to be having some success. Possibly better results will be achieved in programs that provide work experience as a part of the school program as early as age fourteen, or eighth grade.

Some people, including some educators, are not satisfied with accepting the present trends of metropolitan development and adapting the schools to them. They believe that the civic ills of metropolitan growth require fundamental urban renewal. These critics ask that a national megalopolis be designed. They call for plans that will lead to new growth from the center of the city to the suburbs, with parks, shopping centers, libraries, churches, and schools organized to serve people near where they live, and with industry, the central business district, and the centers of residence linked by fast, comfortable transportation, public and private. Billions of dollars are already being spent on bold new shopping plazas, garden villages, high-rise apartment buildings, and expressways.

Urban renewal has the physical goal of restoring areas of comfortable middle-class living in the central city and establishing areas of comfortable, slum-free, lower-class living. Beyond this, urban renewal has the social goal of making the whole of megalopolis a good place for all kinds of people to live in. Leaders of urban renewal often say that their goal is to increase the range and the amount of choice people have among good ways to live.

Among specialists in city planning there is much discussion of the typical physical plan that will make megalopolis a good place to live. It is generally agreed that residential areas should be decentralized, that each area should be self-contained with respect to shopping facilities, schools, libraries, and churches. One type of arrangement is the galaxy, in which constituent communities are spaced more or less evenly over the territory, with a network of highways and transportation lines leading to areas of specialized activity, such as industrial sites, airports, freight docks, and financial centers. Another type of arrangement is the many-pointed star or wagon wheel, with residential areas radiating from a central business district, industry located in certain sectors of the star, and transportation routes leading out from the center, crisscrossing other transportation routes that circle the area at various distances from the center.

There seems to be agreement among city planners on two matters: first, megalopolis should consist of residential areas that meet nearly all the ordinary needs of family and cultural life; second, many residential areas should contain a cross section of the social structure, with people of the upper class, the middle class, and the working class living in the same area. In particular, it is felt that many residential areas near the central business district should be populated by middle-class as well as working-class people.

Several large cities have embarked on major programs of slum clearance with the aim of restoring cross-sectional communities in the central city. Chicago has such areas to the south, the southwest, and the northwest of the central business district. St. Louis has the Mill Creek Valley District, southwest of the city center. New York City has several such areas, including one north of Columbia University. In these and other places slum buildings have been cleared, and land has been made available to private builders for apartment buildings and single-family residences to be sold or rented to people who can afford to pay substantial prices and rents.

The future of these developments is uncertain, however, and further urban renewal is likely to be delayed until these experiments are evaluated. One major question is whether middle-class people with children will move into these renewal areas. Their decision will depend on their attitudes toward the schools. They may want new, modern school buildings, and in many places they will get them because the old buildings are obsolete. Most important, they are likely to want assurance that the status ratio of the schools will be above the critical point. This assurance may be present for elementary schools, which serve relatively small areas, but not for secondary schools, which may serve both a renewal area and a large neighboring working-class area. The secondary school is likely to be the crucial element of the school system. The secondary school may well make or break programs for urban renewal.

Urban renewal of a fundamental nature will require major developments in school policy. The megalopolis of the future will probably have a single area-wide governing and taxing unit, with constituent local communities of fifty to a hundred thousand in population, each with its own local government. School policies and programs will be determined partly by an area-wide educational authority and partly by local community school boards. The following propositions concerning educational policy would seem to fit a rational plan for megalopolitan development:

1. A single area-wide educational authority with its own tax authority should be supplemented by local community school boards with authority to levy supplementary taxes for educational purposes.

2. A metropolitan area educational council or commission should work with the metropolitan area planning council on plans for establishment of new suburban school districts and area-wide educational institutions, such as a university, a teachers college, and technical institutions.

3. The area-wide educational authority should have responsibility for such educational functions as purchasing, teacher certification, pensions, the planning and the construction of school buildings.

4. The school board of the local community should administer its own school system up through the secondary school and probably through the junior college. It should provide a school program suited to community needs and should levy supplementary taxes if the area-wide tax support is inadequate.

Any metropolitan area that commits itself to a fundamental program of urban renewal needs to provide for a transitional period of perhaps twenty years. During this period the local communities would gradually become organized and separated from other communities by green belts, parks, and open spaces; and they would be linked by a system of highways and transportation routes.

Certain educational policies would need to be adopted for the transitional period. The policies should be aimed at stopping the flight of middle-class people from the central city. The goal should be self-contained communities of fifty to a hundred thousand in population, communities made up of a social cross section of the entire area. Some policies would be temporary, while others would become permanent policy for the megalopolis of the future. The principal transitional policies might well call for:

1. A set of regional high schools generously selective on the basis of intelligence and school achievement so as to be open to the top third of the high-school age group. Admission to these high schools should be controlled so that no school would have less than .6. By the end of the transitional period these schools would probably become comprehensive high schools serving local communities and open to all high-school students.

2. A set of work-study centers at the junior high school level for boys and girls who have demonstrated that they cannot profit from the regular academic high-school program. These centers should be located in junior and senior high schools but run on a separate schedule. They should enrol 10 to 20 per cent of the school population at age thirteen or fourteen to sixteen, but enrolment should drop as the elementary schools improve their kindergarten-primary programs.

3. A set of general high schools with strong commercial and vocational training programs for young people who are not attending other types of schools. By the end of the transitional period they would probably merge with the selective schools into comprehensive high schools serving local communities.

4. Special attention at the kindergarten-primary level to children from culturally and emotionally inadequate homes so as to give these children as good a start in school as possible, thus reducing the number who would later go to the work-study centers.

5. A set of regional junior colleges so located that there would eventually be one in each local residential community.

6. An adult education program on an area-wide basis, a program that uses junior colleges and branches of the public library, a program that exploits the educative potential of the metropolitan area and seeks to make adult education available to all kinds of people.

Some of the adaptations now being made in great cities to the problems of metropolitan development can be fitted into a rational plan for urban renewal. There is no need for educators to take sides in a controversy between the two alternatives posed here—that of making the best of existing trends and that of working toward fundamental urban renewal. However, the choice of fundamental urban renewal requires more exercise of rational foresight, more thought about goals of megalopolitan development and about ways of reaching these goals. Educators can impede urban renewal by holding stubbornly to practices that were good before World War II but have now lost much of their value.

REFERENCES

1. Detroit Area Study, "Family Income in Greater Detroit: 1951-1959" (Ann Arbor, Michigan: Survey Research Center, University of Michigan, 1960).
2. Sixtieth Annual Report of the Superintendent of Schools (New York: Board of Education of the City of New York, 1959).

3. J. Cayce Morrison, The Puerto Rican Study (New York: Board of Education of the City of New York, 1958).

4. Patricia Sexton, Education and Income (New York: Viking Press, 1961).

SOCIAL CLASS IN A TEACHERS COLLEGE*

by Durlyn E. Wade

In spite of the controversy over issues related to the social class system in America, research has recently been reported which exposes some of the influences of this phenomenon in the operations of our social institutions. The study to be here reported concerns itself with the distribution of rewards in a publicly supported teachers college.

Hollingshead was one of the investigators who found significant relationship between the rewards distributed to the youth in Elmtown's High School and their social class status. The picture was one of a disproportionate sharing of the rewards in a way that favored the upper classes and penalized those from the lower social class levels. The students from the upper social class levels (levels I and II) received twice their proportionate share of the high grades (above 85) given by the teachers in the high school. On the other hand, the students from lower class backgrounds (class V) received 65 per cent less than their proportionate share of these higher academic rewards.

In the non-academic area this social class bias existed to a large degree. The teachers reprimanded 27 per cent of the upper class youth (class II) for doing poor work; 92 per cent of the lower class students received this treatment. Student participation in athletic events, social gatherings, parties, dances, plays, and musical activities, revealed a bias favoring those from the upper class levels and disproportionately penalizing those in the lower social class groups. The research placed the credo of equal educational opportunity under considerable strain.

Shortly after Hollingshead reported his findings Abrahamson studied the problem at the level of the junior high school. Seven hundred students in junior high schools in the northeastern part of the nation

*From Durlyn E. Wade, "Social Class in a Teachers College," Journal of Educational Sociology, Volume 28 (1954), pp. 131-138. Reprinted by permission.

were included in the research. The rewards and penalties received by these students were compared with the distribution of social class status. Academic as well as non-academic rewards were included. The findings showed that the students in the upper social classes received significantly more than their proportionate share of the high grades distributed by teachers and less than their proportionate share of the low grades. Conversely, the students from the lower social class backgrounds received proportionately less of their share of the high grades and more than their proportionate share of the lowest academic grades given. A statistically significant pattern which repeated the trend was found in the favors teachers distributed to students; the upper social class received a greater proportionate share and the students from the lower social class levels received less than their share. The research tested student participation in clubs found in the junior high school, social acceptance among students, officerships in student government groups, and the honors and scholarships students received. In each of the tests a status was revealed. The results gave overwhelming evidence that somewhere a break had occurred in the fences of democracy.

Lenn included in his study grades below the junior high school level. Part of his research tested the rewards and punishments received by elementary school children according to their social class status. The results substantiated the relationships already known to exist. Academic and non-academic rewards and punishments were distributed with a social class bias that was statistically significant at a high level. Lenn was able to show that consciousness of the problem helped teachers minimize the disproportionate distribution of rewards and opened up useful avenues to assist in the amelioration of unequal educational opportunity.

The three investigations briefly mentioned and other research suggest the high probability that the pressures of the American social class system affect the operation of our public elementary and secondary school in a significant manner. One of the effects is reflected in a system for distributing rewards in a relatively uneven and perhaps unfair manner.

The question was raised whether the pattern discovered to exist in the public elementary and secondary schools would also be in effect at the level of higher education. The selective character of the student population at the college level suggested that it might not. In addition, there is the selective factor with regard to faculty. The instructional staff is usually recruited only from individuals with extensive training and education. The likelihood that the rewards distributed by faculty at this level should be biased according to social class seems remote. No proof, however, existed which would answer the question. The accepted hypothesis was similar to that tested by others in the field: that the academic grades received by students and the amount of student participation in extracurricular activities were biased according to social class status. The hypothesis was extended to state that: this bias favors those in the upper social class levels and penalizes those from the lower social class groups.

To test the contention a form of null hypothesis was assumed and the statistic chi-square employed to determine significance. The criterion of five per cent was set in the design of the study.

The Warner Index of Status Characteristics was employed to social class stratify a sample of 419 student teachers at "Keystone Teachers College." The results showed that five per cent of the students were upper class, nineteen per cent upper-middle class, forty-six per cent lower middle class, twenty-one per cent upper-lower class, and nine per cent lower-lower class.

A comparison was made between the social class distribution and the distribution of the rewards students receive in the following forms: academic grades recorded on the permanent records of the college, social acceptance scores received from fellow students in college courses, participation in extracurricular student activities, and selection by faculty and administration to receive other forms of special recognition.

A proportionate distribution of each of these forms of reward was constructed, and placed in a contingency table. If the differences between the actual number of rewards received and the proportionate number expected, were statistically significant, a bias was judged to exist that could be attributed to social class. If the differences were not significant (the criterion was set at 5 per cent) and bias was not identified, some evidence was present to suggest equity in the distribution of these rewards according to social class.

When the academic grades received by students were examined a social class bias was discovered which proved statistically significant. Table I shows the comparison between the high grades received by students, the low grades they received, both according to their social class status.

The comparison showed that the upper class students received proportionately more high grades, (A's and B's) and less than their proportionate number of the low grades, (D's and E's). This was true for the students in the upper middle class as well; they received more than their proportionate number of high grades and less than a proportionate

TABLE I

ACADEMIC GRADES RECEIVED ACCORDING TO
SOCIAL CLASS STATUS N=419

Social Class	ACADEMIC GRADES			Total Grades
	High	C	Low	
Upper	242	176	56	474
	200	209	65	
Upper Middle	752	766	203	1721
	726	727	238	
Lower Middle	1668	1743	566	3977
	1677	1749	551	
Upper Lower	754	851	254	1859
	784	818	257	
Lower Lower	326	368	150	844
	356	371	117	
Total	3742	3904	1229	8875

number of the low grades. The lower-middle group received less than a proportionate number of high grades, and more than their proportionate share of low grades. This trend was also found in the next two social class levels; the upper-lower social class received less than a proportionate share of the high grades and about their proportionate share of low grades. At the lower-lower social class levels, proportionately more of the low grades were received, thus substantiating the major hypothesis of a social class bias favoring the upper social class levels.

The social acceptance scores which students received from their fellow students were considered as an important part of the reward system at college. When the scores women received from men on the Ohio Social Acceptance Scale were examined in association with social class a statistically significant chi-square resulted. The evidence supported the hypothesis that women from the upper social classes received more (proportionately) of the high acceptance scores and less (proportionately) of the low acceptance scores. Interestingly, when the comparison was made *within* the same sex (acceptance scores women received from women, and men received from men), no significant difference was found.

The college activities were divided into two major types and subjected to analysis. The activities which were open to all students, or represented all students were considered as non-selective college functions; those functions open to only a few students where special selection was in operation were considered as selective college activities.

The first type included memberships in extracurricular clubs, memberships in student government, and offices in college clubs. When the first two of these were placed in association with social class negative results were secured. Offices in extracurricular clubs were studied and tested according to social class. Statistically significant results were obtained. The students in the upper social class levels had proportionately more offices in student clubs than did the students from the lower parts of the social class range. This activity, in isolation, supported the hypothesis.

Since college life is really a total scene the major interest was to learn what the total picture concerning the distribution of rewards looked like. For this reason the three activities just mentioned were combined, and placed in association with social class. The results were statistically significant, supporting the hypothesis at the one per cent level, when the total pattern was considered.

When *each* of the selective activities, memberships in sororities, fraternities, and honor societies, were examined separately according to the distribution of social class, the results obtained were negative. When these were combined the results were also negative. The findings favored the hypothesis, but were clearly outside of the five per cent criterion.

If students are given relative freedom to choose activities, and leaders, social class seems to be a significant factor in their choices. When, however, their choices come within the limits of widely known university policies, and certain mores given wide publicity ("discrimination is wrong") social class appears not to significantly bias the distribution of these forms of rewards.

What about the *total pattern* of non-selective and selective participation in activities at Keystone Teachers College? Now all six college activities were combined and placed in association with social class. The statistical result was significant at the two per cent level. Thus in the *over-all scene* a social class bias existed in the distribution of these rewards to students in the college.

The generalization concerning the choices of students when given relative freedom and the choices made when governed by university and college policies appeared to apply to the action of faculty groups as well.

Comparisons were made between the students selected for student counselors, those selected for dismissal from college and those selected to receive special awards and prizes. None of these classifications, individually, or in combination, gave statistically significant results. It was noted that in each of these distributions of rewards the action of the faculty was guided by quite definite requisites (university and college policies); in these cases a social class bias was not present.

In addition to questioning social class as the important factor influencing the biased distribution of rewards, several other aspects of living were examined. The religious affiliation of the student was found significantly related to the bias distribution of academic grades. It was thought that perhaps religion was more important than social class in explaining the observed relationship. Further study showed however that social class was operative within religion. Social class operated within both dependent variables.

The educational level of the parent was tested in comparison with rewards, and found to be statistically significant. Once again, however, social class was found to be significantly related to the educational level of the parent. It appeared that the social class system incorporated knowledge about the educational level of the person into the system of values which help determine relative degrees of prestige and status.

Foreign and native born parents were tested with the distribution of rewards. The results were statistically significant. Nationality was found significantly related to social class. The inference was made that it was not nationality that influenced the bias distribution of rewards but the social class system utilizing knowledge about nationality that was accountable in this case.

The sex of students was compared with the distribution of rewards and was found to be related in a statistically significant manner. On the other hand when tested with social class it appeared not statistically significant. Sex appeared to be an independent factor influencing the distributions; however, a biased distribution of rewards was found to exist *within* the same sex. The reasonableness of a sex difference was further questioned. It was also noted that the sex differences within the same family could hardly result in different social class membership. In other words although sex seemed not related to social class, and hence an independent factor to be reckoned with, it was reasoned that other factors may be operating with social class to influence this picture.

Age, place of residence, and college major were tested in comparison with the distribution of rewards. The results proved negative. Either the statistical tests failed to substantiate significance or else logical explanations were present to show that social class was more important than any one of these other factors.

The results of the inquiry brought to light some evidence to suggest that a number of students from the lower social classes are present as student teachers, yet published accounts of the social class status of teachers place few if any in these levels. Perhaps enrolment in a teachers' college is the first step of upward mobility for many young men and women.

The investigation showed social class status to be statistically related to the distribution of certain rewards students received in a publicly supported teachers college. The association shown supported the hypothesis that a bias exists in favor of the upper social classes. It was learned that certain of the rewards were protected from typical effects of the system.

It is not known whether such a bias exists in other institutions of higher learning. If it does the question follows: does it exist to a greater or lesser degree? There are some who will contend that the bias shown to exist is a minimum level and therefore not of serious consequence.

Still others, and the writer includes himself in this group, would say that the identification of a social class bias at this level is important from at least two points of view. If equal educational opportunity is to be provided for all qualified youth regardless of their environmental backgrounds, then a social class bias (of any degree) in the distribution of rewards cannot be tolerated.

Secondly, as in all events of a dynamic nature the conditions here identified are moving and changing. At a time when higher education, and teacher education perhaps most of all, is undergoing important changes, the identification and close inspection of this phenomenon is important. Is it likely that the future will witness an increase in the pressures of social class and thus an increased bias in the distribution of rewards? Can an awareness of the problem, and conscious effort to remove this bias help insure that greater equality of educational opportunity will exist for all qualified young men and women?

At a time when the creative genius of man is taxed to release the human resources now available, a greater proportionate sharing of rewards in college may initiate a chain reaction favoring the growth of a more democratic society.

Chapter Six

DEVIANT BEHAVIOR

Both teachers and administrators must eventually come to first-hand grips with the distasteful reality of "deviant" conduct. Yet to encounter such behavior is one matter and to understand it another. In this section we shall analyze two virulent types of norm violations[1] which are especially rife among school-age youth: juvenile delinquency and ethnic prejudice. The question of delinquency will be accorded more heed, not because it is the more prevalent pathology (in fact the statistics attesting to the frequency of delinquency may be so variously interpreted that they are open to serious question), but because (1) so much lucid, non-technical material on the subject is at hand and (2) to comprehend the social dynamics of delinquency is to understand better the dynamics of so many other types of culturally-patterned deviant behavior.

No social problem, not even divorce, has been subjected to more public scrutiny than delinquency; nor has any been subjected to so many and so diverse a series of diagnoses. Emotional instability, broken homes, temperament, body build, intelligence, bad upbringing, poverty, parental neglect, inadequate housing, overindulgence, and heredity: these and infinitely more "causes" have been repeatedly employed in efforts, amateur and professional, to account for delinquent behavior. But if we are to profitably probe the causal features of delinquency and if we hope to gain any degree of coherent understanding of the issue, we must necessarily devote our energies to a three-pronged attack: (1) divest

---

[1]For our purposes, norm-violating behavior may be taken to mean conduct which is contrary to popularly sanctioned values.

ourselves of our prior misconceptions and prejudices (perhaps the most difficult task of all); (2) turn to the contributions of a number of the behavioral sciences—most notably sociology, social psychology, clinical psychology, and cultural anthropology; and (3) integrate these diversified contributions into a meaningful, logical overview. Failing to take this approach, we can only attain a warped, piecemeal picture of the problem. It is to this integrative — and interpretive — mission that the authors of the five selections have addressed themselves.

The initial selection, "Common Misconceptions and Delinquency," is, appropriately, an interdisciplinary undertaking. Although edited by a psychologist (William C. Kvaraceus) and a cultural anthropologist (Walter B. Miller), the study is a joint effort involving the additional collaboration of a sociologist, psychiatrist, pediatrician, and criminologist. The authors' thesis is stated at the very outset: there is a popular inclination to "explain" the causes of delinquency in neat, simple, and unadorned terms; this is unrealistic and, worse, often dangerous. It is the article's purpose to catalogue—and sharply challenge—the more compelling of these man-on-the-street speculations. The enterprise is a challenging one, for many of these suppositions are more than mere bromides; they embody tenaciously held half-truths that are frequently re-echoed by quasi-experts and even sociologists, probation officials, and psychiatrists. Among the more salient points raised by the authors is the reminder that delinquency, like all norm-violating (and norm-abiding) behavior, is not a discrete, black-and-white proposition; there is no hard-and-fast line that clearly demarcates delinquent youths from their non-delinquent peers. We are warned, too, that if we are to regard delinquency as a form of deviant behavior, we must disabuse ourselves of the commonplace notion that every American subscribes to the same middle-class norms.

Albert K. Cohen's contribution, "An Unsolved Problem in Juvenile Delinquency," is adopted from *Delinquent Boys: The Culture of the Gang*—a book that, since its publication in 1955, has re-energized professional concern with the question of delinquency causation. Cohen's basic messages are only now beginning to reach segments of the lay public. In this selection, which comprises the first chapter in his book, the author elaborates his thesis that an understanding of the theory and dynamics of the "delinquent subculture" will afford fruitful insights for the student of delinquency. Delinquency, to Cohen, is far less a question of individually aberrant behavior than it is a distinctive way of life— a culturally patterned form of activity that is far from mysterious to the person familiar with the rudiments of social-class theory, cultural anthropology, and social psychology. Elsewhere in his book Cohen admits that participation in a delinquent subculture can hardly explain all delinquency, but his theory is eminently sound if only because it relates to a slum-area, "corner-boy" phenomenon—the matrix that accounts for the vast preponderance of officially delinquent acts.

"Delinquent Acts and Delinquent Subcultures," by Richard A. Cloward and Lloyd E. Ohlin, is from a book, *Delinquency and Opportunity: A Theory of Delinquent Gangs,* which appeared five years later than *Delinquent Boys.* The authors elaborate on Cohen's conception of delinquent subculture. Although accepting the subcultural thesis, Cloward and Ohlin take exception to Cohen's contention that delinquency results among lower-class boys when access to middle-class goals is thwarted (an assumption that presupposes that many lower-class youths accept the middle class as their reference group). To the authors, a delinquent subculture ". . . is one in which certain forms of delinquent activity are essential requirements for the performance of the dominant roles supported by the subculture"; it is the central position accorded to *delinquent* activity that distinguishes the delinquent subculture from other deviant subcultures. In the selection reproduced here, Cloward and Ohlin describe three basic types of subcultures: urban, lower-class, and teenage. Lacing their narrative with sprightly examples of delinquent jargon, the authors present a sophisticated as well as a concise delineation of the pressures, goals, and aspirations that motivate the sorts of delinquent activities the educator is likely to encounter. And once more much that the reader has encountered in earlier portions of this book—role theory, small-group dynamics, marginality, and the membership-reference group concept—will help clarify the authors' principal emphases.

"Norm-Violating Behavior and Lower-Class Culture," the second selection from the Kvaraceus-Miller study, is adapted from an earlier, much-cited article by the latter author.[2] Miller's basic thesis—implicit in both the Cohen and Cloward-Ohlin essays—amounts to this: (1) the lower class is characterized by distinctive values; (2) these vary markedly from the middle-class values that undergird the official legal code; and (3) the result is that conformity with certain lower-class values may automatically result in violation of the law. In short, it is Miller's opinion that the very lower-class way of life is intrinsically norm-violating, for it runs counter to the definitions of goodness and propriety that prevail in the dominant, middle-class-oriented sectors of society. Miller's dissertation defines and elaborates six "focal concerns"—preoccupations and

---

[2] Walter B. Miller, "Lower Class Culture as a Generating Milieu of Gang Delinquency," *Journal of Social Issues,* 14 (April, 1959).

values—that characterize lower-class boys and predispose them to law-violating activity. Miller's treatise is imaginative and provocative, but some persons would disagree with his tacit subscription to a basic culture-conflict theory of delinquency and his correlative assumption that delinquent gangs are simply a variant of street-corner gangs. In addition to his convincing delineation of focal lower-class dimensions, his analysis of three basic patterns of lower-class adaptations to blocked mobility aspirations will prove of particular value to anyone who must work with and understand "lower-blue-collar" adolescent boys.

Of every 100 American youths, approximately 15 belong to the motley ranks of the "alienated"; these youths are underprivileged, emotionally insecure, often members of ethnic minorities, and, above all, unadjusted to the middle-class orientation of teachers and authorities. These are the children described by Robert J. Havighurst and Lindley J. Stiles in "National Policy for Alienated Youth." This selection is topical, not simply because the majority of delinquents belong to the alienated minority, but because the children the authors describe are the perennial truants and school dropouts who have thus far thwarted virtually every effort to reach, motivate, and educate them.

Our concern is with socio-cultural explanations of delinquency; however, we cannot glibly dismiss psychogenic explanations of social phenomena. "Culture" and "personality," let us remember, represent obverse sides of the same coin. We cannot fathom delinquency in purely sociological or purely psychological terms. Sociodynamics and psychodynamics, in short, are as inextricably interwoven in delinquency as they are in other types of deviant behavior. This will become especially apparent in our analysis of prejudice.

Prejudice, like all else we have examined, cannot be construed as a quality present in some individuals and altogether lacking in others. We are all prejudiced to some degree; some of us are less prejudiced than others. Our concern here is with the person who is "highly" prejudiced. Like the delinquent (or, for that matter, the gifted, neurotic, or the extrovert), the highly prejudiced person is not easily categorized or defined; yet he is very much in our midst, and it is important that we identify and understand him. That the bigoted person is to be found in every classroom—and on some teaching staffs—makes him all the more menacing.

We can better comprehend the person who is highly prejudiced if we turn to a twofold distinction—a distinction not between the prejudiced and the unprejudiced but between the person whose prejudice is of a "culture-conditioned" nature and the person whose prejudice is of a "character-conditioned" nature. Culture-conditioned prejudice is more prevalent and generally more visible; it is typified in the anti-Negro southerner who clings to his prejudice because he has grown up in a culture that propagates and nourishes anti-Negro norms. In fact, within a group where patterns of prejudice prevail, it is characteristically the individual who *conforms* to his group's norms (that is, the most "normal" or "well-adjusted" person) who is prejudiced. Conversely, should a person in such a milieu be unprejudiced, he is likelier to be a non-conformist—a person who does not as readily accept his community as his dominant reference group. Studies of the growth of ethnic prejudice in children suggest that prejudicial complexes arise, in the main, through contacts with prevailing social norms rather than through actual contacts with members of the group in question. Once the child accepts the prejudicial norms of his parents (and, through reinforcement, those of his peers and other adults), these become "internalized"; that is, they slip into his subconscious and become a functioning part of his self-makeup. In his adult years, when he "feels" an aversion for the group he learned to dislike in childhood, he will probably justify his attitude with all manner of "reasonable" rationalizations.[3]

We have been examining the person whose prejudice is culture-conditioned in nature; his counterpart, the person victimized by character-conditioned prejudice, is an altogether different sort. His prejudice is often not only more violent but simultaneously more diffused and generalized; his antipathies are typically directed toward a whole host of targets. It is almost as though he "has" to hate: if one of his scapegoats is somehow eliminated from focus, he will inevitably seek out another. This person is not always easily identified; for example, he may effectively cloak his hostility beneath a veneer of respectability and even charm. The intolerant proclivities of this person are rooted in childhood as are the attitudes of the Negro-condemning southerner (or the northern, middle-class anti-Semite). However, unlike the person whose prejudice is culturally conditioned, the individual warped by character-conditioned prejudices is not so much anti-this or anti-that as anti-"other." His whole outlook on life is (quite subconsciously and seldom obviously) one of threat-orientation. He appears to walk in

[3]There are differences in susceptibility to culture-conditioned prejudice even among those reared in the same general culture; for example, in the south, the anti-Negro is likelier to (1) be older; (2) be engaged in a farming or unskilled occupation; (3) live on a farm or in a small town; (4) be less informed about public issues and less active politically; (5) earn a lesser income; and (6) be a member of the lower-lower class. Analysis reveals the latter to be the underlying, key component. All the same, of course, there are some anti-Negro upper-class southerners and some pro-Negro white sharecroppers.

a hostile jungle and is so plagued by a free-floating sense of insecurity that he seems almost incapable of warm and trusting relationships with others.

The article by Gordon Allport, "The Nature of Prejudice," probes and attempts to explain the psychodynamics of character-conditioned prejudice. Allport's article, from the book of the same name, makes a number of other salient points about prejudice. The reader will gain rather concrete insights into the mental set—the characteristic outlook and manner of perceiving the world—of the person burdened by character-conditioned prejudice. Allport points out that such prejudice is in one very real sense "functional": it serves as a psychic "crutch" that enables its victim to ward off the threats he senses within himself and thinks he senses from those around him. Consequences of such repressive efforts constitute the major part of Allport's article; the reader will note how and why repression is the central defense mechanism in the life of the character-conditioned prejudiced person.

We will see from reading Harold Hodges' article, "Peninsula People" (Chapter Eight), that authoritarianism, which is another way of designating character-conditioned prejudice, is an emphatically class-linked phenomenon. Both types of prejudice are far more prevalent among lower-status than higher-status Americans, although authoritarianism seems likelier to occur at all social-class levels than its culture-conditioned counterpart.

COMMON MISCONCEPTIONS AND DELINQUENCY*

by William C. Kvaraceus and Walter B. Miller

Most people have very definite opinions on delinquency, which usually purport to go directly to the "cause" or "cure" with one deft stroke. Unfortunately, the problems of norm-violating behavior are not so simple; otherwise, delinquency would have long since ceased to be a major topic of national concern.

The previous chapter has indicated that the delinquent and delinquency have a societal function as a hostility target for some segments of the community. Perhaps its continuance as such a target is closely bound up with various myths, half-truths, antidotes, and nostrums that have grown up around its "cause" and "cure." In fact, some of the myths of delinquency are changing with the times and are becoming more sophisticated. Witness the current emphasis on "emotional disturbances," where before discussion centered around "lack of recreation" and "slum areas." Once some unitary factor was assigned as "cause"; now "multiple causation" is glibly cited. For some, the term "unhealthy" has replaced the term "immoral" as a primary deprecatory epithet, but the evaluative overtones remain the same.

It will be necessary in the following sections to explore some of the ideas which are misleading or incorrect but which still, like legends, persist in the folklore surrounding delinquency. Although there may be an element of truth in some of these notions, they are open to serious challenge as absolute or categorical statements concerning the nature and sources of delinquency. Some may contain half-truths which have been falsified through overgeneralization and indiscriminate application. Moreover, many misconceptions have resulted from translating the information obtained from a small and frequently biased sample into universal conclusions and prescriptions.

FALSE DICHOTOMY

All youngsters cannot be filed conveniently into two major categories of "delinquent" and "nondelinquent." Norm-violating behavior exists on a continuum. Most people break a rule or regulation at one time or another, some people more often than others. Some of these violations are minor and infrequent; others represent more serious behavior and may become habitual. But one delinquent act does not necessarily make a delinquent.

DELINQUENCY AS MALADJUSTMENT

From the point of view of the delinquent, most delinquent behavior is purposive and adjustive. From the vantage point of middle-class norms and status, such behavior is frequently seen as a maladaptation. But in looking at this same behavior from the child's point of view, one can see that the child frequently uses it as means of adapting or adjusting in accordance with his essential frame of reference. Occasionally, he may even be solving a serious problem, which has long been confronting him, in the best and only way he knows how — through his delinquency. Delinquent "malbehavior" is usually "adjustive behavior," and only from the outsider's point of view does the child seem "maladjusted."

DELINQUENCY: A PSEUDODIAGNOSTIC RUBRIC

Merely to dub a boy or girl "delinquent" is not to explain anything about his behavior, for the term "delinquent" does not represent a useful diagnostic concept. Series of norm-violating behaviors, which run counter to legal codes and which are engaged in by youngsters, are only symptomatic of something else in the personal make-up of the individual, in his home and family, or in his cultural milieu.

WORKING-MOTHER MYTH

Many people point to the working mother as a major cause of delinquency. This is predicated on the concept of the intact middle-class family in which the mother stays home to rear her children and does not accept employment outside the home lest she neglect her young. The mother-child axis as the basic determinant of behavior and personality is largely a concept that stems from an overly heavy emphasis on certain elements in psychoanalytic theory at the expense of other very important factors. This is not to deny the importance of the mother-child relationship at various points in the child's life.

Current studies on the negative effects of working mothers on their children are far from conclusive. The working mother will not suffice as a simple, neat causal explanation of delinquency. Moreover, the working mother has a very different meaning and effect in the middle-class home than in the lower-class family.

"BROKEN" HOME

Causative pronouncements and inferences concerning the broken home and delinquency are popular and, seemingly, timeless. Although the "broken" home explanation, like the "working-mother" concept, has some utility, more precise definitions of broken homes are required and the precise effects these have in different milieus need to be determined. There is, for example, always the question of the psychologically broken home, even though both parents are living together. There is the question of a lower-class culture pattern in which separation is a standard or an acceptable style and, thus, a broken home has a different connotation in this frame of reference than in others. There is also the need to describe the specific type of household system and then relate this type to the manner in which it is accepted by the youngster. Then, too, there is the question of the impact of the physically broken home on the first four or five years of the child's life, as against the impact of breaks that may occur later in life. Finally, there is the problem created by the physically and psychologically broken home when the child comes before the law and disposition is made in such a manner that the legal agency itself decides to break up the family. And there is readily available evidence that a child with two parents to back him up is more likely to get a break in court and to be treated as a problem child who should be helped by a nearby clinic; but if the home lacks the nuclear design so prominent in middle-class culture, the child is more than likely sent off to a state institution.

Studies on causes of delinquency that are based on court and institution cases carry the heavy built-in bias of the broken home because of this screening process, in which a youngster from an intact home generally goes back home or to the clinic and the youngster from a broken home goes to an institution. Consequently these studies can be frequently misleading.

Labeling a child a potential delinquent simply because he comes from a broken home or explaining away his behavior on this basis is an ever-present danger. Putting all the blame at the door of the broken home is a neat, but too easy, way out. Too often it becomes a respectable, though tricky, way of psychologically dismissing the youngster who is difficult to diagnose and who needs help that cannot be easily prescribed.

MENTAL RETARDATION MYTH

"Delinquents have a lower IQ" is a common statement for which there is little scientific support. It appears even less valid when non-verbal and "culture-fair" tests are used. It is true that many lower-class children may score lower on "intelligence tests" than middle-class children, but the kind of "intelligence" measured frequently involves intellectual capacities especially emphasized in middle-class life—verbal fluency, reading comprehension, and substantive knowledge derived from conventional middle-class interests. However, even these differences tend to fade as more effective and sensitive instruments are devised and as more representative samples of the delinquent population are compared to nondelinquents from the same milieu. Many delinquents turn out to be extremely bright when they are viewed within the context of their own milieu.

PLAYGROUND MYTH

There is a highly organized school of thought which says, "Give the boy a place to play and he won't get into trouble" and "A community with many playgrounds is a community with little delinquency." Several research projects have indicated that there is no direct or discernible relationship between the usual recreation program and delinquency rates. Unquestionably, however, a particular type of recreation program that is carefully planned and administered under certain auspices, direction, and leadership—*if coordinated with other efforts*— can effectively redirect or channel energies away from illegal activity into organized athletics and other leisure-time pursuits.

A special problem is presented by the "rotten apple" or "sinner" who traditionally won't even try the standard groups, partly because he won't be accepted and partly because he would rather join other "rotten apples" or others more willing and ready to decay. A major problem, always to be faced, is how such a youngster can be involved in constructive leisure programs.

Bad Companions and Evil Gang Leader

Parents in both lower and middle classes frequently cite the "bad companion" as the source of their youngster's delinquency. The only difficulty here is that the parents of the alleged "bad boy" make the same claim, but of others in the group. There is also the problem of "the gang" which is labeled "bad" but whose members seldom do much more than hang around street corners or find the back way into a theater, a bowling alley, or a variety store. In many ways, this gang plays a constructive role in the socializing process for any youngster from any class.

The stereotype of the juvenile gang generally includes the idea of one overpowering evil-doer and a group of weak, or sheeplike, followers. This stereotype is often tied to preventive myth which says, "If one can get to the leader, then the gang can be reached and straightened out." This kind of "Little Caesar" leadership does exist, of course, but in the typically organized gang there are usually at least three or four leaders. Depending on the particular situation, one or another member assumes primacy and makes the basic definitions but only after a great deal of interaction and discussion in which almost all members take part. The mythical figure of one evil, powerful leader "manipulating all those weak and spineless kids" does not correspond to the facts and can be classified as less than a half-truth.

Physical Attributes and Heredity

Contrary to many opinions, delinquents are as healthy, if not healthier, than their nondelinquent contemporaries. A theory which has maintained its hold on the public mind is that one can recognize a delinquent by facial or body characteristics. This has little basis in fact; for example, the highly organized gang member must generally be strong, physically skillful, and mentally alert.

The "bad-seed" explanation for delinquency and crime, once so popular among researchers concerned with the blood lines of the Jukes, Kallikaks, Nams and Zeros, never seems to fade away. Updated versions of this thesis continue to appear, generally in the company of modified and modernized adaptations of the Lombrosian tradition. For example, certain differences in physical constitution have been identified recently and related, presumably, to delinquency and nondelinquency. It is true that strength, athletic prowess, and toughness, which center around body constitution, all play a very important and functional role in the concerns of lower-class street-corner society. Here psychological concepts of self and of others based on physical traits in certain social milieu may generate, though only indirectly, a tendency toward norm-violating behavior. There is little solid evidence for any close or direct tie-in of norm-violating behavior and hereditary components. Nevertheless, it is likely that hereditary-biological types will continue to furnish the simplest explanation of all for delinquency and always within an aura of "scientific method." Those who want a handy explanation for delinquency can always invoke the ancestors, particularly the not-so-dear departed. But, as a matter of fact, there should be less concern with the seed and more concern with the soil and the sun which so nurture and develop these youngsters that they are enabled to accept and pattern themselves after those persons in the home, neighborhood, and community who exemplify norm-violating behavior.

THE DETERIORATED NEIGHBORHOOD AND SLUMS

Research has pointed out that slum clearance in itself is not an answer to delinquency. Hot and cold water, central heating, and fresh paint, in and of themselves, neither relate to nor automatically reduce delinquency. Attention should be directed to the inhabitants, to their relationships and culture, not to the number of rooms and the brick and mortar of their residences.

IDLE HANDS

The hue and cry—like that raised for "recreation"—for change in child labor laws to allow the 14- to 17-year-olds to gain employment appears unrealistic when evidence which clearly indicates that there is little room or opportunity for them in the present labor market is taken into consideration. As a preventive, "keeping youth busy," whether through compulsory education, drafting for service in the armed forces, providing fun through recreation, or early employment, can, at best, only temporarily postpone behavior that is symptomatic of more deep-seated or culturally oriented factors. Youngsters need opportunity for meaningful school-work-play activity in the maturation process. More-over, they are quick to detect artificial "busy work" as against vital and genuine activity-experiences. Merely "keeping idle hands occupied" touches only surface symptoms and overlooks underlying factors known to generate norm-violating behavior patterns.

Curfew and Legislation

"Let's change the law" is often heard as a cure for juvenile delin-quency. There is no question that enlightened legislation provides the legal definitions of approved and protective cultural practices in our own and other countries. Nevertheless, a legislative measure will not serve as an antidote for cultural and psychological forces that tend to create norm-violating behaviors; these forces must be understood and offset through carefully planned preventive and control efforts based on valid research.

There is no demonstrated relationship between "curfews" and delinquency reduction. Reliance on some quick legislative "gimmick" will not insure any long-term success in delinquency prevention or con-trol. Carefully thought out legislation can enable the community to support and conduct more promising programs of aid for the delinquent at the local and state level. But good legislation alone is only enabling; it is not curative.

Punishment as an Antidote

Frequent appeals for a resort to severe tactics in an effort to manage the norm-violating behavior of youngsters are heard in every community. Greater reliance on the birch rod, the night stick, and the woodshed is a perennial recommendation for a simple and straight-forward solution to the "delinquency foolishness." Although some delinquents may be impervious to this technique and thus suffer no great harm, others may be only further confused and confounded by harsh punitive and retaliatory methods. Delinquents, as well as nondelinquents, need fair but firm treatment when they step out of bounds. They must also learn the natural consequences of their actions and that they will have to assume responsibility for them. There are effective uses of various types of punishment that may be invoked with the delinquent. However, to overlook causative factors and to capitulate to the punishment routine will neither prevent nor control further expressions of norm-violating behavior.

DELINQUENCY AS ABERRANT OR DEVIATING BEHAVIOR

Delinquency is frequently regarded as a form of deviant behavior. Such a concept assumes the existence of a unitary system of institutional norms. But there are many institutional systems and, hence, many norms. The norms of the dominant middle class serve as the main vantage point (or disadvantage point) for interested and concerned lay and professional workers. Prevalent forms of norm-violating behavior, seen through this window, may appear to be distortion or aberrancy; but if viewed, for example, in terms of lower-class street-corner society, the delinquency may appear as conduct that yields status and prestige—as illustrated by attitudes toward car theft and early sex experience in certain neighborhoods. In Part II, where an attempt will be made to define delinquent behavior and to delineate some of the forces generating it, the implications of the various norms of the different institutional systems in a community will be explored in some detail.

AN UNSOLVED PROBLEM IN JUVENILE DELINQUENCY*

by Albert K. Cohen

The expression, "the delinquent subculture," may be new to some readers of this volume. The idea for which it stands, however, is a commonplace of folk—as well as scientific—thinking. When Mrs. Jones says: "My Johnny is really a good boy but got to running around with the wrong bunch and got into trouble," she is making a set of assump-

---

*Reprinted with permission of the publisher from *Delinquent Boys: The Culture of the Gang* by Albert K. Cohen. Copyright 1955 by the Free Press, New York: the Free Press of Glencoe, pp. 11-19.

tions which, when spelled out more explicitly, constitute the foundations of an important school of thought in the scientific study of juvenile delinquency. She is affirming that delinquency is neither an inborn disposition nor something the child has contrived by himself; that children *learn* to become delinquents by becoming members of groups in which delinquent conduct is already established and "the thing to do"; and that a child need not be "different" from other children, that he need not have any twists or defects of personality or intelligence in order to become a delinquent.

In the language of contemporary sociology, she is saying that juvenile delinquency is a subculture. The concept "culture" is familiar enough to the modern layman. It refers to knowledge, beliefs, values, codes, tastes and prejudices that are traditional in social groups and that are acquired by participation in such groups. Our American language, political habits, sex mores, taste for hamburger and cokes and aversion to horse meat are parts of American culture. We take for granted that the contrasting ways of Hindus, Chinese and Navahos are for the most part a matter of indoctrination into a different culture. But the notion of culture is not limited to the distinctive ways of life of such large-scale national and tribal societies. Every society is internally differentiated into numerous sub-groups, each with ways of thinking and doing that are in some respects peculiarly its own, that one can acquire only by participating in these sub-groups and that one can scarcely help acquiring if he is a full-fledged participant. These cultures within cultures are "subcultures." Thus, within American society we find regional differences in speech, cookery, folklore, games, politics and dress. Within each age group there flourish subcultures not shared by its juniors or elders. The rules of marbles and jackstones live on, long after you and I have forgotten them, in the minds of new generations of children. Then there are subcultures within subcultures. There is the subculture of a factory and of a shop with the factory; the subculture of a university and of a fraternity within the university; the subculture of a neighborhood and of a family, clique or gang within the neighborhood. All these subcultures have this in common: they are acquired only by interaction with those who already share and embody, in their belief and action, the culture pattern.

When we speak of a delinquent subculture, we speak of a way of life that has somehow become traditional among certain groups in American society. These groups are the boys' gangs that flourish most conspicuously in the "delinquency neighborhoods" of our larger American cities. The members of these gangs grow up, some to become law-abiding citizens and others to graduate to more professional and adult forms of criminality, but the delinquent tradition is kept alive by the age-groups that succeed them. This book is an attempt to answer some important questions about this delinquent subculture. The pages which follow will prepare the ground for the formulation of these questions.

A large and growing number of students of juvenile delinquency, systematically developing the implications of Mrs. Jones' explanation of Johnny's "trouble," believes that the only important difference between the delinquent and the non-delinquent is the degree of exposure to this delinquent culture pattern. They hold that the delinquent is not distinguished by any special stigmata, physical or psychological. Some delinquents are bright, some are slow; some are seriously frustrated, some are not; some have grave mental conflicts and some do not. And the same is true of non-delinquents. Delinquency, according to this view, is not an expression or contrivance of a particular kind of personality; it may be imposed upon any kind of personality if circumstances favor intimate association with delinquent models. The process of becoming a delinquent is the same as the process of becoming, let us say, a Boy Scout. The difference lies only in the cultural pattern with which the child associates.

In describing this "cultural-transmission" theory of juvenile delinquency we have already suggested the main features of its principal rival. Mrs. Jones' neighbor may be of a different mind about Johnny's delinquency. "That kid's just never been trained to act like a human being! If I let my kid run wild like Johnny, if I never laid down the law to him, he'd be the same way. Any kid will steal and raise cane if you don't teach him right from wrong and if you let him get away with anything." Or her explanation may run like this: "He never had a chance. The way he's been tossed from pillar to post! The way his folks have always fought with one another and the way they've both beat on him! The one thing he's never had is a little real love. What do you expect of a boy when his own people treat him like dirt and the whole family is all mixed up?"

Again, if we spell out the assumptions underlying these two "explanations," we find that they are two variants of a whole class of theories which we may call "psychogenic." These are the theories which are favored by psychiatrists, especially those of a psychoanalytic persuasion. These theories have in common the idea that delinquency is a result of some attribute of the personality of the child, an attribute which the non-delinquent child does not possess or does not possess in the same degree. One type of psychogenic theory holds that every human being is endowed with a fund of inborn or instinctual anti-social impulses, commonly called the Id. Most people, in the course of growing up, acquire a capacity for circumspection or prudence, commonly called Ego. They also incorporate into their own personalities, as conscience or Superego, the moral code of their society. The Ego and Superego together normally suffice to hold the Id in check. The delinquent and the criminal differ from the normal, law-abiding person in the possession of unusually imperious Id drives or faulty Ego or Superego development, resulting in the eruption of the Id into illegal acts. This imperfect mastery of the Id may be a result of faulty training or parental neglect. Here we recognize the substance of our neighbor lady's first explanation: Johnny's Ego and Superego, through the failure of his family to train and discipline him, are too weak to restrain his bumptious Id.

Another type of psychogenic theory does not assume that the impulse to delinquency is itself inborn. Rather, it views delinquency as a symptom of, or a method of coping with, some underlying problem of adjustment. The delinquent differs from the non-delinquent in that he has frustrations, deprivations, insecurities, anxieties, guilt feelings or mental conflicts which differ in kind or degree from those of non-delinquent children. The delinquency is often thought of as related to the underlying problem of adjustment as a fever is related to the underlying infection. Our neighbor lady's second explanation is a folksy version of this mental conflict variant of psychogenic theory: as a result of a disturbed family situation, Johnny is "mixed up," he has psychological problems, and these problems find their expression through delinquency.

Psychogenic theories of both classes recognize the importance of the child's social environment in producing the character structure or the problem of adjustment, but give it relatively little weight in determining the particular manner in which it finds expression. For the first class of psychogenic theories, the Id is already there at birth in all people. It does not *become* criminal through experience. It is criminal from the very start and never changes. What is acquired through experience is the shell of inhibition. For the second class, delinquency as a symptom or mode of adjustment is contrived or "hit upon" by the child himself, perhaps through one or more of the familiar "mechanisms" of substitution, regression, displacement, compensation, rationalization and projection. If other children exhibit the same behavior it is because they have *independently contrived* the same solution.

We have been discussing kinds of theories. It does not follow that all students of juvenile delinquency embrace one or another of them as an explanation for all delinquency. On the contrary, most students give at least passing acknowledgment to more than one kind of causal process. Thus, many psychoanalysts, the people most strongly wedded to psychogenic theories, recognize the existence of a kind of delinquent who is not just giving expression to his Id or working out a problem of adjustment but who has internalized a "delinquent Super-ego." That is, he has internalized the moral code of his group and is acting in accordance with that code, but it happens to be a delinquent code. It is fairly typical of psychoanalytical writers, however, that they formally concede, so to speak, the existence of this sort of thing but thereafter, in their actual case studies, pay little attention to it. At the same time most sociologists, who are generally disposed to favor a cultural-transmission theory, feel that there are some delinquents whose delinquency cannot be explained in cultural-transmission terms. Many of these sociologists, however, are reluctant to flirt with psychogenic alternatives, particularly those of the more extreme psychoanalytical kind.

It may be that we are confronted with a false dichotomy, that we are not really forced to choose between two conflicting theories. There is the possibility of two or more "types" of juvenile delinquents, each the result of a different kind of etiology or causal process: one, let us say, predominantly subcultural and another predominantly psychogenic. There is the possibility of subcultural and psychogenic "factors" simultaneously but independently at work in the same personality, each providing a separate and distinct "push" in the direction of delinquency, like two shoulders to the same wheel. However, we are especially interested in a third possibility, namely, that in the majority of cases psychogenic and subcultural factors blend in a single causal process, as pollen and a particular bodily constitution work together to produce hay fever. If this is so, then the task of theory is to determine the ways in which the two kinds of factors mesh or interact. We will have a good deal to say about this as our inquiry unfolds.

In the present state of our knowledge, there is room for question and disagreement about the proportion of all juvenile delinquency which depends, in some way, upon participation in the delinquent subculture; about the relationship between cultural-transmission and psychogenic factors; and about the nature of the culture-transmission process itself, that is, about just how persons take over a new subculture. There seems to be no question, however, but that there is a delinquent subculture, and that it is a normal, integral and deeply-rooted feature of the social life of the modern American city.

Now we come to a curious gap in delinquency theory. Note the part that the existence of the delinquent subculture plays in the cultural-transmission theories. It is treated as a *datum,* that is, as something which already exists in the environment of the child. The problem with which these theories are concerned is to *explain how that subculture is taken over by the child.* Now we may ask: Why is there such a subculture? Why is it "there" to be "taken over"? Why does it have the particular content that it does and why is it distributed as it is within our social system? Why does it arise and persist, as it does, in such dependable fashion in certain neighborhoods of our American cities? Why does it not "diffuse" to other areas and to other classes of our population? Similar questions can be asked about any subculture: the values and argot of the professional dance band musician, social class differences in religious beliefs and practice, the distinctive subcultures of college campuses. Any subculture calls for explanation in its own right. It is never a random growth. It has its characteristic niche in our social structure; elsewhere it does not "catch on." It has its characteristic flavor, qualities, style. Why these and not others?

With respect to the delinquent subculture, these questions are of more than theoretical or speculative interest alone. Social control of juvenile delinquency is a major practical problem of every sizable American community. No such efforts at control have thus far proved spectacularly successful. While knowledge does not guarantee power, it is improbable that we will achieve striking successes at control without some understanding of the sources and sustenance of this subculture in our midst. The problem has not, to be sure, been completely ignored but there has been remarkably little effort to account for the delinquent subculture itself. That is the task of this book [*Delinquent Boys: The Culture of the Gang*]. A by-product of our inquiries will be a new perspective on the issue of psychogenic *versus* cultural-transmission theories of delinquency.

DELINQUENT ACTS AND DELINQUENT SUBCULTURES*

by Richard A. Cloward and Lloyd E. Ohlin

Delinquent acts occur in many different social contexts and take many different forms. Before we explain them, we must try to classify them in some meaningful way. There are many aspects of delinquency that might be used as a basis of classification. For example, one could devise a set of categories based on various characteristics of the delinquents themselves, such as age, sex, social class, school achievement, family relationships, emotional stability, intelligence, relationship to other delinquents, personal aspirations, and the like. One might also classify delinquencies in terms of various characteristics of the victim, whether a person, a group, or an institution. Alternatively, one might classify certain features of the behavioral transaction between the delinquent and the victim. For example, did it involve property destruction, assault, theft, or fraud? What was the relative cost to the victim or to the more general interests of dominant power groups in the society?

The way in which one chooses to classify the complex social events that are delinquent acts depends upon what it is that one is interested in doing about these acts. People usually attend particularly to those features of delinquency that seem most relevant to the accomplishment of their objectives. For example, the policeman, interested in controlling crime, will tend to be concerned about the seriousness of the offense, the cost to the victim, the threat of a repetition by the offender, the likelihood of securing a conviction, and the effect of all these upon the public's definition of the police department. The judge, charged with such additional tasks as making an appropriate disposition of the offender, will be concerned about the social background of the delinquent, the motivation and circumstances of the act, the likelihood of a favorable response to different forms of treatment, and so forth. The social worker or psychiatrist concerned with rehabilitation will try to identify the sources of the behavior and its susceptibility to treatment. The research scientist committed to developing explanations of delinquency will seek to establish causal connections or correlations between elements of the total problem: for example, the relationship between various types of act and the social conditions that attend or precede them, or the connections between offenders and their victims.

*Reprinted by permission of the publisher from *Delinquency and Opportunity* by Richard A. Cloward and Lloyd E. Ohlin, pp. 7-13. Copyright 1960 by The Free Press, New York: the Free Press of Glencoe.

Clearly there will be considerable overlapping among these classifications of the facts about delinquents and their offenses by persons charged with these different tasks. However, the classifications of greatest value for one purpose may not be suited to another. Legal codes represent efforts to define and to classify those facts which facilitate the determination of responsibility for illegal acts with the minimal error or cost to the innocent. Although these classifications are essential to the legal definition of persons as delinquents or criminals, they are not necessarily the only categories that might be employed in developing an understanding of the processes which generate the prohibited behavior. The same applies to the distinctions of greatest relevance to the action interests of policemen, judges, and treatment therapists. The research scientist must develop classifications that enable him to understand and explain the events he is investigating without regard to their immediate implications for action, official or otherwise.

In this book, as we have suggested, we are concerned with those forms of delinquent activity which result from the performance of social roles *specifically provided and supported by delinquent subcultures.* There are many thefts, assaults, and other delinquent acts which do not depend upon the prescriptions of a delinquent subculture but are, rather, secondary or incidental to the performance of essentially lawful social roles. The deaths, injuries, or destruction which occasionally result from fraternity initiations are of this sort; they are unintended consequences rather than expected or prescribed consequences. They may occur in the course of carrying out other expected forms of activity but are not the essential types of action upon which the social definition of the role has been constructed. Student pranks following athletic contests, to cite another example, may result in injury and property destruction, but they are not activities which are essential to being a loyal supporter of one's favorite team; one can fully perform this role without committing delinquent acts. Similarly, neurotic or psychotic youngsters often perform acts of violence, sexual assault, or property destruction without involvement in a delinquent subculture. Such youngsters are not necessarily acting out social roles sanctioned and shared by their peers. In fact, severely neurotic and psychotic adolescents are usually estranged from their peers.[1] It sometimes happens that the "lone" offender is able to maintain a role in a conventional group whose members are totally

---

[1] For example, Fritz Redl has observed that some mentally disturbed youngsters are unlikely to be tolerated by delinquent gangs because of their erratic and unreliable performances. (Helen L. Witmer and Ruth Kotinsky, eds., *New Perspectives for Research on Juvenile Delinquency,* United States Children's Bureau [Washington, D. C.: Government Printing Office, 1956], pp. 60, 64-65.)

unaware that they have a delinquent in their midst. Many adolescent shoplifters fall into this category, for they sometimes succeed in concealing their delinquencies from their peers for long periods of time.

THE SOCIAL COSTS OF DELINQUENT SUBCULTURES

In this study, we focus on delinquent subcultures because in our opinion those forms of delinquent activity that are rooted in the prescriptions of a delinquent subculture represent the most costly and difficult problem in the field of delinquency control and prevention. First, acts of delinquency that reflect subcultural support are likely to recur with great frequency. In the delinquent subculture, habitual delinquent behavior is defined as a prerequisite for acceptance and status in the group. The fighting member of the street gang can lay claim to a "rep" only if he continually exhibits skill in the use of violence. The thief must persist in making big "scores" in order to maintain his reputation for dexterity and audacity and thus his social position. The drug addict wins deference by his mastery of the resources and knowledge for maintaining or increasing the esoteric experience of his "kick."

Secondly, access to a successful adult criminal career sometimes results from participation in a delinquent subculture. Delinquent subcultures, as we shall have occasion to note in later chapters, are often integrally linked to adult criminal groups. Through these age-graded relationships, the young are sometimes afforded an opportunity to acquire the values and skills that are prerequisite to competent performance of adult criminal roles. If they excel in criminal learning, they may subsequently be recruited into the adult world of crime. By thus furnishing continuity between juvenile and adult illegal activities, the delinquent subculture promotes careers in crime which might otherwise be successfully controlled. It therefore greatly increases the long-run social costs of juvenile misconduct.

Finally, the delinquent subculture imparts to the conduct of its members a high degree of stability and resistance to control or change. Delinquent activity is an essential feature of the social role which a member must perform in order to maintain his acceptance by other members of the group. As long as he finds satisfaction in these associations, the delinquent behavior can be expected to continue. His actions are integrated with the actions of other members who rely on him to carry out his role. A division of labor is readily apparent in the operation of the three types of delinquent group that we have identified. The member who refuses to perform further delinquencies must expect expulsion from the group. Because of this network of expectations and obligations, it is difficult to change or control one member's behavior without first changing the character of the entire group. Furthermore, efforts to induce a member to feel shame or guilt are blocked by the rationalizations and reassurances which the group provides.

A distinction between acts that are supported by delinquent subcultures and those that are not is implicit in many research investigations and official decisions, although it is seldom recognized. Law-enforcement officials must continually assess the relative social costs of offenses by different types of offender. They tend to regard the occasional or accidental delinquencies of lone offenders as less serious than the aberrant acts of those who have connections with an established delinquent group. Solitary offenders, as we have suggested, appear less likely to pursue adult criminal careers and are more easily encouraged to develop alternative solutions to their adjustment problems. In general, the delinquencies of adolescents who are not members of a delinquent subculture seem to be more transitory phenomena, more susceptible to social control.

Earlier we alluded to the tendency among officials of criminal justice to respond differentially to similar acts of delinquency committed by members of different social classes. This disposition to "bear down" upon lower-class offenders has been interpreted as "class bias."[2] In our opinion, however, it may also reflect a judgment that lower-class delinquency involves greater long-run social costs—at least partly because lower-class offenders are more likely to be enmeshed in a delinquent subculture.[3] The apparent class bias of law-enforcement officials may

---

[2] It has been noted consistently in the criminological literature that officials do not view middle-class and lower-class delinquency with the same degree of alarm. Glaser, for example, points out: "It has been well established that official agencies take a more punitive attitude towards misbehavior by low-status youth than towards the same behavior in higher-status youth. The son of a highly respected family who is caught stealing or in less serious misbehavior often is merely reprimanded or taken to his parents by the victim, or even by police, where similar activity by a youth from 'across the tracks' would lead to official arrest and classification as a delinquent. In general, where the social status of the youth and his family is lower than that of the complainant, the greater the difference between statuses, the more likely it is that the youth's activities will be called 'delinquency' " (Glaser, op. cit., p. 9).

[3] We do not wish to suggest that delinquent subcultures never arise in the middle class. Evidence is accumulating that they do exist but that they are organized principally for relatively petty delinquencies, such as the illicit consumption of alcohol or marijuana, sexual experiences, petty larceny, and auto theft for joy-riding. This behavior seems to occur less frequently, to be more responsive to control and change, and to be less likely to continue in the form of adult criminal careers. See, e.g., A. K. Cohen and J. F. Short, Jr., "Research in Delinquent Subcultures," Journal of Social Issues, Vol. 14, No. 3 (Summer 1958), p. 28.

stem from their feeling that lower-class delinquencies are therefore more likely to recur, to become patterned systems of action, and perhaps even to eventuate in adult careers, since the subculture constitutes a fertile criminal learning environment as well as a source of powerful social controls over the behavior and attitudes of participants. The isolated offender—as the middle-class offender more often is—is not likely to evoke serious concern on the part of law-enforcement officials, who recognize that delinquent behavior tends to be less stable when peer supports are weak or absent. We shall have more to say later in this chapter about the relative frequency and social cost of delinquent behavior among the various classes.

NORM-VIOLATING BEHAVIOR AND LOWER-CLASS CULTURE*

by William C. Kvaraceus and William B. Miller

A bunch of street-corner youngsters are hanging around a variety store. Someone says, "Gee, it's dull around here. What a dead neighborhood. There's never anything to do. Nothing ever happens."

Someone else comes along and says, "Hey, Paul has some cans of beer." The group goes off, starts drinking beer, and becomes engaged in discussion of feats of daring and danger. Then someone says, "Gee, it's dead around here. Let's go and find something to do. Let's pick up a car somewhere and go for a ride." The group agrees, off they go, and the groundwork for a night of "trouble" has been prepared.

The terms "lower class" and "middle class" are used here to refer to systems of behavior and concerns rather than groups defined in conventional economic terms. There are "rich" and "poor" in the lower class as well as in the middle and upper classes. Owning an automobile, even a Buick or a station wagon, is no longer in itself a sufficient symbol or criterion of class status. Wealth, as evidenced by personal possessions or bank books, is becoming less useful as a primary determinant of family status. What are some of the patterned forms of behavior and focal concerns which characterize the culture of the lower class, and

*From William C. Kvaraceus and Walter B. Miller, *Delinquent Behavior,* pp. 62-75. Copyright 1959 by the National Education Association of the United States. Reprinted by permission.

how are these related to norm-violating behavior of lower-class adolescents? [1]

A large proportion of delinquency today has its origins in the street-corner subculture of lower-class society. A close look is needed at the forces in this milieu which often tend to generate norm-violating behavior for a large segment of the delinquent population.

Lower-class culture[2] refers specifically to a way of life which is followed by a large segment of the present-day population of this country, whose concerns, values, and characteristic patterns of behavior are the product of a well-formed cultural system. Preliminary evidence indicates that somewhere between 40 and 60 percent of the total population of the United States share or are significantly influenced by the major outlines of the lower-class cultural system.[3] In this report attention is directed chiefly to this cultural system in an urban setting. In its most representative form, it reveals a distinctive patterning which differs significantly from that of middle-class culture.

Much of the delinquency of lower-class youngsters may be seen as an attempt by the acting individual to adhere to forms of behavior and to achieve standards of value as they are defined within this type of community.

LOWER-CLASS FOCAL CONCERNS

The behavior of those involved in a given cultural system may be said to be motivated by a set of "focal concerns," which receive special emphasis within that culture.[4] "Achievement," for example, is a generally recognized concern of most members of the middle class. In lower-class culture, similarly, certain focal concerns are dominant; these include: *trouble, toughness, smartness, excitement, fate,* and *autonomy*. In relating these concerns to the behavior of lower-class youngsters, each

---

[1] The presentation and description of focal concerns of lower-class culture as well as the discussion of how these concerns influence delinquent behavior are adapted from: Walter B. Miller. "Lower Class Culture as a Generating Milieu of Gang Delinquency." *Journal of Social Issues* 14: April 1959.

[2] The criteria here pertain particularly to large urban communities and are less applicable to certain ethnic groups, such as the Italians and Chinese.

[3] Statistics as to the prevalence of lower-class culture, using educational, occupational and economic indexes, are presented by Walter B. Miller in "Cultural Features of an Urban Lower Class Community," reproduced by Community Services Branch, National Institutes of Health, March 1959.

[4] The "focal concern" as a concept for describing and analyzing subcultural groups in the United States is introduced and discussed in: Miller, *Journal of Social Issues* 14: April 1959, *op. cit.*

concern must be considered as a *dimension* within which a fairly wide range of alternative behavior patterns may be followed by different individuals in different situations. At the same time, it will be necessary to relate the influence of these concerns to the motivation of delinquent behavior by specifying the nature of behavioral orientation in each instance. How concealed (covert) and how direct (overt) is the influence of each of these concerns? Does the individual's behavioral adjustment to his culture stem from a positive orientation toward the particular concern (does he appear to seek out the aspect) or from a negative orientation toward it (does he reject it)?

Norm-violating behavior in this subculture is not to be simply explained on the basis of direct imitative behavior, nor is it solely the outgrowth of a so-called delinquent subculture which arises from conflict with middle-class values which are misunderstood, rejected, and scorned by the delinquent.

Trouble "Getting into trouble" and "staying out of trouble" represent dominant concerns for lower-class individuals. Prestige may often attend a boy or girl's success in achieving or avoiding involvement with authorities of official agencies. "Trouble" is a word that constantly occurs in lower-class conversation: A mother may express relief that her daughter is going steady with a boy "who has never been in trouble"; an unmarried daughter who becomes pregnant is described as having "got in trouble with a man." In spite of the greater prevalence of both official and unofficial norm-violating behavior in lower-class communities, there still remains much leeway in the choices to be made by the adolescent who is raised in this type of environment. Although individuals are often motivated in the direction of getting into trouble, the choice frequently favors staying out of trouble.

Some writers, in referring to the lower-class youngster's propensity for trouble, have said, "These street-corner kids don't know right from wrong." This is far from true. Lower-class adolescents are very conscious of what the official rules of society are. At the actual point of being impelled or motivated to engage in given types of delinquent activity—getting into a gang fight, picking up a hot car, getting drunk, gambling, "hooking" school, all of which may be legally defined as delinquencies—their perception of the potential gains to themselves in terms of prestige, group status, and appropriate or demanded behavior outweighs their perception of the sanctions that can be directed against them for the specific delinquent act. For the youngster born and bred in this cultural milieu the total dynamics underlying choice of alternative forms of behavior, including the individual's perception of potential gains to himself, frequently throws the weight of decision on the side of norm-violating behavior. Other aspects of the dynamics and direction of choice will be discussed later.

Toughness Physical prowess, "masculinity," endurance, athletic ability, strength, all rank high in the concerns of lower-class adolescents and are evident in the kinds of heroes they select. The tough guy, the gangster, the pugilist, the tough cop, the combat infantryman and the "hard" teacher are heroic models.

Feats of toughness and exploits requiring physical and mental endurance are constant conversation pieces in street-corner society. Anything that smacks of the effeminate and the soft is scorned and ridiculed. The street-corner boy will say, "Man, I ain't been home or ain't slept for two nights. I've been on the prowl." Or: "They grilled me and beat me with a hose but I didn't admit nothin'." Similarly: "My old man and me had one helluva fight. Man, he beat me up good." Some aspects of this type of masculine behavior may be explained as attempts by the street-corner boy to accommodate to certain fears relating to "masculine" identity acquired as the result of his early relations with his parents.

Smartness Skill in duping and outsmarting the other guy as well as the ability to avoid being duped by others indicate a lower-class concern with "smartness." Although the "IQ" of the lower-class adolescent —as measured by school-administered intelligence tests, which entail certain types of verbal and academic aptitudes—is almost invariably low, his "duplicity" quotient must be high if he is to operate effectively in the world of the street corner.

In this world the lower-class adolescent will most likely disdain the "academic" wisdom of the teacher. Instead of seeing the teacher as a "person who knows," the lower-class boy may regard him as someone who knows very little about what really goes on in the streets and alleys, the flats and tenements, the street corners and backyards of the city. The models of estimable achievement in the area of "smartness" are the con man, the fast-man-with-a-buck, and the bunco operator, whose victims are seen as suckers and dupes.

Excitement The search for thrill and stimulation is a major concern in the lower-class community, where life often involves monotonous and dull routines in the home, on the job, and in just "hanging around." Frequent complaints about boredom and monotony are related to a recurrent quest for excitement and stimulation. The desire for excitement is reflected in prevalent patterns involving drinking, gambling and playing the numbers, goading ("testing") official authorities such as teachers and policemen, picking up girls, going out on the town, participating in a "rumble," destroying public property, stealing a car, and joy riding. All these acts involve risk, and their perpetrators court "trouble." Much of the delinquency related to this cultural concern involves the quality of high adventure. Although aggression against persons and property may figure in many of these acts, such behavior, from the actor's point of view, can not be interpreted simply as "antisocial"; the aggressive component is one by-product of a complex of motives which includes the quest for "excitement."

Fate Lady Luck is a reigning goddess of lower-class society: "I was unlucky, I was caught" and "He's lucky, the police didn't catch up with him." Every boy hopes that his luck will change and that his number will come up soon. Any evil that befalls him can be explained away by evoking an ill-fated destiny. The prevailing philosophy of Kismet in lower-class culture operates to inhibit directed seeking after certain goals and provides a handy excuse for misadventures. Gambling in its many forms—numbers, pool, cards, dice and horses—nicely combines the element of thrill with that of luck.

Autonomy Many lower-class youngsters indicate in no uncertain terms, "No one is going to boss me, but nobody." Yet lower-class delinquents frequently seek out, through norm-violating behavior, situations in which they will be told what to do, when to do it, how to do it, and whether it is right when done. Overt expression of dislike, disdain, and resentment of external control over behavior apparently runs counter to an implicit seeking out of highly restrictive social environments where rules, regulations, and edicts exert close control over all behavior. The large percentage of lower-class youth in such institutions as the armed forces, the disciplinary school, and the state training school casts doubt on the reliability of their overt complaints against dominant authority. The common use of the term "boss" for landlord, first-line supervisor, or local politician also reflects the pattern of seeking stable sources of dependency accompanied by verbal protest against these same restricting and controlling authorities.

Norm-violating behavior by lower-class pupils which serves to "test" the firmness of school authority may represent an expression of the need for "being controlled," which is often equated with "being cared for" by superordinate authority. If kicking up, talking back, truanting, or running from an institution are dealt with severely, firmly, and quickly, the pupil is reassured, although he may complain bitterly about his "unfair" and "tough" punishment or the "bad luck" of being caught. Moreover, studies of street-corner society indicate that certain restrictive social environments such as the school, after being tested by the norm-violating youngsters, may be rejected for failing to be *strict enough rather than for being too strict*. The problem presented to public schools enrolling many lower-class youngsters is how to preserve and use the coercive controls that are implicitly sought by the very same individuals who elude authority and complain most loudly about being pushed around by the principal and attendance officer. The tough "independence" of many youngsters from this subculture presents a neat exterior camouflage for strong dependency needs and cravings implicit in the recurring lower-class complaint against unjust, coercive, and arbitrary authority.

The Interplay Among Focal Concerns

How does their cultural milieu contribute to the lower-class youngster's involvement in delinquent behavior? Three general processes may be cited. *First,* engaging in certain cultural practices which comprise essential elements of the total life pattern of lower-class culture automatically violates certain legal norms. Examples of this may be seen in the use of profanity, in hanging around or loitering, and in the serial-mating pattern characteristic of many homes. *Second,* in certain instances where alternative avenues to valued objectives are available to the youngster, the law-violating route frequently entails a relatively smaller investment of energy and effort than the law-abiding route. *Third,* the *demanded* response to certain situations recurrently engendered within lower-class culture may call for the commission of illegal acts. For many youngsters the bases of prestige are to be found in toughness, physical prowess, skill, fearlessness, bravery, ability to con people, gaining money by wits, shrewdness, adroitness, smart repartee, seeking and finding thrills, risk, danger, freedom from external constraint, and freedom from superordinate authority. These are the explicit values of the most important and essential reference group of many delinquent youngsters. These are the things he respects and strives to attain. The lower-class youngster who engages in a long and recurrent series of delinquent behaviors that are sanctioned by his peer group is acting so as to achieve prestige within this reference system.

Adjustment to street-corner living is not, by any means, easy. Members of lower-class street-corner groups are often the most fit and the most able youngsters in their community, for this is a tough league in which to make the grade. One must possess both stamina and perseverance as well as the capacity to interact and to subordinate self to the over-all needs of the group. These same qualities, directed to different ends, are often cited as important ingredients for success in school and on the job. Similar skills and drives in the case of the middle-class boy are often directed toward the Eagle Scout badge. It is these motives and qualities of the lower-class boy which may, under the proper circumstances, be channeled into law-abiding activities.

Can a street-corner youngster who is able to adapt effectively to his primary neighborhood reference groups also adapt himself to the classroom? Many of the prestige factors in his peer group have been enumerated. When the same child comes to school, the whole set of definitions as to the basis of prestige is shifted. Now the capacity to apply oneself assiduously and conscientiously to intellectual tasks is of prime importance. To gain status within the academic frame of reference, one must achieve in "book learning" and acquire certain linguistic patterns. But a young male who engages successfully in these types of behavior runs a serious risk of being tagged as effeminate by his neighborhood peers. To the extent that the youngster, thus in conflict, continues to take his peer group as his primary object of reference, to that extent he will be impeded in making an easy or ready adjustment to the school situation. As the schools are discovering, there are a great many youngsters for whom their peer group remains as the reference group of highest priority. The measure of the students' "adjustment" must always depend on the extent to which the other groupings of which the youngsters form an effective part have systems of values resembling those of the groupings in which they receive their early learning experiences.

Some school-connected experiences such as football—with its long, tedious practice periods and drills, interspersed with a weekly battle that calls for a sharp focus of all physical skills and strength in concentrated measure and for a short duration—find analogies in lower-class life and in certain kinds of lower-class occupational roles. A dull, slow, and typical week in this subculture frequently culminates in a "night out on the town" and by "hanging one on." It should also be noted that a substantial portion of the labor force today (about 50 percent) still consists of laborers, unskilled workers, and routine factory operatives. Most of these jobs are filled by lower-class individuals. Graduates of the street corner, as they grow and assume their roles in the world of work, have been prepared to operate within these interactional milieus, for their street-corner and occupational groups share similar sets of ideas, principles, and values. The job routines of the fireman, trucker, soldier, sailor, logger, and policeman reflect the occupational rhythmic pattern characteristic of lower-class community living, street-corner activity, and football—long periods of routine activity broken by intense action and excitement. As one views occupational needs of the future and, at the same time, analyzes the prevailing features of street-corner society, the following conclusion emerges: *The essential outlines, values, and language patterns; the emphasis on "smartness"; the regard for strength and physical prowess, all appear to remain functional, adjustive, and adaptive for these youngsters.*[6]

There are many nondelinquent lower-class youngsters. The same neighborhoods produce cops and crooks, pimps and priests. What factors make the difference between quitting school and going on to college or in becoming a fireman rather than a firebug? The next section presents a hypothesis that may suggest an answer to this question, one of particular importance to the school.

THREE PATTERNS OF ADAPTATION TO SOCIAL CLASS MOVEMENT

Three patterns of adaptation to the problems of aspiration and class movement may be identified within the adolescent lower-class community. These may be delineated in terms of two major factors: first, the extent to which the individual youngster manifests a realistic desire for upward social movement—which involves the actual adaptation of a different set of class-related behavior patterns, and not merely symbols of status such as cars and big houses—and, second, the extent to which such upward aspirations are actually feasible in light of the youngster's early family training and his resultant personality characteristics. On this basis, three patterns of adaptation can be distinguished:

1. *"Stable" lower class.* This group consists of youngsters who, for all practical purposes, do not aspire to higher status or who have no realistic possibility of achieving such aspirations.

2. *Aspiring but conflicted lower class.* This group represents those for whom family or other community influences have produced a desire to elevate their status, but who lack the necessary personal attributes or cultural "equipment" to make the grade, or for whom cultural pressures effectively inhibit aspiration.

3. *Successfully aspiring lower class.* This group, popularly assumed

---

[6] This position is developed and the following typology included in Walter B. Miller's "Implications of Lower Class Culture for Social Work," *The Social Service Review* XXXIII: No. 3, September 1959.

to be most prevalent, includes those who have both the will and the capacity to elevate their status. The familiar educational success story involved here is in the best tradition of the Horatio Alger "rags to riches" dream of American folklore. Moreover, when these cases do appear, they are dramatized and, by implication, presented as the norm. Cases of this type were more frequent during the late nineteenth and early twentieth centuries and were related to the epic migrations from the "old country." As this migration has ebbed and as many of those with upward aspiration have achieved their objective, the number of persons in this category has diminished considerably. At present, the highest untapped potential is probably in the Negro group, most of whom are still in the lower class and thus represent a vast reservoir of potentially upwardly mobile individuals.

At present there is little reliable research evidence as to the relative prevalence of these three types. However, it should be noted that there is evidence that Type 1, the "nonaspiring" lower-class youngster, is far more common than generally supposed, and that this group does not seem to be getting smaller, and may be getting larger. Type 2, the group that is being "stalled," is particularly significant in any consideration of delinquency because of the inevitable frustrations and conflicts associated with this position. Frictions arising when the youngster's levels of aspiration exceed his realistic potential or when serious obstacles thwart realistic levels of aspiration may contribute to the motivation of much delinquent behavior. Here is an important and profitable area for further research and for special attention by the schools.

The factor of aspiration level also relates significantly to the problem of the school drop-out. Usually the youngster who drops out of school as soon as it is legally possible is culturally lower class. The fact that approximately 45 percent of those youngsters completing the fifth grade do not graduate from high school[7] is a good indication of the size of the lower-class adolescent population and indicates clearly that the "drop-out" is not merely a relatively isolated "learning problem," but, in fact, represents a highly prevalent social class group. "Dropping out" is a recurring, standard practice and derives support from the whole cultural system. This often creates a difficult situation for youngsters of Type 2. For example, an adolescent boy may evidence a desire to continue in school, but his older brother will say, "For cripes sake, you

---

[7] U. S. Department of Health, Education, and Welfare, Office of Education. "Statistical Summary of Education." *Biennial Survey of Education in the United States, 1952-54*. Washington, D. C.: Superintendent of Documents, 1957. Chapter 1, p. 10.

still going to school? What do you want to go to school for, you can drop out now? You're old enough." "I never went to school," adds the old man. "Go get a job. Be something beside a book reader."

To the negative pressure that this youngster gets from his family is added the taunts of his peer group who see him carrying his books home for study. They yell at him, "Hey, you still going to school? What kind of a fairy are you?" In such cases where certain influences have caused the adolescent to consider continuing in high school and going on to college as a desirable course of action, the basic definitions of his own cultural environment operate to block and stall him. This youngster must be tough indeed to move out and up. There is always conflict in such a situation. It is perhaps this group that is most likely to strike out in aggressive or norm-violating fashion against school and family.

For the youngsters in Type 1, experience in school is generally regarded as meaningless and useless. They may sit out the school in relatively passive compliance but not without considerable annoyance to school authorities. Their problems and the school's problem end on their sixteenth birthday. School becomes for members of this group another arena in which to demonstrate their toughness, their smartness, their autonomy, their daring—to the great discomfort of the school. To them, most school teachers are "a bunch of real squares."

Many of those lower-class youngsters who are in the "stable" group and even some who are upwardly mobile to a slight degree, in terms of both aspiration and potential, can manage to live out their adolescence as relatively law-abiding youngsters who get into little serious trouble with the law. Many school people tend to see the future lives of these youngsters in terms of only two major alternatives—an essentially lower-class or an essentially middle-class way of life. A third alternative and one which is far more feasible in a large proportion of cases—is to train and prepare the youngster for a *law-abiding lower-class way of life.*

For that segment of law-abiding lower-class youngsters for whom the commission of a delinquent act is relatively rare or infrequent, the school and other community agencies should make every effort to recognize and exploit those elements in their cultural environment and personalities which provide support for a pattern of law-abiding behavior.

In order to discover why some youngsters and not others adopt a pattern of law-violating behavior, it is necessary to look at the youngster's basic childhood experiences, and especially his relationships with his parents and other models for identification.

NATIONAL POLICY FOR ALIENATED YOUTH*

by Robert J. Havighurst and Lindley J. Stiles

If citizens of all occupational, political, and religious affiliations were asked the question, "What should this country do for its young people?" the answer would be unanimous that the United States should give its boys and girls a good chance to grow into productive workers, successful parents, law-abiding citizens, and happy persons—in effect, help them become competent adults.

There would of course be some differences of opinion as to how society should provide opportunities suited to the accomplishment of this goal. In addition, disagreement might prevail as to which tasks are appropriate for the schools to do, which are best left to the family, and what contributions should be made by churches and other agencies. Further, there might be some differences of opinion as to the kinds of opportunities that are appropriate for girls as compared with boys, for Negroes in contrast to white youth, or for the mentally dull as compared with gifted children.

General agreement would probably prevail, however, that opportunity is relative. One boy's chance would be another's burden. The circumstances that spell opportunity to a boy or girl depend on the youth's abilities, on what he has been brought up to want from life, and on which openings or positions in the adult society are likely to be available to him.

Thus young people with below average abilities whose family backgrounds have given them limited contact with books and ideas will more likely experience satisfactory growth if they get stable semi-skilled or unskilled jobs, make stable marriages, and get an income that provides reasonably adequate housing and the standard of living they have learned to want. Nobody can rightly say that they lack opportunity if they drop out of school at age 16 and find a stable job.

On the other hand, many children from culturally inadequate homes do much better in life than their parents did, mainly through using educational and economic opportunity. One should not, therefore, force the children of poor parents into rigid educational or occupational molds that prevent them from showing potential abilities. This premise is

*From Robert J. Havighurst and Lindley J. Stiles, "National Policy for Alienated Youth," *Phi Delta Kappan,* Volume 42, Number 7 (April 1961), pp. 183-291. Copyright 1961 by Phi Delta Kappa, Inc. Reprinted by permission of authors and publisher.

generally accepted and followed. The United States has reason to be proud of practices in its schools and industries which challenge young people to find, develop, and use hidden powers in themselves.

It is generally agreed that the great majority of young people in this country will profit from the educational opportunities afforded by the high school, and that the upper third to half of them will profit from a college education.

Satisfactory growth depends upon appropriate opportunity, while appropriate opportunity depends upon the abilities and the personality of the individual.

How Well Is Our Goal for Youth Achieved?

Opportunity for satisfactory growth is provided to a fairly adequate degree for the great majority of young people. To evaluate a community's performance in this respect it is useful to think about four classifications of youth, each of which has a particular pattern of opportunity, advantages, and disadvantages.

A. The Academically Superior. The Conant report on the American high school[1] speaks of the 15 per cent of boys and girls who are academically superior. Such young people have IQ's generally above 115 and are good "college material"; it is generally agreed that they should be encouraged to achieve well in high-school academic courses and to go on to college.

Academically superior students have been the center of attention in the decade just past. Most of the recent improvements in secondary school programs have been aimed at them. They have been able to profit from the new science and mathematics curricula, from more intensive foreign language teaching, and from college level courses taught in high school or from early admission to college.

Because of the shortage of young adults due to the low birth rates of the 1930's, these young people have been regarded as a precious resource which must be cared for and cultivated to the fullest.

B. The Middle Two-Thirds. In addition to the 15 per cent just mentioned, some two-thirds of young people get along reasonably well under present educational and social conditions. Most of them graduate from high school and some of them go to college. A quarter of this middle two-thirds, or 15 to 20 per cent of the age

---

[1] James B. Conant, *The American High School Today*. New York: McGraw-Hill, 1959.

group, do not graduate from high school, but they manage to get jobs at the age of 16 or 17, or to marry at those ages, and to grow up to adulthood in a fairly acceptable manner.

These young people were the focal point of discussion immediately following World War II before public attention shifted to the gifted in the early 1950's. They are assumed to be able to adapt themselves to school and to the society, and actually most have done so reasonably well. When a multi-track system has been introduced in high school, this group occupies the middle one or two tracks. Some of them do fairly well in college. Most of them found the labor market of the 1950's to be hospitable.

C. The Handicapped. Two or three per cent of boys and girls have serious mental or physical handicaps which obviously interfere with their progress to competent adulthood. Some of them are slow to learn, with IQ's below 75 or 80 that place them in the group defined as the "educable mentally handicapped." Others are deaf, or blind, or crippled, or afflicted with cerebral palsy. While it is next to impossible to provide opportunities that will equate their chances for satisfactory growth with those enjoyed by the "normal" youngster, society has made substantial effort in this direction.

Special provision has been made in most states for the education of those children at a greater-than-average expense. Their teachers obtain special training and are usually paid higher salaries than teachers of normal pupils receive.

D. The Alienated Group. Some 15 per cent of young people do not grow up in a satisfactory way. This group has been identified in several studies. It has been called by various names—the uneducables, the nonlearners, the hard-to-reach, the alienated. The "alienated" is an appropriate name for this group, because it expresses the fact that they are somehow alien to the larger society in which they live. Such youths have been unsuccessful in meeting the standards set by the society for them—standards of behavior, of learning in school, of performance on a job. By the time they reach adolescence these boys and girls are visible as the misfits in school. Either they are hostile and unruly, or passive and apathetic. They have quit learning and have dropped out of school psychologically two or three years before they can drop out physically.

Most alienated youth come from low income homes; most of them fall in the IQ range 75-90; almost all drop out of school at age 16 or before; they tend to come from broken homes, or homes which are inadequate emotionally and culturally. Yet this is not simply a group low in economic status and IQ; two-thirds of working-class children do satisfactory work in school, as do two-thirds of children with below average IQ's. This is a group whose start in life has been poor because of the disadvantages its members face. Their families have been inadequate. Often their physical health has been poor. Their intellectual skills are usually too marginal to compensate for other deficiencies.

It should be emphasized that alienated youth can be found in all IQ ranges from middle and upper class homes, although the percentages are higher in the 75-90 IQ bracket and among groups which are culturally and economically disadvantaged. Any child who lacks recognition at home or in school, or who is emotionally insecure, can become alienated.

Within this alienated group are found the majority of juvenile delinquents. Among the girls of this group are found the majority of 16- and 17-year-old brides.

We call them "alienated" because they do not accept the ways of living and achieving that are standard in our society. As younger children they probably accepted the standard ideas of right and wrong, complied with school regulations and tried to succeed, but the combined and repeated frustrations of failure in school and mistreatment at home have turned them either into members of delinquent subgroups or into defeated, apathetic individuals. The 15 per cent about whom we speak are found in a community which has a normal cross-section of American youth. But in the slum area of a big city the proportion may be doubled. As many as 30 or 40 per cent of the eighth and ninth graders in some of our city schools are alienated youth. On the other hand, this group comprises only a small percentage of youth in the upper middle class suburbs of a metropolitan area.

Members of underprivileged racial or immigrant minorities are likely to be found in the alienated group. Thus Negroes, Mexicans, and Puerto Ricans make up a large proportion of alienated youth in the industrial cities of today, whereas thirty or forty years ago this group would have been composed largely of children of European immigrants. On the other hand, many boys and girls from racial and immigrant minorities are growing up successfully, and these numbers are increasing.

The alienated group seems to be a product of society, its size the resultant of combinations of socioeconomic factors, and its particular composition determined by the presence of one or another social group at the bottom of the social scale. Thus in a Midwestern city of 45,000 this group was found to be present to the extent of about 15 per cent; there were no Mexicans or Puerto Ricans in the community, and few Negroes. The boys and girls in the alienated group carried names that reflected English, Scotch, Irish, or German origin. Their families occupied low status in that particular community.

The alienation of a youth in this community may be illustrated by the case of a boy whose nickname was Duke. He was the older of two boys born to his mother when she was living with her second husband. This man deserted her when the boys were young. She supported them by working and from help provided by the government aid-for-dependent-children program. Duke's IQ was about average as measured by an intelligence test, yet he did poor work in school and was required to repeat the sixth grade. He was regarded by his agemates and by his teacher as a highly aggressive boy. His sixth grade teacher checked the following adjectives as descriptive of him: aggressive, alert, boastful, bossy, cruel, depressed, honest, loyal, revengeful, show-off, tease, touchy, vindictive.

As Duke grew older he became more actively aggressive in school, until in the ninth grade, the records show, he was frequently "sent out" of his classes by his teachers. Finally, shortly after he reached his sixteenth birthday, he decided to quit school. One of his best friends had just been expelled and another had dropped out.

When asked by an interviewer how it seemed to him after he had been out of school several months, Duke said: "I'd rather be in. But when I quit I had a feeling that they were going to kick me out anyway. It was quit or get kicked out because of my bad behavior. I couldn't mind my teachers or they couldn't mind me; I don't know which. Anyway, I had mostly study halls when I quit. They kicked me out of science and social studies and algebra."

Duke's first brush with the law had come when he was 10 years old. On this occasion he was brought before the police matron with some other boys for putting their footprints in some freshly-laid cement. By the time he was sixteen he had accumulated an assortment of misbehaviors on the record, including stealing, fighting, and sexual offenses.

From the time he quit school at 16 and until he was 17 Duke loafed around town with cronies, working at unskilled jobs periodically for a few weeks at a time, and getting into various kinds of trouble. Finally he enlisted in the Navy.

Here we see a boy whose pattern of failing to grow up according to society's expectations became clear to him and to others by the time he was 10 or 11 years old. He reacted to this failure by becoming aggressive, tough, masculine, and boastful. Since he could not hold jobs for any length of time, he stole in order to get money. Within his delinquent gang he was accepted as a leader, and thus earned his nickname. His enlistment in the Navy marked another effort to grow up by doing something active. This did not work out, however, since he lacked the stability and the affirmative attitude required by the military service; he was soon discharged back into his home community, where he resumed his delinquent ways. Not until he reached the age of 19 did he seem to be stabilizing somewhat. At this time he married and became a steadier and more dependable person.

NEED FOR AN ALTERNATIVE PATHWAY TO ADULTHOOD

The essential problem of the alienated group is that they have not found a satisfactory avenue or channel of growth toward adult competence. Since they are failing in school, they cannot grow up by means of the school. They need an alternative pathway to that offered by the school as we now know it.

These boys want the same things in life that are achieved by boys who are growing up successfully. They would like to have money, a job, and as they grow older they want the use of an automobile. They want girl friends, and eventually desire to have a wife and children. Unlike the majority of boys, however, they do not have the combination of family assistance, the intelligence, the social skills, and the good study and work habits necessary to achieve their goal legitimately. Nevertheless, they want to grow up and to have the symbols of manhood, and they become discontented when they do not succeed.

Alienated boys, thwarted in the normal channels, seek illegitimate means to achieve the symbols of manhood. They may turn to the delinquent gang for "moral support" and for instruction in ways to get money, excitement, power, and the feeling of masculinity. These boys, frustrated by the adult society around them, may become hostile and aggressive toward that society. Often they may vent their hostility through such activities as destroying property, burning school buildings, and attacking law-abiding people.

Forty years ago there were many boys who could not grow up through the school system. But at that time there was a clear alternative road to adulthood—the road of work. A boy could quit school at age 14, 15 or 16 and get work on a farm or in a business. In fact, more than half of all boys in 1920 did drop out before graduating from high school; nevertheless, they found work and grew up along the pathway provided by a series of jobs with increasing pay and increasing responsibility. Census records show that in 1920 somewhat more than 50 per cent of boys aged 14 through 17 were employed full-time or part-time. The proportion of 14-year-olds who were out of school and employed full-time was low, but more than half of all boys were out of school by age seventeen and at work. At that time a boy could easily follow a well-traveled highway of work from early adolescence to adulthood.

During the past forty years the number of jobs open to juveniles has been decreasing. Jobs as telegraph messengers, delivery boys, office boys, elevator boys, etc., have grown scarce. The farm population has been reduced greatly and with it the farm as a place where a non-academic boy could be doing a man's work by the age of 16. The proportion of unskilled and semiskilled jobs in the labor force has also decreased. Employers, faced with an oversupply of adult labor during much of this period, have adopted as a standard for employment the minimum age of 18, or high-school graduation. The 1960 census will show that fewer than 35 per cent of boys aged 14 through 17 were employed at that time, and a large proportion of them have only part-time jobs. The unemployment rate is at least twice as high among boys between 14 and 17 as it is among older boys who are in the labor market. During the latter part of the 1950's, while the overall rate of unemployment in the United States was about 5 per cent, the teen-agers' unemployment rate was 10 per cent, while 16- and 17-year-olds who had dropped out of school had an unemployment rate of 20 per cent.

The employment situation for teen-agers is not likely to improve during the 1960's, for the high birth rate of 1947 and later years will cause the numbers of 16- and 17-year-olds to increase by 1963 to a figure 40 per cent above the numbers in this age bracket in the 1950's.

Thus there is a strong prospect that the road to adulthood through juvenile work which has been narrowing since 1920 will become even more constricted during the coming decade. This road will remain in existence, however. It is being followed with fair success by about half of the 35 to 40 per cent of boys who now drop out of school before finishing a high-school course.

What our society must do is to widen this narrow road once more, through finding or creating more juvenile jobs. With work experience, there is a good chance of bringing many alienated boys back into the mainstream of American youth, where they can grow up with confidence in themselves and in the society.

Since jobs in the American economy, as we now define jobs, are not likely to increase in numbers for boys, it becomes necessary to find ways to provide boys with the moral equivalent of work, a kind of work experience that has the growth value of a job, though it is not a job in the narrow sense of the word.

IMPORTANCE OF WORK IN THE GROWING-UP PROCESS

The idea that work experience should be provided for boys outside of the labor market, if the labor market as then constituted could not accommodate them, was generally accepted during the depression of the 1930's. By 1933 the mounting wave of unemployment had engulfed hundreds of thousands of families. Fathers were unemployed, and adolescent boys could not find work. Boys took to the road, partly in the hope of finding jobs elsewhere, and partly to take some of the burden of feeding a family off their fathers' shoulders. Soon a quarter of a million homeless boys were riding freight trains and hitchhiking toward places where work was rumored to be, or where they might at least find a change from the grim conditions at home.

This situation was soon recognized as an emergency and was treated as such by President Roosevelt. The Civilian Conservation Corps was established to place boys over 16 in resident camps under a semi-military regime. In this program boys learned to do socially useful work, under supervision, and were paid a small sum of money, most of which was allotted to the assistance of their families. The program was not related to schools; indeed, school administrators were excluded from its policy-making bodies and top leadership because they were believed by President Roosevelt to be unsympathetic to work experience. This program worked well, but it was limited to boys who had already dropped out of school, it was also rather expensive. In some situations the lack of cooperation between schools and the Civilian Conservation Corps Program tended to hinder the full development of youth who needed and desired both work experience, by which some income could be derived, and academic training. Groping for a type of work experience that would have school-relatedness and which would be available to youth of both sexes, the federal government next created the National Youth Administration plan, which provided for part-time work with pay for students of high-school and college age. The work projects in the NYA program were developed mainly by schools and colleges; the funds for the payment of salaries were provided by the federal government. Program regulations specified that work provided could not compete with ordinary business and industry. The objective was to provide supervised work experience which would have educational value and promote an allegiance to society while permitting young people to continue their schooling.

This experiment in providing youth with jobs continued until the entry of the United States into World War II, when the armed services and war industry quickly absorbed all available youth.

During the late 1930's the American Youth Commission, a group of citizens appointed by the American Council on Education to study the problems of youth in the depression years, made studies of the Civilian Conservation Corps and the National Youth Administration work program. They drew the following conclusions:

> Every young person who does not desire to continue in school after 16, and who cannot get a job in private enterprise, should be provided under public auspices with employment in some form of service . . .
>
> The Commission is impressed with the success of experiments that have been made with combinations of part-time schooling and part-time employment . . .
>
> Public work for young people should be planned with special regard to its educational quality. It should be superintended by persons who are competent to train young people in good work habits as well as in specific skills. It should be carried on in a spirit that will give to the young worker a sense of being valued by and valuable to his country. Finally it should provide an opportunity to try various kinds of work, so that the young person may find his own aptitudes and abilities and may be given some guidance in preparing for private employment in a field where he can be most useful and successful . . .
>
> The Commission recommends, therefore, that in the formulation of public policy at all levels, explicit recognition be given to the social responsibility of seeing to it that all young people are constructively occupied up to some appropriate age. The Commission believes that 21 is the age which ought to be recognized for this purpose. Insofar as any specific age can do so, it corresponds to a real point in the process of maturation for a very large number of individuals, and it has been imbedded in law and custom by centuries.[2]

---

[2] *Youth and the Future*. Washington, D. C.: American Council on Education, 1942.

A NEW NATIONAL EMERGENCY

While we are not in a severe economic depression, and we do not have a quarter of a million homeless boys on the road, we do have almost a quarter of a million alienated boys in each annual cohort—a quarter of a million reaching their fourteenth birthday this year, another quarter of a million becoming 15, and so on. Consequently, alienated youth might be considered a national emergency equal to or worse than that of the 1930's.

Dramatic testimony on the need and desire for work experience for youth was presented last year by Congressman Frank Bow of Ohio, in the following letter, published on September 12, 1960, with his own statement:

> I have an anonymous letter, postmarked Louisville, that reads in part as follows:
>
> "As future taxpayers and voters, my buddies and myself, all teen-agers, are writing this to tell how we feel about the unemployment and juvenile delinquents.
>
> "Our opinion is that if most boys 17, 18, and 19 who quit or finish high school could find work to get them off the streets and supply them with some money; they won't have to steal or rob for it.
>
> "All teen-agers are not delinquents. We looked hard for work of any kind and found very little. If someone took time to do something for us, they would be doing a favor for all.
>
> "Older people said 'look harder' or 'write your Congressman,' so we are. Ohio streets are bad, the parks are not clean. Why not hire teen-agers to do some of this work?"
>
> If I could reply, the first thing I would tell the anonymous teen-ager is that youngsters of his generation should not quit high school, and should make every effort while in high school to equip themselves for productive work in our era. There will not be much future in the "Space Age" for a teen-ager who lacks even the preparation of a high-school education.
>
> I would try to resist a lecture on whether anyone should think for a moment that he must "steal or rob."
>
> But most important, I would ask the community to act on this young man's suggestion. Why not a community project to use the talents and energies of such boys? Encourage them to set up their own central agency for job information. Make a real effort to find work that will help them to keep their self-respect.

CURRENT PROGRAMS AND PROPOSALS

The fact that work experience is important in the process of growing up has not escaped the attention of educators. For a long time, vocational education has contained work experience as an integral part in many courses. What has been called "cooperative education," which combines a job with study, has been practiced in some engineering schools and technical institutes, as well as in some high schools, for more than thirty years. In 1928 there were seventy-eight cities with 5,682 pupils enrolled in cooperative courses under the Smith-Hughes Act. The government-aided diversified occupations-work study program was started in 1933. Since World War II there has been a substantial growth of work experience programs in schools. In a survey of work experience educational programs published by the U. S. Office of Education in 1957, 145 items in the working bibliography of 276 items were produced after 1950. More than 200 articles, books, and research reports on work experience education have been published since 1941.

The following types of work experience are now found in secondary schools:[3]

1. In-school nonremunerative general education work experience programs.

Experience is provided in the school for students as typists, clerks, parking lot attendants, messengers, multigraph operators, library assistants, motion picture machine operators, locker maintenance workers. Students are not paid except for after-school work. In some cases, credit is given toward graduation.

2. Out-of-school, nonremunerative general education work experience programs.

   a. Community service work in noncommercial organizations: libraries, parks, social agencies, elementary schools.

   b. Student learner assignments in physicians' or dentists' offices, architects' studios, hospitals, city or county offices.

3. Remunerative general education work experience programs at the junior high-school level.

This is for youth who are likely to drop out of school at age 16. It is usually provided for 15-year-olds. School credit and "going wages" are given. Typical jobs are as bus boys, messengers, waitresses, car washers, printers' helpers, sales clerks.

4. Remunerative general education work experience for pupils in senior high school.

---

[3] DeWitt Hunt, *Work Experience Education Programs in American Secondary Schools.* Washington, D. C.: Department of Health, Education and Welfare, U. S. Office of Education, Bulletin No. 5, 1957, p. 13.

This type of program is for youth in senior high school who will profit personally and economically from work experience in such a way as to make their schooling more attractive and more successful. Scholastic credit is generally given for work which is coordinated with school studies.

5. Remunerative vocational work experience in senior high schools not subsidized by federal vocational education funds.

A "diversified occupations" type of course is offered, mainly to high-school juniors and seniors over 16 years of age who have good records. Often the course is set up in schools or communities too small to qualify for the federal subsidy. Some of these students will get work experience in selling jobs, some in office assignments, and some in factories. An effort is made to place the student in the field of employment where he is likely to work as an adult.

6. Remunerative vocational work experience programs in high school subsidized from federal vocational educational funds.

Commencing in 1917 with the Smith-Hughes Act (which was amplified in 1946 by the George-Barden Act), a cooperative part-time education and employment program is available to high-school juniors and seniors. Jobs are in the trades, industrial occupations, and distributive occupations. This is the most highly selective program; it is seldom available to a student who has done poor work in school.

NEEDED: PROGRAMS FOR ALIENATED YOUTH

The most widespread programs are for senior high-school pupils, age 16 or over, who have a good school record. Thus they are not open to alienated youth. They are useful programs; but something more is needed.

The kind of work experience program that will be most useful to alienated youth will have the following characteristics:

1. It will commence at age 13 or 14, and continue to age 19, though many boys will graduate from it a year or two before age 18.

2. It will attempt to teach boys elementary work disciplines: punctuality, ability to take orders from a boss, ability to work co-operatively with others in a team, responsibility on the job.

3. It will lead directly into stable adult jobs.

4. It will be a part of the public school program, with the curriculum adapted to the intellectual level, the interest in practical endeavors, and the work-experience program of alienated youth.

A preventive program of this type must of course rest upon a procedure for identifying the future alienated youth at least by the age of 13 or 14. This can be done and has been done in several researches. The identification process consists of finding those boys who show a combination of aggressive maladjustment with failure in school, plus checking in marginal cases by visiting the home and evaluating the nature of family discipline and help given to the boy.

A work experience program will need to be organized in stages which reflect the boys' level of maturity and responsibility, and which at the same time are geared to prevailing child labor legislation. Probably three stages are indicated.

A. The first stage should be work in groups, under school supervision, completely or partially outside of the labor market. For example, boys might work in groups on parks, school grounds, alleys, beaches, thus contributing to community housekeeping. Alternatively, boys might work in a "sheltered workshop" in the school which would contract for jobs with local business and industry. The workshop might take contracts for stuffing envelopes with advertising matter; simple assembly jobs, such as nuts and bolts into packages for sale; processing material with a simple machine. The difficulty with the sheltered workshop idea for boys is that similar facilities are badly needed for handicapped adults and for old people who need employment.

B. A second stage should be part-time work on an individual basis with employers in private or public business or industry. Here the boy would be more nearly "on his own" in the labor market, but he would still work under close supervision by the school.

C. The final stage would be full-time employment in a stable job, aided by some guidance and supervision on the part of school or employment service personnel.

RESPONSIBILITY OF SOCIETY AS A WHOLE

The corollary school program provided for alienated youth would need to be adapted in content, methods of instruction, and learning materials to the ability and orientation of youth involved. The content would need to be appropriate to the goals of instruction and to the age level of the pupils. At the same time, it would, in most cases, need to be presented in textbooks and other learning materials at a lower reading level, and with less abstractness, than is common for high-school courses. Instruction would need to be characterized by practical approaches to problems, shop or laboratory experiences, and an extensive use of audio-visual aids. A close relationship between the program of the school and work experiences would be desirable.

A program of the type just outlined cannot be lodged in the labor force as it is now constituted. There are not nearly enough juvenile jobs, and the trend is toward reduction of juvenile jobs and unskilled jobs. Private business is not in a position to provide all the jobs needed, nor is organized labor in a position to cooperate in a program that might reduce the number of adult jobs in the economy.

Nevertheless, there seems to be good reason for adopting a social policy which guarantees work experience as a part of education to every boy who needs it, just as instruction in mathematics or science or foreign language is guaranteed to youth who need that kind of education. And the society should bear the cost of one kind of education just as it bears the cost of the other kind.

If the provision of juvenile jobs becomes a part of social policy, there are two presently expanding areas of the economy in which jobs for boys may be created fairly easily. One of these areas is that of conservation of natural resources, and the other is that of public service. Assuming that federal, state, and local government funds will be used increasingly on projects for soil and water conservation, and on the maintenance of parks, parkways, highways, beaches, and forest preserves, the respective government agencies might deliberately design work projects in such a way that substantial numbers of boys could be employed on work crews.

A Program Supported by Federal Government

Recently Senator Hubert Humphrey introduced a bill in Congress to set up a Youth Conservation Corps. His proposal was incorporated into the platform of the Democratic Party in 1960. This idea has much in its favor. It might well be developed for boys 16 and over, but if it were limited to work camps, it would not be applicable to boys under 16, where the need is especially great.

Possibly the plan might be developed into a more general Youth Development Program, for boys aged 13 to 20. The program might provide for locally-based work projects in the earlier stages, so that the boys could live at home and go to their regular schools while taking part in a work-study project.

Federal grants might be made to the states for the support of work experience programs meeting certain criteria. The state which received the grant might develop a program with three elements:

1. A program for the big cities, based on elementary or junior high-school units, with a job-creating and job-finding program supported by city-wide civic, business, and labor organizations.

2. A program for the community of 20,000 to 100,000 people, based on a particular junior high school or several elementary schools, and backed by a community commission of business and labor leaders.

3. A program for rural counties and rural sections or urban counties, based on elementary schools or consolidated schools, and developed in collaboration with the county agricultural agent and local community business leaders.

WHAT A WORK EXPERIENCE PROGRAM WOULD NOT DO

The work experience program suggested in these pages is not a panacea for all youth problems. It is merely one element (but a highly important one) in a complex of arrangements which our society should make in order to reduce the number of alienated youth.

Such a program might be expected to cut down juvenile delinquency by as much as 50 per cent. It could not reduce juvenile delinquency more than this, because a substantial proportion of juvenile delinquency is committed by boys who are not aggressive or are not failing in school, and such boys would not be in the program.

A work-study program needs to be supplemented by community agencies, such as Boys' Clubs, Settlement Houses, YMCA, CYO, and other organizations that give boys a chance for wholesome recreation and social life.

Furthermore, a work-study program for adolescent boys may not be needed as much in the future as it is right now. It is likely that the number of boys who fail in school and who become socially maladjusted can be reduced materially by preventive measures taken earlier, when the boys are in kindergarten and first grade.

More work and more effective work needs to be done with these boys and their families when they are five or six years old. A more successful program at this age might cut the numbers of teen-age alienated youth in half, and thus reduce the size of a work-study program.

SUGGESTED STRATEGY FOR COMMUNITIES

Thus the strategy of attack on the problem of alienated youth appears to have the following phases:

1. Development of a work-study program for alienated 13- and 14-year-old boys.

2. Supplementation of the work-study program by social agencies and community organizations which create and maintain a wholesome social situation for alienated youth.

3. Preventive programs for work with young children in the primary grades and their families to help them make more satisfactory progress in school and thus to reduce the future numbers of alienated youth for whom a work-study program is needed.

This country should be doing all three of these things. If we do, we can look ahead with some confidence to a time, ten or twenty years from now, when the unhappiness and frustration of young people and the danger to society of having a large group of alienated youth will be reduced to less than half their present proportions.

THE NATURE OF PREJUDICE*

by Gordon W. Allport

Prejudice, as we have seen, may become part of one's life tissue, suffusing character because it is essential to the economy of a life. It does not always act in this way, for some prejudices are merely conformative, mildly ethnocentric, and essentially unrelated to the personality as a whole. But often it is organic, inseparable from the life process. This condition we shall now examine more closely.

METHODS OF STUDY

Two methods have proved fruitful in the study of character-conditioned prejudice, the *longitudinal* and the *cross-sectional*.

*From Gordon W. Allport, "The Psychology of Prejudice," *The Nature of Prejudice,* Reading, Massachusetts: Addison-Wesley Publishing Co., 1954, pp. 395-408. Copyright 1954 Addison-Wesley Publishing Co., Inc. Reprinted by permission of the publisher.

In the longitudinal approach the investigator attempts to trace back through a given life history factors that might account for the present pattern of prejudice. The technique of interviewing may be used, as in the California studies, or the technique of psychoanalysis, illustrated in the investigation by Ackerman and Jahoda. There is also the ingenious device employed by Gough, Harris, and Martin, who compared the present prejudice level of children with their mothers' ideas on child training, thus revealing situational factors presumably operating in the present prejudice. All these studies are described in Chapter 18.

The cross-sectional method attempts to find out what the contemporary prejudice pattern is like, asking especially how ethnic attitudes are related to other social attitudes and to one's outlook on life in general. Using this method, we uncover some interesting relationships. For example, Frenkel-Brunswik reports that highly prejudiced children tend to endorse the following beliefs (not one of which deals directly with ethnic matters):

There is only one right way to do anything.

If a person does not watch out somebody will make a sucker out of him.

It would be better if teachers would be more strict.

Only people who are like myself have a right to be happy.

Girls should learn only things that are useful around the house.

There will always be war; it is part of human nature.

The position of the stars at the time of your birth tells your character and personality.

When the same method is applied to adults, similar results occur. Certain types of propositions are endorsed by highly prejudiced more often than by tolerant adults.

The world is a hazardous place in which men are basically evil and dangerous.

We do not have enough discipline in our American way of life.

On the whole, I am more afraid of swindlers than I am of gangsters.

At first sight these propositions seem to have nothing to do with prejudice. Yet it is proved that all of them have. This finding can only mean that prejudice is frequently woven firmly into a style of life.

FUNCTIONAL PREJUDICE

In all cases of intense character-conditioned prejudice a common factor emerges which Newcomb has called "threat orientation." Underlying insecurity seems to lie at the root of the personality. The individual cannot face the world unflinchingly and in a forthright manner. He seems fearful of himself, of his own instincts, of his own consciousness, of change, and of his social environment. Since he can live in comfort neither with himself nor with others, he is forced to organize his whole style of living, including his social attitudes, to fit his crippled condition. It is not his specific social attitudes that are malformed to start with, it is rather his own ego that is crippled.

The crutch he needs must perform several functions. It must give reassurance for past failures, safe guidance for present conduct, and ensure confidence in facing the future. While prejudice by itself does not do all these things, it develops as an important incident in the total protective adjustment.

To be sure, not all character-conditioned prejudice serves precisely the same purposes in every prejudiced personality, for "threat orientation" differs in nature from person to person. In some, for example, it may be particularly related to unresolved infantile conflicts with parents or siblings, in others to persistent failure in later years. But in any case, we are likely to find a picture of ego-alienation, longing for definiteness, for safety, for authority. Personalities which for any reason feel threatened are likely to evolve similar patterns of accommodation to life in general.

An essential feature of this pattern is *repression*. Since the person cannot in his conscious life face and master the conflicts presented to him, he represses them in whole or in part. They are fragmented, forgotten, not faced. The ego simply fails to integrate the myriad of impulses that arise within the personality and the myriad of environmental presses without. This failure engenders feelings of insecurity, and these feelings engender, in turn, repression.

Thus an outstanding result of studies of bigoted personalities seems to be the discovery of a sharp cleavage between conscious and unconscious layers. In a study of anti-Semitic college girls they appeared on the surface to be charming, happy, well-adjusted, and entirely normal girls. They were polite, moral, and seemed devoted to parents and friends. This was what an ordinary observer would see. But probing deeper (with the aid of projective tests, interviews, case histories), these girls were found to be very different. Underneath the conventional exterior there lurked intense anxiety, much buried hatred toward parents, destructive and cruel impulses. For tolerant college students, however, the same cleavage did not exist. Their lives were more of a piece. Repressions were fewer and milder. The *persona* they presented to the world was not a mask but was their true personality. Having few repressions, they suffered no ego-alienation, and facing their own calamities frankly, they needed no projection screen.

This study, as well as others, reveals that the consequences of such repression are likely to be the following:

Ambivalence toward parents
Moralism
Dichotomization
A need for definiteness
Externalization of conflict
Institutionalism
Authoritarianism

All of these characteristics can be regarded as devices to bolster a weak ego unable to face its conflicts squarely and unflinchingly. They are accordingly the earmarks of a personality in whom prejudice is functionally important.

AMBIVALENCE TOWARD PARENTS

In the study of anti-Semitic women students cited above, the authors found that "without exception these girls declared that they liked their parents." Yet in their interpretation (Thematic Apperception Test), a preponderance of responses to parental figures accused them of meanness and cruelty, and betrayed jealousy, suspicion, and hostility on the part of the daughter. By contrast, the unprejudiced subjects in the same test were much more critical of their parents when they discussed them openly with the interviewer, but showed less animosity in the projective tests. The sentiments of these latter girls toward their parents was more *differentiated*. That is to say, they saw their parents' faults and openly criticized them, but they also saw their virtues, and on the whole got along pleasantly enough with them. The prejudiced girls were torn: on the surface all was sweetness and light, and this view was held up to public gaze; but deeper down there was often vigorous protest. The sentiment had become bifurcated. The anti-Semitic girls had more fantasies of their parents' death.

In spite of this buried animosity there seems to be less ideological friction between prejudiced youth and their parents. As children they take over the parents' views, especially their ethnic attitudes. They do so because ideological imitation is demanded and rewarded. Earlier we examined the conditions of child training that are likely to prevail in prejudiced homes. There we saw that the themes of obedience, punishment, actual or threatened rejection loom large. A relationship of power rather than love prevails. In such circumstances it is often difficult for the child to identify fully with the parents because his affectional needs are not met. He learns through imitation, coerced by reward, punishment, reproof. He cannot fully accept himself and his failings, but must be ever on guard against slips from grace. In such a family situation a child never knows just where he stands. A threat hangs over him at every step.

MORALISM

This anxiety is reflected in the rigidly moralistic view that most prejudiced personalities take. Strict insistence on cleanliness, good manners, conventions is more common among them than among tolerant people. When asked the question, "What is the most embarrassing experience?" anti-Semitic girls responded in terms of violations of mores and conventions in public. Whereas non-prejudiced girls spoke more often of inadequacy in personal relations, such as failing to live up to a friend's expectation. Also, anti-Semitic girls tend to be harsh in their moral judgments of others. One said, "I would sentence any striker to 50 years in the penitentiary." Tolerant subjects, by contrast, show much greater leniency toward transgression of the mores. They are less condemnatory of social misdemeanors, including violations of sexual standards. They tolerate human weakness just as they tolerate minority groups.

Studies with children show the same tendencies. When asked what makes for a perfect boy or girl, the prejudiced children mentioned usually purity, cleanliness, good manners; the more liberal children are often content to mention merely companionship and good fun.

The Nazis were noted for their emphasis upon conventional virtues. Hitler preached and in many respects practiced asceticism. Overt sex perversion was violently condemned, sometimes punished with death. A rigid protocol dominated every phase of military and social life. The Jews were constantly accused of violating conventional codes—with their dirtiness, miserliness, dishonesty, immorality. But while pretentious moralism ran high, there seemed to be little integration with private conduct. It was sham propriety, illustrated by the urge to make all expropriation and torture of the Jews appear "legal."

The genetic theory underlying such scrupulosity has to do with the child's early failure to live with his own impulses. Suppose he is punished and made to feel guilty whenever he soils himself, whenever he is found handling his genitals (we recall that mothers of prejudiced children are more likely to punish the child for this offense), whenever he has a temper tantrum, whenever he strikes his parent. A child who finds his every impulse wicked—and feels that he is unloved when he gives way to it—is likely to grow up hating himself for his many transgressions. He carries a burden of infantile guilt. As a consequence, when he sees any lapses from the conventional code in others he grows anxious. He wishes to punish the transgressor, just as he himself was punished. He develops a dread of the very impulses that trouble him. When a person grows overconcerned with sin in others, the tendency may be viewed as a "reaction formation." Having had to fight unholy impulses in himself, he cannot be permissive and lenient toward others.

The tolerant individual, by contrast, seems to have learned how to accept socially tabooed impulses early in life. He is not afraid of his own instincts; he is not a prude; he views bodily functions in a natural way. He knows that anyone may fall from grace. In his own upbringing his parents were skillful in teaching him the socially correct line of conduct without withdrawing their love when he failed to toe this line. The tolerant individual, having learned to accept the evil in his nature, does not grow anxious and fearful whenever he sees (or imagines) similar evil in others. His view is humane, compassionate, understanding.

Moralism is only surface compliance; it does not solve the conflicts within. It is tense, compulsive, projective. True morality is more relaxed, integral, and congruent with the life pattern as a whole.

DICHOTOMIZATION

We have reported that prejudiced children, more often than non-prejudiced, hold "there are only two kinds of people: the weak and the strong"; also, "there is only one right way to do anything." Prejudiced adults show the same tendency to bifurcation. Males with ethnic bias more often subscribe to the proposition: "There are only two kinds of women: the pure and the bad."

Those who tend to dichotomize in their cognitive operations are the very people who accentuate the distinction between in-group and out-group. They would *not* agree with the sentiment expressed in the familiar bit of doggerel:

> There is so much good in the worst of us,
> So much bad in the best of us,
> That it scarcely behooves any of us
> To talk about the rest of us.

The functional significance of "two-valued logic" for the prejudiced person is not far to seek. We have noted his failure to accept the criss-cross of good and bad in his own nature. He is therefore chronically sensitized to right and wrong. This inner bifurcation becomes projected upon the outer world. He gives approval or disapproval categorically.

NEED FOR DEFINITENESS

We assert that one of the most important psychological discoveries of recent years is that the dynamics of prejudice tend to parallel the dynamics of cognition. That is to say, the style of thinking that is characteristic of prejudice is a reflection, by and large, of the prejudiced person's way of thinking about *anything*. We have already made the point in connection with the dichotomizing tendency. We may now underline it by citing a series of experiments related to the matter of "tolerance for ambiguity."

An experimenter placed his subjects in a dark room. Only a point of light was visible. Without any visual anchorage or habits to guide them, all subjects under such circumstances saw the light sway in various directions. (Probably internal conditions of the retina or brain are responsible.) The experimenter discovered, however, that prejudiced people soon established a norm for themselves. That is, they reported the light as moving in a constant direction from trial to trial and to a constant number of inches. They require stability, and manufacture it when it does not objectively exist. Tolerant people, by contrast, tend to take longer to establish a norm for themselves. That is, for a longer period of trials they could tolerate the ambiguity of the situation.

Another experimenter studied memory traces in people with high and with low prejudice. He employed a drawing of a truncated pyramid.

Immediately after looking at the design for a brief time the subjects were asked to draw it from memory.

About 40 percent of both groups tended to draw a symmetrical figure, equalizing the two margins of the drawing. This type of symmetrization is normal enough, since our memories do tend to simplify and to reach a level of "better Gestalt." But what is especially interesting is that after a four-week interval, many more of the highly prejudiced subjects equalized the margins. Sixty-two percent of the high-prejudiced and only 34 percent of the low-prejudiced group did so.

Here it seems as though the highly prejudiced could not for long tolerate the ambiguity of the design; they needed a firm, simple, categorical memory. On the other hand, those who were low in prejudice seemed to say in effect, "I know this is a truncated pyramid, but I also know it is not as simple as it might be; there is something individual and unusual about it."

In short, while the low in prejudice also tend to form simplified memory traces, they are relatively better able to hold in mind what William James called "feelings of bus. . . ."

Another manifestation of the need for definiteness is encountered in the way prejudiced persons cling to past solutions. If they are shown a definite line drawing of a cat, and if in a series of subsequent brief exposures this picture gradually undergoes transformation until the line drawing of a dog appears, the more prejudiced subjects *cling* to the image of the cat for a longer time. They do not see the change so quickly; nor do they report, "I don't know what it is."

From this experiment we see that prejudiced people are more given to *perseveration,* which means that old and tried solutions are considered to provide safe anchorage. The experiment also discloses an interesting related phenomenon. Prejudiced people seem afraid to say "I don't know." To do so would cast them adrift from their cognitive anchor. This finding is duplicated in widely different investigations. In one, Rokeach asked his subjects in an experiment dealing with the recognition of names and faces to tell him which name should be associated with which face. Those high in prejudice made many erroneous guesses, while those low in prejudice often admitted defeat and refused to guess. Roper, studying the results of a public opinion poll, reports that individuals high in anti-Semitism give a low proportion of "Don't know" responses when asked their opinions on current events. Prejudiced people, it seems, feel more secure when they "know the answers."

The need for definiteness is likely to lead to a constriction of cognitive processes. The individual fails to see all relevant sides to his problem. Rokeach labels the resulting type of solution "narrow-minded." An experiment illustrates the process.

The ten following concepts were presented in alphabetical order to college freshmen: *Buddhism, Capitalism, Catholicism,*

Christianity, Communism, Democracy, Fascism, Judaism, Protestantism, Socialism. The students were asked to tell in what way any or all of these concepts were interrelated. Rokeach summarizes the results as follows:

"Analysis revealed that the cognitive organization as represented by the descriptions could be ordered along a single continuum ranging from *comprehensive* to *isolated* to *narrow.* A *comprehensive* organization is one in which all 10 concepts are organized into a single whole (e.g., 'all are beliefs'). An *isolated* organization is one in which the 10 concepts are broken down into two or more substructures with little or no inter-communication among substructures (e.g., 'Five are religious. Five are governments'). A *narrow* organization is one in which one or more of the parts objectively present is omitted from the description, the remaining parts being organized into one or more substructures (e.g., 'Only Buddhism, Catholicism, Christianity, Judaism, and Protestantism are related because they all believe in God')."

It turned out to a significant degree that those high in prejudice gave *narrow* groupings, i.e., left out some of the relevant items; those low in prejudice took them all into account and gave *comprehensive* groupings; while those intermediate in prejudice inclined to favor isolated groupings.

The same sort of constrictedness in thinking is reported by Reichard, who notes that prejudiced subjects taking the Rorschach test tend to give responses that are more inhibited, compulsively overmeticulous, as compared with other groups who are more given to seeing wholes and are more productive of associations.

All these experiments point in the same direction. Prejudiced people demand clear-cut structure in their world, even if it is a narrow and inadequate structure. Where there is no order they impose it. When new solutions are called for they cling to tried and tested habits. Wherever possible they latch onto what is familiar, safe, simple, definite.

There are at least two theories as to why this intolerance of ambiguity exists. Both may be right. One holds that the self-image of prejudiced persons is badly confused. From early life they have never been able to integrate their natures; the result is that the ego itself does not provide a fixed anchorage point. By compensation, therefore, the individual must find outer definiteness to guide him. There is no inner definiteness.

The other theory, slightly more complex, holds that when they were children prejudiced individuals suffered much deprivation. Many things were forbidden. They therefore grew apprehensive of delay and gratifications, for delay might mean deprivation. They therefore developed an urge for quick and definite answers. To think abstractly is to risk ambiguity and uncertainty. Better not hesitate; better adopt concrete, if rigid, modes of thinking. In favor of this view, we recall the evidence that prejudiced people do seem more susceptible to frustration. Their low tolerance may well be the reason they want always to see the ground on which they stand, for only with a clearly structured perceptual field can they avoid the threat of frustration.

EXTERNALIZATION

In the last chapter we saw that prejudiced people are given to projection, to seeing qualities in others that they should see in themselves but do not. In fact, all along the line they seem defective in self-insight.

To the prejudiced person things seem to happen "out there." He has no control over his destiny. He believes, for example, that "although many people may scoff, it may be shown that astrology can explain a lot of things." Tolerant people, by contrast, tend to believe that our fate lies not in our stars, but in ourselves.

Prejudiced girls, in telling stories from pictures (Thematic Apperception Test) more often see the events transpiring without the active participation of heroine. The action is determined by fate (for example, the heroine's fiance is killed in battle), and not by herself. When asked the question, "what would drive a person nuts?" prejudiced subjects respond in terms of threats from *without* or else say something like, "ideas which keep running through the head." Both replies indicate uncontrolled external agencies. It is not one's own shortcomings or actions that could "drive one nuts."

To explain this tendency we may again refer to ego-alienation as an underlying factor. It is easier and safer for a person in inner conflict to avoid self-reference. It is better to think of things happening *to* him rather than as caused *by* him. Extropunitiveness, as a trait, is one expression of this generalized tendency. The relation to group prejudice is obvious: it is not *I* who hates and injures others; it is *they* who hate and injure me.

INSTITUTIONALISM

The person with character-conditioned prejudice likes order, but especially *social* order. In his clearcut institutional memberships, he finds the safety and the definiteness he needs. Lodges, schools, churches, the nation, may serve as a defense against the disquiet in his personal life. To lean on them saves him from leaning on himself.

Research shows that, by and large, prejudiced people are more devoted to institutions than are the unprejudiced. Anti-Semitic college girls are more wrapped up in their sororities; they are more institutionally religious; they are more intensely "patriotic." Asked "What is the most awe-inspiring experience?" they usually answer in terms of external patriotic and religious events.

Many studies have discovered a close link between prejudice and "patriotism." As the following chapter will show, extreme bigots are almost always super-patriots. The tie between nationalism and persecution of minority groups was clearly seen in Nazi Germany. It seems to hold for other countries as well. One investigation, conducted by Nancy C. Morse and F. H. Allport in a suburban American community, among middle-class people, is particularly revealing.

These investigators undertook the ambitious task of discovering which of several alleged causes of anti-Semitism was in fact most outstanding and demonstrable. The method was elaborate, requiring a 92-page booklet of tests, scales, questionnaires. The collaboration of 175 subjects was secured by paying into the treasury of their local clubs a certain amount of money for each booklet completed and returned.

First of all, the extensive instrument measured several aspects of anti-Semitism: how much aversion the subjects felt to Jews; how much they would say against them (antilocution); and how far they would actually go in hostile and discriminative behavior (antiaction).

It then tested several hypotheses, such as the following: that anti-Semitism would be associated with insecurity or fear of the future; with actual economic need or uncertainty; with feelings of frustration; with belief in a Jewish "essence"; with "national involvement."

This last variable was measured by a series of propositions asking for agreement or disagreement, one of these being, "Whereas some people feel that they are citizens of the world, that they belong to mankind and not to any one nation, I, for my part, feel that I am, first, last, and always, an American."

By the method employed the investigators discovered a high degree of anti-Semitism among their subjects. In only 10 percent did it seem wholly absent. In about 16 percent it reached an extreme, almost violent, degree.

While there was some evidence that insecurity and frustration do play a part in the nexus of anti-Semitism, the investigators find proof that the *most important single factor* is "national involvement." Only this factor stands up when all other variables are held constant. It alone meets the criterion of "unique covariation" with prejudice. Important too is the "belief in essence"—that Jews at bottom are in some way utterly unlike other people. But this belief is effectively related to prejudice only if strongly nationalistic views are likewise present. Thus "patriotism" may be a mask for bigotry.

The findings of this research are important. It will be noted that the anti-Semite is not merely a bundle of negative attitudes. Rather he is trying to *do* something: namely, to find an island of institutional safety and security. The nation is the island he selects. It is a positive anchorage; it is *his* country right or wrong; it is higher than humanity; more desirable than a world state. It has the definiteness he needs. The research establishes the fact that the higher the degree of nationalism, the higher the anti-Semitism.

Note the emphasis here is upon positive security. Anti-Semitism is not merely the shadow that fear and anxiety cast. Plenty of apprehensive and frustrated people never develop into anti-Semites. What is important is the way fear and frustration are handled. The *institutionalistic* way— especially the nationalistic—seems to be the nub of the matter.

What happens is that the prejudiced person defines "nation" to fit his needs. The nation is first of all a protection (the chief protection) of *him* as an individual. It is his in-group. He sees no contradiction in ruling out of its beneficient orbit those whom he regards as threatening intruders and enemies (namely, American minorities). What is more, the nation stands for the *status quo*. It is a conservative agent; within it are all the devices for safe living that he approves. His nationalism is a form of conservatism. According to his definition, the nation is that which resists change. It follows that he distrusts liberals, reformers, supporters of the Bill of Rights, and other "commies"; they threaten to change his safe conception of what the nation means.

AUTHORITARIANISM

Living in a democracy is a higgledy-piggledy affair. Finding it so, prejudiced people sometimes declare that America should not be a democracy, but merely a "republic." The consequences of personal freedom they find unpredictable. Individuality makes for indefiniteness, disorderliness, and change. It is easier to live in a defined hierarchy where people are types, and where groups are not constantly shifting and dissolving.

To avoid such slipperiness the prejudiced person looks for hierarchy in society. Power arrangements are definite—something he can understand and count on. He likes authority and says that what America needs is "more discipline." By discipline, of course, he means *outer* discipline, preferring, so to speak, to see people's backbones on the outside rather than on the inside. When students are asked to list the names of great people they most admired, prejudiced students usually gave names of leaders who had exercised power and control over others (Napoleon, Bismarck) whereas the unprejudiced listed, more typically, artists, humanitarians, scientists (Lincoln, Einstein).

This need for authority reflects a deep distrust of human beings. Earlier in this chapter we noted the tendency of prejudiced people to agree that "the world is a hazardous place where men are basically evil and dangerous." Now, the essential philosophy of democracy is the reverse. It tells us to trust a person until he proves himself untrustworthy. The prejudiced person does the opposite. He distrusts every person until he proves himself trustworthy.

The same suspicion is seen in responses to the following question: "If I were to express a greater fear of one of the following types of criminals I would say that I am more afraid of (a) gangsters, (b) swindlers." About half of the respondents choose one, and half the other alternative. But those who are more afraid of *swindlers* have higher prejudice scores in general. They feel more threatened by trickery than by direct physical attack. Ordinarily it might seem that fear of gangsters (physical threat) is a more natural and normal type of fear—and it is this that unprejudiced people report.

To the prejudiced person the best way to control these suspicions is to have an orderly, authoritative, powerful society. Strong nationalism is a good thing. Hitler and Mussolini weren't so wrong. What America needs is a strong leader—a man on horseback!

We have evidence that the authoritarian pattern may become set at an early age. Prejudiced children are more likely than others to believe that "teachers should tell children what to do and not worry about what the children want." Even by the age of seven the same type of child is distressed and at loose ends unless the teacher gives him instructions what to do and makes his assignments definite and authoritative.

DISCUSSION

Our portrait of the prejudiced personality (called by some authors "the authoritarian personality") is based largely on the results of recent research. While the outlines of the pattern are clear, the weighting and interlocking of evidence are not yet complete. Contrasting with the authoritarian type, investigators report an opposite pattern of correlated qualities that comprise what is sometimes called a "democratic," a "mature," a "productive," or a "self-actualizing" personality.

Most of the research underlying this comparison is based on the study of extreme or contrasting groups of subjects—those having very high or very low prejudice scores. Median or "average" subjects are usually discarded. This procedure is defensible, but it has the disadvantage of overemphasizing types. We are likely to forget that there are plenty of mixed or run-of-the-mill personalities in whom prejudice does not follow the ideal pattern here depicted.

There is a further methodological weakness in research to date. Most of it takes only one starting point. It creates a cluster of high-prejudice and one of low-prejudice subjects, and then discovers, for example, that the former shows greater intolerance for ambiguity in perceptual or problem-solving tasks. It does not use the desirable reverse control which would be to take a cluster of subjects who have intolerance for ambiguity and then discover whether this group has more ethnic prejudice. There should be a two-way demonstration of correlations claimed, before we can feel entirely sure.

But in spite of these weaknesses—due largely to the youthfulness of this area of research—we cannot possibly explain away the trends reported in this chapter. Our picture may be oversharp and may later need modification and supplementation, but the basic fact is firmly established—prejudice is more than an incident in many lives; it is often lockstitched into the very fabric of personality. In such cases it cannot be extracted by tweezers. To change it, the whole pattern of life would have to be altered.

Chapter Seven

MASS CULTURE

World War II was hardly over when a faint but angry voice was heard; it has been growing in vigor ever since. This is the substance of its indictment: America is less and less a land of individualists and more and more a land of think-alike, act-alike robots. What is more, a parallel argument runs, our "cultural" landscape is increasingly a monochromatic wasteland, ever less spontaneous and original and ever more contrived and synthetic. Although the debate on American culture has been confined in the main to intellectual circles, it will inevitably be broadcast for all to hear. It is imperative that the teacher and the administrator be aware of the question, for the very nature of their calling places them in the vortex of the controversy.

We have already encountered David Riesman's contention that today's suburban, upper-middle-class American (and presumably tomorrow's modal American) is increasingly "other-directed" in orientation, that he is increasingly fearful lest he stand out from the crowd and be taken for a maverick or nonconformist. An analogous case has been made by William H. Whyte, Jr. In his best-selling book, *The Organization Man,* the *Fortune* editor argues that the core American ideology—the congeries of values that combine in the "Protestant Ethic" of thrift, hard work, and self-reliance—is being supplanted by a new ideology: the "Social Ethic." Central to this emergent norm is ". . . a belief in 'belongingness' as the ultimate need of the individual."[1] Like Riesman,

---

[1] *The Organization Man* (Garden City, N. Y.: Doubleday & Co., 1956), p. 7.

Whyte traces this new value system to the functional need for the gregarious, extrovertive "team" man in an era dominated more by the bureaucrat and the organization man than by the old-fashioned, freewheeling individual enterpriser. And just as Riesman writes that ". . . on the whole, contemporary society, especially American, no longer requires and rewards the old enterprise and the old zeal,"[2] so Whyte observes that ". . . people do have to work with others . . . it *is* an age of organization."[3] Others, too, among them E. E. Cummings,[4] Erich Fromm,[5] Clyde Kluckhohn,[6] and Archibald MacLeish[7] have contended that ours is an era of hypercautious conformism and "dictatorship by peers." But our concern here is less with togetherness and the "adjustment ethic" than it is with the correlative charge that America is becoming a "mass society."

The author of "Peninsula People" (See Chapter Eight) reviews the pressures, actual and ideological, that are inevitably homogenizing and "flattening out" the American cultural scene. Harold M. Hodges contends that the very "massification" process that is gradually erasing remaining class, ethnic, regional, and even age and sex differences is also at work in related arenas—and in none more vividly than in the sphere of "cultural"[8] and esthetic values. In "Masscult and Midcult," Dwight Macdonald maintains that the corrosive impulses of what he calls "masscult" are inevitably eroding the lingering cultural survivals of an earlier era. If the differences that once so sharply distinguished American from American are indeed being ironed out (and the evidence is at best tentative and conjectural), we must ask why. The answer, in its simplest terms, is not hard to come by. Mass culture is the twin corollary of mass society, and a mass society is what our nation is unfailingly becoming. American society is not merely a convenient case in point either: it is the paramount example of the mass-type social-economic structure that, it appears, will inevitably take hold in all "post-industrial" societies—in all societies which have evolved what

---

[2] *The Lonely Crowd* (New Haven: Yale University Press, 1950), p. 104.

[3] Whyte, *op. cit.,* p. 13.

[4] "i & self-discovery," *Atlantic Monthly,* May, 1953, pp. 57-62.

[5] "The Psychology of Normalcy," *Dissent,* Spring, 1954, pp. 139-143.

[6] "Have There Been Discernible Shifts in American Values during the Past Generation?" in *The American Style,* ed. by Elting E. Morrison (New York: Harper & Row, 1958).

[7] "The Loss of Confidence," *American Scholar,* Spring, 1953, pp. 141-153.

[8] In this context we shall take "culture" to mean "the enlightenment and refinement of taste acquired by intellectual and esthetic training" *(Webster's Collegiate Dictionary,* Fifth edition, 1940).

David Potter characterizes as an economy of "abundance."[9] When automation and mass communications become the focal element of a society, successive developments in technology—in production, marketing, and transportation—literally transform the organization of group life.

If we recall the multiform pressures—not the least of them mass education—that have forged Americans into an ever more homogeneous people, we can understand what the late Frederick Lewis Allen meant when he remarked of mass culture, " . . . *this is something new; there was never anything like it before.*"[10] And we can sense the logic that impelled Daniel Bell to observe that " . . . America in recent years has become, perhaps for the first time, a truly national society."[11] All this has been made possible, he adds (in what may strike us as too premature an inference), " . . . by the rise of mass production and mass consumption, and the consequent leveling of distinctive class styles of life."[12] Similarly, Macdonald proposes that mass culture is " . . . like nineteenth-century capitalism . . . a dynamic, revolutionary force, breaking down the old barriers of class, tradition, taste, and dissolving all cultural distinctions."[13] Although we may not quite agree with Macdonald, we can hardly dispute Irving Howe's conclusion that " . . . we cannot escape what is so much a part of the atmosphere in which we live."[14] We might agree, too, with Hannah Arendt when she writes that " . . . mass society, whether we like it or not, is going to stay with us into the foreseeable future."[15]

Kitsch—German for mass culture—has not, on the whole, been treated kindly by the social critics who have examined it. Bernard Rosenberg in "Mass Culture in America" and Dwight Macdonald in "Masscult and Midcult" represent the less sanguine (and more typical) intellectual stance. In *Beyond Conformity*, Winston White analyzes and refutes the thesis of critics like Macdonald and Rosenberg that conformism and mass culture are about to engulf humanity. Both

[9] David Potter, *People of Plenty: Economic Abundance and the American Character* (Chicago: University of Chicago Press, Phoenix edition, 1954); see, especially, pp. 66-72.

[10] Frederick L. Allen, *The Big Change, 1900-1950* (New York: Doubleday & Co., 1952), p. 277.

[11] Daniel Bell, "Modernity and Mass Society: On the Varieties of Cultural Experience," *Studies in Public Communication*, No. 4 (Autumn, 1962), p. 55.

[12] *Ibid.*, p. 7.

[13] Dwight Macdonald, "A Theory of Mass Culture," *Diogenes*, No. 3 (Summer, 1953), p. 1.

[14] Irving Howe, "Notes on Mass Culture," *Politics*, 5 (Spring, 1948), p. 120.

[15] Hannah Arendt, "Society and Culture," *Daedalus*, 89 (Spring, 1960), p. 278.

Macdonald and Rosenberg would agree with what White describes as the central proposition of mass culture theory: that mass culture "corrupts the standards of excellence and at the same time effaces the unique quality of folk culture. It is, in short, one more agency of homogenization in modern society."[16] Macdonald, in particular, affirms that mass culture takes the content of high culture as its raw material and debases it so that it will be palatable to the masses. Both Rosenberg and Macdonald fit what White calls the "reformer's approach" to mass culture: both would agree that mass culture " . . . is the result of the *loss of consumer sovereignty:* the masses do not get what they want but instead are 'oversold' ";[17] they are consumers coerced either by the producers of mass culture or by the very nature of the marketplace.

Clement Greenberg, on the other hand, takes what White would designate as the opposite, "elitist" approach.[18] Although Greenberg is mainly concerned with the "new leisure class" emerging with the shorter work week among blue-collar workers, he belongs with T. S. Eliot, Ortega y Gasset, Bernard Iddings Bell, and Daniel Bell in fearing the "rule of the masses"; for the elitist-aristocratic view blames mass culture for the low quality of mass demand. According to this view, it is not the purveyor (Madison Avenue, Hollywood) but the consumer who is responsible for the "cult of mediocrity."

In David Riesman's eyes, neither purveyor nor consumer is altogether responsible for mass culture. Yet it is the latter, he argues—and especially those who have only " . . . recently been released from underprivilege by mass production and mass leisure"—who have won ". . . an often influential voice in the direction of consumption and hence of production." Elaborating on this theme in "Leisure and Work in Post-Industrial Society," Riesman holds that the "new leisure class" is ill-prepared for its demanding consumership role. Facing an ever shorter and less strenuous work week, coupled with an ever increasing standard of living, the new consumers lack the requisite sales resistance—the "consumer sophistication"—to resist successfully the blandishments of

---

[16] Winston White, *Beyond Conformity* (New York: The Free Press of Glencoe, Inc., 1961), p. 53.

[17] *Ibid.,* p. 63; this theoretical stance (which has seen "Madison Avenue" supplant "Wall Street" as a whipping boy) is essentially neo-Marxist in its defense of the duped "masses."

[18] Clement Greenberg, "Work and Leisure under Industrialism," *Commentary,* Volume 16, Number I (July, 1953), pp. 57-61.

"juke-box culture."[19] The problem, Riesman concludes, is no small one; it is one that will increasingly confront us as we attain an economy of abundance.

Captivating as the mass society concept is, many of its core assumptions are heavily tinged with speculative value judgments that have yet to be substantiated. Thus, though Daniel Bell admits that (Marxism apart) the theory of mass society " . . . is probably the most influential social theory in the Western world today," he warns that the idea becomes very slippery when one seeks to apply it analytically.[20] Winston White, too, would question certain assumptions that are basic to the mass culture suppositions: he wonders, above all, if the individual is as much a hapless, manipulatable puppet as he is made out to be. Another case made by many who would challenge the principal mass culture rationale relates to the quality of the mass media. Bell, for instance, contends that a great *proportion* of today's population participates in worthwhile cultural activities—and that the rising levels of education assure increasing appreciation of superior culture. Oscar Handlin calls attention to the fact that American "popular culture" has witnessed bursts of high-level creativity (much of our jazz, for example, and such comedians as Charlie Chaplin, Buster Keaton, and W. C. Fields).[21] Edward Shils would even defend what Macdonald disdainfully calls masscult; "the very growth of *Kitsch,* and of the demand that has generated the industry for the production of *Kitsch* is," he argues, "an indication of a crude aesthetic awakening in classes that previously accepted what was handed down to them. . . ."[22] David Manning White wonders whether the "castigators of mass culture are justified in their shrill pronunciamentos that damn the mass media as all black," and he notes that the " . . . xenophilic critics who discuss American culture as if they were holding a dead vermin in their hands seem to imply that in some other, better age the bulk of people were fair copies of Leonardo Da Vinci."[23] To buttress his point, White cites the many

---

[19] For a witty, tongue-in-cheek lesson on the question of America's cultural levels, see "Highbrow, Lowbrow, Middlebrow," by Russell Lynes, *Harper's,* 198 (February, 1949), pp. 19-28.

[20] Daniel Bell, *The End of Ideology,* (New York: Collier Books, 1961), p. 21.

[21] Oscar Handlin, "Comments on Mass and Popular Culture," *Daedalus,* 89 (Spring, 1960), p. 329.

[22] Edward Shils, "Mass Society and Its Culture," *Daedalus, Ibid.,* p. 294.

[23] David White, "What's Happening to Mass Culture?" *Saturday Review,* 39 (1956), p. 11.

artistic assets of contemporary American mass culture: the television audience of 20 million that watched the premiere of Sir Laurence Olivier's *Richard III,* the burgeoning sales of quality paperback books and classical records, the mushrooming of community orchestras in thousands of small cities, and the massive audiences that greet touring foreign ballet companies. "There has been," White concludes, "such a rehearsal of all that is ugly and bathetic in our popular arts by critics whose sincerity cannot be questioned that it is time that the other side of the coin be examined."[24]

[24] *Ibid.,* p. 13. For an elaboration of this and related themes, see Harold M. Hodges, Jr., *Social Stratification: Class in America* (Cambridge, Mass.: Schenkman Publishing Co., Inc., 1964), pp. 191-195.

MASSCULT AND MIDCULT*

by Dwight Macdonald

MASSCULT

For about two centuries Western culture has in fact been two cultures: the traditional kind—let us call it High Culture—that is chronicled in the textbooks, and a novel kind that is manufactured for the market. This latter may be called Mass Culture, or better Masscult, since it really isn't culture at all. Masscult is a parody of High Culture. In the older forms, its artisans have long been at work. In the novel, the line stretches from the eighteenth-century "servant-girl romances" to Edna Ferber, Fannie Hurst and such current ephemera as Burdick, Drury, Michener, Ruark and Uris; in music, from Hearts and Flowers to Rock 'n Roll; in art, from the chromo to Norman Rockwell; in architecture, from Victorian Gothic to ranch-house moderne; in thought, from Martin Tupper's *Proverbial Philosophy* ("Marry not without means, for so shouldst thou tempt Providence;/But wait not for more than enough, for marriage is the DUTY of most men.") to Norman Vincent Peale. (Thinkers like H. G. Wells, Stuart Chase, and Max Lerner come under the head of Midcult rather than Masscult.) And the enormous output of such new media as the radio, television and the movies is almost entirely Masscult.

I

This is something new in history. It is not that so much bad art is being produced. Most High Culture has been undistinguished, since talent is always rare—one has only to walk through any great art museum or try to read some of the forgotten books from past centuries. Since only the best works still have currency, one thinks of the past in their terms, but they were really just a few plums in a vast tasteless pudding of mediocrity.

*From Dwight Macdonald, *Masscult and Midcult, Partisan Review Series,* No. 4, 1954, pp. 3-15, 38-41. Reprinted by permission of author and publisher.

Masscult is bad in a new way: it doesn't even have the theoretical possibility of being good. Up to the eighteenth century, bad art was of the same nature as good art, produced for the same audience, accepting the same standards. The difference was simply one of individual talent. But Masscult is something else. It is not just unsuccessful art. It is non-art. It is even anti-art.

Masscult offers its customers neither an emotional catharsis nor an aesthetic experience, for these demand effort. The production line grinds out a uniform product whose humble aim is not even entertainment, for this too implies life and hence effort, but merely distraction. It may be stimulating or narcotic, but it must be easy to assimilate. It asks nothing of its audience, for it is "totally subjected to the spectator." And it gives nothing.

Some of its producers are able enough. Norman Rockwell is technically skilled, as was Meissonier—though Degas was right when he summed up the cavalry charge in *Friedland, 1806:* "Everything is steel except the breastplates." O. Henry could tell a story better than many contributors to our Little Magazines. But a work of High Culture, however inept, is an expression of feelings, ideas, tastes, visions that are idiosyncratic and the audience similarly responds to them as individuals. Furthermore, both creator and audience accept certain standards. These may be more or less traditional; sometimes they are so much less as to be revolutionary, though Picasso, Joyce and Stravinsky knew and respected past achievements more than did their academic contemporaries; their works may be seen as a heroic break-through to earlier, sounder foundations that had been obscured by the fashionable gimcrackery of the academies. But Masscult is indifferent to standards. Nor is there any communication between individuals. Those who consume Masscult might as well be eating ice-cream sodas, while those who fabricate it are no more expressing themselves than are the "stylists" who design the latest atrocity from Detroit.

The difference appears if we compare two famous writers of detective stories, Mr. Erle Stanley Gardner and Mr. Edgar Allan Poe. It is impossible to find any personal note in Mr. Gardner's enormous output—he has just celebrated his centenary, the hundredth novel under his own name (he also has knocked off several dozen under pseudonyms). His prose style varies between the incompetent and the nonexistent; for the most part, there is just no style, either good or bad. His books seem to have been manufactured rather than composed; they are assembled with the minimum expenditure of effort from identical parts that are shifted about just enough to allow the title to be changed from *The Case of the Curious Bride* to *The Case of the Fugitive Nurse*. Mr. Gardner obviously has the production problem licked—he has rated his "native abilities" as Very Good as a lawyer, Good as a business analyst, and Zero as a writer, and the last realistic estimate is the clue to his production-line fertility—and his popularity indicates he has the problem of distribution well in hand. He is marketing a standard product, like Kleenex, that precisely because it is not related to any individual needs on the part of either the producer or the consumer appeals to the widest possible audience. The obsession of our fact-minded culture with the process of the law is probably the lowest common denominator that has made Mr. Gardner's unromantic romances such dependable commodities.

Like Mr. Gardner, Mr. Poe was a money-writer. (That he didn't make any is irrelevant.) The difference, aside from the fact that he was a good writer, is that, even when he was turning out hack work, he had an extraordinary ability to use the journalistic forms of his day to express his own peculiar personality, and indeed, as Marie Bonaparte has shown in her fascinating study, to relieve his neurotic anxieties. (It is simply impossible to imagine Mr. Gardner afflicted with anything as individual as a neurosis.) The book review, the macabre-romantic tale, the magazine poem, all served his purposes, and he even invented a new one, the detective story, which satisfied the two chief and oddly disparate drives in his psychology—fascination with horror *(The Murders in the Rue Morgue)* and obsession with logical reasoning or, as he called it, "ratiocination" *(The Purloined Letter)*. So that while his works are sometimes absurd, they are rarely dull.

It is important to understand that the difference between Mr. Poe and Mr. Gardner, or bcween High Culture and Masscult, is not mere popularity. From *Tom Jones* to the films of Chaplin, some very good things have been popular; *The Education of Henry Adams* was the top non-fiction best-seller of 1919. Nor is it that Poe's detective stories are harder to read than Gardner's, though I suppose they are for most people. The difference lies in the qualities of Masscult already noted: its impersonality and its lack of standards, and "total subjection to the spectator." The same writer, indeed the same book or even the same chapter, may contain elements of both Masscult and High Culture. In Balzac, for instance, the most acute psychological analysis and social observation is bewilderingly interlarded with the cheapest, flimsiest kind of melodrama. In Dickens, superb comedy alternates with bathetic sentimentality, great descriptive prose with the most vulgar kind of theatricality. All these elements were bound between the same covers, sold to the same mass audience, and, it may well be, considered equally good by their authors—at least I know of no evidence that either Dickens or Balzac was aware of when he was writing down and when he was writing up. Masscult is a subtler problem than is sometimes recognized.

"What is a poet?" asked Wordsworth. "He is a man speaking to men . . . a man pleased with his own passions and volitions, and one who rejoices more than other men in the spirit of life that is in him." It is this human dialogue that Masscult interrupts, this spirit of life that it exterminates. Evelyn Waugh commented on Hollywood, after a brief experience there: "Each book purchased for motion pictures has some individual quality, good or bad, that has made it remarkable. It is the work of a great array of highly paid and incompatible writers to distinguish this quality, separate it and obliterate it." This process is called "licking the book"—i.e., licking it into shape, as mother bears were once thought to lick their amorphous cubs into real bears; though here the process is reversed and the book is licked not into but out of shape. The other meaning of "licked" also applies; before a proper Hollywood film can be made, the work of art has to be defeated.

II

The question of Masscult is part of the larger question of the masses. The tendency of modern industrial society, whether in the USA or the USSR, is to transform the individual into the mass man. For the masses are in historical time what a crowd is in space: a large quantity of people unable to express their human qualities because they are related to each other neither as individuals nor as members of a community. In fact, they are not related *to each other* at all but only to some impersonal, abstract, crystallizing factor. In the case of crowds, this can be a football game, a bargain sale, a lynching; in the case of the masses, it can be a political party, a television program, a system of industrial production. The mass man is a solitary atom, uniform with the millions of other atoms that go to make up "the lonely crowd," as David Riesman well calls our society. A community, on the contrary, is a group of individuals linked to each other by concrete interests. Something like a family, each of whose members has his or her special place and function while at the same time sharing the group's economic aims (family budget), traditions (family history), sentiments (family quarrels, family jokes), and values ("That's the way we do it in *this* family!"). The scale must be small enough so that it "makes a difference" what each person does—this is the first condition for human, as against mass, existence. Paradoxically, the individual in a community is both more closely integrated into the group than is the mass man and at the same time is freer to develop his own special personality. Indeed, an individual can only be defined in relation to a community. A single person in nature is not an individual but an animal; Robinson Crusoe was saved by Friday. The totalitarian regimes, which have consciously tried to create the mass man, have systematically broken every communal link—family, church, trade union, local and regional loyalties, even down to ski and chess clubs—and have reforged them so as to bind each atomized individual directly to the center of power.

The past cultures I admire—Periclean Greece, the city-states of the Italian Renaissance, Elizabethan England, are examples—have mostly been produced by communities, and remarkably small ones at that. Also remarkably heterogeneous ones, riven by faction, stormy with passionate antagonisms. But this diversity, fatal to that achievement of power over other countries that is the great aim of modern statecraft, seems to have been stimulating to talent. (What could be more deadly than the usual post-Marx vision of socialism as equality and agreement? Fourier was far more perceptive when he based his Utopia on cabals, rivalry, and every kind of difference including what he called "innocent mania.") A mass society, like a crowd, is inchoate and uncreative. Its atoms cohere not according to individual liking or traditions or even interests but in a purely mechanical way, as iron filings of different shapes and sizes are pulled toward a magnet working on the one quality they have in common. Its morality sinks to the level of the most primitive members—a crowd will commit atrocities that very few of its members would commit as individuals—and its taste to that of the least sensitive and the most ignorant.

Yet this collective monstrosity, "the masses," "the public," is taken as a human norm by the technicians of Masscult. They at once degrade the public by treating it as an object, to be handled with the lack of ceremony of medical students dissecting a corpse, and at the same time flatter it and pander to its taste and ideas by taking them as the criterion of reality (in the case of the questionnaire-sociologists) or of art (in the case of the Lords of Masscult). When one hears a questionnaire-sociologist talk about "setting up" an investigation, one realizes that he regards people as mere congeries of conditioned reflexes, his concern being which reflex will be stimulated by which question. At the same time, of necessity, he sees the statistical majority as the great Reality, the secret of life he is trying to unriddle. Like a Lord of Masscult, he is —professionally—without values, willing to take seriously any idiocy if it is held by many people (though, of course, *personally* . . .). The aristocrat's approach to the masses is less degrading to them, as it is less degrading to a man to be shouted at than to be treated as non-existent. But the *plebs* have their dialectical revenge: indifference to their human quality means prostration before their statistical quantity, so that a movie magnate who cynically "gives the public what it wants"— i.e., assumes it wants trash—sweats with anxiety if the box-office returns drop five per cent.

Whenever a Lord of Masscult is reproached for the low quality of his products, he automatically ripostes, "But that's what the public wants, what can I do?" A simple and conclusive defense, at first glance. But a second look reveals that (1) to the extent the public "wants" it, the public has been conditioned to some extent by his products, and (2) his efforts have taken this direction because (a) he himself also "wants" it—never underestimate the ignorance and vulgarity of pub-lishers, movie producers, network executives and other architects of Masscult—and (b) the technology of producing mass "entertainment" (again, the quotes are advised) imposes a simplistic, repetitive pattern so that it is easier to say the public wants this than to say the truth which is that the public gets this and so wants it. The March Hare explained to Alice that "I like what I get" is not the same thing as "I get what I like," but March Hares have never been welcome on Madison Avenue.

For some reason, objections to the giving-to-the-public-what-it-wants line are often attacked as undemocratic and snobbish. Yet it is precisely because I do believe in the potentialities of ordinary people that I criticize Masscult. For the masses are not people, they are not The Man in the Street or The Average Man, they are not even that figment of liberal condescension, The Common Man. The masses are, rather, man as non-man, that is man in a special relationship to other men that makes it impossible for him to function as man (one of the human functions being the creation and enjoyment of works of art). "Mass man," as I use the term, is a theoretical construction, an extreme toward which we are being pushed but which we shall never reach. For to become wholly a mass man would mean to have no private life, no personal desires, hobbies, aspirations, or aversions that are not shared by everybody else. One's behavior would be entirely predictable, like a piece of coal, and the sociologists could at last make up their tables confidently. It is still some time to 1984 but it looks unlikely that Orwell's anti-Utopia will have materialized by then, or that it will ever materialize. Nazism and Soviet Communism, however, show us how far things can go in politics, as Masscult does in art. And let us not be too smug in this American temperate zone, unravaged by war and ideology. "It seems to me that nearly the whole Anglo-Saxon race, especially of course in America, have lost the power to be individuals. They have become social insects like bees and ants." So Roger Fry wrote years ago, and who will say that we have become less apian?

III

Like the early capitalism Marx and Engels described in *The Communist Manifesto,* Masscult is a dynamic, revolutionary force, breaking down the old barriers of class, tradition, and taste, dissolving all cultural distinctions. It mixes, scrambles everything together, producing what might be called homogenized culture, after another American achievement, the homogenization process that distributes the globules of cream evenly throughout the milk instead of allowing them to float separately on top. The interesting difference is that whereas the cream is still in the homogenized milk, somehow it disappears from homogenized culture. For the process destroys all values, since value-judgments require discrimination, an ugly word in liberal-democratic America. Masscult is very, very democratic; it refuses to discriminate against or between anything or anybody. All is grist to its mill and all comes out finely ground indeed.

Life is a typical homogenized magazine, appearing on the mahogany library tables of the rich, the glass cocktail tables of the middleclass, and the oilcloth kitchen tables of the poor. Its contents are as thoroughly homogenized as its circulation. The same issue will present a serious exposition of atomic energy followed by a disquisition on a movie star's love life; photos of starving children picking garbage in Calcutta and of sleek models wearing adhesive brassieres; an editorial hailing Bertrand Russell's eightieth birthday *(A Great Mind Is Still Annoying And Adorning Our Age)* across from a full-page photo of a matron arguing with a baseball umpire *(Mom Gets Thumb);* nine color pages of Renoir paintings followed by a picture of a roller-skating horse; a cover announcing in the same size type two features: *A New Foreign Policy, By John Foster Dulles* and *Kerima: Her Marathon Kiss Is A Movie*

Sensation.[1] Somehow these scramblings together seem to work all one way, degrading the serious rather than elevating the frivolous. Defenders of our Masscult society like Professor Edward Shils of the University of Chicago—he is, of course, a sociologist—see phenomena like *Life* as inspiriting attempts at popular education—just think, nine pages of Renoirs! But that roller-skating horse comes along, and the final impression is that both Renoir and the horse were talented.

IV

The historical reasons for the rise of Masscult are well known. There could obviously be no mass culture until there were masses, in our modern sense. The industrial revolution produced the masses. It uprooted people from their agrarian communities and packed them into factory cities. It produced goods in such unprecedented abundance that the population of the Western world has increased more in the last two centuries than in the preceding two millennia—poor Malthus, never has a brilliantly original theorist been so speedily refuted by history! And it subjected them to a uniform discipline whose only precedent was the "slave socialism" of Egypt. But the Egypt of the Pharaohs produced no Masscult any more than did the great Oriental empires or the late Rome of the proletarian rabble, because the masses were passive, inert, submerged far below the level of political or cultural power. It was not until the end of the eighteenth century in Europe that the majority of people began to play an active part in either history or culture.

Up to then, there was only High Culture and Folk Art. To some extent, Masscult is a continuation of Folk Art, but the differences are more striking than the similarities. Folk Art grew mainly from below, an autochthonous product shaped by the people to fit their own needs, even though it often took its cue from High Culture. Masscult comes from above. It is fabricated by technicians hired by businessmen. They try this and try that and if something clicks at the box-office, they try

---

[1] The advertisements provide even more scope for the editors' homogenizing talents, as when a full-page photo of a ragged Bolivian peon grinningly drunk on coca leaves (which Mr. Luce's conscientious reporters tell us he chews to narcotize his chronic hunger pains) appears opposite an ad of a pretty, smiling, well dressed American mother with her two pretty-smiling-well dressed children (a boy and a girl, of course—children are always homogenized in our ads) looking raptly at a clown on a TV set, the whole captioned in type big enough to announce the Second Coming: RCA VICTOR BRINGS YOU A NEW KIND OF TELE-VISION—SUPER SETS WITH "PICTURE POWER." The peon would doubtless find the juxtaposition piquant if he could afford a copy of *Life,* which, luckily for the Good Neighbor Policy, he cannot.

to cash in with similar products, like consumer-researchers with a new cereal, or like a Pavlovian biologist who has hit on a reflex he thinks can be conditioned. It is one thing to satisfy popular tastes, as Robert Burns's poetry did, and quite another to exploit them, as Hollywood does. Folk Art was the people's own institution, their private little kitchen-garden walled off from the great formal park of their masters.[2] But Masscult breaks down the wall, integrating the masses into a debased form of High Culture and thus becoming an instrument of domination. If one had no other data to go on, Masscult would expose capitalism as a class society rather than the harmonious commonwealth that, in election years, both parties tell us it is.

Midcult

In these more advanced times, the danger to High Culture is not so much from Masscult as from a peculiar hybrid bred from the latter's unnatural intercourse with the former. A whole middle culture has come into existence and it threatens to absorb both its parents. This intermediate form—let us call it Midcult—has the essential qualities of Masscult—the formula, the built-in reaction, the lack of any standard except popularity—but it decently covers them with a cultural fig-leaf. In Masscult the trick is plain—to please the crowd by any means. But Midcult has it both ways: it pretends to respect the standards of High Culture while in fact it waters them down and vulgarizes them.[3]

Midcult is not, as might appear at first, a raising of the level of Masscult. It is rather a corruption of High Culture which has the enor-

---

[2] And if it was often influenced by High Culture, it did change the forms and themes into its own style. The only major form of Folk Art that still persists in this country is jazz, and the difference between Folk Art and Masscult may be most readily perceived by comparing the kind of thing heard at the annual Newport Jazz Festivals to Rock 'n Roll. The former is musically interesting and emotionally real; the latter is—not. The amazing survival of jazz despite the exploitative onslaughts of half a century of commercial entrepreneurs is, in my opinion, due to its folk quality. And as the noble and the peasant understood each other better than either understood the bourgeois, so it seems significant that jazz is the only art form that appeals to both the intelligentsia and the common people. As for the others, let them listen to *South Pacific*.

[3] It's not done, of course, as consciously as this suggests. The editors of *The Saturday Review* or *Harper's* or *The Atlantic* would be honestly indignant at this description of their activities, as would John Steinbeck, J. P. Marquand, Pearl Buck, Irwin Shaw, Herman Wouk, John Hersey and others of that remarkably large group of Midcult novelists we have developed. One of the nice things about Zane Grey was that it seems never to have occurred to him that his books had anything to do with literature.

mous advantage over Masscult that while also in fact "totally subjected to the spectator," in Malraux's phrase, it is able to pass itself off as the real thing. Midcult is the Revised Standard Version of the Bible, put out several years ago under the aegis of the Yale Divinity School, that destroys our greatest monument of English prose, the King James Version, in order to make the text "clear and meaningful to people today," which is like taking apart Westminster Abbey to make Disneyland out of the fragments. Midcult is the Museum of Modern Art's film department paying tribute to Samuel Goldwyn because his movies are alleged to be (slightly) better than those of other Hollywood producers —though why they are called "producers" when their function is to prevent the production of art (cf. the fate in Hollywood of Griffith, Chaplin, von Stroheim, Eisenstein and Orson Wells) is a semantic puzzle. Midcult is the venerable and once venerated *Atlantic*—which in the last century printed Emerson, Lowell, Howells, James, and Mark Twain—putting on the cover of a recent issue a huge photograph of Dore Schary, who has lately transferred his high-minded sentimentality from Hollywood to Broadway and who is represented in the issue by a homily, "To A Young Actor," which synthesizes Jefferson, Polonius and Dr. Norman Vincent Peale, concluding: "Behave as citizens not only of your profession but of the full world in which you live. Be indignant with injustice, be gracious with success, be courageous with failure, be patient with opportunity, and be resolute with faith and honor." Midcult is the Book of the Month Club, which since 1926 has been supplying its members with reading matter of which the best that can be said is that it could be worse, i.e., they get John Hersey instead of Gene Stratton Porter. Midcult is the transition from Rodgers and Hart to Rodgers and Hammerstein, from the gay tough lyrics of *Pal Joey,* a spontaneous expression of a real place called Broadway, to the folk-fakery of *Oklahoma!* and the orotund sentimentalities of *South Pacific.* Midcult is or was, "Omnibus," subsidized by a great foundation to raise the level of television, which began its labors by announcing it would "be aimed straight at the average American audience, neither highbrow nor lowbrow, the audience that made *Reader's Digest, Life, The Ladies' Home Journal,* the audience which is the solid backbone of any business as it is of America itself" and which then proved its good faith by programs mingling Gertrude Stein and Jack Benny, Chekhov and football strategy, Beethoven and champion ice skaters. "Omnibus" failed. The level of television was not raised, for some reason.

MASS CULTURE IN AMERICA*

by Bernard Rosenberg

The late Morris Raphael Cohen, an extraordinarily gifted teacher, was perhaps best known in and out of the classroom as a superb critic of other philosophers. From time to time students would grumble about his negativism; Cohen tore down whole systems of philosophy without offering an alternative world-view of his own. On one such occasion he is said to have answered this charge as follows: "My first name is an Anglicization from the Hebrew for Moses, and like Moses, I can lead you through the wilderness without bringing you to the Promised Land." The editors of this anthology, whose subject matter is not the universe but only an increasingly significant part of it, feel much as Cohen must have felt when he found himself unable to formulate sweeping answers to every question. Mass culture is not only a wilderness—with oases here and there, to be sure—it is largely uncharted. Indeed, whole parts of it remain to be explored.

Moreover, at the end of this *terra incognita,* even if we wander over its surface for forty years, there may be no Promised Land. One can only have hunches—and of these there is a plethora. But any calculation of what lies before us is premature, especially if it proceeds by extrapolating the imperfectly understood situation that we face today. Our purpose in assembling this formidable selection of readings is rather to present the reader with a guide through what is now known, or thought to be known, about extremely problematic matters. Mass culture has reached into the Academy both by its pervasive influence and as a subject of serious study. The former, with such spectacular phenomena as audio-visual education, has been more striking than the latter. But, gradually, academicians and detached intellectuals are being drawn into the vortex by a suction force none can resist. They are beginning to ask themselves whether the quality of life has not been decisively altered by mass-circulation magazines, "comic" books, detective fiction, movies, radio, television—with all their meretricious and/or meritorious accompaniments.

Some thoughtful persons are pleased with machine civilization; many more are alarmed by its destructive force. We wish to suggest that this basic division—those who applaud and those who wring their hands over our technological apparatus—explains why there is such a range of differences in the assessment of mass culture. It tells even more than political position, which is also a fairly reliable index. The political lines that have crystallized are approximately these: radicals (Dwight Macdonald, Clement Greenberg, Irving Howe) who, like the arch-conservatives (Ortega y Gasset, T. S. Eliot, Bernard Iddings Bell), although for opposite reasons, are repelled by what they commonly regard as vulgar and exploitative, and the liberals (Gilbert Seldes, David Riesman, Max Lerner) who take a predictable position in the middle. The parallel between left, right, and center in politics and in the "popular arts" is virtually perfect.

Why, then, something still more fundamental? Because, in the mid-twentieth century, political stances and cultural choices are part of a much larger whole. In none of the archeological ages has human society been so thoroughly revolutionary as at present. Consider that man, for the million years since his origin as a distinct species, has had to struggle like every other beast (and like the postgraduate ape he was) for the means of subsistence. Only now, with mechanized agriculture, artificial photosynthesis, use of algae and other foods from the sea, is it possible to speak of a *well-fed* world population much larger than ours. That everyone could enjoy an adequate diet, with relatively little physical exertion to secure it, would have been unimaginable in any earlier age.

As Toynbee's Great West Wind blows all over the world, which quickly gets urbanized and industrialized, as the birth rate declines and the population soars, a certain sameness develops everywhere. Clement Greenberg can meaningfully speak of a universal mass culture (surely something new under the sun) which unites a resident of Johannesburg with his neighbors in San Juan, Hong Kong, Moscow, Paris, Bogota, Sydney and New York. African aborigines, such as those recently described by Richard Wright, leap out of their primitive past—straight into the movie house where, it is feared, they may be mesmerized like the rest of us. First besieged with commodities, postmodern man himself becomes an interchangeable part in the whole cultural process. When he is momentarily freed from his own *kitsch,* the Soviet citizen seems to be as titillated as his American counterpart by Tin Pan Alley's products. In our time, the basis for an international sodality of man at his lowest level, as some would say, appears to have been formed.

All this comes at a time when the species' dependence upon nature for a steady food supply has virtually disappeared. Simultaneously, the curse of Adam is being lifted. Frank Lloyd Wright half seriously suggests that we will soon develop a paralysis of all our limbs except the pushbutton finger by whose sweat, rather than the brow's, man may soon live. Utopian philosophers used to speculate about who, in their good society, would do the dirty work. That *someone* had to do it was as clearly an immutable fact as the mortality of man. Now our answer, with imminent automation, and not for the world of fancy but for that of reality, is, "Nobody." Manual labor is becoming obsolete.

We can do no more than assimilate a fragment of the change before it leads to another innovation whose significance is likewise imponderable. Of this much one can be certain beforehand: no IBM machine, nor yet a Univac, will tell us whether the latest development is for good or ill. Ambiguity is its key characteristic. If men are freed from manual labor and from the struggle with nature, what will they do? Cultivate their minds? Improve their sensibilities? Heighten their understanding? Deepen and broaden themselves? Possibly. The precondition for transfiguring *Homo sapiens* into a higher species begins to exist. When our physical environment has been subdued we may become hypersentient beings. Drudgery, monotony, inanition and brutishness can then be dispelled along with the animal existence we used to lead.

That such a step in human evolution could take place is what makes the likelihood so much more tragic. Before man can transcend himself he is being dehumanized. Before he can elevate his mind, it is being deadened. Freedom is placed before him and snatched away. The rich and varied life he might lead is standardized. This breeds anxiety, and the vicious circle begins anew, for as we are objects of manipulation, our anxiety is exploitable. The mass grows; we are more alike than ever; and feel a deeper sense of entrapment and loneliness. And even if the incubus of hydrogen war could be lifted, these specters would still hover over us.

In short, the postmodern world offers man everything or nothing. Any rational consideration of the probabilities leads to a fear that he will be overtaken by the social furies that already beset him.

There can be no doubt that the mass media present a major threat to man's autonomy. To know that they might also contain some small seeds of freedom only makes a bad situation nearly desperate. No art form, no body of knowledge, no system of ethics is strong enough to withstand vulgarization. A kind of cultural alchemy transforms them all into the same soft currency. Never before have the sacred and the profane, the genuine and the specious, the exalted and the debased, been so thoroughly mixed that they are all but indistinguishable. Who can sort one from the other when they are built into a single slushy compost? Is there anything beyond a debased remnant of theology *or* of psychiatry left in the mind that has been encased in "peace" and whose soul has been similarly laid to rest?

Ernest van den Haag has suggested that there are two assumptions underlying all mass culture: (1) everything is understandable, and (2) everything is remediable. We might add a corollary to the first assumption: "Everything had better be made understandable." The more arcane a subject the less effort it should require for easy absorption. If education and cultivation are gradual, progressive, orderly processes, then popular education is its opposite. For what makes mass culture so tantalizing is the implication of effortlessness. Shakespeare is dumped on the market along with other authors, and publishers are rightly confident that their audience will not feel obliged to make any greater preparation for the master of world literature than for its latest lickspittle.

II

This general phenomenon, although it frightens some and leaves others relatively undisturbed, has seldom been placed at the center of our attention. Now and then an important nineteenth-century figure such as Nietzsche or Tocqueville would express some sense of what lay in store for us. However, it remained for a novelist, Gustave Flaubert, to set the case before his readers in boldest outline. If this were a two-volume selection of readings on mass culture, *Madame Bovary,* saved from the vultures of condensation, would have to be presented in its entirety as a prolegomenon to the understanding of our subject. For Emma and her husband did not simply spring out of Flaubert's mind; they also sprang out of his times. And his times, as he understood them, were a prefiguration of our own.

As they are revealed to us in the novel, Emma's husband, Charles, suffers from an underdeveloped imagination, Emma from an overheated imagination, and neither of them was born or predestined to be that way. Charles is the familiar type of professional man who scarcely "has time to keep up with his medical journals." He has been given a narrow occupational training, and while this vehicle of his social ascent detaches him from the folk, it does not awaken his sensibilities. Charles, like his father, holds culture in small esteem. It cannot be otherwise: this is what his "embourgeoisement" means.

Emma's origins are as humble as her husband's. Her life slides off-center for the same reason, i.e., external forces impinge upon it, as they were soon to impinge upon and engulf the whole Western world. Charles goes to medical school and Emma to finishing school. Charles learns his lessons but remains otherwise unresponsive. Emma, to her mother-in-law's horror, studies dancing, geography, drawing, embroidery and the piano. With sovereign skill Flaubert spells out for us how Emma's mind was debauched, how her emotions were inflamed.

"For six months, Emma, when she was fifteen, battened on the garbage of those out of date 'Libraries of Choice Fiction.' Later on she came to read Walter Scott [This is a prime target of Flaubert's. Still later Emma is thrown into raptures at a production of *Lucie de Lammermoor* which she witnesses with husband and lover.] and got enthusiastic about historical things, forever dreaming of coffers, guardrooms and minstrels." Again, "In the music class, the songs she had to learn were all about little angels with golden pinions, madonnas, lagoons, gondoliers, compositions in which silly words and shoddy music could not conceal the attractive phantasmagoria of their sentimental substratum."

This is the stuff out of which Flaubert forms Emma's character; without it there is no adequate motivation for the behavior he wishes to describe. More, that background, rather than, or set in relief from, the rural milieu, lends a powerful element of inevitability to the drama. Emma, the little villager with her psyche on fire goes quixotically in search of the joy, passion, and intoxication "which had looked so fine to her in books." These are the first drippings of an osmotic process that has only in our day come into its own as full-blown mass culture. Once bathed in them and their deliquescent values, Emma can only be bored to death. She must seek satisfaction in adultery, and failing, seek it again. Any worldly man on the make can have her. She has learned what our mentors in Hollywood now teach us with even greater proficiency, namely, that love is something which must come suddenly with a great display of thunder and lightning, descending on one's life like a tempest from above, turning it topsy-turvy, whirling away one's resolutions like leaves and bearing one onward, heart and soul toward the abyss.

Denis de Rougemont, a historian of romantic love, while tracing its medieval lineage, finds the aberration, as Flaubert did, a particularly virulent one in our day. The romantic complex thrives on inaccessibility in any prototypic representation of the past. Thus Tristan and Iseult or Romeo and Juliet. Consummation, prompted by boredom, brings more of the same in its wake. Emma might have been able to endure her lot if she had only flirted with Léon or merely dreamed of sleeping with Rodolphe. Wish fulfillment intensifies the original discomfort and renders it incurable. Illusions cannot persist when faced with the reality test of actual contact, and as they crumble there is nothing left to sustain their victim. Hence, one lover is discarded for another around whom the same false aura is soon spun. Emma, who could even romanticize Charles— from a distance—is still better at this game with Léon and Rodolphe, only to have each spell broken by prolonged *contact de deux épidermes*.

And in such a crisis, what does the deracinated woman do? "By moonlight in the garden she recited all the love poetry she knew and sighed and sang of love's sweet melancholy. But afterwards she found herself not a whit more calm, and Charles not a whit more amorous or emotional."

Nothing goes more directly to the core of mass culture than this. Any indictment of sleazy fiction, trashy films, and bathetic soap operas, in all their maddening forms, must come to rest finally on Flaubert's prescient insight. Far from dispelling unrest, all the (admittedly slim) evidence now on hand suggests that mass culture exacerbates it. Once understood, this fact cuts the ground from under those who justify organized distraction by claiming that it satisfies a fundamental need. Dwight Macdonald comes much closer to the point when he says that it *exploits* that need.

Contemporary man commonly finds that his life has been emptied of meaning, that it has been trivialized. He is alienated from his past, from his work, from his community, and possibly from himself— although this "self" is hard to locate. At the same time he has an unprecedented amount of time on his hands which, as van den Haag has pointed out, he must kill lest it kill him. Society abhors a vacuum, and quickly fills this one with diversion. Brutes and mimes achieve an apotheosis in these secular surroundings that they seldom enjoyed even in the late Roman Empire which, after all, had its more ethereal gods. All this is accepted—and celebrated by a certain percentage of the intelligentsia not altogether unrepresented in our anthology—as a highly desirable kind of public stupefaction. It is widely assumed that the anxiety generated by industrial civilization can be allayed, as the nerves are narcotized, by "historical" novels, radio or television programs, and all the other ooze of our mass media.

It is to be expected that someone will discover hidden virtue in the kind of pin-up magazine catalogued by Geoffrey Wagner, a collector of cultural curiosa. The titles tell us enough: *Cover Girls, Paris Models,*

Whirl, Laff, Keyhole, Zip, Wham, Stag, Brief, Bare, Eye, Rave, Wink, Titter, Eyeful, Flirt, etc., etc. Harold Orlans writes, as a contributor to *Dissent* in the winter of 1954, of a situation that has since worsened:

> The postwar flood of pornography shows no signs of abating and, for once, it seems, the dim congressmen, stern churchmen, and stiff-laced ladies are complaining about something real and reckonable. . . . Its recent invasion of the public domain is unmistakable. The most obvious sign is that the two-bit monthlies "glorifying the American girl" which used to be confined to the newsstands around the tracks now overflow the back shelves of the racks in neighborhood drug and candy stores. Six years ago they could not be bought in a dry Southern village, although they were imported from the nearby city to the barber shop, poolroom, and bar. Today they will be found on all the newsstands in a quiet Quaker town—or they were there until a mother, the local editor, and several ministers pounced upon the hapless police chief. They will be back again the day after tomorrow. The magazines are all the same: bosoms and butts, high heels, opera hose, leopard skins, manacles, whips and wrestling ladies. In the back pages, ads for "art photos" sent in plain envelopes via railway express. Was it for this that Peter Zenger stood trial? . . . The bomb is not getting smaller. We have bread. (When do our children die?) On with the circus!

So frightful a juxtaposition of words as "war comics" and "horror comics" may be found in our new lexicon. There is a genre of popular literature—without the written word—that specializes in the representation of lesbians dressed in riding attire with spurs and whips, mercilessly flogging their victims. Yet none of this strikes such terror in the heart as an advertisement Wagner reports having seen for the past few years in *U. S. Camera* side by side with an offer of lewd photographs. This one announces sets of Nazi German atrocity pictures at thirty for two dollars.

Sometimes it seems as if we are overtaking and passing 1984, all unawares. The total obliteration of our privacy is, if not an accomplished fact, one technically easy to accomplish. Here is an illustrative item from *Newsweek* magazine, October 24, 1955:

> The Calbest Engineering and Electronics Co. announced that by the end of the year it would have perfected a cheatproof device for polling television without the set owners' cooperation or knowledge. Called the "Poll-o-meter," it is a compact portable unit with a directional antenna fitted at the end of a gun-type barrel. The operator drives down a residential street, aims his gadget at passing TV aerials, and pulls a trigger. A sensitive electronic detector picks up each station's characteristic frequency signal and automatically records it.

At its worst, mass culture threatens not merely to cretinize our taste, but to brutalize our senses while paving the way to totalitarianism. And the interlocking media all conspire to that end. Wagner: "So Chop-Chop exclaims, as he wrenches a commie's head off in a *Blackhawk* [comic] book, 'Me study wrestling from television set.' "

But Emma Bovary resorts to the garbage on which she had battened as a girl and feels not a whit more calm—and neither do the rest of us when we follow her example. One feels bad because his life seems to be pointless; he is invited to divert himself, and gladly accepts, only to feel still worse afterwards.

Apart from its ghastliness, which is a matter of taste, mass culture must be indicted for this failure. In an anxious age mass culture builds the tension that it is usually credited with relieving. Meanwhile the electronic wonderworld and the rulers thereof, with a large number of collaborators from every entertainment industry, manage to debar the mass man they have created from any really satisfying experience. A genuine esthetic (or religious or love) experience becomes difficult, if not impossible, whenever *kitsch* pervades the atmosphere. And only the genuine experience, as Flaubert realized, can satisfy us. It presupposes effortful participation. In the arts this may mean no more than a willing suspension of disbelief, an *act* of the imagination which projects the reader or the audience into a state of empathy from which man's fate can be viewed with great understanding. Not everyone can achieve such a state today, and it will be argued that for those who cannot, experiences at a lower level may suffice. But surely those who know there are greater delectations than cultural pap and gruel, which cannot be concocted or appreciated without working at them, should say so.

All this applies with equal force to the pursuit of knowledge. Quite often the most "popular" teachers in our universities are those who simplify their material, make it look simple, and thereby foster the illusion that a challenging body of knowledge can be easily assimilated. This is catch-phrase pedagogy: Plato was an Idealist, Aristotle a Realist, Kant a Dialectician. All you need is a label, and every field has its Will Durant who will retail it for you. No discipline, however exacting, is insusceptible to this treatment. So, though we never really come to grips with philosophy this way, the dangerous belief that we have fully embraced it nevertheless persists. A true teacher will say, "No, there is so much more within your reach—only you must stretch yourself to find it." Such an attitude is frequently dismissed as snobbery, an egghead affectation, an expression of contempt for the ordinary man. It may be just the opposite, if we say to the *l'homme moyen sensuel,* "Here is what

many of you could do. Why settle for so much less? What you consume
now may please you for the moment; sub-art and pseudo-knowledge is
shoveled down your open mouth; in another moment it will leave you
ravenous and restless once again." As *kitsch* is institutionalized and we
are robbed of our spontaneity, the likelihood of satisfaction, of tension
followed by distension, gets to be more and more remote. Culturally, we
become hungrier than ever—and our diet, though habit-forming, contains less nourishment than ever. . . .

. . . In 1934 three sociologists, George Lundberg, Mirra Komarov-
sky, and Mary Alice McInerny reported the results of a valuable pioneer
study in their book, *Leisure*. It was already obvious to them that, "There
are, unhappily, many reasons why mere freedom from vigorous physical
toil and long hours of labor will not in itself insure men against heavy
and unhappy lives." They used a few random illustrations which have
a figurative, as well as a literal, significance: the enforced leisure of the
physically handicapped, the blind, the deaf and the convalescent who are
usually wretched in their idleness although they may not have economic
worries; prisoners whose misery is increased by light work or no work;
and millions of the unemployed who find "leisure more burdensome than
work ever was"; the many people who "retire" in good health, and find
only a debilitating vacuum to replace the old occupation. The authors
remind us of Mahatma Ghandi's fear that modern machinery would
leave India's millions with "too much leisure."

Twenty-five years ago, Professor L. P. Jacks asked the key
(rhetorical) question about people with unprecedented leisure on their
hands.

> Will they take as the model for their leisure the sort of life
> now most favored by the "idle rich" and get as much of that sort
> of thing as their means enable them to procure—display, luxurious
> feeding, sex excitement, gambling, bridge, golf, globe-trotting and
> the rest? Or will they spend it in the way the idle poor—by whom
> I mean the unemployed—are now spending the leisure forced on
> them by the industrial crisis, which consists for the most part in
> just stagnating, physically, mentally and morally? Or will it be a
> mixture of the two — stagnation relieved by whatever doses of
> external excitement people may have the cash to purchase?

What "they" or "we" will do remains an open question, but one
that seems to many of us, and to the majority of "highbrows" represented
in this reader, to be closing very rapidly. Maybe not. Any judgment
based upon necessarily faulty and partial perception can have only a
limited validity. However, a few things do appear to be clear. For
instance:

It is necessary to take as holistic a view as possible. No effort to comprehend and evaluate mass culture can start anywhere else than in a large sociocultural context. From such a standpoint we may clear the air of certain obviously erroneous assumptions:

1. *Capitalism is responsible for mass culture.* Not at all. It flourishes wherever the appropriate technological apparatus emerges, whether slowly or suddenly, and nowhere more so than in Soviet Russia which, whatever else it is, cannot be considered capitalist. A strong case could be made for pinpointing the most malignant features of mass culture where music, art, and ideas are publicly expressed only if they conform with a dictator's infantile conception of music, art, and ideas. In this realm, capitalist America has lost its leadership to the communist world. We are no longer the pacesetters. The view that we are is parochial. A cross-mass-cultural survey would dispel it.

2. *America is responsible for mass culture.* Hardly, and for the same reasons. There is nothing in our national character that makes us peculiarly vulnerable to a condition that is sweeping the earth.

3. *Democracy is responsible for mass culture.* Tocqueville was perhaps the first to make this common mistake. It was shared by democrats who thought that vulgarity through leveling was the price that had to be paid for an otherwise beneficial system, and antidemocrats who thought the price too high.

If one can hazard a single positive formulation (in the form of a hypothesis) it would be that modern technology is the necessary and sufficient cause of mass culture. Neither national character nor the economic arrangement nor the political system has any final bearing on this question. All that really matters is the most recent industrial revolution.

The tentative technological determinism implicit in this formulation may be valid only for the present. *Today,* wherever modern tools are introduced and superimposed on any culture, the mixture seems to be deadly. Differences between backward and advanced countries become attenuated. They meet at the same low level. Maybe at a higher stage of development, society will be "ready" for industrialization, with conseqeuences very different from those we see all around us in the here and now. Meanwhile, change, followed by barbarous accommodation proceeds at an accelerated tempo.

LEISURE AND WORK IN POST-INDUSTRIAL SOCIETY*

by David Riesman†

To the rest of the world, the American has characteristically appeared as someone who could not stand being idle or alone, someone who rushes about, whether in work or play, and is preternaturally restless. Tocqueville for instance observed, "No men are less addicted to reverie than the citizens of a democracy."[1] It is important to recall this pre-industrial image of America lest we assume that industrialization, the automobile, or television are responsible for what Clifton Fadiman deplores as "the decline of attention": the "American" way preceded the inventions which gave that way added scope. Like Tocqueville, Lewis Mumford, in his remarkable book, *The Transformations of Man,*[2] discusses these changes from Old World to New World life, suggesting that the Americans, released by social and geographical space from age-old limits and norms, have exhibited from the beginning an exuberance and vitality, a romantic strenuousness, that in their respective ways both Emerson and Whitman represented and celebrated.

---

*From David Riesman "Leisure and Work in Post-Industrial Society." Eric Larrabee and Rolf Meyersohn, *Mass Leisure,* New York: The Free Press of Glencoe, 1959, pp. 363-374; 379-385. Reprinted by permission.

---

†This paper is developed from a lecture, given January 27th, 1958, in a series on "The American Future" sponsored at the University of Chicago by the Division of the Social Sciences and the College. It is a publication of the Center for the Study of Leisure, established at the University under a grant from the Ford Foundation. In footnotes I have sought to take account of some of the points raised in the question-and-answer period which followed the lecture. I have drawn on an earlier article, "Abundance for What?" in *Problems of United States Economic Development, vol. I.* (New York: Committee on Economic Development, 1958), pp. 223-234; reprinted in the *Bulletin of Atomic Scientists,* vol. 14 (1958), pp. 135-139.

[1] *Democracy in America,* Phillips Bradley edition (New York: Knopf, 1945), vol. 2, page 208. Tocqueville had in mind the contrast with the members of an aristocratic society who had a smaller portion of discontent because people knew their place and, whether resignedly or not, remained in it; his view anticipated that of Durkheim.

[2] New York: Harper's, 1956.

I. MASS LEISURE: THE END OF SUMPTUARY TRADITIONS

At the present time, two processes are going on simultaneously. On the one hand, a decline of exuberance is just barely noticeable in America, making itself felt particularly among the more highly educated and the well-to-do in a loss of appetite for work and perhaps even for leisure. On the other hand, the spread of industrialization and of the mass media are bringing both the residual pockets of traditionalism within this country and the great areas of it outside into a more "American" pattern. Whatever a nation's political or religious ideology, mass culture continues to spread, even ahead of industrialization, bringing the disruption of old ways and the lure of a new hedonism (as most dramatically seen in the cargo cults of the Pacific islanders which combine a nativist revival with the belief that the white man's goods can be obtained, without the white man himself, by appropriate rituals[3]).

I recently saw a documentary film focused on a family living in the hills of Tennessee in the 1930s—a family with many children and many dogs, eking out a bare existence. Despite efforts to insure minimal schooling, knowledge of the outside world scarcely percolated. Today, despite remaining pockets of abysmal misery, many of the very Tennessee shacks where, before the coming of the TVA, life resembled that in other peasant and pre-industrial cultures, are equipped with television aerials that now bring in not only the local boys who made good with a guitar, like Elvis Presley, but all the insignia of making good which pass as currency in the nation at large: cars, clothes, washers (which are often put on the front porch), and general styles of life and leisure. Some of the farms even in this area have become nearly as over-mechanized, and hence engaged in "conspicuous production," as the richer agricultural areas of the North; horses and mules are disappearing, and the South is catching up with the rest of the country in per capita ownership of automobiles. (In that sense, the North is finally winning the Civil War, whatever resistances can be focused around racism—a theme that W. J. Cash already foresaw in his prophetic book, *The Mind of the South*.)

Indeed, Southerners coming North, white or Negro, Caribbean or native, have replaced the immigrants from Southern Europe as fodder,

---

[3] Cf., e.g., Margaret Mead, *New Lives for Old* (New York: William Morrow, 1955); also Daniel Lerner, *The Passing of Traditional Society* (Glencoe, Ill.: The Free Press, 1958).

not for the machines of production so much as for those of consumption; for coming from a pre-industrial culture they lack sales resistance, let alone consumer sophistication: entering, if not the high-wage economy, at least the high-credit one, they are being "processed" as consumers, while escaping, because of their late arrival, some of the drill and exhausting hours that met earlier pre-industrial cadres entering the work force of industrial society.

They enter a society which has over the past eighty years taken in the form of leisure or free time approximately a third of the gains in productivity which industrialism and organization have achieved. (The average work-week now hovers around forty hours, as contrasted with seventy hours in 1850 and, in many industries and on the farms, nearly as much as that as late as 1920.) When the Bantu who works, let us say, in Johannesburg, has attained an increment over his old standard of living, he is likely to quit and return to the reservation; few of these Americans have a reservation to return to;[4] consequently, the Americans remain rather steadily at work while having time enough left on their hands for learning how to spend money in accordance with, and just beyond, their new wages.

This injection at the bottom is, I believe, responsible for much of the American economy of leisure, and more than makes up for the withdrawal of those people in the educated strata (whose attitudes we shall discuss more fully later) who no longer find in the purchase of possessions a sufficient agenda for living. (There still remain in America some more or less permanently underprivileged enclaves, principally among the old, the infirm, and among the less agile and mobile Negroes and poor whites in the south.)

But it is those who have recently been released from underprivilege by mass production and mass leisure who have gained, along with an often meaningless political vote, an often influential voice in the direction of consumption and hence of production. It is, for instance, the very millions whom Henry Ford helped release from drudgery who eventually defeated his ascetic and still rural canons of taste; it is they who like borax furniture or juke-box culture; their aesthetic is akin to that of all

---

[4] To be sure, something analogous to a reservation exists in our urban and rural slums to which migrants come and in which they seek, despite pressures and temptations, to preserve enclaves of traditionalism. Conversely, even in Africa, the reservation, though geographically more stable, proves fragile in the face of the inducements and pressures of industrialism and urbanization.

deracinated peasants whose folk culture crumbles at the first exposure to mass-produced commodities.[5]

Even in countries formerly run by an elite or presently run by a dictatorship, the same democratization and vulgarization of taste make themselves felt. The British mass press and the Butlin Holiday Camps are more than the equal of our Hearst papers and our own vacation

---

[5] The consequences of this overexposure, in the short and in the long run, are complex and are the themes of passionate debate (cf. the contributions to *Mass Culture* and especially Clement Greenberg's article, "Work and Leisure under Industrialism." While I agree with Lyman Bryson that it is not right to judge a culture by its peaks of art and artisanship alone but that one must also judge it in terms of the total quality of its life [cf. *The Next America* (New York: Harper's, 1950)], Bryson is readier than I to sacrifice the peaks of aristocratic attainment to the plateaus of popular contentment, in part because perhaps we differ on how long the latter can last without the former.

Certainly, the role of the artist changes when his patrons are no longer the few but the many. In a traditional society with a small elite, he is ancillary to the elite: they patronize him and he serves them, and may remain unaffected by the attitudes and desires of the mass of the people—save as these furnish folk themes for his music or imagery. Even if patronized, he moves among those who count, whereas today the successful artist may be rich and famous and still not feel he knows anybody who counts. Artists and intellectuals in our time have a choice of constituencies: they may try to serve the traditional elite of culture and taste or the mass of people who for the first time in history have money enough to become patrons. This dilemma has driven some artists towards willful efforts to stave off mass understanding, whether by obscurities, sadism, or serious attitudes which are unpopular. The results of this have not always been bad for art—on the contrary—but they do curtail some of the possibilities for the artist by making obscurities sometimes seem attractive per se. Conversely, such artists as, let us say, the typical jazz musician who plays popular, feel that they have sold out to the largest purse; the same with painters who go commercial. Sometimes artists are thrown back upon their fellow artists as the only ones who understand this dilemma, but this does not always save an artist from being caught in the enormous machinery for disseminating his work if it catches hold. Indeed, if popular taste were utterly debased, then what is "high" and "low" could be clearly differentiated; but we have a situation of an infinite series of minute gradations in which it is not easy to say what is high-brow and upper-middle-brow and so on; thus, the Book-of-the-Month Club may circulate a very good book at times. As a result, the climate for the most intensive achievements of art and intellect has a good deal of smog in it: the artist does not necessarily starve but may be all too well patronized without giving him any sense that he has a genuine audience. Moreover, in an age of plenty, it may require more conviction for an artist to remain poor than when all but a few were poor. (I have profited from the clarifying discussion of these issues in Nathan Glazer's, "Technology, Mass Culture, and High Culture," a paper delivered at the American Sociological Society meetings, August, 1958.)

"culture."[6] Likewise, although the newly urbanized in the Soviet Union may read a few more books and go to fewer movies, and will surely spend less time aimlessly driving about, their Parks of Culture and Rest are hardly more elevating than Coney Island; their privileged youth appears to be even more bored and delinquent; and the documentary realism of their art and its general lack of subtlety are being steadily outgrown in America. What distinguishes the Soviet Union is that it still has the goal of catching up with America and still possesses millions of unsatiated and eager buyers.

II. Technological Overprivilege

As many thoughtful people have recognized, our society offers little in the way of re-education for those who have been torn away from their traditional culture and suddenly exposed to all the blandishments of mass culture—even the churches which follow the hillbillies to the city often make use of the same "hard sell" that the advertisers and politicians do. In the past, the relatively voluntary nature of the immigration to this country, and the belief in progress of natives and immigrants alike, have tended to blind us to the casualties of transplantation. There are a few exceptions. For example, in the 1930s I admired the Rust brothers, inventors of the cotton picker, who hesitated to market their invention because they were worried about technological unemployment among Southern workers. (They were as unconvinced of the gospel of progress as were the members of the Advisory Committee which recommended under Oppenheimer's leadership against proceeding with the H-bomb.) It is ironical to reflect that this invention came along just in time to save some Southern fields from utter desertion—not only because Negroes and poor whites were leaving for the cities in the North but also because the cotton picking machine, as a form of conspicuous production, frees its operator from work which has long been considered dirty work and thus raises the status of the operator: it is the counterpart on the production side of today's Tennessee shack, electrified and gadget-filled. Even so, I think that the Rusts' scruples were well taken: people should not be ruthlessly torn away even from their incapacities and given the industrial bends: this country is rich enough and inventive enough to

---

[6] This situation in Britain has recently been described in Richard Hoggart's eloquent *The Uses of Literacy: Changing Patterns in English Mass Culture* (Fairlawn, New Jersey: Essential Books, 1957).

make social provision for a moratorium and retraining in those instances where uprooting is inescapable.

For many people today, the sudden onrush of leisure is a version of technological unemployment: their education has not prepared them for it and the creation of new wants at their expense moves faster than their ability to order and assimilate these wants.[7]

III. The Conservative Belief in Progress

In the mercantilist era, and even today in the countries of grinding poverty, the creation of new wants has been a first step towards a better life and wider horizons of choice. But in the United States today, the belief that one cannot stop invention, cannot stop technological progress, has itself become a tradition, indeed a form of realistic insanity, or what C. Wright Mills calls "crackpot realism." Although adult Americans, contrary to European impression, are not dazzled by machines as such— but simply want to have those appurtenances that betoken an appropriate style of life—we are nevertheless half-willing slaves of the machine process itself. Even big business, thanks to the anti-trust laws and to the potential competition of small business, does not quite have sufficient control of the market to plan to its own liking the sequence of applied technology. A fortiori, it seems inconceivable to Americans that we could reduce the aggression our technology keeps up against our traditions and the texture of our lives—and we can always use the competition of the Russians to counter any tendency within ourselves to relax the rate of growth or to question the belief in growth as a value per se.

To be sure, the optimism of the booster was once much stronger in America than it is now. The ideal of manifest destiny, which took us

---

[7] Since the writing of this paper, John Kenneth Galbraith's clarifying book, *The Affluent Society* (Boston: Houghton Mifflin Company, 1958) has appeared. With superb understanding, Professor Galbraith shows how the fear of economic insecurity which haunts Americans makes us the victim of our own productive processes—processes which create and then supply the "wants" as well as the leisure we choose because we don't want the wants that much. Galbraith also shows that the very primacy given to full production and full employment in the United States robs the economy of the flexibility that would permit diverting some of the surplus to wiping out the residual but stubborn poverty in this country and to making a dent on the vast and apparently increasing poverty of the non-industrialized world. And Galbraith sketches some of the political and ideological reasons why "high production" has become a goal, not only for dairy cows, but for human beings—a goal which is now shared by liberals and conservatives and, almost by definition, by economists.

across the continent and held the South bound to the Union in the Civil War, infects now only those perpetually adolescent males who are eager to conquer space or the planet Venus.[8] But the booster psychology has for so long been built into our culture and into our patterns of individual and group achievement that we tend to take for granted the notion that growth in population, in assets, in national income, is inevitable if not always desirable. Imagine the outcry, for instance, and not only from Catholics, against any suggestion that people be encouraged in this country to practice birth control, let us say, by removing the tax concession for child dependents or by instituting a sales tax on children's toys and clothes, or even by pointing out forcefully to people some of the less happy consequences of an exploding population.[9] For most Americans still believe that the future can take care of itself, or at any rate that we are not required to do anything to make it easier, less crowded, less full of friction, for our descendants. (In the same way, on a far smaller and simpler and less controversial issue, it seems almost impossible to cut down the growth of our autos in size and horsepower, let alone to forbid them from entering our downtown areas without good cause shown. Instead, everything else has to adjust to the auto: our central cities must tear down homes and tear up parks to provide those highways that, as Mumford has often pointed out, only brings more cars in an endless vicious spiral.)[10]

In other words, we have become a conservative country, despite our worldwide reputation for seeking novelty, in that we are unable to envisage alternative futures for ourselves. In an illuminating essay, John Kouwenhoven has suggested that a certain style of extrapolative thinking and designing is characteristically American.[11] He referred there to the

---

[8] The space age is not a safety valve for the luxury economy and for our overflowing energies. Although the comparison is often made, I believe there is a real difference between our space age and the exploration of this continent in the fifteenth and sixteenth centuries; at that time Europe was cramped and bound in all kinds of traditional constraints, and could find in colonization an opening for its growing population, its growing energies, its growing rationalism; the "best" use of the space frontier today would be to deflect our weapons—we can bombard Venus rather than each other.

[9] For a better grasp of some of these problems, I am indebted to the writings of John R. Platt, Harrison Brown, and Richard L. Meier.

[10] Cf. for a fuller discussion, Riesman and Eric Larrabee, "Autos in America: Manifest and Latent Destiny," in Lincoln Clark, ed., *Consumer Behavior* (New York: Harper's, 1958), pp. 69-92.

[11] "What's American about America?" *Harper's*, vol. 213, no. 1274 (July, 1956).

way we have laid out our cities in gridiron blocks, to our assembly lines
and consecutive sections, to our skyscrapers in serried stories. He
pointed to our continuous flow of comic strips, movies, the stanzas of
our popular music; he might have added our football cheers, and our
seriatim credits and terms as one passes through the educational plant.
Though no one of these is unique to America, it can be argued that our
way of thinking tends to be extrapolative: we add one story to another,
one thing to another, one frame to another: we think in terms of addi-
tives.

IV. THE ABYSS OF LEISURE

So, too, it has been until recent years in the field of leisure time—
so much so that my collaborators and I in *The Lonely Crowd* took it for
granted that it was impossible to reverse the trend towards automation;
we assumed that the current efforts to make work more meaningful—
which by and large succeeded only in making it more time-consuming
and gregarious but not more challenging—might as well be given up,
with the meaning of life to be sought henceforth in the creative use of
leisure. We failed to see, in the famous Marxist phrase, that "quantity
changes into quality" and that there would come a point where additional increments of leisure would prove more stultifying than satisfying
and that the mass of men would be incapable of absorbing any more.

The situation confronting Americans—and, as already indicated, in
due course the rest of the industrially advanced countries .also — is
historically unprecedented. In pre-industrial cultures leisure is scarcely a
burden or a "problem" because it is built into the ritual and groundplan
of life for which people are conditioned in childhood; often they possess
a relatively timeless attitude towards events. Likewise, the tiny leisure
classes of the past would sometimes be able to absorb what seems like
an overdose of leisure because they lived in an era when work itself was
thought demeaning and when free citizens engaged in physical and intellectual self-cultivation and in the arts of war and government—they,
so to speak, exercised their leisure on behalf of the whole society. During
this era, which lasted throughout most of history, it was inconceivable
that the mass of men could support a large and growing leisure class, let
alone join such a class themselves. Yet today we live in such a world.
The rich and leisured are no longer drastically set apart, but seek for the
sake of their souls as well as their public relations to work with relative

sobriety and consume with relative modesty and inconspicuousness; thus, they no longer set an example for either good or ill.[12]

At the present time, the closest thing we have to the traditional ideology of the leisure class is a group of artists and intellectuals who regard their work as play and their play as work. For such people, and for the larger group of professional people whom we shall discuss later, work frequently provides the central focus of life without necessarily being compartmentalized from the rest of life either by its drudgery and severity or by its precariousness. At best, the painter may always be seeing and the poet and writer always envisaging, although with greater or lesser intensity and concentration.

V. WORK AS A PSYCHOLOGICAL STABILIZER

Such considerations and reconsiderations led the Center for the Study of Leisure to decide in 1957 to examine the prospects of the four-day week in manufacturing industry and to initiate conversations with union officials concerning the bearing of such a pattern of work on the leisure activities of the workers. At that time Walter Reuther and the UAW were contemplating such a week and other union leaders were also interested in it as a possibility. We were curious about the effects on employees of receiving an unexpected and unplanned-for dividend of leisure. Accordingly, when a small aircraft parts manufacturer in Southern California unilaterally decided to give its employees a four-day week at the beginning of each month, with Monday off (to be made up by working one Saturday at the end of the week), Rolf Meyersohn, Research Director of the Center, went to the spot and began to question workers concerning their reactions to the new plan. The periodic interviewing of these employees is presently under way; and *in medias re* it is, of course, not possible to say just what the research will turn up. But, so far, it would seem that the employees have accepted the idea of a four-day week readily enough and without Puritan inhibitions or mis-

---

[12] It is however a very different story when one views the rich, not in their individual capacity, but in their collective capacity, whether corporate or national. For a brief discussion of the two economies, that of luxury and that of subsistence, which exist side by side even in America see my article, "The Suburban Sadness" in William Dobriner, ed., *The Suburban Community* (New York: G. P. Putnam, 1958), pages 393 and *sec.* And for discussion of America's wealth as a barrier in our relations with other nations, see my Introduction to Daniel Lerner's book, *op. cit.*, and "Human Relations and National Boundaries," *Comprendre,* 1958.

givings; the only major problems appear to arise from the fact that the rest of the family is not as yet on a similar schedule. One could argue indeed that Southern California can absorb increments of leisure more readily than can other parts of the country: many of the employees have camps in the hills or boats in the water.

In fact, in a Roper Poll taken in the summer of 1957 concerning attitudes toward a possible four-day week, it turned out that there were some distinct regional differences as well as differences among people of different age and economic levels (although differences in education were the most pronounced). Strikingly enough, in the Far West a third of the respondents would use an additional day to take another job—in part apparently to get still more money to spend in the remaining time off or in a later stage of the life cycle. Contrastingly, the Southerners were least able to come up with ideas about what they would do with the extra day: do-it-yourself was less in evidence, as were hobbies, sports, and trips. College graduates incidentally were the most trip-prone: 47% would take trips as against 19% who had had only a grade school education; likewise, the college graduate also had a far greater interest in participant sports. Older people (who are also people of lesser education) were somewhat more worried about the possibility that people would get soft and lazy while younger people were somewhat more likely (27% to 19%) to believe that with the extra time people would relax more, enjoy themselves more, and be happier.

On the whole, this survey did not turn up great eagerness for an extra day (nor did a somewhat comparable Gallup survey). In our own more limited inquiries we have discovered many wives who are aghast at the thought of having their husbands around the house for a still-longer "lost weekend"—and not a few husbands who are not notably eager for what they term "honey-do" days; that is, days at home when their wives ask them, "Honey, do this!" and "Honey, do that!"

An informal poll of a union local (conducted by James Carper) found that the leaders did want a shorter work week whereas the rank and file did not. This was interpreted as suggesting that the leaders, better educated and more enterprising, feel cramped for time to do everything they want to—to read more books, to see more of their families, to take more adult education courses. Such men already had many hobbies, including being union leaders. But the less active members (no doubt including many who might tell the union leaders that they "lack time to go to meetings") had no similar feeling of wanting the days to be longer. Such men, asked what they would do with an extra day, sometimes say, "sleep"; others could use it in hunting season—and already did so to the dismay of the foreman.

Union leaders have pointed out to me that a lack of any experience with extensive leisure may be responsible for the frequent breakdown and anomic reactions among men forced to retire, regardless of the medical and recreational facilities that may be provided for the retired. Moreover, these officials have envisaged the impact of automation on their industry as well-nigh complete, and they have described to me what was already occurring: namely, the creation of many jobs which consist of little more than half-attentive dial watching of nearly self-corrective automatic machinery—machinery which, if it does break down, requires the services of specialists.[13] Envisaging a continuing decline in working hours, either through a four-day week or the six-hour day of the rubber workers, these thoughtful men have felt that leisure has to take up the slack in work, providing both the challenges and the variations of monotony that can no longer be found in work.

Certainly, there is plenty of evidence that even as things stand, unskilled industrial workers do not like their work, although some enjoy the companionship it provides.[14] In a study by Nancy Morse and Robert Weiss,[15] some 80% of such workers stated that they, in effect, kept on working for lack of alternatives, not for positive satisfactions. These workers were asked whether they would go on working even if there were no financial need to do so, and they said they would, although also indicating that the job itself (and in many cases any job they could imagine) was boring and without meaning in its own terms. This cling-

---

[13] This is not to say that the machine as such is bad for man. I don't share the imagery of *Brave New World;* it is rather that we need more *social* science fiction, more social science imagination as well as technological imagination in the design of our work routines. What I am opposed to is unidimensional so-called technological progress which is measured purely in the easily defined terms of output and fails to take account of the total constituency involved in that output. Thus, some automation serves to reassemble jobs and makes severe demands on intelligence, analogous to working or at the switchboard of a power grid or programing a computer. Such work is meaningful and much more demanding of course than routinized assembly-line work. What we must do is make just this sort of judgment about the consequences for the worker and not simply plow ahead in what is wrongly called "automation," namely, further specialization and not quite total elimination of human beings.

[14] The extent of this companionship may be exaggerated at present by industrial sociologists. See the study by Robert Dubin, "Industrial Workers' Worlds," in *Social Problems,* vol. 3 (1956), pp. 131-140, and reprinted in this volume.

[15] "The Function and Meaning of Work and the Job," *American Sociological Review,* vol. 20 (1955), pp. 191-98. I am indebted to Mr. Weiss for many helpful suggestions.

ing to the job is not simply a legacy of the Puritan ethic: it is rather a legacy of industrialism itself, of the old structures it has destroyed and the new structures it has created. Nor, in Mr. Weiss's opinion, is it merely the feeling of shame in not having a job which is involved (although this is certainly an element). Work may not be an active presence in the life of these workers, but its absence would be an active absence. Or, more accurately, it is not so much "work" that would be missed as having a job: it doesn't have to be, and should preferably not be hard work, nor need it even be gregarious work, but rather the self-definition (these data refer only to male workers) that comes from holding a job and the punctuations of life provided by regular employment. Putting together the still incomplete data from the four-day week studies and from the study by Nancy Morse and Robert Weiss, it would seem that there is a difference in kind between a four-day or three-day week and a no-day week — a difference which leisure in its present versions and for people of this level of education cannot possibly fill.[16] These workers, in other words, are too intelligent and too well educated to accept the routine of most factory work, while being still a long way away from the education of the artist or intellectual who can in some measure create his own work with a minimum of outside structuring.[17]

Such considerations concerning the limits of leisure suggest that it might be easier to make leisure more meaningful if one at the same time could make work more demanding. When work itself is infiltrated with leisure (as it is today in many jobs where the time-study man has been stymied), leisure may lose its savor, often becoming not much more than a continuation outside the plant of the sociability and inanity that go on within the plant. It might be slightly less difficult to reorganize work routines so that they become less routine, more challenging, and hence more instructive, than to cope all at once with the burdens placed on

---

[16] Spanish-American workers are reported as being different in this respect: their feeling of masculine purpose and dignity does not depend on holding a job. See "Spanish Americans of New Mexico, U.S.A.," in Margaret Mead, ed., *Cultural Patterns and Technical Change* (New York: Mentor Books, 1955), pp. 164-165.

[17] Many of the workers in the Morse-Weiss study harbor the vague hope of some day having a small business of their own, such as a gas station or television repair shop. So too the practice of "moonlighting" or holding two jobs testifies not only to the continuing inflation of consumer wants and of the corresponding prices, but also to the fact that many factory workers are like the Russian peasants who were drafted into the collective farms: they give a minimum quantum of their work to the factory as the peasants did to the farms, and save up their real energies for the "private plots" of their work outside. Cf. Ely Chinoy, *Automobile Workers and the American Dream* (New York: Doubleday, 1955), and Charles R. Walker and Robert H. Guest, *The Man on the Assembly Line* (Cambridge, Mass.: Harvard University Press, 1952).

leisure by the evaporation of the meaning of work. This evaporation has occurred as a result of the same commercial and industrial developments that have turned leisure from a communal affair, celebrated by festivals or other shared activities, into an individualized pursuit, hence a "problem." Thus, we have lost not only, as already indicated, the folk traditions that have in many cultures integrated work and leisure, but also those that have integrated leisure with the community's framework (in Fromm's terms) or orientation and devotion. In this situation, I believe that we cannot take advantage of what remains of our pre-industrial heritage to make leisure more creative, individually and socially, if work is not creative, too. And not only have we lost the folk and peasant traditions: we are rapidly losing those which have developed under industrialism itself—whether of the John Henry variety or of the free-swearing, free-swinging construction engineer who gets roads and dams built: such legends hold little allure in an opulent society, even when building continues at a rapid pace. It is from the Soviet Union that the story comes of a mill foreman who, though complaining of his pay, says he "must be content with the 'thrill of producing something anyway.' "[18] Though he may have been speaking in part for the record, there is no doubt that production remains exciting for many where industrialism is the unfinished business of a rising power. Americans, however, cannot artificially recreate that atmosphere; we cannot make factory or other industrial and commercial work over on the model of army basic training or campcraft just to make it hard (though in fact many workers do enjoy making a game of output, for instance, working up the line on an assembly-line, in order to establish control and dramatize their activity). One alternative is to redesign our factories with an eye to the educational or challenging quality of each job, following the example set by some industrial units which have eliminated assembly lines and are giving workers larger units to assemble, or what is sometimes termed "job enlargement." The march of specialization which had originally been based on steam production but has in our day become an end in itself with its own dynamic and momentum could thereby be reversed.[19] Un-

---

[18] See Max Frankel, *New York Times,* September 21, 1957, p. 3, col. 1.

[19] See, e.g., Peter Drucker, *Concept of the Corporation* (New York: Harper's, 1946), and the brilliant discussion by Daniel Bell, *Work and Its Discontents: The Cult of Efficiency in America* (Boston: Beacon Press, 1956).

To be sure, there would always be a question whether the work were being complicated only by the energy of the work force to create a plot for the daily drama of life or because the total configuration had been reorganized so that the work and the workers were seen as a "single" product. Assuredly, such reorganization, like anything else, could become a gimmick of management but it need not do so.

doubtedly, work flows could be redesigned to maximize the demands on the worker's intelligence, while retaining present advances in making work quiet, free of dirt, and relatively unstrenuous.[20]

VI. LEISURE — SOCIETY'S BLOTTING PAPER

It has become clear that post-industrial society no longer requires arduous and routinized work on the one hand, or, on the other hand, that kind of seemingly varied work, such as that of the salesman, in which the worker is compelled to exploit his own personality. Nevertheless, I have been arguing that Americans remain too unequivocally the children of industry, even when automation threatens to disinherit us, for us to be able to resort to leisure as a counterbalance for the deficiencies of work. Even so, leisure is coming to occupy for adults something of the position the school already occupies for youngsters, of being the institution which seems "available" to bear the brunt of all society's derelictions in other spheres. Thus, just as schools are asked to become quasi-parental, quasi-custodial, quasi-psychiatric, and quasi-everything else, filling in for tasks other institutions leave undone or badly done, with the result that the schools often cannot do their job of education adequately; so leisure is now being required to take up the energies left untapped everywhere else in our social order, with the result that it often fails in its original task of recreation for most of us most of the time and of creativity for some of us some of the time. The hopes I had put on leisure (in *The Lonely Crowd*) reflect, I suppose, my despair about the possibility of making work in modern society more meaningful and more demanding for the mass of men—a need which has come upon us so rapidly that the taste of abundance we have had in the past now threatens to turn into a glut.

My despair on this score, I must add, was not greatly alleviated by the feeling in the group of union leaders mentioned above that it was impossible either to get unions or management in the least interested in making work more humanly satisfying. I hoped the union leaders might cooperate with management in, so to speak, turning the engineers around, and forcing them to design men back into their machines rather than out of them. In this connection, I recall talking with aircraft engi-

---

[20] Nelson Foote tells me of a case in Detroit some years ago where workers through their union insisted on their right to sing at work against the objections of a Puritanical management. I am indebted to Mr. Foote, and particularly to his unpublished paper on "Stultification at Work," for much illumination concerning the themes discussed in this paper.

neers who were irritated with the "human factor," and eager to put a machine wherever a man might go wrong, rather than to design equipment that maximized the still enormous resourcefulness of the human mind. I recall the highway engineers who designed thruways that would look good to other engineers or to engineering-minded Americans—until the death toll made them realize that boredom could be a greater danger to man than speed and obstacles. And I thought of the subdividers who bulldozed down all trees to make it easier to build a road or a suburb, with no authorities around to forbid such wanton simplification of their own task along with such destruction of history and life. As the discussion with the union officials continued, it became clearer to me that the workers themselves were too much of this same school of engineering thought really to believe in the reorganization of industry.[21] The kind of Utopia of meaningful work pictured in Percival and Paul Goodman's book, *Communitas*,[22] made no sense to them.

In this perspective, the rebellion of workers against modern industry is usually mere rebellion, mere goofing off. Many are quite prepared to go on wildcat strikes (Daniel Bell notes that in 1954-55 there were forty such in just one Westinghouse plant in East Pittsburgh); they are quite prepared to deceive the time-study man and to catch forty winks on the night shift, and otherwise to sabotage full production while still "making out" in terms of the group's norms—being in this like students who might cheat on exams or cut classes but could not conceive of reorgani-

---

[21] It may be asked (and was) whether we can reverse our technical impetus and the trend towards automation without losing the very source of our leisure and our high productivity. In my opinion, we are already far past the point where we must be bound by such alternatives. In the great world of impoverished people with a very low life expectancy and the annual income of, let us say, an Indonesian villager, the question would answer itself: many people would be willing to sacrifice much for the greater amenity and ease of life Americans have. But if in America the changes I am recommending would make industry less productive, which I doubt, I think many of us would be willing to pay the price of working harder and having less so that we might have a more meaningful life at work. In fact, however, we have no evidence it would lower our overall productivity to re-design our industrial pattern. Instead, I am convinced that ideology dominates factory and machine design to such an extent that we have a dream or myth of efficiency whose long-run cumulative costs are enormous in the sabotage and resentment of the work force, in boredom, in absenteeism, and so on. Engineers still act as if workers were as undisciplined and inefficient a group as they were before mass education and before industrialism—and by so doing they make our industry less productive than it might be even in its own terms.

[22] *Communitas: Ways of Livelihood and Means of Life*, (Chicago: University of Chicago Press, 1946). Compare my discussion in "Some Observations on Community Plans and Utopia," *Yale Law Journal*, vol. 47 (1947), reprinted in *Individualism Reconsidered* (Glencoe, Illinois: The Free Press, 1954).

zation of the curriculum or of asking for heavier assignments. The great victory of modern industry is that even its victims, the bored workers, cannot imagine any other way of organizing work, now that the tradition of the early nineteenth century Luddites, who smashed machines, has disappeared with the general acceptance of progress. We must thus think of restriction of output and other sabotage of production as mere symptoms.[23]

Furthermore, the resentment which manifests itself in these symptoms helps engender a vicious circle, since it confirms the opinion of management that workers must be disciplined by bringing them together in great factories and subjecting them to the relentless pressure of assembly lines—as against the possibility, for instance, that work could be decentralized so that workers would not have to commute long distances and could proceed more at their own pace and place.[24] In the high-wage industries given over to "conspicuous production," management has the resources to be concerned with the amenities of work — the group harmony, the decor, the cafeteria and other ancillary services — and to make provision for the worker's leisure, such as bowling teams, golf courses, and adult education courses too; in fact, a whole range of extra-curricular pleasures and benefits. Sometimes these benefits include profit-sharing, but they are much less likely to include decision-sharing, for of course managers object less to giving away money, especially money that would otherwise go to stockholders or to the government in taxes, than to giving away power and prestige and freedom of action to workers whose unionized demands reflect merely their discontent and scarcely at all their desires for reconstruction.[25]

It is obvious in addition that managers are not free to reorganize their plants in order to provide their workers with a more satisfying work environment, if this might risk higher costs, unless their competitors are

---

[23] For an understanding of how to look for and interpret such symptoms in a whole society or subculture, I am indebted to the work of Erich Fromm. Compare especially *The Sane Society* (New York: Rinehart and Co., 1955).

[24] Cf. Daniel Bell, *Work and Its Discontents, supra;* also "The Evasion of Work" in *Work and the Welfare Age,* L.P.E. Papers #4, July 1956, pages 23-30.

[25] What is General Motors to make, for instance, of some of the UAW locals' demands which are being presented in the current negotiations as these pages go to press, e.g., that the scores of World Series and other baseball games be announced at the end of each inning over the public address system or that motor scooters be furnished for union committeemen, or that workers be allowed to buy GM products at 40% off! Another demand, that schedules be adjusted to allow employees wanting to go deer hunting to take time off (as in fact many do anyway), has a pre-industrial ring to it but hardly betokens a new rearrangement of work and leisure. See *Time,* June 9, 1958, page 84.

Lest I be misunderstood, let me make clear that I am not recommending arduousness per se nor do I object at all to the steps workers and unions have taken to make life pleasanter and less exhausting.

prepared to go along. Yet competition is not the whole story, for the situation is hardly better and is often worse in nationalized industries in Great Britain and Western Europe generally, while the situation of industrial workers in the Soviet Union today reminds one of the worst excesses of the Victorian era and the earlier days of the Industrial Revolution in the West. Managers of whatever ideological stripe seek to measure themselves against a single, uni-dimensional standard by which they can judge performance and thus are drawn to simplified work routines and an unremitting drive for maximum output. To open the possible consideration of factories as making not only things but also men, and as providing not only comfort and pay but also challenge and education, this would itself be a challenge to the way we have assimilated technology for the last three hundred years; and it would compel us to search for more Gestaltist and amorphous standards, in which we were no longer so clear as to what is process and what is product. There have, to be sure, been paternalistic employers (such as the Lowell mills in the 1840s or the Pullman plant a half-century ago) concerned with the education and uplift of their operatives—often to the eventual resentment and unionization of the latter (who felt it was enough to have to work for the bosses without imitating their preferred inhibitions). But these were efforts to compensate outside the plant for the dehumanization regarded as inevitable within. What I am asking for now is hardly less than reorganizing work itself so that man can live humanely on as well as off the job.

*   *   *

IX. ABUNDANCE FOR WHAT?

Even the most confident economists cannot adequately picture a society which could readily stow away the goods likely to descend upon us in the next fifteen years (assuming only a modest rise in annual productivity), with any really sizable drop in defense expenditures. People who are forced by the recession or by fear of their neighbors' envy or by their own misgivings to postpone for a year the purchase of a new car may discover that a new car every three years instead of every two is quite satisfactory. And once they have two cars, a swimming pool and a boat, and summer and winter vacations, what then?

Increasingly, as we all know, the motivation researchers are being pressed to answer these questions, and to discover what the public does not yet know that it "wants." Just as we are lowering our water table by ever-deeper artesian wells and in general digging ever deeper for

other treasures of the earth, so we are sinking deeper and deeper wells
into people in the hope of coming upon "motives" which can power the
economy or some particular sector of it. I am suggesting that such
digging, such forcing emotions to externalize themselves, cannot continue
much longer without man running dry.

Even now, some of the surplus whose existence presents us with
such questions is being absorbed in the very process of its creation but
by what I have termed the "conspicuous production" of our big corporations, acting as junior partners of the welfare state and absorbing all
sorts of ancillary services for their own members and their own
communities.[35]

Defense expeditures loom so large in our political as well as economic horizon because they do offer an easy and seemingly feasible way
out by creating goods which do not themselves create other goods. (They
are "multipliers" only in a Keynesian sense.) But of course the international consequences as well as the long-range domestic ones point the
way only to lunacy and the alternatives of destruction or the garrison
state. Indeed in a recent article, "Economic Implications of Disarmament," Gerard Colm argues that it would be difficult to deploy for
public services our rising productivity even without reducing defense
expenditures.[36] He sees education as potentially absorbing much the
largest part of the surplus (education must be seen even now as the
greatest leisure time-killer we have, keeping out of the labor force an
increasingly large portion of the young). And Colm presents figures for
highway and other transport, along with other public works, hospitals,
and water conservation—yet these altogether hardly make up in ten
years what we spend in one year for our armed forces. I would contend
that expenditures which serve no real social imperative, other than prop-
ping up the economy or subduing the sibling rivalry of the armed
services, will eventually produce wasteful byproducts to slow that
economy down in a tangle of vested inefficiencies, excessively conspicuous production, lowered work morale, and lack of purpose and
genuine inventiveness.[37] The word "to soldier" means "to loaf" and

---

[35] As Professor Galbraith makes abundantly clear in his book (*supra*, note 7),
these corporations along with their employees are actually "senior partners," with
the State and its subdivisions in contrast living shabbily as a very junior partner
in a period of inflation. See *The Affluent Society,* ch. 14, 18, and elsewhere.

[36] *Illinois Business Review,* 14 (July 1957), pp. 6-8.

[37] Discussion period question: "Isn't there a good deal of cynicism or debunk-
ing among workers concerning the product they are making?" Answer: "You are
right that the problem of meaning and work lies not only in its intellectual or
physical gamesmanship but in its relevance to the total social context. Thus, one
could make work in an aircraft plant or missile plant more intriguing without in

conscription gives training in soldiering to a large proportion of the future work-force (despite islands of asceticism in the Strategic Air Command or the air-borne "brushfire" infantry). For a time, men will go on producing because they have got the habit, but the habit is not contagious. Men will scarcely go on producing as mere items in a multiplier effect or conscripts in an endless Cold War, nor will they greatly extend themselves to earn more money which they are increasingly bored with spending. To be sure, many workers have little objection to getting paid without "earning" it by traditional standards of effortfulness. And while those standards are usually irrelevant in a society of advanced technology and high expenditures on research and development, there are certainly many parts of the economy, notably in the service trades, whose gross inefficiency we only conceal from ourselves by contrasting America with pre-industrial societies or with those possessing far less adequate resources of men and machines—if we compare ourselves with the West Germans, for instance, or with the Canadians, the advance in our economy since 1946, great as it is in absolute terms, is unimpressive. The pockets of efficiency in our society are visible and made more so by the myth that we are efficient; hence, the evidence of disintegration and incompetence that is all around us strikes us as temporary or aberrant.

X. The Dislocation of Desire

Correspondingly, some of our desires have been made highly visible by advertising and market research and lead to equally visible results such as good cars and, intermittently, good roads to drive them over. But other desires, which require cooperation to be effective, are often lamely organized and all but invisible. Thus, while some of us have a missionary zeal for learning, which we regard as the basis of later leisure as well as later employment, we have not been helped even by the push of sputnik to get a bill for school construction past the same Congress which eagerly voted Federal money for highways (in part, no doubt,

---

all dimensions making it more meaningful. Of course it does not prove that something is a good product because it gets bought. Cynicism among advertising men comes out of the feeling that the work they do, although creative in many ways— artistic, imaginative, ingenious in terms of research methods—is not meaningful or is actually harmful so that they don't enjoy it. Surely this is the feeling of many intellectuals, whose work, although demanding and challenging, is not worthwhile. We must proceed on both fronts: to make the work more invigorating and pleasant in its own terms, that is, in terms of technical operations, and in terms of its bearing on what adds to human growth and development."

because the annual maintenance of schools falls upon a local tax base which grows constantly more inadequate while the maintenance of highways can be more easily financed from gasoline and registration taxes).[38] Other services, not so clearly "a good thing" as secondary and university education, are even more lacking in organized institutional forms which would permit the channeling of our surplus in ways which would improve the quality and texture of daily life. For example, even the great demand for scenic beauty (anemically reflected in the new highways) cannot make itself politically felt in preserving the countryside against roadside slums and metropolitan expansion, while men of wealth are missing who could buy up whole counties and give them to the nation as a national park. We see one consequence on summer weekends when millions pour onto the roads and breathe each other's fumes and crowd each other's resorts. And we see too that leisure is cut down by the time taken to get to and from work—commuting time increased by the desire to live in the suburbs in order to enjoy leisure! As our resources dwindle in comparison with population and as individual abundance creates social blight, we will increasingly find little solace in leisure without privacy. It is extraordinary how little we have anticipated the problems of the bountiful future, other than to fall back on remedies which did not work in the less bountiful past, such as individualism, thrift, hard work, and enterprise on the one side, or harmony, togetherness, and friendliness on the other. Meanwhile, we stave off the fear of satiation in part by scanning the technological horizon for new goods which we will all learn to want, in part by the delaying tactic of a semi-planned recession, and, as already indicated, in part by the endless race of armaments.

That race has its cultural as well as Keynesian dynamic: as poll data show, a majority or large plurality of Americans expect war, though perhaps in a rather abstract way—war is one of those extrapolations from the past; like technological progress, we find it hard to resist. And, on the one hand, the threat of war is one factor in discouraging long-term plans, while, on the other hand, the continuation of the Cold War provides a sort of alternative to planning. Thus, there tends to be a state of suspended animation in the discussion concerning the quality of life a rich society should strive for; social inventiveness tends to be channeled into the defense of past gains rather than into ideas for a better

---

[38] On this point, as on so many others of this paper, Professor Galbraith's discussion adds clarity and perspective. See *The Affluent Society*, chs. 11, 13, 22, 25, and passim.

proportionality between leisure and work. Like soldiers off duty, "as you were," we subsist in default of more humane hopes.

But I should add that no society has ever been in the same position as ours, of coming close to fulfilling the age-old dream of freedom from want, the dream of plenty. And I want to repeat that millions of Americans, perhaps still the great majority, find sufficient vitality in pursuit of that dream: the trip to the end of the consumer rainbow retains its magic for the previously deprived. It is only the minority where, looking further ahead, we can see already the signs of a generation, prepared for Paradise Lost, which does not know what to do with Paradise Found. Regrettably, it will not be given a long time to come to a decision. For, by concentrating all energies on preserving freedom from want and pressing for consumer satiation at ever more opulent levels, we jeopardize this achievement in a world where there are many more poor nations than rich ones and in which there are many more desires, even among ourselves, for things other than abundance.

Chapter Eight

SOCIAL CLASS

Were a turn-of-the-century American teacher to walk into today's representative classroom, it is probable that one feature above all others would evoke his curiosity: the awesome *diversity* of the students sitting in front of him. Never before has one educational system been faced with such an array of cultural differences: Negro, Mexican-American, Caribbean, new urban dwellers from the Deep South or from farms, and—included in each of these groups—members of the very bottom segment of the socio-economic hierarchy.[1] The middle-class Protestant Anglo-Saxon—the selected few that comprised the characteristic classroom of 1900—is in many of today's schools little more than another minority.

Without gainsaying the significance of ethnic, racial and rural-urban differences, an impressive and ever-mounting body of evidence suggests that the most profound of the cultural differences that characterize today's Americans are *social-class* differences. If we recognize the significance of this testimony, we hardly need ask why those who will work with today's students (and, more so, tomorrow's) must be more than merely aware of the roots, the dynamics, and the implications of social class in American culture.

---

[1] Immediately before and after World War I, it is true, the teacher in metropolitan public schools faced a greater variety of nationality backgrounds. But never has so impressive a *proportion* of "minority" students—Negro, Puerto Rican, Mexican-American, and lower-blue-collar—(1) attended our schools and (2) gone beyond the junior high school level.

The two selections in this chapter describe, assess, and analyze these and other provocative facets of our class structure. But before reading the selections by Robert J. Havighurst and Harold M. Hodges, it is well to remind ourselves of a set of biases that might otherwise muddle our vision. For social stratification, plainly, is not a matter that evokes unruffled reactions. In fact most persons, when they first come to solid grips with the question of "social class," assume a posture that is curiously either "for" or "against" in inclination. In a word, they are characteristically somewhat awe-struck or somewhat skeptical.

The first, and certainly the more naive, response is to exaggerate beyond all reason the salience of what we choose to call class: to neatly class-type friend, foe, and stranger, to see "status symbols" lurking behind every car grill or hi-fi component, and "status striving" motivating every purchase of a color television set. Or worse, to imagine that each and every person is a powerless automaton, forever in the grasp of class-induced pressures to conform according to type. The unbeliever, on the other hand, is variously prone to regard class as (1) a restatement of the obvious—disguised in the beguiling mystique of sociological gobbledegook; or (2) an ominous myth that would deny individual differences (and stereotype each of us as one more statistic on an IBM punch card); or (3) an alluring but really worthless intellectual fad; or perhaps (4) an outright deception foisted on us by the "people watchers."

Somewhere midway between such dispositions, but nearer the skeptical pole, is a question that is too frequently dismissed or easily glossed over: can we precisely identify every Tom, Dick, and Oswald in pure social-class terms? The answer must be a quite candid "no!" Yet to admit this is not to question the validity of "social class" as a concept —a concept every bit as valid as such other useful notions as "national character" and "ethnic," "delinquent," or "adolescent" subculture. It is merely to contend that the student of social stratification is dealing not with iron-clad absolutes but with probabilities, not with differences of black and white, but with differences of pitch, tenor, and intensity. Like the insurance actuary who is concerned with risk groups, the student of social class is interested in central tendencies: the characteristic, the representative, and the customary.

To acknowledge the reality of the class divisions in our midst is not to assume class consciousness or even awareness of the fact that class divisions exist (in like manner another concept—that of "personality"— does not require that we *know* what we are to *be* what we are). To realize the potency of class is not, furthermore, to ignore the overriding consequence of individual differences. Nor is it to declare that class-typed distinctions and class-linked behavior in hamlet, village, and metropolis, in the Negro community and the Mexican-American, or in the Ozarks and the San Francisco Peninsula are all cast of the same mold. We cannot precisely class-type Ashmead Goodwin, Donald Garske, or Godric Pontefract any more than we can unerringly pinpoint their deep-seated fears and compulsions, or say with confidence why and how they differ because of race or residence. The realm of social class, finally, is substantially uncharted and unexplored. That is perhaps why, at heart, it is so annoying a subject to some and so beguiling to others.

SOCIAL CLASS IN THE UNITED STATES: AN OVERVIEW*

by Robert J. Havighurst

A majority of the readings in this book have social class as a central or important element in them. Why are educators so keenly interested in social class? Why do they think that all teachers should understand social class?

In the first place, *everybody* is interested in social class. Like sex, it is a fascinating topic, and also, like sex, it is just slightly taboo, and therefore all the more interesting. Nobody is bored by social class. People feel involved. They react to discussions about it. Some are for it, others are against it.

By the time a person is in college he has had enough experience in society and enough personal experience to be aware of the influence of social class in himself and in others he meets. If he is at all interested in people, he has learned to notice things about them that mark them as from one social class or another. And he has begun to realize that social classes are very important elements in society.

In the second place, people are puzzled and a little worried about social class. Having been brought up with the idea that equality is an important aspect of democracy, the obvious inequality of social classes disturbs them. They feel bound to make a moral judgment about the social stratification that they discover in society. They ask themselves whether such stratification is consistent with democracy. They ask themselves whether they should work to abolish social classes, and how they should act, as citizens and as prospective teachers, in a society of this sort.

THE BASIC FACTS

There are certain facts that are by now common knowledge to anyone who reads the literature of sociology. Dozens of sociologists and anthropologists have studied dozens of communities and reported on their social structure.

---

*This commentary was written for publication in this book.

These communities have a visible group structure. People fall into groups. They work in groups, they worship in groups, they play in groups, and these groups cut across and overlap one another, so that some people belong to one set of groups, other people to another set of groups, and so on. Lawyers tend to see other lawyers not only in the courts, but also in certain clubs, certain churches, and at certain parties; factory workers tend to see other factory workers in certain parks, certain churches, and certain union meetings. Furthermore, the community's physical structure reflects these groups. The community is cut up into areas by the railroad tracks, the highways, and factory districts, and the people living in one district appear to be different kinds of people from those living in other districts.

There are cultural differences between the different social groups. A culture is a common and standardized set of ways of behaving and believing. The sociologists find that the different social groups in America have somewhat different cultures, even though they also share certain common culture traits—such as the English language, a liking for ice cream, and a belief in democracy. It is useful to make a distinction between the general national culture—which is the system of common and standardized ways of behaving and believing shared by the great majority of Americans—and the various sub-cultures—which are sets of culture traits shared by the people within sub-groups in the country.

There are a number of sub-cultures in the United States, in addition to the social-class sub-cultures. There are regional sub-cultures, ones that make Southerners and Midwesterners different. There are religious sub-cultures, which make Methodists and Lutherans different. But from the point of view of a student of education, the most interesting and the most important sub-cultures are the social classes. The reason for this is that the social classes differ from one another in many ways that are important for education. They also differ in other respects, such as their religious habits, their leisure activities, their taste in food and drink and in the interior decoration of their homes.

Social mobility is a basic fact about our social structure. People are born into a certain class, but a considerable number move into another class during their adolescence or early adulthood. Education is an important means of achieving social mobility—more important now than it was at the beginning of this century. The secondary school and the college provide the major avenues in our society for social mobility.

Through these institutions a person accomplishes two things that will tend to make him mobile upward in social status. He prepares for an occupation that will place him higher in the social scale, and he learns the attitudes and manners of a higher social class by playing and working with other boys and girls and with teachers from the higher social class.

What do these facts about social class and social structure mean for democracy? If democracy means that all people are equal, then there cannot be a democracy with social class. But if democracy means that people have equal opportunity to "pursue happiness," whatever that may signify, then social classes may be compatible with democracy provided people have equal opportunity to move from one class to another.

Equal opportunity means equal educational, economic, political and recreational opportunities; and the educational system, if it is doing its work well, tends to equalize opportunity in all these respects.

The fact of social class position is one of the most important characteristics of a boy or girl, because it tends to determine his values and to determine his motives for education. Teachers need to know how to assess social class position quickly when they are studying children and dealing with adults. This enables them to anticipate some of the attitudes toward school and its discipline, and some of the attitudes of the individual toward himself and toward people in authority over him.

THE BASIC CRITERION OF SOCIAL CLASS POSITION

Every community of people that we know about consists of people with different degrees of power and prestige. There is a hierarchy of power and prestige in every modern society, and in every primitive society that has evolved to the stage of division of labor. In the hierarchy different people have different roles in the economic and political and religious life of the society.

When people have different degrees of power or prestige in a society we say that the various positions of power and prestige that they occupy constitute a part of the *structure* of the society. When groups of people have various positions of power and prestige, then the society has a *group structure*.

What is it that gives a person or a group a high status or position in a society, and what is it that leads to a low status?

In a cave-man society, no doubt physical strength and courage give a man higher status, but in a modern society this is no longer true. Many sociologists see economic power as the basic criterion of social position. The people with the most money are at the top, and those with the least money are at the bottom. This means that people with highly paid occupations have high social status, while people with low-paid occupations have low status.

The Middletown Study[1]* reflects the view that economic power is basic to social prestige, and therefore that the occupation of a person is the best clue to his social position.

A good deal of research has been done in this country and in other countries on the prestige of various occupations, with the finding that big property owners and industrialists and medical doctors and lawyers are rated at the top of the occupational hierarchy, while garbage collectors and unskilled workers and farm laborers are at the bottom. Generally speaking, there is a close relation between the income of an occupation and its prestige, though there are exceptions. A priest or clergyman is apt to be rated higher than the owner of a burlesque theater, even though the latter earns more money.

The Yankee City[2] and other studies by Warner and his colleagues have taken the basic criterion of social class as *social participation,* which places them in theoretical disagreement with the scholars who prefer economic position as the basic criterion. Warner's studies demonstrate that in the modern American community there is a consensus as to who is at the top of the social scale, who is just below this, who is further down, and, finally, who is at the bottom of the scale. When he studies the people at the top of the scale he finds that money is not the thing that differentiates them from the people just below them. Rather, the basic criteria are membership in a family which has had money for several generations, living in a certain section of the community, belonging to certain exclusive clubs, and being related by marriage to other high status families.

Therefore, the Warner studies map out the social structure by finding out who associates with whom in a social clique, which families intermarry, what clubs and other societies they belong to. Then a group of residents in the community are asked to rank certain key persons on what they perceive to be the social scale of the community. The people who are asked to judge the social position of the key persons show a high degree of agreement.

With the key persons placed on the scale, it is a simple matter to locate the remainder of the people in the community on the same scale by finding out whom they associate with among the key persons. The

---

*Footnote references will be found at the end of the article.

Yankee City and Jonesville[3] and Deep South[4] studies were made with this method.

However, this procedure is cumbersome and expensive, and Warner and his colleagues developed a short-cut method, using several indices of social status which can be obtained fairly easily. Their composite index correlates very highly with the method of *evaluated social participation,* which is Warner's basic method.

The Index of Status Characteristics, described in *Social Class in America,*[5] uses such information as the following: occupation, house-type, residential area in the community, amount of education, and source of income. Each of these elements serves as the basis of a rating scale, and the ratings for a person are combined into a single score for his social status.

This method of Warner's relies quite heavily on economic facts, and therefore does not differ very much, operationally, from the method favored by the economic determinists.

When comparisons must be made between social classes in different countries or even in different cities or states, the criterion of social participation can hardly be used, and the general method is to use one or more socio-economic indices, such as occupational rating, amount of education, and amount of income.

There is a third type of criterion for social class position, namely, a person's own perception of his position. By this method, a person is asked—To what social class do you think you belong? Professor Richard Centers has used this procedure, with interesting results. Many people who would be rated objectively as lower class or upper class say that they are "middle class" when asked this question. Others who would be rated objectively as middle class say that they are "upper class."

Objections to Social Class Studies

Some take exception to the emphasis on social class that is so general in educational sociology. These objections are of two types:

1. One objection is based on the observation or the conviction that social class is unimportant. If it is not important in the lives of pupils or teachers, why study about it? This objection is sometimes raised by people who work in rural areas. The study of *Midwest*[6] by Roger Barker and others, tends to take this line. The work done in the hamlet of Midwest is a model of systematic observation of children and their relations with one another. Midwest is a small village of about 700 population in a midwestern state, and it

is fairly clear that there are few social class distinctions in this community and they are not very important in the lives of children while they live in Midwest. It seems likely that a village like Midwest does not have much of a class structure. Probably the community would have to exceed 1,000 in population in order to be complex enough for class structure to be important. In villages between one and two thousand in size, such as *Plainville, USA,*[7] studied by James West, and *Seneca, Illinois,* described by Havighurst in *The Social History of a War Boom Community,*[8] there is a rather vaguely outlined three-class structure that has some significance for the lives of the children.

Studies of social structure have been made in communities of various size from the rural villages just mentioned to the metropolitan areas of Kansas City and San Francisco. In the larger cities, a five or six class structure has been found, with interesting subdivisions within these classes.

2. The other objection turns on the definition of a social class. Some scholars insist that a class must be a class. A person is either in a class or not in it. He cannot be halfway in, or in today and out next year. If a social class exists as a definite sub-culture, it must have a definite membership, and all the members must have all the traits of that sub-culture.

If this definition of a social class is insisted on, then there is no system of social classes in the United States, or in any other modern country. Only a very simple society with a few social groups who maintained rigid formal relations with other groups could qualify as a society with social classes by this definition.

With social classes defined as they are in the studies cited above, there are always people on the border between two classes. One investigator will place these people in Class B, another in Class C. Or the same investigator may place a person in Class B one time and a similar person in Class C the next time.

The differences between classes are expressed in two ways. Sometimes a class is described as though all of its members were like a typical person right at the middle of that class. The upper middle class person is described as though he must be a college graduate with an income of ten thousand dollars, because many upper-middle class people are like that. Yet there will be some who have barely graduated from high school, who make five thousand dollars a year, but have other characteristics which are definitely those of the upper-middle class.

The lower-middle class person is described as though he must be a high school graduate who makes seven thousand dollars a year. Yet there will be some lower-middle class people who are college graduates and make ten thousand dollars a year, but have other characteristics which are definitely those of the lower-middle class. Thus it is misleading to describe a social class as though all its members were alike in every respect.

Another way of describing the differences between social classes is to do it in statistical terms. The upper-middle and the lower-middle classes differ by a certain number of years of education, *on the average;* by a certain number of dollars of income, *on the average;* and by a certain number of points on a scale of occupational status, *on the average.* Yet, being contiguous classes, they overlap slightly on all three variables.

If a person can feel comfortable with a statistical definition of a social class, and with the recognition that the sub-culture representing a given social class has some things in common with the sub-culture representing another social class, then he can be comfortable with most of the studies reported in this Reader.

Social Class and Education

Social class studies are important for the teacher because there are so many important educational factors which are closely related to social class. In the studies cited here, it is seen that social class is related to IQ, school achievement, social adjustment, peer status, probability of dropping out of school before high school graduation, probability of going to college, choice of college, participation in extra curricular activities.

If the teacher and the school are to do a good job of teaching all kinds of boys and girls, they need to know a good deal about social class in general, as well as a good deal about the individual boys and girls in their classes.

Is Social Class Becoming Less Important in the U.S.A.?

There is some evidence that social class differences are decreasing in the U.S.A. Several factors seem to be acting to reduce class differences. One is the rise in standard of living of the working class. With increased real income, the working-class man or woman is able to buy the same clothing, the same make of automobile, the same gadgets for the kitchen, as the middle-class person does.

The studies of social class differences in child-rearing practices suggest that the differences between classes are being reduced in this very important area. If so, this may be due to the widespread use of pediatricians and their advice given orally or in books, in place of reliance on more traditional sources of norms for child-rearing, which show large class differences.

Another factor is the spread of information and entertainment through the mass media. If everybody watches the same TV programs, this may tend to reduce differences between social classes.

There is some basis for the idea that a "common-man" culture is spreading over the former lower-middle and upper-lower classes, to make them very much alike. This may be especially true in the sections of the country where new industry pays high wages and there is not much social distinction between office work and factory work. The airplane and electronics industries may be examples, and Southern California may be a place where class distinctions are being reduced between lower-middle and upper-lower classes. Since these two groups together make up about 70 per cent of the population, if they should merge culturally the practical significance of social class differences would be decreased. It is well to ask whether the differences between middle class and working class goals are decreasing. Harold M. Hodges, Jr.'s study of social stratification and mobility in the Peninsula area south of San Francisco (Peninsula People)[9] suggests that they are.

IS SOCIAL MOBILITY DECREASING?

Another question of major concern to education is whether the degree of social mobility in decreasing in the U.S.A. In his popularized book, *The Status Seekers,*[10] Vance Packard claims without presenting evidence that the chances of being upward mobile in America have decreased substantially during the past two decades. It is possible to argue heatedly either for or against the truth of this proposition. But some good empirical studies of the extent of social mobility need to be made in order to settle the issue. One study by Coleman of social mobility in Kansas City indicated that in a sample of middle-aged adults in the 1950's, 33 per cent were one or more classes higher than their parents on a 4-class scale, while 12 per cent were one or more classes lower, leaving a net upward mobility rate of 21 per cent. This is fairly high, but there is no comparable study of an earlier period. Warner and Abegglen, studying the social origins of business leaders about 1950 found some evidence of increased upward mobility among business leaders as compared with 30 years earlier.

Hodges' study also throws some light on this question.

Importance of Intra-Class Factors

If the differences within a social class are as great as the differences between social classes, then it becomes useful to study the intra-class differences. For example, in the studies of social class differences in child-rearing practices, some class differences are found, but it is clear that there is a wide range of variation in child-rearing practices within a social class. Miller and Swanson, in their book, *The Changing American Parent,*[11] suggested that the differences within the middle class might be more important to study than the differences between middle and lower class. They proposed that within the middle class there are two quite different styles of life. One style, the bureaucratic, involves the head of the family as an employee of a bureaucratic organization such as a government office, or a school system, or a factory. A quite different style of life, the entrepreneurial, involves the head of the family as a self-employed person, who must take risks and depend on his initiative and energy to make good in life. They suggested that child-rearing practices would be different in these two types of family, and these differences would be more significant than class differences.

Their study is somewhat related to the concept of "The New Middle Class" which C. Wright Mills has treated.[12] We need a number of studies looking for major sub-cultural differences within the upper-middle class, which is growing so large that it may be harboring some interesting and important sub-groups.

Hodges' study of *Peninsula People* finds the upper-middle class to contain two quite different sub-groups—a group who were born into upper-middle class and another group who have been upward mobile into this class. They differ significantly in such things as religious behavior, leisure activities, political liberalism, and rigidity of personality.

Within the lower class there may also be some important intra-class differences. For instance, we know that most juvenile delinquency is found among boys of the lower-lower class. Yet two out of three boys of this class do not become delinquent. In the readings on Delinquency, it is useful to look for clues as to the intra-class differences that produce delinquency in one family and not in another.

CONCLUSION

The literature on social class shows how rapidly a basic theme in sociology can develop in a society which respects and supports research in the social sciences. Studying the pioneer work of the Lynds in Middletown in the 1920's, together with that of Warner and his colleagues in the 1930's and 1940's and the studies of intra-class differences in the 1950's gives a person an understanding, not only of social class in relation to education, but also of the movement and intensity of social science in the middle of the twentieth century.

REFERENCES

1. Robert S. and Helen M. Lynd, *Middletown*. New York: Harcourt, Brace and Company, 1929.
2. William Lloyd Warner and Paul S. Lunt, *The Social Life of a Modern Community*. New Haven: Yale University Press, 1941.
3. William Lloyd Warner and others, *Democracy in Jonesville*. New York: Harper and Brothers, 1949.
4. Allison Davis, *Deep South*. Chicago: The University of Chicago Press, 1941.
5. William Lloyd Warner, *Social Class in America*. Chicago: Science Research Associates, 1949.
6. Roger Barker and others, *Midwest and Its Children: The Psychological Ecology of an American Town*. Evanston, Illinois: Row, Peterson and Company, 1954.
7. James West, *Plainville, U. S. A.* New York: Columbia University Press, 1945.
8. Robert J. Havighurst and H. G. Morgan, *The Social History of a War-Boom Community*. New York: Longmans, Green and Company, 1951.
9. Harold M. Hodges, Jr., *Peninsula People: Social Stratification in Suburbia* (in press). (For an extended summary of this work, see selection immediately following.)
10. Vance Packard, *The Status Seekers*. New York: David McKay Company, Inc., 1959.
11. Daniel R. Miller and Guy E. Swanson, *The Changing American Parent*. New York: John Wiley and Sons, 1958.
12. C. Wright Mills, *White Collar*. New York: Oxford University Press, 1951.

PENINSULA PEOPLE:
SOCIAL STRATIFICATION IN A
METROPOLITAN COMPLEX*

by Harold M. Hodges, Jr.

"We are a classless people": of all the venerable American myths, few, it would appear, have demonstrated more remarkable staying power than this.

That it has endured as so cherished an element in the American dream is not altogether illogical. For our democratic heritage and its accompanying ideology are premised on the compelling assumption that our worth is determined not by our ancestry, but by what we, as individuals, accomplish in our own lifetimes by dint of our own efforts.

But to deny that we are a classless people, to assert that in fact social classes are salient ingredients in the American social fabric, is not to deny the worth of the doctrine of equality; it is rather, in an important sense, to affirm it.[1] Nor is such an assertion fraught with ugly Marxian overtones of class consciousness and class conflict. It is a neutral statement of fact, devoid of connotations of inferiority and superiority. It is a valid statement of fact, and not the mere fanciful creation of theorists, because copious evidence increasingly corroborates both the conclusive reality and the substantial everyday consequence of social-class divisions in American society.[2]

---

[1] Because social as much as economic rank is determined, in the long run, by talent and marketable skills rather than hereditary privilege, it can be argued that the American stratification system has functioned more as an elevator than a barrier—that despite obvious flaws and short-term exceptions, it has made for de facto equality.

[2] Historical experience virtually ordains that social stratification connotes one thing for Americans and another for the peoples of the Old World. Particularly in such agrarian, semi-feudal states as Spain or tradition-permeated societies as England, survivals of the three-estate system of stratification—hereditary nobility and "gentlemanly" occupations and schools are prime examples—make class divisions more tangible and class consciousness more pervasive; the nearest American equivalent is our own "deep south." Correlatively, what Talcott Parsons has called the "particularistic" style of social outlook—the popular division of men into categories based on inherited differences—is generally more prevalent in Europe than in the United States.

For many Americans—educators, for example—or social workers, psychiatrists, clergymen, probation officers, personnel and advertising men, social classes[3] are not simply forces, such as death and taxation, that one must live with; they are decisive elements which help shape and color virtually every facet of our lives. As such, they must be comprehended with clarity and insight. Helpful as it is for the person who would know the behavior, motives, and values of others to understand the "typical" American, it is infinitely more critical that he understand, say, the "middle-class," and, better, the "lower-middle-class" American. We shall shortly see why.

Yet what knowledge of social classes is available is, on the whole, piecemeal and fragmentary. To date, for example, there has been no comprehensive investigation of the American class structure on a national scale. Numerous accounts, among them August Hollingshead's "Elmtown's Youth" and Lloyd Warner's "Yankee City,"[4] have treated the question of social stratification on the level of the local community.[5] But "Main Street, U.S.A."—small-town America—typifies our country more in fiction and memory than in fact. Contemporary America, and even more certainly tomorrow's America, may be better visualized in terms of sprawling metropolitan complexes: of central cities, their suburban peripheries, and neighboring satellite communities. Accordingly, the descriptive portrait of social-class differences which follows is postulated on the conviction that urban-suburban America is sociologically more meaningful than the Elmtowns, Yankee Cities and similar small and stable communities described 15 and 20 years ago.

The report is based on the findings of a still-continuing investigation[6] into the relationships between social-class membership and a di-

---

[3] The concept of "social class," it must be warned, is neither (1) universally accepted in the social sciences, (2) conceived in precisely the same way by all students of social stratification, nor (3) commonly designated by the same label.

[4] Captivating as such sociological accounts may be, the subtle texture of social class is often more readily amenable to the stylistic graces of the novelist. For richness of insight and deftness of contrast, few have better described upper-class Americans than Henry James, Edith Wharton, F. Scott Fitzgerald, and J. P. Marquand; Sinclair Lewis remains the unparalleled chronicler of the middle classes, while the varying nuances of lower-class behavior have been variously conveyed by William Faulkner, John Dos Passos, Erskine Caldwell, Nelson Algren, John Steinbeck, James T. Farrell, and John O'Hara.

[5] In addition, hundreds of studies appear annually which are devoted to such class-related facets of life as infant-training and child-rearing procedures, recreational habits, political orientation, consumer behavior, formal affiliations, friendship patterns, and a multitude of attitudinal and psychological variables.

[6] The study will be reported in detail in two books: *Social Stratification*: *Class in America,* and *Peninsula People*: *Social Stratification in Suburbia* (forthcoming).

verse array of attitudinal, behavioral, and life-style factors.[7] (See Table, pp. 418 and 419.) In the course of the undertaking, now in its sixth year, a random sample of more than 3,000 "heads of household" in the populous (1960 population: approximately 2,000,000) three-county San Francisco "Peninsula area" completed comprehensive questionnaires (forced-choice and open-ended) and a variety of clinical and depth-type tests.[8]

Despite a deliberately minimal use of such standard sociological cautionary terms as "typically" and "generally," it must be remembered that the class-linked differences described are, without exception, differences not of kind, but of degree. Although the verbal sketches are, for illustrative purposes, broad-stroked, the actual qualities which differentiate class from class are—with some notable exceptions—commonly less striking and vivid.

Just as the boundaries which separate one class level from the next are not hard-and-fast, but insensibly blurred, overlapping, and imprecise, so is the complex of values and behavior which characterizes an "upper" or "lower-middle" individual energized by other than purely class-related considerations: it is compounded, too, of hereditary and constitutional elements, of such diverse subcultural forces as age, sex, family, ethnic, and regional influences, and, above all, of those uniquely idiosyncratic factors which make all of us mavericks as much as conformists.[9] As with social class, so too with comparisons between Dane and Greek, Ozark hillbilly and Bronx-dweller: each such affiliation is of undeniably critical import, yet other cultural impresses are similarly at work in qualifying and modifying these national and regional biases.[10]

---

[7] Although the variables derived in the main from the findings and theories of earlier students, many were suggested by the initial, "free-exploration" phases of the present study.

[8] A more detailed and technical description of the investigation's research design, sampling techniques, and statistical procedures is available upon request from the author; space considerations preclude their inclusion here. Footnoted technical references have been pared to the barest minimum for the same reason.

[9] Nor, of course, can every last individual be precisely class typed; conscious rebels and zealous individualists aside, many are simply "marginal": en route between one class level and the next, or indeterminantly on the fringe of two levels. Similarly, there are many who are Europeans more than Germans, or cosmopolites more than Texans.

[10] Like "nation" and "region," the concept "social class" comprises considerably more than some such statistical *category* as 20-24-year-old, female, or Democrat; each class level is more nearly a subculture, and the members of a given class, although unknown to one another, are linked because they share similar life experiences, occupational roles, styles of life, educational backgrounds, formal affiliations, consumption behavior, leisure-time preferences, and choices of mass media. They tend to think and act alike because they share common "universes of discourse."

The "class portraits" which follow must, finally, be recognized for what they are: mere partial vignettes, tapping what appear to be certain class-related characteristics among given people (residents of the San Francisco Peninsula) at a given time (the late 1950s and early 1960s). They cannot be safely generalized to the whole of the American population. Some distinctions will seem ruthlessly pat and others makeshift and tentative. The vast majority of the conclusions are based on statistical examination of empirical evidence; others are more impressionistic, deriving from analyses of tape-recorded interviews, responses to open-ended questions, and Rorschach protocols. The reader, lastly, must constantly remind himself that tags of identity, no matter what their technical "validity," are forever in danger of glossing over a central truth: however else we might define or categorize him, every last person on earth is an individual, unlike any other human who has ever existed.[11]

LOWER-LOWER CLASS: DESPAIR, ANGER, APATHY

Of every six Peninsula families, at least one inhabits this lowermost position in the class hierarchy.[12] In the broad occupational sense the occupant of this level is an unskilled "lower-blue-collarite"; but his employment is characteristically sporadic and marginal, his marketable talents are few, and he is the last to be hired and the first to be fired. He entered the labor arena in his middle teens after dropping out of school just short of the eighth grade,[13] he was still a teenager when he married (a legal formality bypassed by at least one "husband" in ten at his class

---

[11] The humanist might object to sociological efforts to "pigeonhole" what are after all individuals with private souls; yet pigeonholing is an honorable occupation, at least as ancient as Herodotus and Plato, and it has been utilized, often magnificently, by philosophers, playwrights, poets, and novelists: by Kant and Sartre, Moliere and Strindberg, Keats and Eliot, Dickens and Faulkner. The "I.B.M." or questionnaire sociologist, armed with calculating machine, infertile imagination, and a mystical language of inelegant gobbledygook, is in part a genuine spectre, in part a straw man. For in sociology as in history, belles-lettres, philosophy, and the arts, there are not only sharply conflicting schools of thought, but scholars whose talents, inclinations, and modes of discourse vary radically.

[12] The term "lowermost" is not so subjective a designation as it appears; for at least one thoroughgoing national opinion survey corroborates what common sense dictates: unskilled occupations enjoy materially lesser prestige than do occupations in other categories.

[13] That his younger brothers will remain in school two years longer than he points up a matter of consequence to the educator: the burgeoning floodtide of lower-class youngsters who pose problems altogether unique, for their subculture is drastically different from that of the heretofore typical middle-class child's.

level), and he fathered the first of his four or five children before he was old enough to vote. He had achieved social and legal adulthood at an age when his upper-middle-class contemporaries faced another five years of schooling and celibacy. If his marriage has endured—and the odds are just short of even that it has not or will not—he is likely to find that it is strife-ridden; he rarely admits an abiding love for his wife and children, and he is plagued by in-law troubles.

The lower-lower-class Peninsula dweller lives in cramped quarters: typically in a dilapidated tenement, a jerry-built "suburban" slum, or in a fast-deteriorating postwar government housing development—a dwelling littered with debris and enjoying at best a minimal level of sanitation. Although the monthly family income of the "LL"—some $250— is the most he has ever realized (more than two wives in three at this level are gainfully employed outside the home), it is consumed more rapidly than it is earned. Only occasional items in his household have not been purchased on an installment plan, and he is perennially in debt. This, then is the objective plight of the LL. His subjective predicament —his private world of dreams, goals, cravings, and frustrations is no less severe because it is less visible to the untutored eye.[14]

Virtually every one of the lower-blue-collarite's major life goals— geared, apparently, to a middle-class frame of reference vividly portrayed for him by the mass media, the advertising industry, and even the schools—has somehow been stifled or thwarted. Reluctantly and for the most part subconsciously, he realizes that he has fallen short of the American dream occupationally, educationally, residentially, and in the realm of material possessions. Although his childhood aspirations in each of these spheres were markedly less pretentious than those entertained by his middle-class counterparts, his actual achievements have, in relative terms, lagged even more markedly.

To ask precisely why the LL has failed to achieve upward occupational-economic mobility is to pose a question which, given our present state of knowledge, is inherently unanswerable; it will nonetheless be worth while to consider a few of the partial clues afforded by the research. In the first place, the LL's lowly position in the class[15] hier-

---

[14] For a more thoroughgoing analysis of the subjective lower-class world, see the recent article by Albert K. Cohen and Harold M. Hodges, Jr., *"Characteristics of the Lower-Blue-Collar Class,"* Social Problems, X (Spring, 1963), 303-304.

[15] Throughout this paper the concept "class" will be used loosely; in truth it has many components, among them, as Max Weber suggested, economic wherewithal (class), social esteem (status), and the ability to influence the destinies and decisions of others (power).

archy is due infinitely less to intellectual deficiency or slothfulness than
to what, for want of a more precise term, may be called "cultural
deficiency." Unassimilated and marginal, the LL is encumbered by
deeply ingrained values and life-styles which are inevitably at odds with
the middle-class values and life-styles which facilitate upward mobility.
Unskilled, ill-educated—often tethered by the additional incubus of skin
color—he is frequently trapped in a vicious circle which effectively sup-
presses his haphazard and infrequent efforts to break through the class
barrier.

It may be hypothesized that the "cultural deficiency" which inhibits
so many LLs (some, remember, will achieve a measure of upward mobility) is due in the main to (1) a set of values and traditions "inherited"
from his three in four grandparents who came from rural or village
areas and/or (2) a simple adaptation on the part of a vulnerable and
insecure person to what must certainly seem an omnipotent and brutal
environment. And of all the rural survivals (or adaptations) which most
persistently impede movement into higher reaches of the class system,
none would appear more an incumbrance than the LL's pervasive sense
of closeness to kin. Despite the frequency of bitter husband-wife conflicts, the LL seems especially fearful of venturing beyond the familiar
confines of his family group; although he "neighbors" more frequently
and intimately than those in other levels, he derives the greater part of
his psychic support from intimate interaction with relatives: from visits
to taverns, front-porch gossip, and watching the fights on television with
brothers, brothers-in-law, or same-sex cousins. In consequence, he is
more unwilling than any to leave "home" for better employment opportunities,[16] he possesses an abiding sense of loyalty toward kinfolk (an
unwritten code of mutual aid prescribes that near-relatives come to one
another's unstinting assistance in times of trouble), and, perhaps most
importantly, his network of lower-class convictions, habits, and life styles
is consistently reinforced and insulated by his like-minded relatives. The
latter, predictably, live near: almost half of all LLs—in comparison to
one in ten middle-class Peninsulans—claim close relatives living within
a four-block radius of their own dwellings.

If he is less removed from a rural heritage, we might expect that the
LL would subscribe to such "patriarchal" values as husband-father
dominance and wife-child subservience. And it is he, indeed, who most
readily concurs that "the wife's place is in the home" (with LL wives in

---

[16] The "ethic of workmanship"—pride and ego-involvement in the work
sphere—is even rarer in the lower-lower than in the upper-lower ranks; work for
the LL is merely an unpleasant means to an end and it is rarely "brought home"
and discussed at the dinner table.

hearty accord!),[17] that the husband should "run the show," and that the child is ideally obedient, quiet, and even servile to parental dictates. The LL parent appears to abide by this dogma in practice as much as in theory. Consistent with the pithy yet representative comment of one respondent that "my pa did it that way and, by God, what's good enough for him is good enough for me," the lower-blue-collar mother knows nothing of Dr. Spock or "new-fangled" ways of infant-training. Instead, she does as her mother did: the errant baby or child is punished with dispatch and often with harshness for "being bad"—for toilet accidents, messiness, crying, fighting, and, above all, sassing or talking back.[18]

But it is the deeper-seated, less manifest recesses of the LL's personality configuration that most tellingly distinguish him from his white-collar counterparts. The LL is at the very nadir of the American class, status, and power hierarchy; yet he is, we will recall, at the threshold of this system because he has incorporated many of its central values. His status is thus as marginal as it is "lowly": he is on the outside looking in. He subscribes to certain middle-class ideals (in particular such goals as material well-being, progress, and upward mobility), yet he is simultaneously attached to antagonistic and even contradictory convictions taught him by his agrarian forebears. The consequence can only be a cruel impasse: he is at once seduced by the success ethic and balked in his efforts to realize its rewards. The resultant frustration, conscious or not, is very real. In congruence with much of contemporary theory and research, it would seem to go far in helping account for the psychodynamics of LL status. Space limitations will not allow a full exposition of the matter, but certain central components in the "LL personality" can be profitably analyzed in this light.

Chief among the hypothetical responses to the frustrations experienced by the study's lower-lower-class subjects are three generalized reactions which proved in fact to be characteristic: (1) a fusion of cynicism, distrust, despair, and pessimism; (2) hostility and anger focused on "others"; and/or (3) apathy and withdrawal from the larger social arena. The first constitute basic ingredients in what has come to be known as "misanthropy"; the misanthrope, by dictionary definition,

---

[17] For a more extensive discussion of this point—and the apparent contradiction between practice and ideal—see Cohen and Hodges, *Ibid*.

[18] Perhaps in partial consequence of such authoritarian relationships, there proved to be more overt conflict between parents and their adolescent offspring at the lower-lower level than at any other; and at no other level did teenage and pre-teen boys so readily turn to all-male "gangs" (not necessarily "delinquent" gangs) for leisure and as guidelines to values and conduct. It is possible, too, that the basic LL distrust of authority figures—policemen, teachers, and "bosses," for example—is also due in part to such parent-child interaction.

is one who hates or distrusts people in general. Other people (except for intimates and relatives), the LLs concurred, are simply not to be trusted: they are selfish and are out to cheat or take advantage of one's weaknesses. "People," they seemed to assert, "are no good." Success of any sort is best accomplished by connections, pull, or underhanded dealing, and no one—television repairman, doctor, butcher, union official, businessman—is truly honorable and worthy of trust. The dog-eat-dog specter of the jungle, it seems, is very real in the lowermost echelons of the Peninsula blue-collar world. Coupled with this outlook was an ill-defined sense of pessimism, aloneness, and despair, of what the sociologist defines as "anomie." "Human nature being what it is," the LL characteristically agreed, "there will always be war and conflict"; the future is bleak and hopeless, and there is nothing we little men can do to avert it.

For many LLs the reaction was less muted but almost as indirect; to them, something was not only vaguely "wrong," but some one or some thing—scapegoats—must be blamed. Theirs, in a word, is what students of personality call an "extrapunitive" reaction (the "intrapunitive" person, in contrast, fixes the blame on himself when things go wrong).[19] Although misanthropy is considered by many to be one form of extra-punitiveness, what has come to be popularly known as *authoritarianism* is an even more personalized, hate-infused way of fixing the guilt on others.

Much has been written about the causes and dynamics of authoritarianism since the concept came into prominence shortly after World War II. Suffice it at this point to remark that the distorted attitudes which warp the authoritarian's vision are in large part deeply imbedded products of early childhood experiences.[20] The authoritarian tends, among other things, to be one who thinks, perceives, and structures most of his life in a categorical, black-and-white sort of way. His world is peopled by weak and strong, pure and impure, good and bad. He wants his heroes (typically strong and tough-minded men who are leaders of the good — or majority — cause) to be unequivocally heroic, and his villains (weak, pussyfooting members of minority causes: "un-Americans," intellectuals, artists, homosexuals, long-hairs) to be clearly villainous. The investigation's LL was patently the most authoritarian

---

[19] It was as though the LL was plagued by a diffused but constant "chip-on-the-shoulder" sense of repressed hostility.

[20] That harsh, punitive infant-training and child-rearing is a corollary of authoritarianism poses a provocative question about the relationship between authoritarianism and social class; see Harold M. Hodges, Jr., *Social Stratification: Class in America*, pp. 210-217.

subject in the entire sample.[21] The world for him is not simply divisible into two hard-and-fast categories, but those in the wrong category, transgressors of the mores—delinquents, alcoholics, beatniks, opiate addicts, perverts—are deserving of harsh punishment, for they are what "ails this world."

For many LLs, particularly the elderly, the most effective way of coping with life appears to be a reaction blended of apathy and resignation. They belong to few or no formal organizations except for the Roman Catholic or Baptist churches (for a growing minority, especially those Negroes who have recently migrated from the Deep South, fundamentalist or emotion-laden sects afford a religious outlet). Some of the younger LLs are disinterested members of trade unions and a sparse handful of the older still claim memberships in fraternal orders, but for most social life is limited to relatives and occasional neighbors. Nor is the lower-blue-collar Peninsulan ego-involved in his community. "Girlie" and movie magazines, the television and comic sections of the newspaper: these are among his rare links with the larger world of affairs. Even the 1960 presidential election, which evoked more interest in his ranks (because of the religious overtones for Catholics and fundamentalists[22]) than any contest since the F.D.R. era, witnessed a scant 25 per cent turnout at the polls. His, it seems evident, is a fatalistic what-can-I-do-about-it, why-bother? universe; he has retreated into the comfortable womb-like sanctuary of the cocoon.

UPPER-LOWER CLASS:
MARLBORO MAN . . . OR MILQUETOAST?

There is a sharper hiatus between the lower-lower class and the upper-lower than between the world of the latter and the world of the lower-middle. Yet in many telling and predictable ways the upper-blue-collarite (approximate statistical markings: he comprises one-third of the Peninsula's residents, completed 10 to 11 years of schooling, reaps

---

[21] To affirm that the LL is "more" authoritarian is not to declare that those at the other extreme of the class scale—the uppers and upper-middles—are altogether lacking in this quality; it is simply to assert that a significantly higher proportion of lower-blue-collarites proved to be authoritarian according to the measures used to assess this characteristic in this study.

[22] At no other class level did the election evoke such strong and vocal religiously hued sentiments; more than four in five LLs who had voted against Eisenhower-Nixon in 1956 voted for the Nixon-Lodge ticket in 1960. Perhaps more significantly, the LL vote was rarely a "proletariat" vote; he did not find the *system* wanting, merely other people.

a $5,500-$6,500 annual family income, and occupies a semi-skilled or skilled occupational status) is less like the white collarites just above him than he is like his LL peers.[23] Thus in comparison to subjects in the middle and upper class levels, the UL is like the LL—only "less so"— in his proclivity for authoritarian, anomic, misanthropic, and patriarchal values; he is almost as intolerant of Mexican-Americans, Oriental-Americans, and Negroes, and is even more anti-Semitic (the most prejudiced of all toward Jews is the lower middle).

But undue stress on the similarities between those in the two blue-collar levels might belie the even more numerous dissimilarities which amply warrant the conclusion that the UL inhabits a class level distinctly his own. To illustrate the point more vividly, we shall first remark on the "uniquely" UL attributes—those which are not merely intermediate between LL and LM characteristics but are more or less singular.

In sharp contrast to the LL, the upper-blue-collarite seems infinitely more confident and ebullient; he is less concerned with his self image among strangers and, unlike the LL, rates himself as aggressive and friendly rather than shy and "uncomfortable among people I don't know." Whether such "self-ascriptions" are valid—are truly the way the typical UL honestly sees himself—is in good part academic; the important issue is that he seems confident to the point of brashness and "inner-directed" in terms of David Riesman's typology.[24] It is as though he walks boldly rather than timidly, that he is vigorously self-assertive, almost pugnacious. By way of amplification, the UL is the apparent personification of the "Marlboro Man": he describes himself as "strong and silent," "tough-minded," and "manly"; he is less forgiving than any of "sissiness" in men and boys; his favorite movies and television shows

---

[23] Although the time-honored blue collar-white collar distinction is fast losing meaning in an increasingly automated work world which may soon see the bulk of all employees classifiable as "dial-watching," button-pushing technicians; the two lower classes share numerous similarities which legitimately mark them as a sphere apart; in like manner, we may refer to "the" middle class. Yet much is lost in such sweeping distinctions, just as the concept of the "average" American must gloss over Vermonter, Hoosier, Brooklynite, Texan, and Southern Californian.

[24] For comments on the relationships between the Peninsula findings and Riesman's character types, see David Riesman, *The Lonely Crowd* (Yale paperback edition, 1961, p. XXI) and Seymour M. Lipset, and Leo Lowenthal, *Culture and Social Character* (Glencoe, Illinois: The Free Press, 1961, p. 435); an attempt at "measuring" Riesman's "other," "tradition" and "inner"-directed types was essayed during the investigation.

are horse operas; John Wayne and Clark Gable are his professed ideals. He is far and away the most avid outdoorsman, hunter, and fisherman, the heaviest of smokers. He more than any likes beer, and poker is his card game.

Yet in a puzzling reversal of form, and in particular contradiction to his independent, devil-may-care stance, the upper-blue-collarite is apparently plagued by "status concern." One of life's most important goals, he declares, is "raising one's social position"; and most vital of all in choosing a career (even more vital than income and job satisfaction) is the prestige which attaches to it. Neighborhood "status competition" is also of disproportionate concern to the UL, and he more than any would admit to "extreme disappointment" were his similarly circumstanced neighbors to acquire newer and bigger cars,[25] extensively remodel their homes, or buy their wives "expensive furs." Somewhat perversely, too, this self-styled "he-man" is likelier than the male at any other level to help his wife with such "womanly" domestic chores as grocery shopping, dishwashing, and table setting.[26]

The upper-blue-collarite's leisure time pace is less restricted than the LL's; not so given to such passive entertainment as movies and television (the LL watches the latter more than four hours a night and, alone among the others, appears to be enjoying television more and more),[27] he is an ardent baseball, boxing, and wrestling fan, bowler, and "do-it-yourself" addict. He has, in comparison to his neighbors in the white-collar ranks, little or no truck for gardening, and he is only reluctantly being converted to back-yard barbecuing. Likelier than the LL to entertain friends he met at work, more than four in five of his and his wife's most intimate acquaintances are themselves classifiable as upper-lower class.[28] And when he and his wife do act as hosts, they eschew bridge, rarely serve hard liquor, and tend to break up into all-male or all-female gossip groups. The UL is more active in clubs than

[25] His car is apparently a prepotent "status symbol" for the UL; and among second-hand buyers, a greater proportion in his ranks than in any own Cadillacs, Lincolns, and Chryslers.

[26] The UL's is the only class level where husbands tend to adopt their wives' religious preferences.

[27] Aside from western (especially "Gunsmoke" among the men and "Maverick" among the women), the ULs more than any prefer comedies (Red Skelton, Bob Hope, Lucille Ball) and variety shows (Lawrence Welk, Ed Sullivan).

[28] The percentages of "four closest friends" occupying the same social-class positions as the subjects: LL: 81; UL: 72; LM: 63; UM: 75, and U: 80.

the LL; he tends to prefer such veterans' organizations as the American Legion .or V.F.W. and occasional fraternal orders (in particular the Elks); she is especially active in the P.T.A.[29] and in auxiliaries to her husband's clubs.

His new-found affluence—no level in the entire sample has obtained such marked yearly income increases as his (between 1950 and 1960 his average annual wages increased more than 50 per cent)—has witnessed what may prove to be far-reaching changes in the upper-blue-collar way of life. For one thing many in his ranks have moved into the same suburban tracts occupied by lower-middle-class families, and an increasing proportion boast the basic amenities traditionally associated with the American middle-class style of life. The physical move to suburbia rarely, at the time of the study, connoted an actual move into middle-class ranks (absolute social-class mobility requires more than the mere material symbols of middle-class status; it involves what amounts to a social-psychological absorption of the most subtle middle-class values, life-styles, and behavior patterns—a conquest which few can essay in less than a generation). But because many UL children grow up with middle-class children,[30] it may be safely predicted that many will themselves bridge the gap. In the meanwhile their parents frequently become "marginal" cases: "lower-middle class" to the outward eye, yet still, in the main, actually "upper-lower class" in the important realms of friendships and deep-seated values. The leap from blue-collar to white-collar status (and the move amounts to a leap in social and psychological terms) warrants brief analysis less because of the strains which attend it than because of its apparently increasing frequency: no Peninsula class level has "lost" more members to the next highest class than the upper-lower—and no level has gained more from the next lowest than the lower-middle.[31]

---

[29] P.T.A. groups in the Peninsula appear to derive their principal numerical support from UL and LM parents; many upper and upper-middle parents explain that other obligations preclude such activities.

[30] Yet even in neighborhoods where LM and UL children live in approximately equal numbers, more than two-thirds of pre-teenagers' "best friends" are drawn from their own class levels.

[31] Census data indicate, however, that the relative proportions of America's male work force in blue-collar and white-collar occupational categories have remained fairly constant during the past half century; this is largely because the skilled occupational level—the upper-lower—has drawn heavily from the diminishing ranks of farmers, semi-skilled, and unskilled. The most frequent UL-to-LM jump in the Peninsula study consisted of a move from skilled laborer (e.g., electrician) to small businessman (e.g., electrical contractor); yet the mortality rate among such starts was high: of every ten who had attempted such a move, five had been unsuccessful and had returned to blue-collar work.

LOWER-MIDDLE CLASS:
PURITANISM, FRUGALITY, AND THE BIBLE

If his upper-lower next-door neighbor stands out as a distinct sort, so does this salesman, clerical worker, foreman, lathing contractor, and proprietor of the corner drug store. In a real sense his social-class level is the most unique and variant of all; yet in another, concrete context, he represents that most illusive of all animals: the "typical" American.

His is what has been called the "level of the common man." And though barely one in three Peninsula-dwellers are members of his class, his common-ness is not a qualitative matter, but a quantitative one. For he is the mythical average man in many ways. His traits include an annual income of between $8,000 and $9,000, a high-school diploma,[32] and a tract home in the suburbs. In fact "suburbia"—an illusive and hard-to-pinpoint geographic entity[33]—"is," in a statistical sense, the lower-middle class; for more than three-fourths of the Peninsula's "non-urban" single-family dwelling units are evaluated at $15,000 to $20,000, and an estimated two-thirds of these are occupied by families designated as "lower middle." But the LM is average in other respects than income, education, and residence. He, many market analysts have come to realize, is virtually the "common denominator" that purveyors of the mass media speak of so fondly. Take, for example, his consumption preferences in four of the media. More than those in other class levels, "his" magazines—*Life, Reader's Digest, Saturday Evening Post,* and *Ladies' Home Journal* . . . his television menu—Perry Mason, The Untouchables, Gunsmoke, Jack Benny, and Groucho Marx . . . his pet comic strips—Gasoline Alley, Dixie Dugan, Mary Worth, Dick Tracy, and Joe Palooka . . . his cinema preferences—for five successive years, his favorite movie stars were rated first in "box-office appeal" by *Variety* have time and again been recognized as *national* favorites.[34]

---

[32] The traditional emblem of white-collar status has been the high-school diploma; yet more than two in five Peninsula UL youngsters are now completing the twelfth grade, while the LM boy and girl are steadily expanding their educational horizons: approximately one in every two of the latter are now completing two years of "college" (typically, junior college) and, within 10 to 15 years, will apparently be earning a bachelor's degree. But in a proportional sense, the true floodgates on the school scene are opening toward the bottom of the class ladder.

[33] Despite the numerous caricatures of the "kaffee-klatsching robots" who presumably people suburbia (see, for example, *Time* magazine, June 20, 1960, or *The Atlantic Monthly,* April, 1960), the suburbs in the Peninsula area proved to be far more heterogeneous than homogeneous according to dozens of measurable characteristics; "the suburbanite," in short, was nonexistent.

[34] Respondents at other levels occasionally named the above as their favorites, too; but the LMs made the same choices with greater frequency.

Undue emphasis upon the lower middle's typicality might, however, obscure his uncommon aspects. And these are many. For one thing, perhaps most importantly of all, the investigation's LM appears to be a "reincarnation" of the nineteenth-century American; if the LL's essential bent was old world and agrarian, the LM's may be said to be middle western and small town.[35] It is almost as though he had stepped into the mid-twentieth century through the pages of Booth Tarkington or Sinclair Lewis. His orientation appears, in short, to be rear-guard (where the upper-middle's, we shall see, is more avant-garde).

A person who is puritanical is, according to one dictionary definition, one who is "extremely or excessively strict in matters of morals and religion";[36] this would seem an apt description, too, of the modal lower-middle-class Peninsulan. At no other level, certainly, was there such rigid insistence upon toeing the ethical and sexual line: upon righteous conduct and conformance with accepted standards of goodness and honesty. And for many LMs, the feeling ran deeper; for them such rectitude meant an unforgiving demand that others be incorrupt and virtuous. Thus, in the words of one questionnaire item, the LM was least willing of all to "remain on friendly, first-name terms with a person who . . . drinks heavily . . . has poor table manners . . . swears . . . has secret extramarital affairs . . . expresses disbelief in God and the Bible." Atheism and profanity, in particular, are cardinal sins to LM eyes. "Sex" is a naughty word to many a LM, and he is less at home than most with an off-color joke. In a somewhat related sense, he expresses the greatest degree of fear that his own son or daughter might depart from his or her appropriate sex role—that his son might be thought a sissy or his daughter a tomboy and unladylike.

If puritanism is a central lower-middle trait, so is the "Protestant Ethic." The characteristic LM belief that hard work, frugality, saving for a rainy day, and proving oneself in the market place are virtues: these are central to the aggregate of values made famous by Max Weber and R. H. Tawney and epitomized earlier by Ben Franklin in *Poor Richard's Almanack*. That the LM should hold such qualities to be worthy makes sense, for his ranks are heavily peopled by the entrepreneurs and small businessmen for whom the Protestant Ethic is a historical article of faith. Yet there is a minority within the Peninsula lower-middle class—a growing minority—who are less willing to abide

---

[35] In fact the LM was likelier than any other to have grown up in (a) the middle west and (b) a small or middle-sized town.

[36] *Webster's New World Dictionary of the American Language, College Edition* (Cleveland and New York: The World Publishing Company, 1959), p. 1182.

by these tenets: these consist, by and large, of the many younger LMs who are salaried employees of large enterprises—the occupational grouping which C. Wright Mills included in his designation "new middle class."[37] Incongruously, however, the majority of LMs—whatever their occupations, salaried or self-employed—*behaved* as though thrift and frugality were mere lip-service ideals. For comparisons of mean annual incomes at each level with estimated values of dwelling units and cars and amounts spent on furnishings and clothes point to an inescapable conclusion: it is above all the lower-middle who spends above his means. Particular manifestations of what Veblen labeled "conspicuous consumption" vary with each class level; but at no other level did respondents spend so high a proportion of their incomes on such commodities as did the LMs. The contradiction between ideal and practice was glaring.[38]

A third major component of the lower-middle value system is religiosity. For religion, at least as the LM conceives it, is a dominant motif in his life. He claims the most frequent church attendance (half his numbers attend weekly), active memberships in church-related clubs, Bible reading, and beliefs that Biblical precepts are of paramount importance for children and adults alike. Like the blue collarites, his ranks include more Roman Catholics than adherents of any other single faith; yet in a relative sense the most characteristic LM denominational preference is Methodist.[39]

At no level is political-economic conservatism so deeply entrenched as at the lower middle. That barely less than one-half of the LM voters cast their lot with the Nixon-Lodge ticket in 1960 (the LM figure was identical to that of the actual Peninsula-wide vote[40]) belies the proportion at this class level who favor Goldwater (one-third of registered LM Republicans) or Byrd (one-fourth of LM Democrats) as presidential nominees in 1964. On other measures of conservatism, too, the LM more than any opposed increased social security legislation, the growing

---

[37] There is evidence, albeit fragmentary, that members of the Peninsula's "new" middle class—such "organization men" as corporation employees, military personnel, salaried salesmen, and teachers—adhere more readily to that constellation of values which William H. Whyte, Jr. has termed the "Social Ethic."

[38] An interesting, but as yet unanswerable question arises: is the LM's professed puritanism and sexual morality practiced as well as it is preached?

[39] Two-thirds of LMs change to their spouses' faiths when they marry; the same pattern prevails at all levels except for the LL, where the two in five who shift faiths are largely non-Catholics.

[40] The lower-middle vote was, in fact, the only vote which almost exactly paralleled the local vote during the past five presidential elections; he appears to be the ephemeral "pivotal voter."

power of trade unions, the employment of "intellectuals" at cabinet level, and the general encroachment of the federal government on states' rights.[41]

Less "organization prone" than the UMs, but more so than the blue-collarites, the lower-middle belongs to many clubs; but his favorites, at least in numerical terms, are the fraternal order (especially the Elks, Shriners, Masons, and Oddfellows), the chamber of commerce, and assorted religious auxiliaries. He, more than any, is a baseball afficianado, and it is his sons who provide the bulk of local Pony and Little League rosters. But whatever his propensity for extracurricular activities, no one is more of a homebody than the LM; he spends more time than any at the family dinner table, on family vacations and weekend auto trips, and barbecuing and gardening in the "back yard." His, in fact, is the sole level where husbands claim greener thumbs than wives.

In conclusion, one final and rather sober inference is adducible about the status of the lower-middle in the Peninsular socio-economic hierarchy: his position is more precarious and ill-defined than ever before. That he clings so tenaciously to the images of the "white collar" and small-town America—and their attendant symbols of respectability —may be symptomatic of the fact that he is at least subliminally aware of his plight.

In a stark economic context he is this era's "forgotten man." Most consequentially, his is the only level where the value of the "real" dollar has actually shrunk; to purchase basic staples he, unlike the majorities in other class levels, must work longer hours in the 1960s than he did in the 1950s. In the critical dimension of power, too, his lot appears to be worsening; in the battle of giant vested interests his chamber of commerce is certainly no match for the N.A.M. on the one side and the A.F.L.-C.I.O. on the other.

Finally, the composition—and thus the traditional value orientation —of the lower-middle class is also in a process of profound permutation. As the well-defined dikes which once separated skilled blue collar from white collar callings become ever hazier, and as the "new" middle class eclipses the "old," the qualities which have historically differentiated the lower-middle class as a class apart are certain to undergo radical changes.

---

[41] Both the John Birch Society and the Christian Anti-Communist Crusade derived their heaviest Peninsula-area support from the LM class, notably from its entrepreneurial elements; but intensive analysis reveals that the appeal of ultra-conservatism is as much "psychological" as it is class or group-linked.

UPPER-MIDDLE CLASS: TOMORROW'S AMERICAN

If the Peninsula's lower-middle class citizen approximates the "average" American, his peer in the next-highest status niche may—at the calculated risk of too glib an analogy—be said to depict the American of "tomorrow." The comparison is dictated less by foresight than hindsight. For it is well documented that yesterday's UM Peninsulan was the first to adopt what have now become nation-wide fancies: the split-level ranch home, the Ivy-League style in men's clothes, the sports car, the barbecue addiction, and the hi-fi craze, to mention the more obvious.

But this is merely part of the UM's many-faceted makeup. Scarcely one subject in seven, characteristically the professional, semi-professional, independent businessman, or corporate employee who has gone a year or two beyond his A.B. degree, belongs to the upper-middle level.[42] Yet his numerical insignificance is abundantly offset by his disproportionate influence in the market place, political arena, and the amorphous world of life-styles.[43]

What, in thumbnail style, are the more distinctive qualities which prevail in the Peninsula's upper-middle level? Variegated as they are, at least one intrinsic theme seems to consistently thread its way through the whole of the UM ethos. It relates essentially to interpersonal relations and a basic way of perceiving others. No one word describes it. But the words flexible, trusting, democratic, tolerant, and non-dogmatic come most quickly to mind. Its antithesis is most relevantly represented by the lower-blue-collarite's character: rigid, defensive, authoritarian, parochial, and suspicious, to re-phrase some of the major traits reviewed earlier. Because this is the rule, there are, of course, exceptions: the outlook of *some* UMs is indistinguishable from *the* "lower-class" outlook. But the mood we have described is the prevailing upper-middle-

---

[42] This representative UM subject is, like those in the other levels, between 40 and 41 years old; many of the older men in this level, especially those in their 60s and 70s, have completed as few as 11 or 12 years of formal schooling. That some of the study's younger lower-middle subjects had completed college calls our attention to the fact that social-class membership is determined by far more than formal education.

[43] Before examining the UM, we must once again remind ourselves of two cardinal points which, if overlooked, would grossly distort our perception of social stratification: (1) "the" American cannot be fully comprehended until his many component memberships (among them, regional, ethnic, and age as well as class) are understood, and (2) the concept social class, like the concepts "girl," "teenager," or "Jew," embraces a multitude of sub-types and variations—not to mention wholly unique individuals. In truth, then, there is no such thing as "a" Negro, "a" Texan, or "a" lower-middle-class American.

class temper, and it helps explain much of what we shall take to be the upper-middle character.

Thus, though by several measures the most "child-centered" of all subjects, the UM parents appeared to be less anxious and more easy-going in the sphere of child-rearing and disciplining. They are, for example, more tolerant and understanding of children's tantrums, messing, fighting, and sassing. This general aura of permissiveness (the often caricatured dominant-child-submissive-parent was rarely encountered) was observable, moreover, through the entire span of parent-child relationships. Less apprehensive and hurried than lower-class mothers in the realms of weaning and toilet-training infants, UM parents were more democratic in later phases of their children's lives. The "children-should-be-seen-but-not-heard" dictum was as rare among UMs as it was common among LLs, and even in adolescence upper-middle youngsters were youngest of all when allowed to go out on their first unchaperoned dates.[44]

Deviates, too—delinquents, homosexuals, and drug addicts as well as such lesser norm-flaunters as people who swore, drank excessively, professed atheism, or engaged in extra-marital affairs—incurred less wrath from UMs than from those at other levels. If, in fact, the LMs were the most puritanical and Victorian of all, the UMs were the least so. In related vein, the upper-middles displayed the greatest degree of faith in their fellow-humans' motives, were the least pessimistic and despondent in outlook, and were by far the most forgiving of others' frailties and discerning of their own: they were the least "anomic," "misanthropic," and "authoritarian" of all. And where the LLs had preponderantly described themselves as shy and retiring, the average UM respondent depicted himself as one who is "at ease" among others: as gregarious and sociable. If, on the other hand, the LL purports to be inner-directed in inclination (and we must recall the conflicting evidence), the logical inference that the prevailing UM tenor is more other-directed is not warranted by the data. For in consequence of efforts to tap at least some dimensions of Riesman's three character constructs, "other-directedness"—a compelling need to "do as those around us do"

---

[44] As in the whole of the United States so among the Peninsula people, adolescence appears to be increasingly prolonged; this was notably so among the upper-middles where—according to parental admission—adolescence is more and more intruding into the "pre-teen" years in the form of earlier dating, drinking, smoking, high heels, mascara, and lipstick; it is protracted, too, at the other end owing to the tendency of UM boys to undertake graduate work and delay their entry into the labor market and marriage. Less volitional and of far more critical consequence is the impasse encountered by the LL adolescent when he is unable to find full-time employment.

—appeared to be more of an upper-lower and even lower-middle than an upper-middle propensity. The member of the latter level seemed, in contrast, less impressionable and more certain of himself. Nor was the UM so self-conscious as those in other levels; he was at least willing to agree, for instance, that ". . . it is difficult, when in a crowd of strangers, not to be concerned with how I look to them—about the sort of impression I am making." Neither (professedly) was he as concerned as the others with what neighbors or strangers thought of his garden, home, car, and clothes.[45] Lest the UM be mistakenly taken as a flawless paragon of virtue, it is only fair to remind ourselves that the "tests" designed to measure various components of personality are at best imperfect stabs at reality.[46] What is more, the descriptions of such findings, if not quite caricatures, are written in consciously bold relief in order to highlight the more relevant and contrasting class-linked qualities. There exists the possibility, finally, that like so many "character" and "intelligence" tests, such measures (together with their criteria of "goodness") are not altogether culture-free: free of a bias which might best be characterized in terms of "seeing—and judging—the world through middle-class glasses."[47]

Almost three-fifths of the Peninsula upper-middles were, in terms of their parents' class levels, "upward mobile." And the key to their mobility, especially if they were 45 years of age or younger, was the college diploma. As much an instrument of status validation to the UM as the white collar is to the LM, the bachelor's degree predictably dominated much of the upper-middle-class vision. "Education" and "career" —and the two are indissolubly linked—may be said, in fact, to be the most focal UM concerns. At the family dinner table, at parties, in terms of values they would instill in their children, "career" crops up again and again as a central UM value. And when he is not talking "shop," it appears, the man at this level is talking education—especially to his

---

[45] Illustrative of UM opinions are two statements which respondents at this level emphatically disagreed with: "it would be embarrassing to arrive at a party and find that I had worn entirely the wrong sort of clothes," and "it would be embarrassing to discover that my neighbors considered me 'different' or an 'oddball'." Riesman, it must be recalled, did not intend his typologies to be confused with individual personality propensities; rather, they represent character types which are common to particular societies (and subcultures) at particular times.

[46] Although major conclusions are based on a variety of measurements—on depth and clinical tests as well as open-ended personal interviews—their validity has yet to be confirmed.

[47] The "bad" boy, in the eyes of far too many teachers, is simply the lower-class boy: bored, restless, noisy, unkempt, dirty, trouble-making, rude; this is but one of many instances in which teachers must ideally combine psychological with sociological "know-how" if they are to effectively deal with their charges.

children. Even as early as the kindergarten-primary years, he appre-
hensively scans his children's school performances less—as with the UL
and LM—for signs of social adjustment than for indications of academic competence. Especially if he himself is a graduate of a state college or university, he wants his offspring to go to some such "prestige"
school as Stanford, Harvard, Yale, or Princeton,[48] yet admittance to
such institutions is increasingly limited to only the ablest students.[49] He
knows this and his consequent concern amounts, at times, to a virtual
panic; it would appear meaningful, then, that it was he, especially, who
led the many local fights for a curtailment of "progressive education"
practices; his characteristic answer to the question "what is wrong with
our public schools?" was the "life-adjustment ideal"! Where, at lower
levels, the lower-class parent might stress toughness and obedience and
the lower-middle parent morality, frugality, and religiosity, the representative upper-middle parent urged his children to attain top academic
marks and win out in classroom competition.[50]

Count Alexis de Tocqueville, Lord James Bryce, and countless observers ever since have observed that Americans are passionate "joiners"
—that the man without some sort of formal affiliation is a virtual pariah.
Had they observed with greater caution, they might have more precisely
qualified this characteristic with the hedge, "certain" Americans: the
Americans we would classify today as "upper-middle." For it is unquestionably at this level that (to borrow from sociological gobbledygook) "organization proneness" most emphatically prevails. It is not,
however, the lodge or fraternal order which claims upper-middle allegiance, but the service club: Rotary, especially, and the likes of Kiwanis,

---

[48] The two in five UMs who "inherited" their status were, in fact, preponderantly graduates of such schools as these (far more, too, had majored in
liberal arts and had belonged to "name" fraternities or sororities). Sons and
daughters of upper-middle professionals and business executives, the whole style
of life of these "core" UMs differed so radically from that of the "parvenu"
(upward-mobile) UMs that their "level" almost constituted a class within a class.
In essence, they were simply "more upper middle" than their parvenu counterparts; yet they were less innovative, future-oriented, gregarious in inclination, and
geographically mobile. For a more detailed analysis of this core-parvenu distinction, see Ruth Shonle Cavan, *The American Family* (3rd ed.; New York: Thomas
Y. Crowell Co., 1963), pp. 86, 132-34.

[49] Whether the UM concern that children attend "Ivy-tinged" preparatory
schools and colleges is actuated more by status than educational motives is a
matter of conjecture; but the further we ascend the class ladder the greater the
likelihood that parents will send their sons to "St. Grottlesex"-type prep schools:
if not to St. Paul's, St. Mark's, Grotton, or Middlesex, then to such California
equivalents as Thacher or Cate. And unlike other parts of the country Peninsula
girls, especially, are sent to private schools.

[50] Almost one-half of the upper-middle spouses, significantly, first met "at
school."

Lions, professional societies, and the big-city chambers of commerce. Upper-middle wives, too, are the most avid clubwomen. If not all Helen Hokinson sorts, they certainly prove likeliest of all to pack the seats at neighborhood improvement meetings, to belong to garden, alumnae, and bridge clubs, and to campaign vigorously for charitable enterprises. What is more she, like her husband, is frequently elected "president" of some such group.[51] And her children, too, are elected to school offices more frequently than others and belong to more such organizations as Boy Scouts and Girl Scouts. Predictably, the UM's civic consciousness and involvement is mirrored in the voting booth; in seven cases in ten a Republican,[52] more than 85 in every 100 at his class level turned out to vote at the 1960 presidential election.

The UM is not very "religious"; not, that is, in the manner of the LM; he attends church (and his children Sunday school) almost as frequently as those in other levels. But there is abundant evidence—including his own testimony—that he takes his religion more socially than literally, more ceremoniously than moralistically; liturgy, ritual, and tradition: these appear to be the most telling religious pulls for the UM. Even among his numbers baptized and raised in the Catholic church, there are far more "faith shifters" than at any other social-class level. And it is *into* three denominations in particular that upper-middle respondents have elected to move: Presbyterian, Episcopal, and Congregational.[53] And that childhood religious background is less and less compelling as one ascends the class ladder is hinted by the respective proportions of respondents at each level who were baptized, confirmed, and reared as Roman Catholics yet who married non-Catholics (LL: 18%; UL: 22%; LM: 47%; UM: 84%). While the matter of marriage is relevant, it should be noted that the broken-marriage rate is lowest of

---

[51] Here again, it seems, we uncover another clue into the characteristic UM personality syndrome: gregarious, hyperactive, socially at ease, he is a diametric counterpart of lower-class torpor, non-involvement, and lack of assurance.

[52] If the LM tended to be conservative in political stance, the UM is more "liberal" in inclination; thus (to cite one of several measures) the Republicans in his midst were likeliest of all to favor Rockefeller and Lodge to Goldwater, and the Democrats to prefer Stevenson and Humphrey to Byrd. It is at the UM level, nonetheless, that the most vocal opposition to President Kennedy has been expressed.

[53] Even more "upper-middle" in membership, but smaller numerically, are the Christ Scientist and Unitarian churches; the percentages of all respondents who claim to have "inherited" their religious faiths—to have followed parental faiths varies denominationally: Roman Catholic: 99%; Methodist: 80%; Baptist: 76%; Episcopalian: 60%; Presbyterian: 35%; Congregational: 11%. Whatever her current religious faith, the lower the class level of the wife, the likelier she is to follow the faith of her parents.

all at the upper-middle-class level: less than one marriage in ten had been dissolved by divorce, separation, desertion, or annulment. The important question, "why?" is too complex to allow the analysis it merits; yet certain circumstances which research has linked with marital success especially predominate at the UM level and warrant mention: upper-middle subjects are presumably more "mature" because they marry later (he averaged 25 and she nearly 23); prior to marriage each had dated for a longer time and had dated a larger number of partners; the parents of each had, according to their children, experienced "happier" marriages, and, perhaps most importantly of all, both more readily subscribed to the "democratic-companionship"—in contrast to the autocratic-patriarchal—ideal-type marital union.

If the Peninsula's upper-middles differed from subjects at other class levels in the realms of attitudes, deep-seated value complexes, organizational activity, and political and religious bents, they differed, too, in their leisure-time proclivities.

And it is here that what behavioral scientists shun as "value judgments" almost necessarily impinge on any attempt at description and analysis.[54] Reservations notwithstanding, the undertaking's UMs were plainly more sophisticated and more discriminating than any but the "uppers" in the arena of leisure. The "fine arts," for example—ballet, opera, symphonic music, the theater, poetry, literature, and graphic art —drew their most enthused devotees from people at this level. They read more books—an average of at least one a month and, more consequentially, they read what arbiters of literature would certainly define as "superior" books. They rarely attended motion pictures, but when they did (from four to six times a year) they typically preferred foreign and "art" fare or sophisticated domestic comedy; representative of their favorite actors and actresses were Greta Garbo, Marlene Dietrich, Barbara Bel Geddes, Grace Kelly, Audrey Hepburn, Cary Grant, Jack Lemmon, Alec Guinness, Jimmy Stewart, and Peter Sellers.[55] Their television tastes were similar to their cinematic: they rarely watched television and the one half who did watch on other than special occasions averaged less than 20 minutes a night in front of their sets. What is more, the viewers at the UM level were becoming weary of television (during recent years television watching has dramatically decreased at the "top"

---

[54] For in the purest terms of "relativism" and "ethical neutrality" nothing—no work of art or literature, cuisine or nature—is inherently superior or inferior; truth and beauty, these concepts would dictate, are not eternal verities but are humanly defined by given people at given times.

[55] A sizable minority of UM men preferred the "sexy-sultry" type: Sylvano Mangano, Sophia Loren, Marilyn Monroe, Kim Novak.

of the class ladder and increased at the bottom); commercials as well as the fare had alienated a significant number of them to the point of vocal disgust.[56] Aside from "Channel 9"—an educational-cultural outlet in the San Francisco area—their favorite fare, even after its demise, was Playhouse 90; other representative upper-middle preferences were discussion panels (their first choice in 1962 was Open End), news analyses (none devoted as much allegiance to Huntley and Brinkley as they), and sportscasts (notably college and professional football).[57]

Magazine likes were just as sharply class-linked. Thus where those in the lower classes were inclined to indulge in the "pulps" and the LMs were fondest of the giant mass-circulation periodicals, the characteristic UM preferences were *Time, Sunset,*[58] *U.S. News and World Report, Sports Illustrated, New Yorker, Harper's, Atlantic,* and *Saturday Review.* Newspaper choices were more variegated, although blue-collarites tended to prefer evening papers and white-collarites morning papers (except for the group, largely those who commuted to San Francisco, who read both morning and evening newspapers); the former expressed a greater interest in local and community news, whereas those in the middle classes, especially the UMs, were more partial to national and international doings.[59] In a word, the LLs and ULs were generally more "localistic" and the UMs more "cosmopolitan" in outlook.[60]

The generic cultural-esthetic bent among the upper middles roughly corresponds to what Russell Lynes has identified in tongue-in-cheek manner as "upper-middlebrow"; it is from this social-class level, too, that the vast majority of "highbrows" are drawn.[61] But the latter, who

---

[56] Although the center of gravity among local video viewers has been visibly shifting toward the blue-collar pole of the class hierarchy, open-ended interviews and unsolicited comments from LMs as well as UMs indicate that a "hungry" market exists for upper-middle-class-type fare; the television market, like those in the other media, is thus not one but many.

[57] These represented relative (and unique) UM choices; in the purely numerical sense the favorite UM options included Gunsmoke, Maverick, and Perry Mason (with the latter two eliciting their most enthusiastic support from wives).

[58] A west-coast magazine devoted to gourmet-type food, travel, and gardening.

[59] Even so mundane a matter as liking for comic strips proved to be class-tinged; characteristic preferences at each level: UM: Gordo, King Aroo, Peanuts, Dondi; LM: Skeezix, Joe Palooka, Judge Parker, Dick Tracy, Mary Worth, Dixie Dugan, Our Boarding House, and Out Our Way; UL: Will-Yum, Smokey, Dilly, Mark Trail; LL: Skymaster, Alley Oop.

[60] In newspaper as with magazine and book preferences, the UMs' interests were also quantitatively different; they read a greater number and variety of sources and they spent more time at reading.

[61] For Lynes' amusing yet informative account of "brow-level" differences, see his "Highbrow, Lowbrow, Middlebrow" in *Harper's* (September, 1949); a more serious and discursive analysis in the same vein: Dwight Macdonald, *Masscult, Midcult* (New York: Partisan Review, 1961), 78 pp.

by definition are virtually classless (for their often self-conscious in-
tellectual-esthetic tastes tend to transcend class as well as national
boundaries), are a distinct minority even in UM circles in San Francisco.
Yet it has been they (more recently identified by Lynes as "upper
bohemians") who in many instances have first supported what have
eventually become major UM interests: high-fidelity music, for example, and modern ballet and opera, the "little theatre," poetry recitals,
contemporary jazz, the *haute cuisine,* and "serious" paperback books.[62]

Before inquiring into the qualities of the last of the Peninsula class
levels—the "upper"—it will be relevant to examine certain contentions
advanced by William H. Whyte, Jr. in his much-quoted *The Organization Man.* Perhaps middlewestern and Atlantic-seaboard "suburbia"
differs radically from its Pacific-slope counterpart. But even in neighborhoods predominantly peopled by middle-management employees of such
giant concerns as I.B.M., Ford, and Lockheed, there was little or no
evidence of the hyper-conforming "organization man." There was only
infrequent "neighboring" in such areas; intimate acquaintances with
next-door neighbors were uncommon, and individuality—not cautious
conventionality—overwhelmingly prevailed. Concordant with Whyte's
hypotheses, the upper-middles were the most "geographically mobile"
of all: less than one in 25 had lived in their current dwellings for as long
as a decade, and the average span of local residence was less than five
years. Yet a sense of "rootlessness" appeared to be rare and only occasional friendships stemmed from first encounters at work or in the
neighborhood. In like vein, we have already noted that "the" Peninsula
suburbanite is—whatever his income or class level—a mythical being.
He lives in suburbia more out of circumstance than choice; he identifies
far more with "the city" than with his immediate environs, and if he is
indeed similar to those who live nearby, it is not because he mirrors his
neighbor: it is because both share a common social-class heritage. Somewhat similarly, some students of American society believe social-class
"cultures" to be little more than "occupational cultures." The allegation,
if the undertaking's findings have been read aright, is in part quite valid.
For if there is one central determinant of social-class membership it is
(except, perhaps, at the uppermost levels) occupational role. Yet it is
possible to interpret such a diagnosis too neatly. The basic LL and UL
callings might be definable, respectively, as "unskilled" and "skilled."
But the LM and, especially, the UM occupational duties are certainly

---

[62] Yet, though a numerically sparse element, the "highbrows" appear to exert
a disproportionate influence on UM tastes in literature, poetry, music, and the
stage. There is evidence, too, that their influence is increasing.

far too motley in every important context to "explain" what we have described as class-related values and behavior. Occupation in the general and abstract sense certainly accounts for social-class membership; but the consequences of such membership—especially for the entire family—surely transcend mere occupational values. There is, finally, nothing sacrosanct about such labels as "upper" and "upper middle"; although traditional usage suggests such names, other designations—perhaps alphabetical or numerical—are no less worthy. Nor is the term "social class" necessarily the best; "culture unit," "socio-economic division," and "subcultural level" are among many which might prove equally as suitable.

UPPER-CLASS:
ECCENTRICITY, ANCESTOR WORSHIP, AND INSOUCIANCE

Of all the social-class designations, none has been simultaneously so apparent yet so misunderstood and misused. For "upper class" connotes many things for many people: privilege, power, and wealth justly or unjustly gained; ostentation, snobbery, immorality, gentility, lavish leisure, and inconspicuous consumption: in fact, the entire catalog of the commendable and uncommendable, the esteemed and the begrudged. The image, like so many popular impressions of the renowned and envied, is concocted of part truth and good part fiction. Yet what the "truth" is must remain unanswerable until "upper class" has been faithfully defined; and opinions are sharply divided even among the more diligent students of the matter. Thus for some, membership "at the top" is conceived in terms of power: massive, selfish, conniving power in the eyes of orthodox Marxians; interlocking, mutually buttressing powers— a complementary meshing of interests among such power elites as the military, industrial, and governmental—to the late C. Wright Mills, or conflicting yet "countervailing" power blocs (i.e., big labor, big government, big business) according to John K. Galbraith.[63] For others, upper-class rank is more a corollary of high esteem or status; to them the elite is made up of families which have enjoyed sufficient generations of prestige (blended, of course, with wealth and power) to merit the designation "aristocratic." A similar but variant opinion holds that a "new" society is taking the place of the "old." The old consists of stable, conservative, old-guard families, and is as inevitably represented in the

---

[63] Akin to Galbraith's definition is the political "balance of powers" concept.

sacrosanct pages of the *Social Register* as it is in the membership lists of the ultra-exclusive clubs: San Francisco's Pacific Union, Boston's Somerset, or Philadelphia's The Philadelphia clubs, for example; they are the "Proper Bostonians" and Philadelphia's "Main Liners." The new society is younger and less inhibited; blended of European blue bloods, international celebrities, café society, the very rich, and the very powerful, its membership is more fluid and its stance less snobbish and far less staid.[64]

The *Social Register,* "old society" criterion was elected as this study's measure of upper-class membership, but only after considerable pre-testing and preliminary analysis. For the Peninsula's "power elite," though tacitly admitted to exist, was found to be too ill-defined and amorphous to measure. And the "rich"—those with annual incomes of $50,000 or more—were found to be little more than wealthy UMs: people whose basic values differed so slightly from those of the upper middles that they simply did not warrant a separate class designation.[65]

Numerically insignificant—less than one in every 500 Peninsula families is listed in the pages of the *Social Register*—the upper class is nonetheless highly influential as a "reference group": a membership to which many aspire and which infinitely more consciously or unconsciously imitate. Its characteristics may be delineated briefly.

The ranks of the upper class—of the "Us"—are only rarely characterized by conspicuous and showy consumption: costly debuts, mansions, hosts of servants, gala parties, glittering limousines and furs; this is the rare but publicized side of the coin. Not opulence and certainly not ostentatious display, but more nearly "inconspicuous" consumption— "tweeds," flat shoes, battered stationwagons, quiet parties: these are Peninsula upper-class earmarks. There is, of course, a minority "jet set" which boasts a faster, more public life, and there are many in the U ranks who are ultra-fashionable in the realms of clothes, homes, and cars, and others still who boast chauffeurs and $100,000 homes. But the

---

[64] Characteristic of the heterogeneous "new society" membership: shipping magnate Aristotle Onassis, Princess Margaret and Lord Snowdon, the Duke and Duchess of Windsor, Elsa Maxwell, Jack and Jackie Kennedy, Noel Coward, Henry Ford II; the "old," although the boundaries often overlap, would include such names as Lodge, Saltonstall, Harriman, Belmont, Rockefeller, Biddle, Carnegie, DuPont, Vanderbilt, and Stettinius.

[65] In fact the UM core-parvenu dichotomy proved far more discriminating than the "middle"-"high" income measure; this would appear to be one more convincing demonstration that not income, but basic, deeply incorporated values and life-styles are the essential, cataclysmic ingredient in what we call social-class membership. See Harold M. Hodges, Jr., *Social Stratification: Class in America,* Chapters VII and VIII.

upper class, if it is to be judged accurately, cannot be legitimately assessed in such terms.

However conservative or however flamboyant, the U is heavily addicted to a seemingly unending chain of parties big and small, dances, charity balls, first nights at the theater and opera, and frequent sorties to the Sierra ski slopes, resort homes at Lake Tahoe or the beach, and his box seats at the San Francisco Giants' Candlestick Park. He drinks more frequently—and more heavily—than those at other levels, but he is less given to smoking. When he entertains, he is likelier to host bigger parties than the UMs—or smaller; for most typically he and his wife will entertain another couple with dinner followed by bridge ("the" UM game, incidentally) or dominoes. He likes formality: white-tie affairs and, at work, dark or banker's grey suits with vests; his wife often prefers simple and "basic" black.[66]

The modal upper-class Peninsulan is likeliest of all to live in "the city": notably in San Francisco's exclusive Pacific Heights area or, if not, in more spacious and grandiose Hillsborough (less than half an hour's freeway time south of the city) or "exurban" (and quite "horsey") Woodside. Half his numbers are California born and half have lived in their present homes for eight or more years: longer, in both instances, than any, even those at the lowermost class level. He attended school at either Stanford, California, Yale, or Harvard (his mean educational attainment is equal to that of the UM, and like the UM, he has done at least some post-graduate work); she was likelier than he to have gone to a private school (Burke's, for example) and thence to Stanford, California, Vassar, or a two-year "finishing" school in the East. Fewer Us attend church than those at any other level. More than half are nominally Episcopalian, but fewer find themselves at church on Sunday than for weddings.

The U, finally, is in many ways more akin to the UL and LL than to his middle-class peers. Like the LL, for example, he is more tradition-oriented (although more given to ancestor worship, heirlooms, and insignia—or intimations—of high status in earlier generations); and like the Ls in general he claims to be tougher-minded,[67] more introvertive, and in accord with the ideals that husbands and parents should be

---

[66] "Tweeds and flats" are more her wear for neighborhood walks or the country.

[67] Yet he, and in particular his wife, devote more time and energy than any to charitable endeavors; her Junior League (the one national upper-class organization) is a prime example. See Hodges, *op. cit.*, pp. 106-107.

dominant. He is less permissive than the UM parent toward infants and children, and like the L favors obedience and quietness. Nor is he so wedded to his career; likelier to follow in his father's occupational footsteps, even when he has not "inherited" the job, he, more than the UM with a similar educational background, is found in such callings as banking, stockbroking, medicine, or architecture. Yet even more than the upper middle, the U appears to be "at home" among others, more insouciant and at ease no matter what his current social surroundings. Not quite so flexible and democratic, certainly not as gregarious and empathic, he seems in many ways the most non-conforming and individualistic of all Peninsulans. Much of his social life and public decorum is rigidly straitjacketed by custom, yet he is frequently given to eccentricities which are rare at all levels except the "upper bohemian" segment of the middle class: to a curious blend of formality and casualness, diffidence and outspoken candor, of reverence and irreverence toward tradition. Like the upper middle, he is "at home abroad," yet he feels less compulsion to smile at strangers.

This, in brief, is the class system which prevails on the "Peninsula." It is still ill-defined, its boundaries imperceptibly merge, and the whole of its substance is in a constant state of dynamic flux. At no level are its members rigidly governed by its unwritten norms, yet at all levels deeply embedded values as well as everyday behavior are class-typed beyond our faintest comprehension.

What of the future? None but seers can vividly foretell. But an educated guess will allow a terse if rough-hewn prophecy of things to come.

Most saliently of all, America's social-class affiliations should simultaneously become less—and yet more—consequential in shaping their destinies, perceptions, and behaviors. Less consequential because the American people, like all who belong to industrialized "mass" societies, are fast becoming an ever more homogeneous people with a mass, common-denominator culture. And yet more consequential because the very forces which are making them "more alike" are at the same time making social class a relatively (if not absolutely) more potent instrument.[68]

A word of amplification is in order. Toward the end of the nineteenth century and the beginning of the twentieth, no society on earth seemed more heterogeneous—composed of more diverse racial and ethnic elements—than the United States. But even before immigration

---

[68] As the forces making for sameness and homogenization shatter the once-formidable dikes—regional, racial, ethnic, religious, social-class, and even age and sex—which historically cast Americans into so many distinct types, the role enacted by social class has, in relative terms, become increasingly transcendent.

had dwindled to a trickle, the massive pressures which were to cast Americans into more and more of a look-alike mold were at work.[69]

The pressures are too numerous to detail, but among them were increasingly effective means of mass production (and its correlative mass-marketing operations), transportation, and communication. Simultaneously, the once-potent differences on the American cultural landscape were being flattened by the world's first truly democratic system of mass education. This movement was in turn indissolubly linked with mass literacy, the mass production and marketing of books and periodicals, and an ever more vigorous and pervasive advertising industry.[70] In the meanwhile unionization and federally legislated social security and taxation measures were, together with an economy which benefitted the "have nots" more than any element in the population,[71] shaping an economic structure which bulged the more in the middle as it became narrower at its peak and its base.

These were the more tangible, "real-life" elements making for homogenization. They were hastened and buttressed in turn by certain "American" experiences and ideological commitments which have blunted and distorted our vision of social stratification. Each merits brief analysis.

(1) Lack of a feudal, aristocratic heritage: because our nation was started, in at least one sense, from "scratch," we have not faced the trenchant feudal survivals—both legal and psychological—which have impeded the growth of social democracy in so much of Europe and Latin America; nor have we ever known a native hereditary aristocracy; we have, in fact, been consciously anti-aristocratic. (2) Democratic idealism: the doctrine of democracy is, of course, the very pith of our official philosophy and the heart of the libertarian concept that all citizens are legal equals. (3) Frontier psychology: If the frontier closed with the advent of this century, the "psychology" which accompanied it—the "go-west-young-man" faith in individual initiative, survival of the fittest, and ever-available abundance—did not die. (4) The

---

[69] This is not to forecast a grim Orwellian world of other-directed automatons, but merely to point out the direction in which we have moved and, apparently, will continue to move.

[70] A nearly identical trend is visible wherever industrialization and a psychology of abundance is an increasingly puissant force; thus the so-called "westernization" of Japan and "Americanization" of so much of western Europe.

[71] During the past half century the discrepancies between the wealthiest and most impoverished tenths of the American population have been drastically reduced; what is more, the "deprived" elements—Negroes, Mexican-Americans, sharecroppers, itinerant and unskilled laborers—have realized the most dramatic gains of all in "real income."

TABLE 1. SOCIAL STRATIFICATION IN CALIFORNIA SUBURBS*

Level	Markings	Personality	Habitat	Diversions
Upper .2%	Listing in the Social Register	Conservative; indulges in "inconspicuous consumption"	Doings in "the city"	Partying, gin-rummy, watching baseball; foreign films
Upper-middle 10-15%	Professional or executive position, college diploma; $11,000 per year	The "joiner"—gregarious, hyperative, socially at ease; concerned with "career" and "school"; child-centered and easy-going with children; takes his religion more socially than literally.	Service clubs like Kiwanis and Lions	Do-it-yourself projects, *Time*, *Harper's* Playhouse 90 on TV; bridge, golf
Lower-middle 35%	Whitecollar clerk, neighborhood businessman, or foreman; 7,600 per year; a tract home in the suburbs	Togetherness—active church-going; the "typical" American. *Says* he saves for a rainy day, but more likely than anybody else to own a Cadillac, Lincoln or Buick.	Church, lodge, PTA	Bible-reading; gardening (Mr. says he has a greener thumb than Mrs.); the "national favorites"—*Life*, *Reader's Digest*, *Saturday Evening Post*; on TV, Perry Mason, Ed Sullivan, 77 Sunset Strip; canasta, watching football

Level	Markings	Personality	Habitat	Diversions
Upper-lower 35-40%	A union man; skilled or semi-skilled blue-collar worker; 11 years schooling; $5,500 per year	Closest to the cigarette-ad ideal of the two-fisted, tatooed he-man; ill-at-ease among strangers; wants to improve social position. Likes masculine men and feminine women, but helps with dishes and diapers; has migraine headaches, insomnia.	1) The great out-of-doors 2) Sears, Ward's, Penney's (buying everything on time)	On TV, westerns like Cheyenne and Gunsmoke; poker
Lower-lower 15-20%	Usually unskilled laborer; 8 years schooling or less; $3,000 per year	A misanthrope—pessimistic about the future, wary of strangers. Apathetic towards politics. Loyal to family and kinfolk. Wants to be liked; fearful of being an odd-ball or unpopular. "Children should be seen, not heard."	In front of the TV (and waits up for the late-late show)	Bowling; pool; on TV, westerns such as Wagon Train, wrestling and boxing. For wife: romantic magazines.

*Based on sample of about 2,000 heads of households in the "peninsula area," from San Francisco to San Jose. Originally appeared in Robert J. Havighurst and Bernice L. Neugarten, *Society and Education* (Boston: Allyn and Bacon, Inc., 1962), pp. 32-33. Reprinted by permission. (This chart was constructed by Havighurst and Neugarten on the basis of an earlier report on the "Peninsula People" data.)

Protestant Ethic philosophy: akin to the other ideological commitments was the Protestant Ethic belief which vitalized the commercial and industrial revolutions; for it sanctioned salvation via individual effort rather than hereditary privilege or redemption in the next world. (5) The Horatio Alger myth: the Alger legend, finally, was of a piece with the "log-cabin-to-White-House" and "rags-to-riches" themes; for each ordained that "Every-man" could, like Jackson, Lincoln, Ford, and Carnegie, struggle from humble beginnings to the very pinnacle by dint of grit, determination, and hard work.

Because each of these beliefs has so much in common with the others, they have effectively blended into the national article of faith which we know as the American creed. They have not only obscured the cold realities of social class and class differences, but they have served as the very incentives which have helped so significant a proportion of Americans to actually bridge the gaps in our socio-economic structure.

Chapter Nine

OUR NATIONAL PURPOSE
AND EDUCATION

The question "what do we Americans value and what should we value"—and "how can our values be translated into national and educational goals"—does not want for writers on the topic. The eloquent prose of Adlai Stevenson provides us with a restatement of our classic, traditional goals and urges us to strive for a convincing model of a free society.

Several social commentators have interpreted our ideals into specific goals: they cannot be dry, abstract phrases. Max Lerner states that there must be possible for the individual a sense of mission, a feeling of commitment, of being on fire for things worthwhile, or our greatest national goals will wither. The individual must go beyond the mere consumption of things; those who "have privileges and material benefits which are unshared are in danger of personal corruption."[1] Another writer, Eric Johnston, calls for the creation of a true Atlantic Community within the next decade and suggests that this goal is the most compelling challenge to education devisable.[2]

That we live with contradictions in our democratic society is illustrated in two ironic, implicitly unpleasant, brief articles; one, by

---

[1] Dan W. Dodson, "Reassessing Values in the Present Age," *Journal of Educational Sociology,* XXXII (October, 1958), 49-61.

[2] Eric Johnston, "A New Outlook for Education," an address at Marshall University, Huntington, West Virginia, October 8, 1962.

Robert Lynd, is as cogent today as when it was written some years ago. Lawrence G. Thomas's article takes a similar approach without stating the ideal beforehand; his contention is that we hold the ideal, but————.

George D. Spindler, an educator-anthropologist, explains that not only are our basic values changing in American culture; but this change, in large part, is resulting in strong attacks on our schools. Spindler describes a continuum of values ranging from those "traditional" to those "emerging." He sees our culture—as do many other anthropologists—as a goal-oriented system. He does not predict an easy transitional period, nor does he argue for one end of the continuum in preference to the other.

The concluding selection of the book, "The Central Purpose of American Education," is the most recent policy formulation of the Educational Policies Commission of the National Education Association. The members of the Commission seek achievement of the goals set by earlier Commissions[3] but seek them within a framework designed to develop the rational powers of the student.

Abstract goals, however, offer little challenge to even the most dedicated person. What is wanting is a sense of purpose (Max Lerner's sense of mission) as in, for example, the desire of Peace Corps members to help underdeveloped nations and, specifically, the desire to help the people in underdeveloped nations. It is no wonder that the challenge of the Peace Corps idea has caught the attention and imagination of the nation; here our skills, our attitudes, our understandings—and our rational powers—are directed toward meaningful, even noble goals. An Atlantic Community? A World Community! With "an educational system that in all ways supports human dignity for all races, castes, and classes."[4]

We can ask no less of ourselves and of all mankind.

---

[3] The Objective of Self-Realization; The Objective of Human Relationships; The Objective of Economic Efficiency; and The Objective of Civic Responsibility —represent the "four great groups of objectives" of an earlier Commission report. Educational Policies Commission of the National Education Association, *The Purposes of Education in American Democracy*. Washington, D. C.: NEA, 1938, pp. 39-48.

[4] Theodore Brameld, "World Civilization: The Galvanizing Purpose of Public Education," *Phi Delta Kappan,* Volume 44, Number 2 (November 1962), p. 58.

OUR NATIONAL PURPOSE*

by *Adlai Stevenson*

It is not too difficult, I think, to state the classic goals and purposes of American society. We probably cannot improve on the definition offered by our Founding Fathers: "to form a more perfect Union, establish Justice, insure domestic Tranquility, provide for the common defense, promote the general Welfare, and secure the Blessings of Liberty." Add Tom Paine's words—"My country is the world"—to give our goals universal application, and we have distilled the essence out of all the rhetoric about the freedom and the democratic self-government for which we proudly stand.

But the difficulty is that aims in the abstract mean little. A society is measured by what it does, and no Fourth of July oratory will make its purposes great if in fact they are small, or change them into a moving element in the world's passionate dialogue of destiny if they are meager and private and unconcerned.

We have therefore to look at our noble purpose of freedom—and surely no one would deny that it is the organizing principle of American life—in terms of the concrete, practical content which Americans give to the concept. As one might expect in a free society, we find at once that freedom itself has many meanings and has implied different things to different people at different times in our national life. In fact one can observe something of a rhythm in the nation's mood, a swing from one definition of freedom almost to its opposite, recurring regularly throughout the almost 200 years of our independent history.

The first mood reflects the private aspect of freedom—the right of men to choose their own ideas and pursuits, to be free from the arbitrary interventions of government, to "do what they like with their own."

---

*From Adlai E. Stevenson, "Our National Purpose," *Life Magazine,* May 30, 1960, pp. 87-102. Reprinted by permission.

Many early immigrants escaped the arbitrary restraints of governments in Europe and came to set their money and their wits to work in the new climate of freedom. This sense of the link between "freedom" and private business has indeed been so strong that at some periods they have been virtually equated, as when Calvin Coolidge thus defined the American purpose: "The business of America is business."

But equally freedom has had its public aspect as the organizing principle of a new kind of society. In the Declaration of Independence, the basic charter of the modern world, the picture is of a great civic order in which governments, deriving their authority from the consent of the governed, help to secure the inalienable preconditions of the good life: equality before the law and in human respect, life, liberty and, most precious yet intangible of rights, the pursuit of happiness. This positive vision of society in which public authority plays its essential part in bettering the lot of all citizens was as inherent as freedom itself in the vision of our founders.

There is no inevitable contradiction between these public and private aspects of American society. Indeed, they are the essential poles of energy in a vigorous social order. Without individual decision and inventiveness, without widely dispersed centers of authority and responsibility, the social order grows rigid and centralized. Spontaneity withers before the killing frost of public conformity. Individual citizens with all their varied relationships—as parents, neighbors, churchgoers, workers, businessmen—are reduced to the single loyalties of party and state. In this century we are not likely to underestimate that danger. We have seen free societies destroyed in this way by totalitarians of both the right and the left.

Yet the pursuit of private interest and well-being does not, as the 18th Century sometimes naively believed, automatically add up to the well-being of all. The strong pursuit of my interest can override the vital interests of others, if nature, health, energy and property have weighted the odds in my favor. Social evils pile up when little more than unchecked private interest determines the pattern of society.

At best, the result is a "pressure group" state in which each organized group jostles for its own intereses at the expense of the weak, the isolated or the unorganized. At worst, the power and influence of the few can violate the fundamental rights and decencies of the many, as they did in the long survival of human slavery and in the long resistance of industry to child labor laws and minimum wages. In our own prosperous days a new possibility has arisen: that the many can smugly over-

look the squalor and misery of the few and tolerate, in the midst of unparalleled plenty, ugly slums, rural destitution and second-class citizenship.

It is the often mediocre and sometimes intolerable consequences of
unchecked private interest that have led to the reassertion, at regular
intervals in American history, of the primacy of public good. Sometimes
the swing occurs because evil has become so obtrusive that only vigorous
public action can check it in time. The conviction that the spread of
slavery endangered the Union itself helped precipitate the Civil War. The
demoralization of the entire economy after 1929 led to the experiments
and reforms of Roosevelt's New Deal.

Sometimes the swing seems to occur in response to subtler prompt-
ings. Early in this century, for instance, under Theodore Roosevelt and
Woodrow Wilson, it was not imminent social collapse but disgust at the
materialism which was devouring America that aroused people once
more to demand the restatement of America's public purposes and a
new vision of the common good.

Whatever the reasons for America's recurrent swing in emphasis
from private interest to public responsibility, it has always had a significant external consequence. It has aroused both in America and in
the world at large a sense that the American experiment has significance
far beyond its own frontiers and is in some measure a portent for all
mankind.

Man needs 'a convincing working model of a free society'

Today I don't suppose anyone will deny that mankind is in acute
need of a convincing working model of a free society. Never in human
history has there been an epoch of such profound and sudden social upheaval on so universal a scale. Never has the working model of tyranny
made such claims for its own effectiveness; never has monolithic discipline attacked so savagely what it calls the pretensions of the free way of
life. The whole of human society has become plastic and malleable in
the flames of social revolution. Thus there has never been a time when
the public aspect of American liberty as the organizing principle of a
great social order has needed to be more studied and stressed.

But what do we find? Never before in my lifetime—not even in the
days of Harding and Coolidge—has the mystique of privacy seemed
to me so pervasive. The face which we present to the world—especially
through our mass circulation media—is the face of the individual or the
family as a high consumption unit with minimal social responsibilities—

father happily drinking his favorite beer, mother dreamily fondling soft garments newly rinsed in a wonderful new detergent, the children gaily calling from the barbecue pit for a famous sauce for their steak.

No doubt many of the world's peoples want and mean to get more of this. But it is not all they want, and they have to look hard to find the balancing picture of America's wider purposes and to learn that high private consumption is not our ultimate aim of life, nor our answer to all man's evils and disorders in a time of breathtaking social change. For all these good "things" do not solve the problems of urban decay and congestion. Behind the shining child in the advertisement lurks the delinquent in the slum. Nor does high consumption guarantee to America's children the teachers or the schools that should be their birth-right. It does nothing to end the shame of racial discrimination. It does not counter the exorbitant cost of maintaining health, nor conserve the nation's precious reserves of land and water and wilderness.

The contrast between private opulence and public squalor on most of our panorama is now too obvious to be denied. Yet we still spend per capita almost as much on advertising to multiply the private wants of our people as we do on education to enable them to seek a fuller, wiser and more satisfying civic existence. Nor is this imbalance simply a matter of drift and the unmeant consequence of our fabulous new opportunities for wealth creation. It is in real measure the result of deliberate government policy. Except for defense, American public expenditure today is proportionately lower than it was in 1939. And while we raise a cheer at the fact that we are spending less, let us also remember that this means a relative decline in support for such basic needs as schooling, research, health, small-income housing, urban renewal, and all forms of public services—local, state and federal—at a time when there has been steadily more inocme to spend on every private want, or unwant.

With the supermarket as our temple and the singing commercial as our litany, are we likely to fire the world with an irresistible vision of America's exalted purposes and inspiring way of life?

Even where public spending has been high—for defense and economic aid—our performance has been more defensive than indicative of freedom's positive purposes. We have stressed so much our aim of stopping Communism for our own security that self-interest has often contaminated our generous aid programs. And even in the vital field of military security, the Administration's concern for the citizen as a private consumer, rather than as a mature responsible American who will accept the unpleasant facts about his country's safety, leaves one with the lurking suspicion that budgetary considerations, rather than the stark needs of strategy, are determining our defense effort.

'We Seem Becalmed in a . . . Storm, drifting Through a Century of mighty dreams'

In short, at a time of universal social upheaval and challenge, our vision of our own society seems to be of limited social significance. An air of disengagement and disinterest hangs over the most powerful and affluent society the world has ever known. Neither the turbulence of the world abroad nor the fatness and flatness of the world at home is moving us to more vital effort. We seem becalmed in a season of storm, drifting through a century of mighty dreams and great achievements. As an American I am disturbed.

It is arguable that after the shocks and rigors of the 1930's and '40's, we as a nation needed a period of relaxation—though I would note that the Russians and the Chinese after far greater shocks have had no opportunity for a cozy nap. Now, however, we have had our rest, and I sense the stirring of a new vitality, possibly the beginning of that traditional swing of the political pendulum away from private pursuits to a concern for the nation's broader purposes.

I am persuaded that he who speaks clearly to the Americans of their social responsibilities, as well as their private wants, will now command a more attentive hearing. I believe the old idea of America and its government as a positive instrument for the common weal is being restored once again after all the cheap sarcasm about "bureaucracy" and "creeping socialism." And if a change of mood and attitude toward our public needs and institutions is in fact on the way, I do not think there can be much question about the fields in which the new sense of responsibility must quickly go to work.

At home we must ask ourselves again what quality of life we want, both public and private, as citizens of this great republic. Education and the arts are the starting point, for it is only here that the citizens of tomorrow can learn to demand and live a fuller life. A respect for excellence and a sense of discipline in the attainment of knowledge are virtues not just because the Russians pioneered the space age and photographed the other side of the moon, but because the new society that technology is building demands a grasp and competence among the mass of citizens undreamed of in earlier civilizations.

'New standards of respect and reward for intellect and culture'

By education and the arts we mean something more than better school buildings, higher teachers' salaries, and more scholarships for the intelligent. We mean a reorientation of our ideals and tastes, the strenuous stretching of mental and artistic talent, the exaltation of excellence above social approval, and of mental achievement above quick material success. We mean, in short, new standards of respect and reward for intellect and culture. And we mean more stable financing for basic research, more concern for advancing knowledge for its own sake. We mean cooperation with other communities of scholars and creative thinkers, as in the International Geophysical Year, in order that our pursuit of truth may be an adventure we share with all mankind. And we mean that the pursuit of truth in itself is the highest activity of man.

Here, then, in all its ramifications of expense, of standards, content and opportunity, is a top priority for a great new America and a national purpose few would dispute.

I would include not far below a reconsideration of our urban life. We are adding a city the size of Philadelphia to our population every year. From every large urban center the suburbs spread out and out, without shape or grace or any centered form of civic life. Many are so built that they are the slums of tomorrow. Meanwhile town centers decay, racial divisions destroy harmony, commuters jam the city approaches and a strange, half life of divided families and Sunday fathers is growing up. If we accept both the fact of our rapid growth in population and the fact that most people will live in the cities, we can begin a serious attack upon our congested, ugly, inconvenient metropolitan sprawl. We can create the preconditions of a good urban life that could become a new model for an urbanizing world.

Restoration of compassion is a clumsy way to describe another great embracing national purpose. In the past, evils and miseries have been the driving force of majority discontent. But now, for the first time in history, the engine of social progress has run out of the fuel of discontent. We have therefore to mobilize our imagination, our personal sense of indignation, if we are to act on the conviction that gross poverty, curable illness, racial indignity, mental disease and suffering in old age are a disgrace amidst the surrounding luxuries, privileges and indulgence of such a wealthy society as ours.

> Gap 'between rich and poor is as great a threat to peace as the arms race'

And here our top priorities must reach beyond our shores. For it is not chiefly in America or in the fortunate North Atlantic basin that the world's miseries are to be found. On the contrary, we confidently predict a doubling and tripling of our high living standards. But in Asia, Africa and Latin America live scores of millions who, on present forecasts, may have no such expectations. This disparity in living standards between the rich and the poor is as great a threat to peace as the arms race, and narrowing the gap is as imperative as arms control.

Our aid programs should therefore be designed not primarily to counter Communism—though they will do this too—but to create conditions of self-respect and self-sustaining growth in economics still behind the threshold of modernization. The needs are so staggering that to achieve this will demand not only the greatest intelligence, perseverance and financial enterprise, private and public, but also a much broader cooperation and joint effort with other advanced nations. If we accept this as fundamental American foreign policy, not on a year-to-year basis but for the next critical generation, we shall develop the perspective and staying power to reach real solutions, not doles, handouts, bad debts—and dislike.

And in doing so, we shall do more than set the processes of modernization in healthy motion. I believe that this is the chief way open to us to extend our vision of a "more perfect Union" to all mankind. It is a commonplace that in a world made one by science and the atom the old national boundaries are dissolving, the old landmarks vanishing. We can't have privacy and the hydrogen bomb too. A workable human society has to be fashioned and we must start where we can—by setting up the institutions of a common economic life, by using our wealth and wisdom to spark the growth of production in poorer lands, by working together with like-minded powers to establish the permanent patterns of a workable world economy. In this way we can hope to establish one of the two main preconditions of peaceful human society—economic solidarity and mutual help.

The other precondition of peace—and this, of all priorities, is our highest—is our unwavering search for peace under law which, in our present context, means controlled and supervised disarmament. Only a disarmed world offers us security worth the name any longer.

I do not believe, even now, that the world accepts the idea that genuine disarmament is America's primary, public purpose. We talk of peace and our devotion to it. But there is far more hard, unremitting effort in the task than speeches or protestations or journeys—however distant. What seems to be lacking is sincere and sustained dedication to this goal and unwearying pursuit by our highest officers, both military and civilian. There is a widespread impression that the United States has been "dragging its feet."

I believe that the American people are prepared to face the cost, the rigors, the efforts and the challenge which are involved in recovering the public image of a great America. The cost in physical terms—in hard work, in discipline, in more taxes if need be—is hard to estimate precisely. Any arms control would release resources. Our growing gross national product will certainly provide wider margins out of which vital public expenditures could be met. But if the cost is higher than our present level of public spending, I frankly believe that education and health for our children, dignity, and beauty in our civic lives, and security and well-being in the world at large are more important than the "things" which might otherwise have priority.

But still more important is America's need to face squarely the facts about its situation. If freedom is really the organizing principle of our society, then we cannot forget that it is not illusion, propaganda and sedatives, but truth, and truth alone, that makes us free. Under the influence of the politics of sedation and the techniques of salesmanship I believe that in recent years self-deceit has slackened our grip on reality. We have tended to shirk the difficult truth and accept the easy half-truth. Perhaps it is always that way. As the old humorist Josh Billings used to say: "As scarce as truth is, the supply has always been in excess of the demand."

But we know from our own lives that reality entails hard choices and disappointments: that it measures real achievement not in terms of luck but in terms of difficulties overcome. I don't believe our national life can follow any other pattern.

No preordained destiny decrees that America shall have all the breaks and soft options. Neither greatness nor even freedom lies that way. So we must surely return to the reality principle, to the bracing, invigorating, upland climate of truth itself. I think we are ready now to move forward into the rigors and glories of the new decade with open eyes, eager step and firm purposes worthy of our great past.

That something has gone wrong in America most of us know. We are richer than any nation before us. We have more Things in our garages and kitchens and cellars than Louis Quatorze had in the whole of Versailles. We have come nearer to the suppression of grinding poverty than even the 19th Century Utopians thought seriously possible. We have wiped out many of the pests and scourges which afflicted humanity. We have advanced science to the edges of the inexplicable and hoisted our technology to the sun itself.

We are in a state of growth and flux and change in which cities flow out into countryside and countryside moves into cities and new industries are born and old industries vanish and the customs of generations alter and fathers speak different languages from their sons. In brief, we are prosperous, lively, successful, inventive, diligent—but, nevertheless and notwithstanding, something is wrong and we know it.

The trouble seems to be that we don't feel right with ourselves or with the country. It isn't only the Russians. We have outgrown the adolescent time when everything that was wrong with America was the fault of the Russians and all we needed to do to be saved was to close the State Department and keep the Communists out of motion pictures. It isn't just the Russians now: it's ourselves. It's the way we feel about ourselves as Americans. We feel that we've lost our way in the woods, that we don't know where we are going—if anywhere.

I agree—but I still feel that the diagnosis is curious, for the fact is, of course, that we have a national purpose—the most precisely articulated national purpose in recorded history—and that we all know it. It is the purpose put into words by the most lucid mind of that most lucid century, the 18th, and adopted in 1776 as a declaration of the existence and national intent of a new nation.

Not only is it a famous statement of purpose: it is also an admirable statement of purpose. Prior to July 4, 1776, the national purpose of nations had been to dominate: to dominate at least their neighbors and rivals and, wherever possible, to dominate the world. The American national purpose was the opposite: to liberate from domination; to set men free.

All men, to Thomas Jefferson, were created equal. All men were endowed by their Creator with certain inalienable rights. Among these rights were life, liberty and the pursuit of happiness. It was the existence of these rights which justified American independence from King George and justified also the revolution which would have to be fought for that independence. It was the existence of these rights which would provide a foundation for the government to be established when independence was secure.

We not only have a national purpose: we have one of such aspiration, such potentiality, such power of hope that we refer to it—or used to—as the American Dream. We were dedicated from our beginnings to the proposition that we existed not merely to exist but to be free, and the dedication was real in spite of the fact that it took us three generations and a bloody war to practice our preachment within our own frontiers. It was real in spite of the fact that its practice is still a delusion in numerous pockets of hypocrisy across the nation.

> 'Human freedom . . . is as infinite as the human soul which it enfranchises'

To be free is not, perhaps, a political program in the modern sense, but from the point of view of a new nation it may be something better. The weakness of political programs—Five Year Plans and the like—is that they can be achieved. But human freedom can never be achieved because human freedom is a continuously evolving condition. It is infinite in its possibilities—as infinite as the human soul which it enfranchises. The nation which seeks it and persists in its search will move through history as a ship moves on a compass course toward a constantly opening horizon.

And America did move steadily on before it lost headway in the generation in which we live. The extraordinary feel of liveness which the Americans communicated, whether agreeably or not, to their early European visitors came from that sense of national expectation. We were never a very philosophical people politically after Jefferson and his contemporaries left us. We were practical men who took instruction from the things we saw and heard and did. But the purpose defined in our Declaration was a reality to us notwithstanding. It gave us aim as the continent gave us scope, and the old American character with its almost anarchic passion for idiosyncrasy and difference was the child of both. Those Missouri militiamen Parkmen describes in *The Oregon Trail* slogging their way west to the war with Mexico, each in his own rig and each in his own way, could have constituted an army nowhere else. When, at Sacramento, a drunken officer commanded his company to halt and a private yelled "Charge!" the company charged, knocking five times their number of Mexicans out of prepared entrenchments. The anarchy didn't matter because they were all headed in the same direction and the name of that direction was West or freedom. They had a future in common and they had a purpose in common and the purpose was the enfranchisement of men—of all men—to think for themselves, speak for themselves, govern themselves, pursue happiness for themselves and so become themselves.

Why then do we need to rediscover what our national purpose is? Because the words of the Declaration in its superb housing in the National Archives have become archival words, words out of history? Because the Bill of Rights of the American Constitution belongs, like the Magna Carta, in an airtight case? No one who reads the newspapers could think so. There has never been a time when courts and Congress devoted more of their attention to the constitutional guarantees of individual freedom than they do today, and as for the Declaration of Independence, its language is more alive in the middle of the 20th Century than it was even when it was written. It is not Communism, however Communism may attempt to exploit them, which has begotten the new nations of Asia and Africa or the new nationalistic stirrings in South America and the Caribbean and even in Europe. The Marxist dream is a dream of economic machinery, not of living men: of a universal order and system, not a proliferation of nationalities. No, the dream which has set the jungle and the cane on fire is different and older. It is Thomas Jefferson's dream—the dream which he and his contemporaries believed would change the world. It is changing the world—and not later than one might expect. Two hundred years is a short time in the history of institutions.

If the American Dream is out of date today it is out of date only in America—only in America and in the Communist countries in which the political police have extinguished it. But is it really out of date in America? Is its power to direct and draw us really so faint that we are lost in the blaze of our own prosperity and must enlist the aid of learned men to tell us where the future lies? That, I think, is a question for debate in these discussions.

Have we lost our sense of purpose or have we merely lost touch with it? Have we rejected the arduous labor to which our beginnings committed us? Or are we merely confused and bewildered by the volcanic upheavals which have changed the landscapes of our lives? Or is it neither rejection nor confusion? Is it nothing more than the flatulence and fat of an overfed people whose children prepare at the milk-shake counter for coronary occlusions in middle age? Are we simply too thick through the middle to dream?

I doubt for myself that we have rejected the American Dream or have even thought of rejecting it. There are minorities, of course, who have little enthusiam for the actualities of the American commitment to freedom, but this is largely because they do not understand what the struggle it culminated was all about. Certain areas on the fringes of Europe were preserved by their geographical location from the necessity of living through the crisis of the Western mind which we call the Reformation, and American stock from these areas tends to find the master-mistress idea of the American Revolution— the idea which raised it from a minor war for independence to a world event—incomprehensible if not actually misguided. It is not a question of religion. Catholics from the heart of the European continent understand Jefferson as well as any Protestant. It is a question of geography. Men and women whose ancestors were not obliged to fight the battle for or against freedom of conscience cannot for the life of them understand why censorship should be considered evil or why authority is not preferable to freedom.

But all this does not add up to a rejection of the American dedication to liberty—the American dedication to the enfranchisement of
the human spirit. The Irish Catholics, who are among the most persistent and politically powerful advocates of increasing censorship in
the U.S., and who are brought up to submit to clerical authority in
matters which the American tradition reserves to the individual conscience, are nevertheless among the most fervent of American patriots.
And if their enthusiasm for freedom of the mind is restrained, their
passion for freedom of the man is glorious. Only if a separate system
of education should be used to perpetuate the historical ignorance and
moral obtuseness on which fear of freedom of the mind is based would
the danger of the rejection of the American Dream from this quarter
become serious. As for the rest, the only wholehearted rejection comes
from the Marxists, who, both Mr. Hoovers to the contrary notwithstanding, have no perceptible influence on American opinion.

   'But the whole country is not lost in a sluggish, sun-oiled
   sleep'

I cannot believe that we have rejected the purpose on which our
Republic was founded. Neither can I believe that our present purpose-
lessness results from our economic fat and our spiritual indolence. It is
not because we are too comfortable that the dream has left us. It is true,
I suppose, that we eat better—at least more—than any nation ever has.
It is true too that there are streaks of American fat, some of it very
ugly fat, and that shows most unbecomingly at certain points in New
York and Miami and along the California coast. But the whole country
is not lost in a sluggish, sun-oiled sleep beneath a beach umbrella, dreaming of More and More. We have our share, and more than our share, of
mink coats and prestige cars and expense account restaurants and oil
millionaires, but America is not made of such things as these. We are an
affluent society but not affluent to the point of spiritual sloth.

   No one who has taught, as I have been doing for the past ten years,
can very seriously doubt that the generation on the way up is more intelligent than the generation now falling back. And as for the materialism
about which we talk so much, it is worth remembering that the popular
whipping boy of the moment among the intelligent young is precisely
"Madison Avenue," that mythical advertising copy writer who is supposed to persuade us to wallow in cosmetics and tail-fin cars. We may
be drowning in Things, but the best of our sons and daughters like it
even less than we do.

   What then has gone wrong? The answer, I submit, is fairly obvious
and will be found where one would expect to find it: in the two great

wars which have changed so much beside. The first world war altered not only our position in the world but our attitude toward ourselves and toward our business as a people. Having won a war to "make the world safe for democracy," we began to act as though democracy itself had been won—as though there was nothing left for us to do but enjoy ourselves: make money in the stock market, gin in the bathtub and whoopee in the streets. The American journey had been completed. The American goal was reached. We had emerged from the long trek west-ward to find ourselves on the Plateau of Permanent Prosperity. We were there! It took the disaster of 1929 and the long depression which followed to knock the fantasy out of our heads but the damage had been done. We had lost touch with the driving force of our own history.

> 'Freedom is never an accomplished fact. . . . It is always a process'

The effect of the second war was different—and the same. The second war estranged us from our genius as a people. We fought it be-cause we realized that our dream of human liberty could not survive in the slave state Hitler was imposing on the world. We won it with no such illusions as had plagued us 25 years before: there was another more voracious slave state behind Hitler's. But though we did not repeat the folly of the '20s we repeated the delusion of the '20s. We acted again as though freedom were an accomplished fact. We no longer thought of it as safe but we made a comparable mistake: we thought of it as some-thing which could be protected by building walls around it, by "contain-ing" its enemy.

But the truth is, of course, that freedom is never an accomplished fact. It is always a process. Which is why the drafters of the Declaration spoke of the pursuit of happiness: they knew their Thucydides and there-fore knew that "the secret of happiness is freedom, courage." The only way freedom can be defended is not by fencing it in but enlarging it, exercising it. Though we did defend freedom by exercising it through the Marshall Plan in Europe, we did not, for understandable reasons in-volving the colonial holdings of our allies, defend freedom by exercising it in Asia and Africa where the future is about to be decided.

The results have been hurtful to the world and to ourselves. How hurtful they have been to the world we can see in Cuba where a needed and necessary and hopeful revolution against an insufferable dictator-ship appears to have chosen the Russian solution of its economic diffi-culties rather than ours. We have tried to explain that ominous fact to ourselves in the schoolgirl vocabulary of the McCarthy years, saying that Castro and his friends are Communists. But whether they are or not

—and the charge is at least unproved—there is no question whatever of the enormous popular support for their regime and for as much of their program as is now known. Not even those who see Communist conspiracies underneath everyone else's bed have contended that the Cuban people were tricked or policed into their enthusiasm for their revolution. On the contrary the people appear to outrun the government in their eagerness for the new order. What this means is obvious. What this means is that the wave of the future, to the great majority of Cubans, is the Russian wave, not the American. That fact, and its implications for the rest of Latin America, to say nothing of Africa and Asia, is the fact we should be looking at, hard and long. If the Russian purpose seems more vigorous and more promising to the newly liberated peoples of the world than the American purpose, then we have indeed lost the "battle for men's minds" of which we talk so much.

As for ourselves, the hurt has been precisely the loss of a sense of national purpose. To engage, as we have over the past 15 years, in programs having as their end and aim not action to further a purpose of our own but counteraction to frustrate a purpose of the Russians is to invite just such a state of mind. A nation cannot be sure even of its own identity when it finds itself associated in country after country—as we have in South Korea and Turkey—with regimes whose political practices are inimical to its own.

What, then, is the issue in this debate? What is the problem? Not to discover our national purpose but to exercise it. Which means, ultimately, to exercise it for its own sake, not for the defeat of those who have a different purpose. There is all the difference in the world between strengthening the enemies of our enemies because they are against what we are against, and supporting the hopes of mankind because we too believe in them, because they are our hopes also. The fields of action in the two cases may be the same: Africa and Asia and Latin America. The tools of action—military assistance and above all economic and industrial and scientific aid—may look alike. But the actions will be wholly different. The first course of action surrenders initiative to the Russians and accepts the Russian hypothesis that Communism is the new force moving in the world. The second asserts what is palpably true, that the new force moving in the world is the force we set in motion, the force which gave us, almost two centuries ago, our liberating mission. The first is costly, as we know. The second will be more costly still. But the second, because it recaptures for the cause of freedom the initiative which belongs to it and restores to the country the confidence it has lost, is capable of succeeding. The first, because it can never be anything but a policy of resistance, can only continue to resist and to accomplish nothing more.

There are those, I know, who will reply that the liberation of humanity, the freedom of man and mind, is nothing but a dream. They are right. It is. It is the American Dream.

THE INDIVIDUAL AND NATIONAL GOALS*

by Max Lerner

I want to start with one aspect of national purpose, the aspect that I call élan. I use a French term because I don't know of any English term. What I mean by élan is the feeling of commitment, the feeling of being on fire, a sense of mission, a sense that there are things worth dying for and worth living for. . . .

If you look back at the history of the rise and fall of civilizations you will find, I think, that civilizations have died of two things. They've died of rigidity, of a kind of arteriosclerosis of their master institutions. But they've also died because of the failure of nerve. I take the phrase "failure of nerve" from Gilbert Murray who used it about Greek civilizations and about classical antiquity in the face of ruthless and organized power. The great cultures of antiquity showed a failure of nerve. And we need to understand some of these causes of the death of civilization if we are to understand the second thing that should interest us, and that is, "What does a people, and what does a nation live of?" I would say a people lives of its dreams, lives of its visions. It lives of a sense of possibility and meaning.

I was going through some letters of Henry Adams, and there is one letter written in the 1870's or 1880's to one of his brothers in which he talks of the experience that they had during the Civil War. And he said in his letter, "At that time I understood what it was all about. There was war, there was excitement, and I knew what it was all about. But may I be hung up to dry for the next fifty years if I know what it's about now." This is one of the difficulties with civilizations—that it is in a time of

*With permission of the author and McGraw-Hill Book Co., Inc., from the presentation by Professor Max Lerner at The 1961 Cubberly Conference, School of Education, Stanford University, in *Education: An Instrument of National Goals,* The Board of Trustees of the Leland Stanford Junior University. Copyright © 1962 by The Board of Trustees of the Leland Stanford Junior University.

crisis, in a time of planetary wrack and turmoil, that they begin to understand what it is about.

Henry Adams and his brother Brooks Adams were part of a little circle which included Theodore Roosevelt and young Oliver Wendell Holmes. It was Holmes, later Justice Holmes, for whom the Civil War was also one of the great experiences of his life. And he was to write about it as being the time when our lives were "touched with fire." The problem is to see whether, not just in war but in peace, not just for war power and destruction but for purposes of a peaceful society, we can again make our lives ringed with fire. . . .

I am very heartened by the response of American youth to this notion of a peace army, because not only does this peace army represent an effort on the part of these young people to identify themselves with the fortunes and the possibilities of undeveloped countries abroad, but also it means that in the process these young people are willing to undergo risk and danger, and this is no children's crusade, believe me. This is tough, tough and difficult. Food isn't good and the climate is terrible. They're going to be homesick. They're going to find things awfully hard. But in the process they will learn to stretch themselves. Perhaps in the process they may recapture what Holmes meant when he said that in our youth our lives were touched with fire. . . .

We've got to recapture what seems to me the élan of American history, and that's the authentic idea of a revolutionary America. I think it means that we've got to stop being afraid of the term "revolution." I had some experience in Asia when I spent a year in India teaching there at a graduate school of international studies. I had the experience of talking to my students there and also traveling around the universities of India, and I found that the image of America they had was the image of a fat, rich, prosperous, complacent country which was the last bulwark of the status quo, and they didn't like it.

I talked to them in somewhat different terms. I talked to them in terms of the great revolutionary tradition of America. . . . I asked them, for example, whom they considered a more meaningful figure for a new revolutionary nation like India. Did they regard Lenin as the meaningful figure or Woodrow Wilson, who lived at the same time as Lenin? Lenin gave to the world the doctrine of class struggle. Wilson gave to the world the doctrine of self-determination. It's the very seed bed of revolutionary modern nationalism. It came from Wilson. And if we think in terms of this authentic revolutionary tradition and if we keep alive, as I hope we will keep alive, the life of the mind and the spirit so as to give meaning to these dynamic energies of ours, then I think that we can answer the problem of élan. And with this energy we have great tasks to perform. I wish I had time to talk about them in specific terms, . . . but I think that I can put them all in a single phrase, and the phrase for me is that of finishing the unfinished business of democracy.

I break down the concept of national purpose into a second portion. To this also I give a foreign name, elite, the idea of an educated, creative elite. . . . If we are to win what I regard as the crucial race, not the weapons race but the entire intelligence race, it can be done only by using our educational plant and resources for the development of the best potentials of our most promising youngsters.

I talk partly in terms of political leadership. We live in a time when the traditional kind of leadership will no longer save our country and our culture or the free world. There are two kinds of leaders, the event-responding leader and the event-creating leader. It's only the event-creating leadership which can give America and the free world the kind of resourcefulness and flexibility and resolve which we shall need. But I'm going beyond the problem of political leadership itself. I'm going to the question of creativeness in every aspect of American life. . . .

The problems of the school system of a generation ago, two generations ago, three or four or five generations ago are no longer the problems of today. We've gone through a great educational revolution, a revolution of trying to give a substratus of necessary cohesion to the society. We are, as Walt Whitman said, not just a nation but a nation of nations. America was built up by streams of immigration from every part of the world. And it was necessary during our history to use our educational system in such a way that youngsters coming from families with different religions, with different ethnic traditions, with different cultural traditions, should have something in common, they should have some cohesion, some cement. The problem today is different. It is that of a creative America.

When I speak in these terms, some of my colleagues ridicule me a bit. They talk of American mass culture. I think I know along with them some of the tawdriness, mediocrity, slackness and sleaziness of American mass culture. But I think I know also that this does not exhaust American culture. This is not the whole thing. There is not only a mass culture in the press and radio and television and all the rest, there is also a minority culture. In every realm of activity, in every discipline of our lives, there is a small group of people who are training themselves, educating themselves, stretching themselves in order to transcend the tradition and transcend themselves. I see emerging in America, if only we cleave to the potentials of it, a new creative America which is able to develop a democratic creative elite and is able to make use of it for strengthening the culture. I go back to Thomas Jefferson's conception of a natural aristocracy of virtue and talent. And I see no reason why that basic concept should not be of great utility in our own time.

I've spoken of élan and of a creative American elite. I end by suggesting a third element of the larger concept of national purpose. That is an ethos, a sense of values to live by and to die by if necessary. . . .

In our society we have developed a set of goals that I'm not very happy about. I don't mean that they are entirely empty. I do suggest that part of the problem of education is to understand the national and personal goals by which we live and die, and where they are weak and inadequate, to channel them into a different direction. When I wrote my America as a Civilization I talked of the five-goal system that we have in America, of success and power, and money and prestige, and security, and I added that we are a happiness civilization. We use happiness as the test of so much.

There is nothing basically wrong with success if you are talking of the capacity to see your problem through, but if you mean by success that others should recognize you as having arrived, if you mean by success that you have been able to trample upon others, then I see very little in it. . . . Instead of power for the individual, I would suggest that we shift to a sense of the functioning of the individual to the limit of his powers, . . . of reaching to the very depth of his capacity.

Instead of money as a goal, I suggest the doctrine of work and, through work, achieving the things that money cannot buy. . . . Instead of prestige, which we largely think of in terms of seeing ourselves in the mirror of the esteem of others, I suggest that we care about the good opinion only of our fellow craftsmen, of our friends, the people who form part of us and of whom we form a part, so that we are not continually bedeviled by the question of what the world as a whole thinks of us. Instead of security, I suggest that we shift to the capacity for risk, for a sense of selfhood, sense of identity.

Instead of happiness, I suggest joyousness, a feeling for nature, for the tent of the sky, for the carpet of the earth, for the world of sight and sound and sense all around us. In our industrialized urban society we very badly need a re-education of the senses.

If you put these together, and if along with this you take a creative America with a creative elite, and if along with that you take a sense of élan, a sense of a country still unfinished, a sense of the authentic revolutionary tradition which is in our history and which we can project into the future—if you put those together then I suggest to you that perhaps we'll be able to do something with our youngsters in our educational system. Perhaps we'll be able to win the future.

CONTRADICTION IN AMERICAN IDEALS*

by Robert Lynd

The following suggest some of these outstanding assumptions in American life:

1. The United States is the best and greatest nation on earth and will always remain so.

2. Individualism, "the survival of the fittest," is the law of nature and the secret of America's greatness; and restrictions on individual freedom are un-American and kill initiative.

But: No man should live for himself alone; for people ought to be loyal and stand together and work for common purposes.

3. The thing that distinguishes man from the beasts is the fact that he is rational; and therefore man can be trusted, if let alone, to guide his conduct wisely.

But: Some people are brighter than others; and, as every practical politician and businessman knows, you can't afford simply to sit back and wait for people to make up their minds.

4. Democracy, as discovered and perfected by the American people, is the ultimate form of living together. All men are created free and equal, and the United States has made this fact a living reality.

But: You would never get anywhere, of course, if you constantly left things to popular vote. No business could be run that way, and of course no businessman would tolerate it.

5. Everyone should try to be successful.

But: The kind of person you are is more important than how successful you are.

6. The family is our basic institution and the sacred core of our national life.

---

*From Robert Lynd, *Knowledge for What?* Princeton, New Jersey: Princeton University Press, 1939, pp. 60-62. Copyright 1939, Princeton University Press. Reprinted by permission.

But: Business is our most important institution, and, since national welfare depends upon it, other institutions must conform to its needs.

7. Religion and "the finer things of life" are our ultimate values and the things all of us are really working for.

But: A man owes it to himself and to his family to make as much money as he can.

8. Life would not be tolerable if we did not believe in progress and know that things are getting better. We should, therefore, welcome new things.

But: The old, tried fundamentals are best; and it is a mistake for busybodies to try to change things too fast or to upset the fundamentals.

9. Hard work and thrift are signs of character and the way to get ahead.

But: No shrewd person tries to get ahead nowadays by just working hard, and nobody gets rich nowadays by pinching nickels. It is important to know the right people. If you want to make money, you have to look and act like money. Anyway, you only live once.

10. Honesty is the best policy.

But: Business is business, and a businessman would be a fool if he didn't cover his hand.

11. America is a land of unlimited opportunity, and people get pretty much what's coming to them here in this country.

But: Of course, not everybody can be boss, and factories can't give jobs if there aren't jobs to give.

12. Capital and labor are partners.

But: It is bad policy to pay higher wages than you have to. If people don't like to work for you for what you offer them, they can go elsewhere.

13. Education is a fine thing.

But: It is the practical men who get things done.

14. Science is a fine thing in its place and our future depends upon it.

But: Science has no right to interfere with such things as business and our other fundamental institutions. The thing to do is to use science, but not let it upset things.

16. Women are the finest of God's creatures.

But: Women aren't very practical and are usually inferior to men in reasoning power and general ability.

17. Patriotism and public service are fine things.

But: Of course, a man has to look out for himself.

18. The American judicial system insures justice to every man, rich or poor.

But: A man is a fool not to hire the best lawyer he can afford.

19. Poverty is deplorable and should be abolished.

But: There never has been enough to go around, and the Bible tells us that "The poor you have always with you."

20. No man deserves to have what he hasn't worked for. It demoralizes him to do so.

But: You can't let people starve.

AN EMPIRICAL THEORY OF DEMOCRACY*

(as inferred from present practices)

by Lawrence G. Thomas

1. The solution preferred by the majority is ipso facto the democratic solution.

2. The democratic way to treat people is to give them what they want, e.g., soap operas, comic books, new post offices, lower taxes regardless of the budget, foreign loans out of sympathy but no lowering of tariffs for repayment, etc. . . .

3. A conviction that each person deserves what he gets through his own efforts, and an open-hearted generosity for anyone in trouble through no fault of his own.

4. A warm sympathy for handicapped persons but a strong reluctance to change the social conditions which handicap them.

5. A persisting belief that equality of treatment means identity of treatment, endorsed by rich and poor alike.

6. An inarticulate feeling that democracy is intended for homogeneous groups of people but not for the mixing of heterogeneous types.

*Printed by permission of the author, Lawrence G. Thomas, "An Empirical View of Democracy."

7. A system of checks and balances, not so much to get group projects accomplished of general value, but to prevent too much interference in the life of individuals.

8. Politics is for professionals and is usually an unsavory career. Politics is of concern to decent citizens only on election days, which must be frequent to keep politicians in line and frequently changed.

9. The personality and character of the candidate is almost always more important than the platform or principles of his party.
a. Very seldom does a philosophy or economic theory arise which exists beyond one generation and which is voted for rather regardless of its leadership at the time.

10. Issues are defined by "leaders" and sold to the people, especially in times of dissatisfaction with the present situation. Practically never is an issue defined by a grass-roots movement and assigned in mandate form to a leader for proper execution.

11. Participation in civic affairs at the community level is practiced by a small minority—a civic elite composed largely of prosperous supporters of the status quo, public-spirited do-gooders, and intellectual malcontents who try to "live" their impossible ideals. The normal people composing the majority stay home evenings with their children and hobbies, or got out to the movies or lodge meetings.

12. Civil liberties receive wide popular support when the topics involved are relatively harmless and superficial (e.g., disputes between Republicans and Democrats, disputes between established religions, prohibition, cutting taxes, wage disputes), but are maintained only by an alert minority when the topics really make a difference in our way of life (e.g., the private profit system, the middle class sex code, aliens who criticize us, atheism).

EDUCATION IN A TRANSFORMING
AMERICAN CULTURE*

by George D. Spindler

The American public school system, and the professional educators who operate it, have been subjected to increasingly strident attacks from both the lay (non-educationist) public, and from within the ranks. My premise is that these attacks can best be understood as symptoms of an American culture that is undergoing transformation—a transformation that produces serious conflict. I shall discuss this transformation as a problem in culture change that directly affects all of education, and everyone identified with it.

The notion of social and cultural change is used persuasively, if carelessly, by too many writers to explain too much. Generalized allusions to technological change, cultural lag, the atomic age, and mass society, are more suggestive than clarifying. We must strike to the core of the change. And my argument is that this core can best be conceived as a radical shift in values.

The anthropologist, and I speak as one but not for all, sees culture as a goal-oriented system. These goals are expressed, patterned, lived out by people in their behaviors and aspirations in the form of values— objects or possessions, conditions of existence, personality or character-ological features, and states of mind, that are conceived as desirable, and act as motivating determinants of behaviors. It is the shifts in what I believe are the core values in American culture, and the effect of these shifts on education today, that I wish to discuss. I will present these shifts in values as the conditions of life to which education and educators, whether progressives, experimentalists, conservatives, or in-betweens, must adapt—and to which they are adapting, albeit confusedly. My emphasis within the value frame-work will be upon shifts in the conception of the desirable character type, since education can never be freed from

*From George D. Spindler, "Education in a Transforming American Culture," *Harvard Educational Review,* Volume 25 (Summer 1955), pp. 145-156.

the obligation to support, if not produce, the kind of personality, or social character deemed desirable in society.

But first I must specify what sources are to be used as the factual baseline for generalization, even though there is no avoiding the necessity of going beyond these facts in the discussion to follow. There is a body of literature on American culture, as a culture, and the changes within it. I have drawn most heavily from the anthropologists, like Margaret Mead, Clyde and Florence Kluckhohn, Gregory Bateson, Lloyd Warner, and Geoffrey Gorer, and a few sociologists, like David Reisman. Their writings range from the highly intuitive to the relatively observation-based. Though there is consensus, and a surprising degree of it, on the part of these students of American culture, little they say can be or is intended by them to be taken as proven.

These writings are useful, but most emphasize static patterning in values more than change in values. To extend my factual baseline I have been collecting relevant data from college students for the past four years. The sample consists of several hundred students, ranging in age from 19 to 57 years, mainly graduates in professional education courses, and representing socio-economic strata describable as lower-middle to upper-middle class. The sample is as representative of this professional group and these economic strata as any regionally biased sample can be. I have used two simple value-projective techniques. The aim has been to find out what features of social character (the term I will use to designate those personality elements that are most relevant to social action) the students in the sample hold as being valuable and that presumably determine much of their behavior in classrooms. The first of these techniques is a series of 24 open-ended statements; such as "The individual is ....," "Intellectuals should ....," "All men are born ...." The second of these techniques is to require each student to write one brief paragraph describing his (or her) conception of the "Ideal American Boy."

The various qualifications, problems, and discrepancies in analysis appearing in the treatment of the results cannot be discussed here. Let it suffice to say that I have subjected the responses of the students in the sample to a straightforward content analysis — counting numbers of responses that fall into certain categories appearing from the data themselves. Perhaps some examples will illustrate both the techniques and the kinds of materials from which I am going to draw in the rest of this article.

From the open-ended sentence value-projective technique, results like these have been obtained: "All men are born ....", "equal" (70% of all responses) "wolves", "stupid", "dopes", "hot-blooded" (a miscellaneous negative category of 28%—provided mainly by females in the sample); "Artists are ....", "queer", "perverted", "nuts", "effeminate" (a negative-hostile category of 38% of all responses), "different", "people", "few", (a neutral category of 35%), "creative", "smart", "original", "interesting", (a positive category of 25%); "Intellectuals should ....", "be more sociable", "be more practical", "get down to earth" (a mildly derogative category of 36%), "keep it under cover", "drop dead", "shut up" (an openly hostile category 20%), "apply their intellect", "study", "create", "think" (a neutral to positive category of 40%); Nudity is ...., "vulgar", "obscene", "profane", "repulsive", (a negative-moralistic category of 43%), "pleasant", "self-expressive", "beautiful", "healthy" (an enthusiastic-positive category of 20%), "depends on how interpreted", "alright in some places," "depends on who is looking" (a relativistic category of 30%).

The values are self-evident, and do not call for discussion, as such, for the moment. What is more important is that this fairly homogeneous sample of students provides a wide range of response to each of these statements, excepting for the purposefully stereotyped "All men are born ...." And not only is there a wide range of response evidenced, but many of the categories of response to a single statement can be considered as contradictions with respect to each other. This suggests that although there are clear modalities of values in this sample, there are also differences between people and groups of people in respect to what they believe is good.

The material gathered together as results from the "Ideal American Boy" technique are even more suggestive. A sentence-content analysis procedure reveals that the desirable features of character are ranked in the following order, from highest number of mentions, to lowest number; He should be *sociable,* like people, and get along well with them; he must be *popular,* be liked by others; he is to be *well-rounded,* he can do many things quite well, but is not an expert at anything in particular; he should be *athletic* (but not a star), and healthy (no qualifications); he should be *ambitious* to succeed, and have clear goals, but these must be acceptable within limited norms; he must be *considerate of others,* ever-sensitive to their feelings about him and about events; he should be a *clean-cut Christian,* moral and respectful of God and parents; he should be *patriotic;* and he should demonstrate *average-academic ability,* and *average intellectual capacity.*

These are the characteristics of the ideal American boy seen as most important by the students in the sample. Leadership, independence, high intelligence, high academic ability, individuality, are mentioned relatively infrequently (in about 20% of the descriptive paragraphs). But individuals do vary in the pattern of characteristics that are combined in the paragraph. Some emphasized the high achievement and individualized characteristics just mentioned. Some include elements from the modal list and combine them with these latter items. But the majority emphasize the sociable, well-rounded, average characteristics ranked above.

The implications seem clear. The keynote to the character type regarded as most desirable, and therefore constituting a complex of values, is *balance, outward-orientedness, sociability,* and *conformity* for the sake of harmony. Individuality and creativity, or even mere originality, are not stressed in this conception of values. Introspective behavior is devaluated (even intellectuals are suspicioned by many). Deviancy, it seems, is to be tolerated only within the narrow limits of sociability, of general outwardness, of conformity for harmony ("Artists are perverts"). The All-American Boy is altogether average.

The materials just cited not only serve to illustrate the technique, but more important for present purposes, indicate rather clearly the fabric of the social character values in American culture (providing one can assume, as I am here, that the middle-class culture is the core of our way of life—the pattern of norms against which lower and upper class cultures are seen as deviations). From this point on, I shall use the implications of this data, along with the content of anthropological and sociological writings on American culture, without further reference to the factual baseline itself. The purpose is to sketch in bold strokes the major dimensions of culture changes in our American society and relate them in explanatory style to the contretemps of modern public education and educators.

In doing this, I cannot indicate all of the logical and analytic steps between data and generalization, since this is not a research report. The statements I will make now about American values, their shift, and the effect on education, are based upon the varying responses of different age groups in the sample, upon person-to-person variation in responses, and upon variations in response and particularly contradictions of response within single individual protocols (the total set of responses for a single individual).

On the basis of these kinds of data, and in the light of the perceptive works of the fore-mentioned writers on American Culture, I believe it is clear that a major shift in American values has, and is taking place. I find it convenient to label this shift as being from *traditional* to *emergent*. The values thus dichotomized are listed under their respective headings on page 449, with explanatory statements in parentheses.

TRADITIONAL VALUES	EMERGENT VALUES
Puritan morality (Respectability, thrift, self-denial, sexual constraint; a puritan is someone who can have anything he wants, as long as he doesn't enjoy it!)	*Sociability* (As described above. One should like people and get along well with them. Suspicion of solitary activities is characteristic.)
Work-Success ethic (Successful people worked hard to become so. Anyone can get to the top if he tries hard enough. So people who are not successful are lazy, or stupid, or both. People must work desperately and continuously to convince themselves of their worth.)	*Relativistic moral attitude* (Absolutes in right and wrong are questionable. Morality is what the group thinks is right. Shame, rather than guilt-oriented personality, is appropriate.)
Individualism (The individual is sacred, and always more important than the group. In one extreme form, the value sanctions egocentricity, expediency, and disregard for other people's rights. In its healthier form the value sanctions independence and originality.)	*Consideration for others* (Everything one does should be done with regard for others and their feelings. The individual has a built-in radar that alerts him to other's feelings. Tolerance for the other person's point of view and behaviors is regarded as desirable, so long as the harmony of the group is not disrupted.)
Achievement orientation (Success is a constant goal. There is no resting on past glories. If one makes $9,000 this year he must make $10,000 next year. Coupled with the work-success ethic, this value keeps people moving, and tense.)	
Future-time orientation (The future, not the past, or even the present, is more important. There is a "pot of gold at the end of the rainbow." Time is valuable, and cannot be wasted. Present needs must be denied for satisfactions to be gained in the future.)	*Hedonistic, present-time orientation* (No one can tell what the future will hold, therefore one should enjoy the present — but within the limits of the well-rounded, balanced personality and group.)
	Conformity to the group (Implied in the other emergent values. Everything is relative to the group. Leadership consists of group-machinery lubrication.)

I believe American Culture is undergoing a transformation, and a rapid one producing many disjunctions and conflicts, from the traditional to the emergent value systems outlined above. It is probable that both value systems have been present and operating in American Culture for some time, perhaps since the birth of the nation. But recently, and under the impetus of World Wars, atomic insecurities, and a past history of "boom and bust," the heretofore latent tendencies in the emergent direction have gathered strength and appear to be on the way towards becoming the dominant value system of American Culture.

Like all major shifts in culture, this one has consequences for people. Culturally transitional populations, as anthropologists know from their studies of acculturating Indian tribes, Hindu villages, and Samoan communities (among others), are characterized by conflict, and in most severe form—demoralization and disorganization. Institutions and people are in a state of flux. Contradictory views of life are held by different groups and persons within the society. Hostilities are displaced, attacks are made on one group by another. And this applies as well to the condition of American culture—the context of American education.

The traditionalist views the emergentist as "socialistic," "communistic," "spineless and weak-headed," or downright "immoral." The emergentist regards the traditionalist as "hidebound," reactionary," "selfish," or "neurotically compulsive." Most of what representatives of either viewpoint do may be regarded as insidious and destructive from the point of view of the other. The conflict goes beyond groups or institutions, because individuals in our transitional society are likely to hold elements of both value systems concomitantly. This is characteristic, as a matter of fact, of most students included in the sample described previously. There are few "pure" types. The social character of most is split, calling for different responses in different situations, and with respect to different symbols. So an ingredient of personal confusion is added that intensifies social and institutional conflict.

I hypothesize that the attacks upon education, which were our starting point, and the confusion and failure of nerve characterizing educators today, can be seen in clear and helpful perspective in the light of the conflict of traditional and emergent values that has been described. It is the heart of the matter. The task then becomes one of placing groups, institutions and persons on a continuum of transformation from the one value system to the other. Without prior explanation, I should like to provide a simple diagram that will aid at least the visual-minded to comprehension of what is meant. With this accomplished I will provide the rationale for such placement and discuss the implications of it in greater detail.

The diagram is meant to convey the information that different groups operating in the context of relations between school and community, educator and public, occupy different positions on the value continuum, with varying degrees and mixtures of traditional and emergent orientations. It should be understood that the placements indicate hypothecated tendencies, that no one group representing any particular institution ever consists of "pure" value types, but that there is probably a modal tendency for the groups indicated to place on the transformation, or continuum line, in the way expressed in the diagram.

TRADITIONAL VALUES			EMERGENT VALUES
	General public and Parents	School administrators	
School boards	Students		Students
		Older Teachers	
			Younger teachers

The rationale for the placement of the various groups on the value continuum is fairly complex, but let me try to explain some salient points. School boards are placed nearest the *traditional* end of the continuum because such boards are usually composed of persons representing the power, *status-quo,* elements of the community, and of persons in the higher age ranges. They are therefore people who have a stake in keeping things as they are, who gained their successes within the framework of the traditional value system and consequently believe it to be good, and who, by virtue of their age, grew up and acquired their value sets during a period of time when American culture was presumably more tradition-oriented than it is today.

The general public and parent group, of course, contains many elements of varying value predilection. It is therefore unrealistic to place this public at any particular point in the value continuum. But I hypothesize that the public *tends* to be more conservative in its social philosophy than the professional education set. The placement to the left of center of the continuum ("left" being "right" in the usual sense) takes on further validity if it is seen as a placement of that part of the public that is most vocal in its criticism of educators and education— since most of the criticisms made appear to spring out of value conflicts between traditionalist and emergentist positions. Parents complain that their children are not being taught the "three R's" (even when they are), that educators want to "socialize" the competitive system by eliminating report cards, that children are not taught the meaning of hard work. These all sound, irrespective of the question of their justification or lack of it, like traditionalist responses to change in an "emergent" direction.

Students are placed at two points on the transformation line because it is clear that those coming from traditionalist family environments will tend to hold traditionalistic values, but hold them less securely than will their parents (if our hypothesis for over-all change is valid), while other students who come from emergent-oriented families will tend to place even further, as a function of their age and peer groups, towards the emergent end of the line than their parents would. This is only partially true, indeed, for such a rationale does not account for the fact that offspring in revolt (and many American children from 6 to 16 are in a state of revolt against parental dictums) may go to extremes in either direction.

School administrators, older, and younger teachers, place at varying points on the emergent half of the transformation line. I have placed them there because I believe that the professional education culture acquired in the schools and colleges of education has a clear bias toward an emergent-oriented ethos. Many of my educationist colleagues will reject this interpretation, and indeed, such interpretations are always guilty of over-generalization. Others of my colleagues will welcome such a characterization, but still question its validity. My case must rest on the basis of contemporary educational philosophy, theory, and practice. The emphasis is on the "social adjustment" of the individual, upon his role as a member of the group and community. Most of the values listed under the *emergent* heading are explicitly stated in educational literature as goals. Some of them, such as conformity to the group, are implicit. This value, in particular, grows out of the others, is more or less unintended, and constitutes a *covert* or *latent* value, by definition. This is, admittedly, a little like accusing a man of hating his mother, but not knowing it, and such accusations are usually rejected, or rationalized out of existence. But I believe that it is literally impossible to hold the other values in this system and avoid placing a strong emphasis on group harmony, and group control of the individual. My data, at least, gathered largely from graduate students in professional education courses, indicate that this is the case.

But educators and schools do not all come off the same shelf in the supermarket. Older teachers will tend, I hypothesize, to hold relatively traditionalist views by virtue of their age, and time of their childhood training (when they acquired their basic values)—a period in American culture when the traditionalist values were relatively more certain and supported than they are at present. Younger teachers were not only children and acquired their personal culture during a relatively more emergent-oriented period of American history, but they have been (I hypothesize) exposed to a professional education culture that has become rapidly more emergent-oriented in its value position. They are therefore placed near the extreme of the transformation line of the emergent direction.

School administrators come from a different shelf in the same section of the supermarket. They, to be sure, range in age from young to old, come from different family backgrounds, and have been exposed in varying degrees to the professional education culture. But sociological and anthropological studies of the influence of status and role on behavior and perception indicate that these factors tend to over-ride others, and produce certain uniformities of outlook. The school administrator's role is a precarious one—as any school principal or superintendent knows. He faces toward several different audiences, each with different sets of demands—school boards, parents, power groups, teachers, and students—as well as other administrators. He has to play his role appropriately in the light of all these demands. The fact that many cannot, accounts for the increasingly short tenure of personages like school superintendents. But to the extent that he plays *across the board* he will place somewhere toward the center of the line of transformation. Furthermore, his dependence upon the school board, and the power groups in the community, in many cases will tend to make his outlook relatively more conservative, and probably more traditionalistic, than that of his teachers—at least the younger ones. There are many exceptions, of course. I am only claiming *tendencies*.

My thesis, I hope, is clear by now. I am attempting to explain, or help explain, the increasingly bitter and strident attacks on schools and educators, and the conflict and confusion within the ranks. I have claimed that this situation can better be understood as a series of complex but very real conflicts in core values. And I have tried to show the direction of the values shift in American culture and place the various actors in the drama upon a transformation line within this shift.

In this perspective, many conflicts between parents and teachers, school boards and educators, parents and children, and between the various personages and groups within the school system (teachers against teachers, administrators against teachers, and so on) can be understood as conflicts that grow out of sharp differences in values that mirror social and cultural transformation of tremendous scope—and for which none of the actors in the situation can be held personally accountable. This is the real, and perhaps only, contribution of this analysis. If these conflicts can be seen as emerging out of great sociocultural shifts—out of a veritable transformation of a way of life—they will lose some of their sting. To understand, the psychiatrist says, is to forgive.

But now, though it seems indeed improper at this point, permit me to add another complication to an already complicated picture. I have tried to make it clear that not only are there variations in values held by groups and different parts of the social body and school institutions, but that there are also various values, some of them contradictory, held by single individuals as diverse streams of influence in their own systems. This is always true in rapid culture-change situations, as the anthropologist and philosopher knows.

This means that the situation is not only confused by groups battling each other, but that individuals are fighting themselves. This has certain predictable results, if the anthropological studies of personal adaptation to culture change have any validity. And I believe that those results can be detected in the behaviors of most, if not all, of the actors in the scene. Let me try to clarify this.

I will deal only with teachers, as one of the most important sets of actors on this particular stage. I hypothesize that the child training of most of the people who become teachers has been more tradition than emergent-value-oriented. They are drawn largely from middle to lower-middle social class groups in American society, and this segment of the class structure is the stronghold of the work-success ethic and moral respectability values in our culture (even in a culture that is shifting away from these values). Furthermore, it seems probable that a selective process is operating to draw a relatively puritanistic element into the public school teaching as an occupation. Self-denial, altruism, a moralistic self-concept, seem to be functional prerequisites for the historically-derived role of school teacher in American society (I might have said "school-marm").

If this can be granted, then only one other ingredient needs to be added to explain several persistent types of personal adaptation to value conflicts observable among school teachers. That ingredient is one already spelled out—the relatively heavy emphasis, within the professional education culture, on this emergent-oriented value system. Teachers-to-be acquire their personal culture in a more tradition-oriented familiar environment, but they encounter a new kind of culture when in training to become school teachers—in the teacher-training institutions. There is, in this experience, what the anthropologist would call a discontinuity in the *enculturation* of the individual. This is a particular kind of culture-conflict situation that anthropologists have recently begun to study, but mostly in non-western societies undergoing rapid change towards a western way of life.

On the basis of observation of a fair sample of teachers in coastal communities and in the Middle West, I hypothesize that three types of adaptation to this personal culture-conflict situation and experience are characteristic.

Ambivalent: This type is characterized by contradictory and vascillating behavior, particularly with respect to the exercise of discipline and authority. The type tends to be *laissez-faire* in some classroom situations, and authoritarian in others, depending upon which behavior is called into being as a defense against threat of loss of control.

Compensatory: This type is characterized by one of two modes of behavior. The teacher overcompensates consistently either in the direction of the emergent or the tradition-centered values. In the first mode he (or she) tends to become a member of a *group-thinkism* cult—a perversion of progressive educational philosophy in action. The total stress is placed on social adjustment. Individuality is not sanctioned to any significant degree. Conformity to the group becomes the key to success. The type, in its extreme form, is a caricature of the better features of the emergent-centered value set. The second type compensates for internal culture-conflict in the opposite direction, and becomes an outright authoritarian. Tight dominance is maintained over children. All relationships with them are formalized and rigid. No deviation is allowed, so curiously enough, there is a convergence in the end-results of both types. This type is a caricature of the better features of the tradition-centered values set.

Adapted: This type can be either traditional or emergent value-oriented. But the compensatory and ambivalent mechanisms operating in the first two types are much less intense, or absent. The teacher of this type has come to terms with the value conflict situation and experience, and has chosen (consciously or unconsciously) to act within the framework of one or the other value set. There is consequently a consistency of behavior, and the mode of classroom management and teacher-student relationship is not a caricature of either value system.

No one is in a position to say which of these types is represented in greatest numbers among American public school teachers today, and there are few "pure" types. Certainly there are many traditional and emergent-oriented teachers who have adapted successfully to the personal culture-conflict situation and discontinuity of enculturative experience described. But equally certainly there are many school teachers who fall more clearly into one or the other typologies. It would be asking too much to suppose that a cultural values-conflict situation as intense as the one transforming American culture could be handled without strain by the key agent of the culture-transmission process—the school teacher. But again, to understand is to forgive.

In any event, it seems clear that if conditions are even partially of the nature described, the group culture-conflict situation resulting in attacks by representatives of those groups upon each other is intensified and at the same time confused by the personal culture-conflict problem. Both processes must be seen, and understood, as resultants of a larger culture-transformation process.

In conclusion to this by-far unfinished analysis (the next 20 years may tell the more complete story), let me make it clear that I am not castigating either the emergentists, or the traditionalists. Value systems must always be functional in terms of the demands of the social and economic structure of a people. The traditional mode has much that is good about it. There is a staunchness, and a virility in it that many of us may view with considerable nostalgia in some future time. But rugged individualism (in its expedient, ego-centered form), and rigid moralism (with its capacity for displaced hate) become non-functional in a society where people are rubbing shoulders in polyglot masses, and playing with a technology that may destroy, or save, with a pushing of buttons. The emergentist position seems to be growing in strength. Social adaptability, relativistic outlooks, sensitivity to the needs and opinions of others, and of the group, seem functional in this new age. But perhaps we need, as people, educators, anthropologists, and parents, to examine our premises more closely. The emergentist can become a group conformist—an average man proud of his well-rounded averageness—without really meaning to at all.

And lastly I would like to reiterate the basic theme of this article. Conflicts between groups centering on issues of educational relevance, and confusions within the rank and file of educators can be understood best, I believe, in the perspective of the transformation of American culture that proceeds without regard for personal fortune or institutional survival. This transformation, it is true, can be guided and shaped to a considerable degree by the human actors on the scene. But they cannot guide and shape their destiny within this transformation if their energies are expended in knifing attacks on each other in such a central arena as education, or if their energies are dissipated in personal confusions. I am arguing, therefore, for the functional utility of understanding, and of insight into the all-encompassing transformation of American culture and its educational-social resultants.

THE CENTRAL PURPOSE OF AMERICAN EDUCATION*

by The Educational Policies Commission of the NEA

In any democracy, education is closely bound to the wishes of the people, but the strength of this bond in America has been unique. The American people have traditionally regarded education as a means for improving themselves and their society. Whenever an objective has been judged desirable for the individual or the society, it has tended to be accepted as a valid concern of the school. The American commitment to the free society—to individual dignity, to personal liberty, to equality of opportunity—has set the frame in which the American school grew. The basic American value, respect for the individual, has led to one of the major charges which the American people have placed on their schools: to foster the development of individual capacities which will enable each human being to become the best person he is capable of becoming.

The schools have been designed also to serve society's needs. The political order depends on responsible participation of individual citizens; hence the schools have been concerned with good citizenship. The economic order depends on ability and willingness to work; hence the schools have taught vocational skills. The general morality depends on choices made by individuals; hence the schools have cultivated moral habits and upright character.

Educational authorities have tended to share and support these broad concepts of educational purposes. Two of the best-known definitions of purposes were formulated by educators in 1918 and 1938. The first definition, by the Commission on the Reorganization of Secondary Education, proposed for the school a set of seven cardinal objectives: health, command of fundamental processes, worthy home membership, vocational competence, effective citizenship, worthy use of leisure, and ethical character. The second definition, by the Educational Policies Commission, developed a number of objectives under four headings: self-realization, human relationship, economic efficiency, and civic responsibility.

The American school must be concerned with all of these objectives if it is to serve all of American life. That these are desirable objectives is clear. Yet they place before the school a problem of immense scope, for neither the schools nor the pupils have the time or energy to engage in all the activities which will fully achieve these goals. Choices among possible activities are inevitable and are constantly being made in and for every school. But there is no consensus regarding a basis for making these choices. The need, therefore, is for a principle which will enable the school to identify its necessary and appropriate contributions to individual development and the needs of society.

Furthermore, education does not cease when the pupil leaves the school. No school fully achieves any pupil's goals in the relatively short time he spends in the classroom. The school seeks rather to equip the pupil to achieve them for himself. Thus the search for a definition of the school's necessary contribution entails an understanding of the ways individuals and societies choose and achieve their goals. Because the school must serve both individuals and the society at large in achieving their goals, and because the principal goal of the American society remains freedom, the requirements of freedom set the frame within which the school can discover the central focus of its own efforts.

FREEDOM OF THE MIND

The freedom which exalts the individual, and by which the worth of the society is judged, has many dimensions. It means freedom from undue governmental restraints; it means equality in political participation. It means the right to earn and own property and decide its disposition. It means equal access to just processes of law. It means the right to worship according to one's conscience.

Institutional safeguards are a necessary condition for freedom. They are not, however, sufficient to make men free. Freedom requires that citizens act responsibly in all ways. It cannot be preserved in a society whose citizens do not value freedom. Thus belief in freedom is essential to maintenance of freedom. The basis of this belief cannot be laid by mere indoctrination in principles of freedom. The ability to recite the values of a free society does not guarantee commitment to those values. Active belief in those values depends on awareness of them and of their role in life. The person who best supports these values is one who has examined them, who understands their function in his life and in the society at large, and who accepts them as worthy of his own support. For such a person these values are consciously held and consciously approved.

The conditions necessary for freedom include the social institutions which protect freedom and the personal commitment which gives it force. Both of these conditions rest on one condition within the individuals who compose a free society. This is freedom of the mind.

Freedom of the mind is a condition which each individual must develop for himself. In this sense, no man is born free. A free society has the obligation to create circumstances in which all individuals may have opportunity and encouragement to attain freedom of the mind. If this goal is to be achieved, its requirements must be specified.

To be free, a man must be capable of basing his choices and actions on understandings which he himself achieves and on values which he examines for himself. He must be aware of the bases on which he accepts propositions as true. He must understand the values by which he lives, the assumptions on which they rest, and the consequences to which they lead. He must recognize that others may have different values. He must be capable of analyzing the situation in which he finds himself and of developing solutions to the problems before him. He must be able to perceive and understand the events of his life and time and the forces that influence and shape those events. He must recognize and accept the practical limitations which time and circumstance place on his choices. The free man, in short, has a rational grasp of himself, his surroundings, and the relations between them.

He has the freedom to think and choose, and that freedom must have its roots in conditions both within and around the individual. Society's dual role is to guarantee the necessary environment and to develop the necessary individual strength. That individual strength springs from a thinking, aware mind, a mind that possesses the capacity to achieve aesthetic sensitivity and moral responsibility, an enlightened mind. These qualities occur in a wide diversity of patterns in different individuals. It is the contention of this essay that central to all of them, nurturing them and being nurtured by them, are man's rational powers.

The cultivated powers of the free mind have always been basic in achieving freedom. The powers of the free mind are many. In addition to the rational powers, there are those which relate to the aesthetic, the moral, and the religious. There is a unique, central role for the rational powers of an individual, however, for upon them depends his ability to achieve his personal goals and to fulfill his obligations to society.

These powers involve the processes of recalling and imagining, classifying and generalizing, comparing and evaluating, analyzing and synthesizing, and deducing and inferring. These processes enable one to apply logic and the available evidence to his ideas, attitudes, and actions and to pursue better whatever goals he may have.

This is not to say that the rational powers are all of life or all of the mind, but they are the essence of the ability to think. A thinking person is aware that all persons, himself included, are both rational and non-rational, that each person perceives events through the screen of his own personality, and that he must take account of his personality in evaluating his perceptions. The rational processes, moreover, make intelligent choices possible. Through them a person can become aware of the bases of choice in his values and of the circumstances of choice in his environment. Thus they are broadly applicable in life, and they provide a solid basis for competence in all the areas with which the school has traditionally been concerned.

The traditionally accepted obligations of the school to teach the *fundamental processes*—an obligation stressed in the 1918 and 1938 statements of educational purposes—is obviously directed toward the development of the ability to think. Each of the school's other traditional objectives can be better achieved as pupils develop this ability and learn to apply it to all the problems that face them.

Health, for example, depends upon a reasoned awareness of the value of mental and physical fitness and of the means by which it may be developed and maintained. Fitness is not merely a function of living and acting; it requires that the individual understand the connection among health, nutrition, activity, and environment, and that he take action to improve his mental and physical condition.

Worthy home membership in the modern age demands substantial knowledge of the role that the home and community play in human development. The person who understands the bases of his own judgments recognizes the home as the source from which most individuals develop most of the standards and values they apply in their lives. He is intelligently aware of the role of emotion in his own life and in the lives of others. His knowledge of the importance of the home environment in the formation of personality enables him to make reasoned judgments about his domestic behavior.

More than ever before, and for an ever-increasing proportion of the population, *vocational competence* requires developed rational capacities. The march of technology and science in the modern society progressively eliminates the positions open to low-level talents. The man able to use only his hands is at a growing disadvantage as compared with the man who can also use his head. Today even the simplest use of hands is coming to require the simultaneous employment of the mind.

Effective citizenship is impossible without the ability to think. The good citizen, the one who contributes effectively and responsibly to the management of the public business in a free society, can fill his role only if he is aware of the values of his society. Moreover, the course of events in modern life is such that many of the factors which influence an individual's civic life are increasingly remote from him. His own first-hand experience is no longer an adequate basis for judgment. He must have in addition the intellectual means to study events, to relate his values to them, and to make wise decisions as to his own actions. He must also be skilled in the processes of communication and must understand both the potentialities and the limitations of communications among individuals and groups.

The *worthy use of leisure* is related to the individual's knowledge, understanding, and capacity to choose, from among all the activities to which his time can be devoted, those which contribute to the achievement of his purposes and to the satisfaction of his needs. On these bases, the individual can become aware of the external pressures which compete for his attention, moderate the influence of these pressures, and make wise choices for himself. His recreation, ranging from hobbies to sports to intellectual activity pursued for its own sake, can conform to his own concepts of constructive use of time.

The development of *ethical character* depends upon commitment to values; it depends also upon the ability to reason sensitively and responsibly with respect to those values in specific situations. Character is misunderstood if thought of as mere conformity to standards imposed by external authority. In a free society, ethics, morality, and character have meaning to the extent that they represent affirmative, thoughtful choices by individuals. The ability to make these choices depends on awareness of values and of their role in life. The home and the church begin to shape the child's values long before he goes to school. And a person who grows up in the American society inevitably acquires many values from his daily pattern of living. American children at the age of six, for example, usually have a firm commitment to the concept of fair play. This is a value which relates directly to such broad democratic concepts as justice and human worth and dignity. But the extension of this commitment to these broader democratic values will not occur unless the child becomes aware of its implications for his own behavior, and this awareness demands the ability to think.

A person who understands and appreciates his own values is most likely to act on them. He learns that his values are of great moment for himself, and he can look objectively and sympathetically at the values held by others. Thus, by critical thinking, he can deepen his respect for the importance of values and strengthen his sense of responsibility.

The man who seeks to understand himself understands also that other human beings have much in common with him. His understanding of the possibilities which exist within a human being strengthens his concept of the respect due every man. He recognizes the web which relates him to other men and perceives the necessity for responsible behavior. The person whose rational powers are not well developed can, at best, learn habitual responses and ways of conforming which may insure that he is not a detriment to his society. But, lacking the insight that he might have achieved, his capacity to contribute will inevitably be less than it might have become.

Development of the ability to reason can lead also to dedication to the values which inhere in rationality: commitment to honesty, accuracy, and personal reliability; respect for the intellect and for the intellectual life; devotion to the expansion of knowledge. A man who thinks can understand the importance of this ability. He is likely to value the rational potentials of mankind as essential to a worthy life.

Thus, the rational powers are central to all the other qualities of the human spirit. These powers flourish in a humane and morally responsible context and contribute to the entire personality. The rational powers are to the entire human spirit as the hub is to the wheel.

These powers are indispensable to a full and worthy life. The person in whom—for whatever reason—they are not well developed is increasingly handicapped in modern society. He may be able to satisfy minimal social standards, but he will inevitably lack his full measure of dignity because his incapacity limits his stature to less than he might otherwise attain. Only to the extent that an individual can realize his potentials, especially the development of his ability to think, can he fully achieve for himself the dignity that goes with freedom.

A person with developed rational powers has the means to be aware of all facts of his existence. In this sense he can live to the fullest. He can escape captivity to his emotions and irrational states. He can enrich his emotional life and direct it toward ever higher standards of taste and enjoyment. He can enjoy the political and economic freedoms of the democratic society. He can free himself from the bondage of ignorance and unawareness. He can make of himself a free man.

THE CHANGES IN MAN'S UNDERSTANDING AND POWER

The foregoing analysis of human freedom and review of the central role of the rational powers in enabling a person to achieve his own goals demonstrate the critical importance of developing those powers. Their importance is also demonstrated by an analysis of the great changes in the world.

Many profound changes are occurring in the world today, but there is a fundamental force contributing to all of them. That force is the expanding role accorded in modern life to the rational powers of man. By using these powers to increase his knowledge, man is attempting to solve the riddles of life, space, and time which have long intrigued him. By using these powers to develop sources of new energy and means of communication, he is moving into interplanetary space. By using these powers to make a smaller world and larger weapons, he is creating new needs for international organization and understanding. By using these powers to alleviate disease and poverty, he is lowering death rates and expanding populations. By using these powers to create and use a new technology, he is achieving undreamed affluence, so that in some societies distribution has become a greater problem than production.

While man is using the powers of his mind to solve old riddles, he is creating new ones. Basic assumptions upon which mankind has long operated are being challenged or demolished. The age-old resignation to poverty and inferior status for the masses of humanity is being replaced by a drive for a life of dignity for all. Yet, just as man achieves a higher hope for all mankind, he sees also the opening of a grim age in which expansion of the power to create is matched by a perhaps greater enlargement of the power to destroy.

As man sees his power expand, he is coming to realize that the common sense which he accumulates from his own experience is not a sufficient guide to the understanding of the events in his own life or of the nature of the physical world. And, with combined uneasiness and exultation, he senses that his whole way of looking at life may be challenged in a time when men are returning from space.

Through the ages, man has accepted many kinds of propositions as truth, or at least as bases sufficient for action. Some propositions have been accepted on grounds of superstition; some on grounds of decree, dogma, or custom; some on humanistic, aesthetic, or religious grounds; some on common sense. Today, the role of knowledge derived from rational inquiry is growing. For this there are several reasons.

In the first place, knowledge so derived has proved to be man's most efficient weapon for achieving power over his environment. It prevails because it works.

More than effectiveness, however, is involved. There is high credibility in a proposition which can be arrived at or tested by persons other than those who advance it. Modesty, too, is inherent in rational inquiry, for it is an attempt to free explanations of phenomena and events from subjective preference and human authority, and to subject such explanations to validation through experience. Einstein's concept of the curvature of space cannot be demonstrated to the naked eye and may offend common sense; but persons who cannot apply the mathematics necessary to comprehend the concept can still accept it. They do this, not on Einstein's authority, but on their awareness that he used rational methods to achieve it and that those who possess the ability and facilities have tested its rational consistency and empirical validity.

In recent decades, man has greatly accelerated his systematic efforts to gain insight through rational inquiry. In the physical and biological sciences and in mathematics, where has most successfully applied these methods, he has in a short time accumulated a vast fund of knowledege so reliable as to give him power he has never before had to understand, to predict, and to act. That is why attempts are constantly being made to apply these methods to additional areas of learning and human behavior.

The rapid increase in man's ability to understand and change the world and himself has resulted from increased application of his powers of thought. These powers have proved to be his most potent resource, and, as such, the likely key to his future.

THE CENTRAL PURPOSE OF THE SCHOOL

The rational powers of the human mind have always been basic in establishing and preserving freedom. In furthering personal and social effectiveness they are becoming more important than ever. They are central to individual dignity, human progress, and national survival.

The individual with developed rational powers can share deeply in the freedoms his society offers and can contribute most to the preservation of those freedoms. At the same time he will have the best chance of understanding and contributing to the great events of his time. And the society which best develops the rational potentials of its people, along with their intuitive and aesthetic capabilities, will have the best chance of flourishing in the future. To help every person develop these powers is therefore a profoundly important objective and one which increases in importance with the passage of time. By pursuing this objective, the school can enhance spiritual and aesthetic values and other cardinal purposes which it has traditionally served and must continue to serve.

The purpose which runs through and strengthens all other educational purposes—the common thread of education—is the development of the ability to think. This is the central purpose to which the school must be oriented if it is to accomplish either its traditional tasks or those newly accentuated by recent changes in the world. To say that it is central is not to say that it is the sole purpose or in all circumstances the most important purpose, but that it must be a pervasive concern in the work of the school. Many agencies contribute to achieving educational objectives, but this particular objective will not be generally attained unless the school focuses on it. In this context, therefore, the development of every student's rational powers must be recognized as centrally important.

INDEX

INDEX

ABOUT THE EDITORS

W. Warren Kallenbach is Associate Professor of Education at San Jose State College. He received his B.A. degree from Drury College and his M.A. and Ed.D. degrees at Stanford University. He teaches graduate and undergraduate courses in the social foundations of education, has published several articles on education, is Chairman of the Research Committee, Division of Education, San Jose State College, and is currently engaged in research on teaching effectiveness and its evaluation.

Harold M. Hodges, Jr. is Associate Professor of Sociology and Anthropology at San Jose State College. He received his B.A. **degree** and his M.A. and Ph.D. degrees in sociology from the University of Southern California. Dr. Hodges has published a number of articles in his field, and his six-year study, "Peninsula People," which is included in article form in this book, will eventually be published in expanded form as a book. He is also the author of the recent *Social Stratification: Class in America.*

This book is set in Times Roman, a versatile type face of simple design and even weight, which was created by Stanley Morrison in 1932 for *The Times* of London. The display type used is Spartan, a strong, clear, sans serif face, which combines with Times Roman in a cleanly attractive and highly legible page.